Worlds of Work

Building an International
Sociology of Work

PLENUM STUDIES IN WORK AND INDUSTRY

Series Editors:
Ivar Berg, *University of Pennsylvania, Philadelphia, Pennsylvania*
and Arne L. Kalleberg, *University of North Carolina, Chapel Hill, North Carolina*

WORK AND INDUSTRY
Structures, Markets, and Processes
Arne L. Kalleberg and Ivar Berg

A Chronological Listing of Volumes in this series appears at the back of this volume.

A Continuation Order Plan is available for this series. A continuation order will bring delivery of each new volume immediately upon publication. Volumes are billed only upon actual shipment. For further information please contact the publisher.

Worlds of Work

Building an International Sociology of Work

Edited by

Daniel B. Cornfield

Vanderbilt University
Nashville, Tennessee

and

Randy Hodson

Ohio State University
Columbus, Ohio

Kluwer Academic / Plenum Publishers
New York   Boston   Dordrecht   London   Moscow

Library of Congress Cataloging-in-Publication Data

Worlds of work: building an international sociology of work/edited by Daniel B. Cornfield and Randy Hodson.
     p.   cm. — (Plenum studies in work and industry)
     Includes bibliographical references and index
     ISBN 0-306-46605-8
     1. Work—Social aspects—Case studies. 2. Industrial sociology—Case studies. I. Cornfield, Daniel B. II. Hodson, Randy.   III. Series.

HD6955 .W68 2001
306.3'6—dc21

                                       2001038335

ISBN 0-306-46605-8

©2002 Kluwer Academic / Plenum Publishers
233 Spring Street, New York, N.Y. 10013

http://www.wkap.nl/

10 9 8 7 6 5 4 3 2 1

A C.I.P. record for this book is available from the Library of Congress

Printed in the United States of America

Contributors

Jacques Bélanger, Department Industrial Relations, Université Laval, Quebec, Canada G1K 7P4

Sharit K. Bhowmik, Department of Sociology, University of Mumbai, Vidyanagari, Santacruz (East), Mumbai 400 098, India

Juan-José Castillo, Department of Sociology, Faculty of Political Science and Sociology, Universidad Complutense, 28223 Madrid, Spain

Daniel B. Cornfield, Department of Sociology, Vanderbilt University, Nashville, Tennessee, 37235 United States

Enrique de la Garza Toledo, Department of Sociology, Metropolian University of Mexico, Ixtapalapa, 09340 México, D.F., Mexico

Pierre Desmarez, Centre de Sociologie du Travail de l'Emploi et de la Formation, Free University of Brussels, 1050 Brussels, Belgium

Paul K. Edwards, Industrial Relations Research Unit, Warwick Business School, University of Warwick, Coventry CV4 7AL, United Kingdom

Anthony Giles, Department of Industrial Relations, Université Laval, Quebec, Canada G1K 7P4

Nadya Araujo Guimarães, Department of Sociology, University of São Paulo, 05.508-900 São Paulo–SP–Brazil

Sandra Harding, Faculty of Business, Queensland University of Technology, Gardens Point, Brisbane Qld 4001, Australia

Randy Hodson, Department of Sociology, Ohio State University, Columbus, Ohio 43210, United States

Arne L. Kalleberg, Department of Sociology, University of North Carolina at Chapel Hill, Chapel Hill, North Carolina 27599-3210, United States

Ilona Kovács, Department of Social Sciences, Faculty for Economics and Management, Technical University of Lisbon, 1200 Lisboa, Portugal

Kevin T. Leicht, Department of Sociology, University of Iowa, Iowa City, Iowa 52242-1401 United States

Marcia de Paula Leite, Department of Social Sciences and Education, University of Campinas, Campinas–SP–Brazil–CEP 13083-970

György Lengyel, Department of Sociology, Budapest University of Economic Sciences and Public Administration, 1093 Budapest, Hungary

António Brandão Moniz, Industrial Sociology Section, Faculty of Sciences, and Technology, New University of Lisbon, P-2825-114 Caparica, Portugal

Walther Müller-Jentsch, Fakultät für Sozialwissenschaften, Lehrstuhl Mitbestimmung und Organisation, Ruhr University of Bochum, D44780 Bochum, Germany

László Neumann, National Labour Centre, Research Unit, Budapest, Hungary

Richard B. Sappey, Mapleton, Queensland, 4560, Australia

Ho Keun Song, Department of Sociology, Seoul National University, Seoul, Korea 151-742

Doowon Suh, Graduate School of International Studies, Korea University, Seoul, 136-701 Korea

Casten von Otter, National Institute for Working Life, S-171 84 Solna, Sweden

Edward C. Webster, Sociology of Work Unit, University of Witwatersrand, Wits 2050, Johannesburg, South Africa

Carol Wolkowitz, Department of Sociology, University of Warwick, Coventry CV4 7AL, United Kingdom

Preface

Global economic integration and workplace restructuring have led to the rapid rise of the sociological study of work in most world regions. Since its inception, the field of sociology has been inspired by the human problems and theoretical and practical challenges posed by deep and pervasive reorganization of workplaces and labor markets. Indeed, the sociology of work has arisen during eras of industrialization and democratization, its research agendas often residing implicitly within the geopolitical outlines of nations and world regions. Presently, the advent of transnational economic production and market integration compels sociologists of work to look beyond national boundaries to examine these transnational developments and to compare their patterns and human impact among nations and world regions. In short, we believe that sociologists of work must build an international sociology of work in order to address the human, scientific, and practical challenges posed by global economic transnationalism.

The purpose of *Worlds of Work* is to promote transnational dialogue about the sociology of work and to help build an international discipline in this field. The chapters in this volume promote transnational dialogue by describing both the commonalities and distinctive characteristics of the sociology of work as it is practiced across different national settings. The study of the workplace has been a leading subdiscipline in the development of sociology. Industrialization, development, and stratification are central driving forces of social change. The study of work and the workplace has thus been central to the development of sociological theory and sociology as a discipline.

Studies of the workplace have also provided a key interface between sociology and both other academic disciplines and other societal institutions. In university settings, the sociology of work interfaces with economics, industrial relations, organizational psychology, and management studies. Within the broader society, studies of work, development, unemployment, job training, work attitudes, discrimination, and related topics have provided some of sociology's most important contributions to governmental policymakers, institutional leaders, trade unionists, and corporate leaders.

In studying the workplace, sociologists have taken on three distinct but overlapping roles: objective social scientist, trusted advisor, and advocate for less privileged groups. Some sociologists specialize in one role, while others move between roles with relative fluidity. Similarly, sociology as an area of study within a nation may take on predominantly one approach or operate in all three arenas.

In our research and teaching in the sociology of work, we have often found ourselves wishing for a more systematic overview of international differences in approaches to workplace problems and concerns. This book is a response to that felt need. Available sources on international differences in sociological approaches to workplace issues are often highly sketchy, focusing only on a few selected nations. Other international comparisons are more comprehensive in the coverage of nations but are organized thematically around particular issues such as unemployment policy, family leave policy, or child labor laws. In this book we bring together for the first time integrated statements on the history and current concerns of sociologists of work as these have developed across a wide range of national settings.

We hope that this volume will continue the tradition of international scholarly exchange stimulated by the publication in 1998 of a series of books commissioned by the International Sociological Association to highlight sociology in the various world regions.* The statements and analyses presented in the chapters of this book provide a starting platform for the development of a truly international sociology of work that has the ability to rise above local parochialism and to produce new insights and synergies for understanding the complex, ever-changing, and increasingly international world of work.

One goal of this volume is thus to stimulate increased awareness of international contributions and differences in the sociology of work and to encourage cross-fertilization of ideas. This goal will be met if an increased number of researchers benefit from the insights of international research in the sociology of work and share these insights with their students through an increased internationalization of course content and curriculum.

An additional goal is to provide detailed and specific information about institutional contacts, specific journals publishing articles in the sociology of work, and even specific authors spearheading research on important topics in

---

*Immanuel Wallerstein. 1998. "Is Sociology a World Discipline?" *Contemporary Sociology* 27(4):325–326.

various nations. Toward this goal, we have asked each chapter author to include an appendix listing relevant national research institutes that focus on the sociology of work and to provide contact information for these institutes. We hope that this information and these contacts will facilitate international contacts, collaborations, exchanges, and internships. If these seeds are successfully planted and cultivated by scholars and researchers interested in the sociology of work, then our goal of encouraging a truly international sociology of work will be met.

We have attempted to be comprehensive in our coverage of major world regions and believe we have achieved this goal to a reasonable extent. The differential development of the sociology of work across world regions, however, has sometimes made comprehensive coverage difficult to attain. Within nations, we have solicited contributions from the editors or past editors of the major journals specializing in the sociology of work or from the directors of research institutes focusing on the sociology of work. We were gratified that so many senior and distinguished scholars made themselves available to contribute to the volume; the breadth of their visions is clearly visible in the chapters that follow.

We have organized the fourteen national chapters into three geographical world regions: the Americas; Asia, Africa, and the Pacific; and Europe. Geographical proximity of nations, however, is often unrelated to the similarity and dissimilarity between the type of sociology practiced in any two nations. There is great cross-national variation in the type of sociology practiced within each of these three world regions.

Some nations are not represented because we could not identify journals or research institutes within the nation that focus on work from a sociological standpoint. Other nations are missing because of the failure of our efforts to establish contacts and successfully solicit involvement. Space limitations also constrain the total number of nations that can be included, forcing the selection of certain nations as representatives of broader regions.

Compiling and editing these chapters has been a labor of love for us and a source of considerable intellectual growth. We hope that it is a similarly rewarding experience for you.

DANIEL B. CORNFIELD
RANDY HODSON

Contents

PART III: ASIA, AFRICA, AND THE PACIFIC

PART IV: EUROPE

PART V: CONCLUSION

Worlds of Work

*Building an International
Sociology of Work*

I
Introduction

1

Building an International Sociology of Work

Daniel B. Cornfield and Randy Hodson

The sociology of work has thrived during eras of fundamental economic, political, and social change. During eras of industrialization, labor mobilization, and democratization, sociologists of work have applied their rigorous social scientific techniques to wrestle with and resolve wrenching human problems and thorny theoretical issues associated with new social relations in workplaces, labor markets, and societies. Among the pioneers of the sociology of work, for example, Karl Marx analyzed sharpening class inequalities that accompanied capital concentration and accumulation; Emile Durkheim examined the impact of the increasing complexity of the division of labor on anomie and community; and Max Weber characterized the new bureaucratic social order as an "iron cage."

The current, and global, meteoric rise of sociology of work reflects important changes that are occurring in work, workplaces, labor markets, and economies. In all regions of the world, a sociology of work has arisen to address a wide range of human problems and theoretical issues associated with

Daniel B. Cornfield · Department of Sociology, Vanderbilt University, Nashville, Tennessee 37235. **Randy Hodson** · Department of Sociology, Ohio State University, Columbus, Ohio 43210.

Worlds of Work: Building an International Sociology of Work, edited by Daniel B. Cornfield and Randy Hodson. Kluwer Academic/Plenum Publishers, New York, 2002.

fundamental institutional changes, including increased global economic competition and economic transnationalism, democratization, changing gender-role attitudes, the shift from corporatist to deregulated markets associated with the advent of neoliberal state policies, the decline and revitalization of national labor movements, and increasing gender and ethnic/racial diversity of national labor forces linked to women's, civil rights, and democratic social movements. Fueled by these fundamental institutional changes, a host of human problems in workplaces, labor markets, and families have inspired and challenged the sociologists of work to deepen the analysis of their causes and to fashion solutions for improving human livelihoods, life chances, and dignity. These human problems pertain to income inequality, poverty, and unemployment; emotional stress and mental health; social relations between women and men, ethnic/racial and age groups; violence in the workplace; and interpersonal relations within families. Indeed, sociologists of work are actively developing new theories and visions of humane and efficient workplaces, labor organizations, and worker involvement, as well as a wide range of public policies for worker training, new production technologies and organizational networks, labor–management relations, equal employment opportunity, work and family integration, and social welfare.

In light of the global forces that galvanize the sociology of work, sociologists are rapidly developing a transnational dialogue among themselves (Wallerstein, 1998). Indeed, the tradition of cross-national comparative research is of long-standing and growing importance.

CORE TOPICS IN THE SOCIOLOGY OF WORK

The original organizing theme in the sociology of work has been the process of *industrialization* and attendant changes and dislocations. A focus on the process of industrialization continues as a core topic today in many nations under the rubric of development or modernization, with particular attention being paid to the nature of the insertion of nations within the global economy (Amin, 1976; Bélanger, Edwards, and Haiven, 1994; Briceno-Leon and Sonntag, 1998; Frank, 1967; Keyder, 1998). From industrialization and development emerge new forms of stratification and distinct occupational cultures. Studies of these topics have also provided an integrative transnational focus for the sociology of work (Castillo, 1995, 1996, 1997a, 1997b; Cornfield and Kane, 1998; Edwards, 1992; Hodson, 2001; Proudhon, 1969).

The process of *democratization* is often intertwined with industrialization and workplace actors often play leading roles in this process. Accordingly, democratization and the role of trade unions in both the economic and political spheres have provided another convergent focus for the sociology of work across nations (Ackers, Smith, and Smith, 1996; Adler and Webster, 1995; Bertilsson and Therborn, 1998; Cornfield, 1997; Neumann, 1997; Seidman, 1994).

Following initial periods of industrialization and during periods of relative stability, the focus of sociological studies of work often turns toward work life concerns. Such studies highlight workers' attitudes of job satisfaction and the role these play in commitment to the firm and productivity (Hodson and Sullivan, 1995; Lincoln and Kalleberg, 1990). Similarly, issues of labor force demography and worker training also take precedence during periods of stability and growth. How are new workers recruited, and how will they be trained for the changing needs of the economy?

The increased movement of both women into the paid labor force in many nations and peoples in search of employment has brought another set of concerns to the fore across a range of nations. The historic migration of women from home duties to paid employment has accelerated in recent decades. The importance of this migration and its differential progress across nations has fueled a wealth of studies in the sociology of work about the gendered nature of work and about work and family concerns (Christiansen-Ruffman, 1998; Cockburn, 1991; Collinson and Hearn, 1996; Hakim, 1996; Parcel, 1999; Parcel and Cornfield, 2000).

Changes in the available labor force as a result of international migrations have also taken on a central role in many national sociologies of work. Uneven economic development in the modern world, coupled with falling transportation costs, has resulted in unprecedented population flows between nations as people move in the search for better paying work. Political instability and violence in many regions have also accelerated these migrations. The integration of new immigrant populations into national economies has thus become an important focus of the sociology of work in many nations.

Economic globalization and the decline of manufacturing employment constitute a final set of topics that have become an increasingly urgent focus of concern across a wide range of nations. Employment in manufacturing industries has declined as a share of total employment across a wide spectrum of national economies. The spread of computer-assisted automation is a central cause of this decline. The spread of "lean production" models inspired by the Japanese concept of full utilization of labor has also contributed substantially to reduced employment and to rising problems of unemployment in many nations (Castillo, 1996; Kovács, 1996; E Silva and Sitas, 1998). Conversely, the service sector has grown in many societies, bringing with it an increase in marginal employment and associated problems of poverty and underemployment.

In the former communist nations of the world, attention is focused on the search for viable forms of economic organization to replace centrally

planned economies. The need for new legal, regulatory, and banking structures to organize work and to regulate interorganizational relations has become increasingly apparent in these nations. Emerging forms of capitalism in
these areas have proven difficult to govern in the absence of these institutional structures (Keister, 2001; Kornai, 1992; Sztompka, 1998).

In all parts of the world, the increasingly tight interconnections within
international manufacturing, service, and financial markets have focused attention on the need for theories that are truly global in nature. Increasing
attention is thus being paid to international product chains and to the role of
international actors, such as the World Bank and the International Monetary
Fund, and their often decisive involvements in national economies.

In addition to a common core of topics, sociologists of work share a common set of methods that also bind them together into a cohesive intellectual
tradition.

CORE METHODOLOGIES

What holds the sociology of work together as a coherent intellectual field
is as much its methods of analysis as its topic areas, which are sometimes
shared with other disciplines. Empirical analysis of workplace issues has always been at the heart of the sociology of work and is our most universal tie to
other sociologists. Some of the earliest works in the field are those of Karl
Marx and Max Weber, who wrote about early factory conditions and agrarian
labor, respectively. These early analyses—often referred to as historiographic
studies—relied heavily on secondary accounts. Although such analyses are
still undertaken by sociologists of work, the methodological focus of the discipline has clearly shifted to firsthand empirical accounts using both qualitative
and quantitative methods.

Sociologists of work were early pioneers in both field observation and
survey methodologies (Hodson, 1999, 2001; Miller, 1991; Schwartzman, 1993).
Factory studies and plant observations uncovered rich worlds of meaning and
social relations that were hidden to more casual observers. Similarly, systematic surveys of employees and of broader samples have allowed generaliza-
tions to be made to broader populations of interest. Such populations include
the available labor force, the unemployed, and those not currently in the labor
force for reasons of age, gender, disability, unemployment, or discouragement.

The increased availability of governmental and private data on economic
and labor force concerns has sparked the development of new methods for
analyzing such data. Such methods include time-series methods shared with
economists and methods for the analysis of large-scale census data and area-
specific data. The availability of high-quality data has increased the ability of

sociologists to generate informed reports on current labor force and economic issues such as unemployment, layoffs, injuries, new hires, wages, and discrimination.

Sociologists of work pursue their research topics through their roles in specific institutional settings. As the sociology of work has grown as an area of study, so too have the institutional settings in which sociologists of work are employed.

INSTITUTIONAL SETTINGS

Most sociologists of work are employed as academics in university settings. In such settings, their work typically combines teaching and research activities. The sociology of work is often a mainstay in sociology department curriculums. Sometimes sociologists of work are also employed in business schools, where they teach organizational behavior and related topics in personnel management.

Researchers working for government ministries, especially departments of labor and education, have also significantly advanced the sociology of work. Nonprofit research institutes are an additional locus of employment for sociologists of work. In these settings, they contribute position and policy papers that help inform government and public debate on issues such as unemployment, training, and equal access to employment for different groups.

In nations that practice economic codetermination involving formal participation by corporations, the government, and trade unions, sociologists of work have also found employment on the research staffs of the institutions of codetermination. From this location, they have been able to contribute to the development of strategies leading to partnerships between capital and labor based on the principle of shared rewards (Bertilsson and Therborn, 1998).

Finally, smaller numbers of sociologists of work are employed in unions, religious organizations, and corporations. In unions, they address issues of bargaining, member benefits and union revitalization. In religious organizations, they work in research and advocacy roles, addressing issues of employment, unemployment, and poverty. In corporations, they are employed mainly in personnel departments, where they are involved in human relations work, positions they often share with organizational psychologists.

THEORIES OF WORK

The sociology of work has played a leading role in the development of general sociological theory because of its attention to key issues of industrialization, inequality, and democratic participation. The theoretical roots of the sociology of work extend to the writings of Durkheim, Marx, and Weber. Durkheim highlighted the anomic and dysfunctional consequences of the unregulated division of labor typical of industrialization. Marx highlighted the differential power of the capitalist class, its exploitation of workers, and the role of class conflict in moving society ahead. Weber highlighted the alienating aspects of large modern bureaucracies and the difficulties of escaping from these. Contemporary theorists in the sociology of work typically trace their intellectual roots to one or more of these traditions but they have gone well beyond these initial insights.

The critical tradition in the sociology of work has been significantly advanced in recent years by analyses of the gender-based nature of the division of labor. Sociologists from many nations have contributed new research and new concepts to understanding the gendered nature of work roles and gender-based allocation processes (Cockburn, 1991; Hakim, 1996). The critical approach to work has also been advanced by action research in which researchers function as collaborators with workers (often under the sponsorship of joint union–management programs) to develop programs for job and workplace redesign. Such programs have created giving a new avenue for the voice of workers to be heard in workplace decisions (Bertilsson and Therborn, 1998).

New workplace theories are also being inspired by rational choice theory in sociology, by organizational demography, by institutional economics, and by theories of the regulation of state and economy (Fligstein, 1996; Littek and Charles, 1995; Maruani and Reynaud, 1993; Thompson and Warhurst, 1998). These theories address not only relations between workers and owners but also relations among economic organizations and between states and economic organizations.

Sociologists of work make use of a wide range of theoretical orientations in their investigations of the workplace. Although one or another approach may be dominant in a nation during a given period, there has been sufficient transnational exchange of ideas among practitioners in the field that most researchers and scholars are keenly aware of the different major theories and their potential contributions.

DIVERGENCES

We have outlined some of the core topics, methods, theories, and institutional locations that give integration and coherence to the sociology of work as a transnational field of study. There is also, however, considerable international variation in the mix of ideas and methods used in each nation and in the weights given to various ideas and approaches. It is thus appropriate to ask if there are multiple sociolo*gies* of work rather than a single worldwide sociology of work. We argue that both a common core of theories and methods exists and also that national variations constitute cohesive, integrated, and distinguishable approaches. In the following section, we provide a model for understanding some of the most important of these national differences and how they structure the problems and methods that constitute the various national approaches to the sociology of work.

A close reading of the national and regional chapters presented in this book suggests three principal roles occupied by the sociology of work: scientific, advisory, and advocacy. Each national sociology of work contains some elements of each of these approaches but its particular character is determined by the mix of these roles, with one or two roles tending to dominate.

Why does one or another of these roles tend to emerge as the primary orientation of the sociology of work in a nation? The answer lies in the political, social, economic, and institutional situation characteristic of each nation. In other words, the answer can be revealed through the application of standard sociological tools.

A first role for the sociology of work is to follow the dictates of basic science. The problems to be investigated are identified based on either theoretical or practical interest, and the sociologist applies theoretical and methodological tools to solve the problem or derive an answer. Knowledge is seen as value neutral, as cumulative, and a given research project need have no immediate practical utility. The contributions of the sociology of work in such settings are seen as part of the complex mosaic of knowledge necessary for the operation and further development of technically advanced democratic societies.

A second role for the sociology of work is as a direct policy advisor to government and economic actors. In such settings, the sociology of work plays an important role as technical advisor. Sociologists of work in such settings often serve as de facto administrators of field experiments in social engineering in the workplace and in related institutions, such as schools and child care settings.

The third major role of the sociology of work is as an advocate for exploited groups in society or those excluded from equal access to the economic life of the society. This role emerges in response to exploitation, disenfranchisement, or injustice for some identifiable group or groups in society, including workers, women, racial/ethnic groups, or immigrants. Sociologists of work have often served as activists giving voice to the grievances of such groups. In many settings, sociologists of work have been principal advocates for the rights of workers and for democratic reforms. In some settings, speaking out for the disenfranchised and for economic reforms has resulted in sociologists being labeled as subversives and sometimes suffering repression themselves. Where sociologists strongly identify with the role of advocate, they often act more like independent intellectuals committed to a social movement or to a social change program than professionals committed to the standards of a professional/scientific occupation.

DEVELOPING A TRANSNATIONAL DIALOGUE

The purpose of *Worlds of Work* is to facilitate the growth of a vital and dynamic transnational dialogue in the sociology of work. In order to facilitate this dialogue, this book presents the recent intellectual history of the sociology of work in 14 nations from all regions of the world. We asked each of the distinguished representatives of the 14 nations to describe the enduring and recent research themes in the sociology of work in their nations, as well as the social context that encouraged the pursuit of these themes, the relationship between the sociology of work and related intellectual disciplines, and the institutional context that supports research and the teaching of the sociology of work in their nations. We also asked the authors to append to their chapters a list of the most important centers of research on the sociology of work in their nations. We did not impose a substantive or theoretical framework on the chapter authors. Rather, the 14 national chapters reflect the authors' understandings and perspectives on the unfolding of the sociology of work in their nations, expressed within the constraints on chapter length imposed by space limitations. The only framework we did impose on the authors was the presentation of *enduring* and *recent* research themes and *methodological foundations* of the sociology of work in their nations. The concluding chapter presents analysis and interpretation of the 14 national chapters by a distinguished international scholar in the sociology of work.

In the remainder of this chapter, we distill similarities and differences in the origins and recent developments in the sociology of work in the 14 nations represented in this book. Our analysis is based on the information provided by the authors of the 14 national chapters. We refer the reader to the 14 national chapters in order to examine the source of our characterizations of the sociology of work in these nations.

We developed a three-dimensional framework for making cross-national comparisons of research in the sociology of work. The three dimensions capture the chief objects of observation and themes in this discipline. The first dimension is the concept of the *worker as a social actor*, that is, a member of a group that acts on the basis of group interests. Sociologists of work have tended to conceive of workers as economic actors (e.g. members of social classes, occupations, industries, firms, labor organizations) and as actors whose group identities derive from their gender and ethnic and racial backgrounds. The second dimension is the *institutional context of work* and the social relations associated with work. Among the many institutional contexts examined by sociologists of work are business enterprises (e.g., factory, office, mine), occupations, labor organizations and movements, labor markets, and communities. The third dimension consists of the many *research themes* pursued by sociologists of work. The broadest of these themes include worker subjectivity (e.g., work attitudes and worker consciousness), the structure of workplaces (e.g., Taylorism, bureaucracy, post-Fordism), the development of labor organization and labor–management relations, and the dynamics of labor markets.

ORIGINS

The sociology of work first emerged, according to the authors of the 14 national chapters, during two broad time periods associated with the timing of fundamental social changes, such as industrialization and democratization, in the respective world regions. The first period is the late 19th and early 20th centuries, when the sociology of work emerged in Canada, France, Germany, Hungary, Sweden, the United Kingdom, and the United States. The second period is the late 20th century, when the sociology of work emerged in Australia, Brazil, India, Korea, Mexico, Portugal, and South Africa.

Regardless of when the sociology of work began, sociologists of work tended to conceive of the worker as an economic actor at the start of the discipline in each of the 14 nations represented in this book. The concept of worker *qua* economic actor, however, varied across the 14 nations due partly to national differences in the institutional contexts of work and research themes pursued by sociologists. It is important to note that no single institutional context, and no single research theme, wholly characterized the early sociology of work within any of the 14 nations.

The concept of the worker as an economic actor emerged in *four patterns*. First, in almost all of the 14 nations, the worker was originally conceived as an employee of a large bureaucratic business enterprise. The institutional context and research themes about the bureaucratic employee varied cross-nationally. The pioneering work of German—Marx and Weber—and French—Durkheim—sociologists addressed the rise of large-scale, capitalist societies and impersonal bureaucratic business enterprises, and the impact of these social changes on worker alienation and life chances, and on the social integration of the worker. In several nations, the research, often from the perspective of the "human relations school of management," focused on the social psychological impact of bureaucracy on worker attitudes toward work, coworkers, and employers, and on worker productivity and performance. These nations include South Africa, Sweden, the United Kingdom, and the United States. The "labor process" tradition of research on deskilling and degradation in the workplace, often associated with the 1974 publication of Harry Braverman's *Labor and Monopoly Capital*, is another variant of the bureaucratic work life theme. Labor process research contributed to the emergence of the sociology of work in Australia, Mexico, and South Africa. In Portugal, worker self-management was an important research theme at the start of the discipline.

Second, in several nations, the sociology of work originally addressed the worker as a class actor and developed the theme of working-class mobilization within the institutional context of the labor movement and labor organizations. These nations include Brazil, India, Korea, Mexico, and Portugal. The research themes included the development and institutionalization of the labor movement, worker class consciousness, democracy within the labor movement, labor movement militancy, and the relationship between the state and the labor movement.

Third, in a few nations, the worker was originally conceived as a member of an occupation. A variety of occupational perspectives flourished in Canada, Hungary, and the United States. Generally, occupational sociology addressed the development of occupations, the occupational consciousness and identity of workers, occupational norms and role socialization, and the status of occupations in society. In English Canada, early occupational studies focused on the development of professions, such as doctors and lawyers, and the emergence of a societal occupational status hierarchy. In French Canada, early occupational sociology addressed rural occupations, such as lumberjacks, and structures of occupational status and social mobility in industrializing rural communities. Hungarian sociologists focused their attention on peasants, miners, and metal workers, their employment and living conditions, and their class consciousness. In the United States, sociologists focused on the development of the professions and the processes by which they organized and reproduced themselves.

Fourth, workers were viewed as labor market participants. From this perspective, workers worked in the context of labor markets and industrial relations systems that determined their livelihoods and constrained their life chances. Research themes included rural-to-urban migration and the development of segmented labor markets, income inequality, and variations in unemployment rates and collective bargaining practices and outcomes. These themes contributed to the emergence of the sociology of work in Australia, Korea, Mexico, and the United States.

RECENT DEVELOPMENTS

The contemporary sociology of work focuses on addressing the theoretical, empirical, and policy challenges posed by economic globalization, democratization, the changing social and demographic composition of labor forces, and neoliberal state deregulation of markets. In order to facilitate a transnational dialogue among sociologists, we emphasize here the *common* dynamic research themes and their policy-relevant practical applications among the 14 nations. Again, we distill this commonality from the 14 national chapters in this book and refer the reader to each of these chapters for more detail. Note that the set of research themes within each of the 14 nations is considerably more complex and diverse than the set of research themes we discuss below.

Four common research themes among the 14 nations characterize the recent global trajectory of the sociology of work. Despite the commonality of these research themes, their local manifestations vary cross-nationally. First, and most encouraging for the future of the transnational dialogue among sociologists of work, research themes in the sociology of work have *globalized*. Globalization of research, which consists of cross-national comparative research and international institutional sponsorship and stimulation of research, is discussed in almost all of the 14 national chapters in this book. In several nations, cross-national comparative research themes have become highly salient. For example, cross-national comparative research on the production and reproduction of organizational life has been designed in Australia; on flexibility and job insecurity in Canada; on the "societal effect" on workplace organization in France; on automotive factory organization in Hungary; on plant closings and downsizing in Sweden; on employment and industrial relations in the United Kingdom; and on the determinants of income inequality in the United States.

Institutionally, the sociology of work has been promoted by public and private international agencies and professional associations across multiple nations. For example, the authors of the chapters on Brazil and Mexico note the development of a Latin American sociology of work manifested in the recent establishment of the Asociación Latinoamericana de Sociología del Trabajo, an international professional association with its own scholarly journal. The chapters on Germany, Portugal, and the United Kingdom note the impact of the European Union and the emergence of a single European market on the globalization of the sociology of work.

The second common research theme is the *gendering* of workers, work, and workplaces. In almost all of the 14 nations, sociologists now view workers as gendered actors—that is, actors who enact and pursue their interests as members of gender groups—in addition to viewing them as economic actors.

Sociologists have addressed the theme of "gender and work" in several ways. Gender differences in pay and employment conditions have been examined in most of the nations. The themes of "work and family"—gender differences in the mutual influence of work and family roles—and the marginalization and segregation of women in nonstandard and low-status employment arrangements have been studied in Australia, Brazil, France, Mexico, South Africa, the United Kingdom, and the United States. Swedish research has contributed to the formulation of national policies on child and elder-care for employees.

The third common theme is workplace *restructuring*, which concerns the development of "post-Taylorist/post-Fordist" decentered, loosely coupled, non-union organizations and networks. Sociologists are reexamining the theme of the bureaucratic employee and revisiting bureaucracy as the chief institutional context of workplace social relations. The general research questions being pursued concern cross-cultural variations in the prevalence and shape of post-Taylorist/post-Fordist bureaucracies and employment relations, and the impact of post-Taylorist/post-Fordist organizations on employment conditions, career opportunities, productivity and efficiency, and, more generally, worker livelihoods and dignity.

The wide variety of approaches to workplace restructuring is associated with cross-national differences in political, economic, and social conditions. What follows are only a few examples of cross-national variations in approaches that have been taken. For example, South African research addresses the transition from racial Fordism to racial neo-Fordism, and how new institutional arrangements reproduce enduring racial inequalities and segmentation of the labor market. With democratization, South African research has examined how traditional African culture can be harnessed to promote positive organizational change. In Korea, research is addressing the transformation of the large *chaebols* (Korean corporate conglomerates) and the development of multiple forms of trade unionism. With the privatization of state enterprises in Hungary, sociological research has turned to the analysis of emerging social relations in privatized enterprises and the impact of privatization on worker commitment and livelihoods. In Portugal, sociologists have applied sociology to a wide range of important, practical organizational issues, including adoption of new production technologies, industrial democracy, and trade union strategies, and have promoted the importance of a consideration of sociocultural factors in the revitalization of the national economy. Among the several themes on restructuring pursued by the "new labor studies" in Mexico are technological change, flexibility in the *maquiladoras*, the reorganization of the labor movement, management strategies, and the development of organizational production chains. The decentralization of business enterprises and the diffusion of worker participation in Germany has led researchers to reexamine the dual, industrial relations system of collective bargaining and codetermination through works councils.

Fourth, and closely linked to restructuring, sociologists are examining *nonstandard employment arrangements*. These arrangements are nonstandard in that they consist of a lower mutual commitment between employer and employee than that associated with the "standard," full-time, long-term employment relationship of the bureaucratic internal labor market. Examples include contingent work, part-time and temporary work, outwork, and other types of flexible and casual employment arrangements. Research addresses the diffusion and cross-national, gendered, and ethnic/racial variations in nonstandard employment arrangements, labor–supply issues such as training, and the socioeconomic impact of these employment arrangements on worker livelihoods. Research on these themes is reported in all of the 14 national chapters in this book. Sociologists of work are increasingly focusing on the labor market as the institutional context of workplace social relations and on the concept of the worker as labor market participant.

In summary, fundamental social, economic, and political changes have led sociologists of work in all world regions to reexamine the concept of the worker as a social actor and the institutional context of workplace social relations. In doing so, sociologists from all world regions have developed several broad research themes in common, each with its unique national manifestations, that constitute a platform for launching more cross-national comparative research projects on work, employment, and labor themes.

What is more, the institutionalization of the sociology of work in all world regions serves as a social infrastructure for further globalization of the discipline. According to the authors of the 14 chapters, research and teaching of the sociology of work occur in universities—in sociology departments, other social science departments, and interdisciplinary labor studies and management programs—and in public and private research centers. Research tends to be financed and supported by national scientific agencies, private foundations, international agencies such as the International Labor Organization, the European Institute for the Improvement of Working Conditions, and the Consejo Latinoamericano de Ciencias Sociales, and, to a lesser extent, by labor movements and private corporations. In all regions of the world, sociologists of work have developed and affiliated with sociological and specialized, interdisciplinary professional associations and publish their research nationally and internationally in sociological and interdisciplinary journals. Several Research Committees of the International Sociological Association—including Research Committees 30 (sociology of work) and 44 (labor movements)—are important points of international networking in this discipline. Further information about important national research centers is appended to each of the 14 national chapters.

Sociologists of work have already taken three major, practical steps toward institutionalization. First, in several nations, the discipline emerged as an important policymaking discipline for developing and strengthening national social–welfare and economic institutions, and revitalizing labor and democratic political institutions. This path is especially pronounced in Brazil, Germany, Hungary, India, Korea, Mexico, Portugal, South Africa, and Sweden. Second, sociologists have developed specialized, publicly accessible, national statistical data sets on work, employment and labor themes in several nations, including Australia, Brazil, Canada, France, Germany, Mexico, Sweden, the United Kingdom, and the United States. Third, sociologists have helped to establish and participate in the operations of specialized, interdisciplinary journals in all regions of the world.

In conclusion, the sociology of work has entered an opportune period for promoting transnational dialogue about workplace social relations. The discipline is flourishing in an era of fundamental social, political, and economic change; it has institutionalized in all regions of the world; and, sociologists of all world regions, faced with important theoretical and empirical challenges, are pursuing broad research themes in common that lend themselves to transnational dialogue and to the reconstitution of viable, efficient, and humane economic and political institutions.

REFERENCES

Ackers, Peter, Chris Smith, and Paul Smith, eds., 1996. *The New Workplace and Trade Unionism*. London: Routledge.
Adler, G., and Eddie Webster. 1995. "Challenging Transition Theory: The Labour Movement: Radical Reform and Transition to Democracy in South Africa." *Politics and Society* 23(1):75–106.
Amin, Samir. 1976. *Unequal Development*. London: Harvester.
Bélanger, Jacques, P.K. Edwards, and Larry Haiven, eds., 1994. *Workplace Industrial Relations and the Global Challenge*. Ithaca, NY: ILR Press.
Bergmann, Joachim, and Rudi Schmidt, eds., 1996. *Industrielle Beziehungen: Institutionalisierung und Praxis unter Krisenbedingungen*. Opladen: Leske and Budrich.
Bertilsson, Margareta, and Goran Therborn. 1998. *From a Doll's House to the Welfare State: Reflections on Nordic Sociology*. Madrid: International Sociological Association.
Beynon, Huw. 1973. *Working for Ford*. Harmondsworth, UK: Penguin.
Brandt, Gerhard, Otto Jacobi, and Walther Müller-Jentsch. 1982. *Anpassung an die Krise: Gewerkschaften in den siebziger Jahren*. Frankfurt: Campus.
Braverman, Harry. 1974. *Labor and Monopoly Capital: The Degradation of Work in the Twentieth Century*. New York: Monthly Review.

Briceno-Leon, Roberto, and Heinz Sonntag. 1998. *Sociology in Latin America*. Madrid: International Sociological Association.

Castillo, Juan José. 1995. "¿A Dónde Va la Sociología del Trabajo." *Revista Latinoamericana de Estudios del Trabajo* 1(1):13–42.

Castillo, Juan José. 1996. "Presentación: 'Un Fantasma Recorre Europa'...de Nuevo, la Producción Ligera." *Sociología del Trabajo* 27 (Primavera):3–21.

Castillo, Juan José. 1997a. "El Paradigma Perdido de la Interdisciplinariedad: Volver a los Clásicos." *Revista Latinoamericana de Estudios del Trabajo* 3(5):19–39.

Castillo, Juan José. 1997b. "Looking for the Meaning of Work." *Work and Occupations* 24:413–425.

Christiansen-Ruffman, Linda. 1998. *The Global Feminist Enlightenment: Women and Social Knowledge*. Madrid: International Sociological Association.

Cockburn, Cynthia. 1991. *In the Way of Women*. Basingstoke, UK: Macmillan.

Collinson, David, and Jeff Hearn, eds., 1996. *Men as Managers, Managers as Men*. London: Sage.

Cornfield, Daniel. 1997. "Labor Transnationalism? An Editorial Introduction to 'Labor in the Americas'." *Work and Occupations* 24:278–287.

Cornfield, Daniel, and Melinda Kane. 1998. "Sociological Approaches to Employment Research." Pp. 239–251 in *Researching the World of Work: Strategies, Methods and Critical Views*. edited by Keith Whitfield and George Strauss. Ithaca, NY: Cornell University Press.

de Almeida, Ana Nunes. 1998. *Terra Nostra: Challenges, Controversies and Languages for Sociology and the Social Sciences in the Twenty-First Century*. Madrid: International Sociological Association.

de la Garza, Enrique. 1993. *Reestructuración Productiva y Respuesta Sindical en México*. Mexico City: Instituto de Investigaciones Económicas–Universidad Nacional Autónoma de México.

de la Garza, Enrique, ed. 2000. *Tratado Latinoamericano de Sociología del Trabajo*. Mexico City: Fondo de Cultura Económica.

Edwards, P. K. 1992. "La Recherche Comparative: L'apport de la Tradition Ethnographique." *Relations Industrielles* 47:411–438.

E Silva, Teresa Cruz Maria, and Ari Sitas. 1998. *Gathering Voices: Perspectives on the Social Sciences in Southern Africa*. Madrid: International Sociological Association.

Fligstein, Neil. 1996. "Markets as Politics." *American Sociological Review* 61(August):656–673.

Frank, Andre Gunder. 1967. *Capitalism and Underdevelopment in Latin America*. New York: Monthly Review.

Friedmann, Georges. [1956] 1978. *The Anatomy of Work: Labor, Leisure, and the Implications of Automation*. Westport, CT: Greenwood.

Giles, Anthony, and Gregor Murray. 1988. "Towards an Historical Understanding of Industrial Relations Theory in Canada." *Relations Industrielles* 43:780–811.

Hakim, Catherine. 1996. *Key Issues in Women's Work*. London: Athlone.

Haraszti, Miklós. [1979] 1988. *Darabbér: Egy Munkás a Munkásállamban* [Piece-wages: A Worker in a Worker's State]. Budapest: Téka K.

Hodson, Randy. 1999. *Analyzing Documentary Accounts*. Quantitative Applications in the Social Sciences, No. 128. Newbury Park, CA: Sage.

Hodson, Randy. 2001. *Working with Dignity*. New York: Cambridge University Press.
Hodson, Randy, and Teresa A. Sullivan. 1995. *The Social Organization of Work*, 2nd ed. Belmont, CA: Wadsworth.
Keister, Lisa. 2001. *Chinese Business Groups*. New York: Oxford University Press.
Keyder, Caglar. 1998. *Tradition in Modernity: Southern Europe in Question*. Madrid: International Sociological Association.
Kornai, János. 1992. *The Socialist System: The Political Economy of Communism*. Oxford, UK: Clarendon.
Kovács, I. 1996. "The Sociology of Work in Portugal: Situation and Perspective." *Proceedings of the World Meeting of Labor Studies and Sociology of Work*, Mayaguez University, Puerto Rico.
Lee, Su-Hoon. 1998. *Sociology in East Asia and Its Struggle for Creativity*. Madrid: International Sociological Association.
Lincoln, James R., and Arne L. Kalleberg. 1990. *Culture, Control, and Commitment*. New York: Cambridge University Press.
Littek, Wolfgang, and Tony Charles, eds., 1995. *The New Division of Labour: Emerging Forms of Work Organisation in International Perspective*. Berlin: de Gruyter.
Maruani, Margaret, and Emmanuele Reynaud. 1993. *Sociologie de l'emploi*. Paris: La decouverte.
Miller, Delbert C. 1991. *Handbook of Research Design and Social Measurement*. Newbury Park, CA: Sage.
Moniz, A. B., and I. Kovács. 1997. *Evolução das Qualificação e das Estruturas de Formação em Portugal*. Lisbon: Instituto do Emprego e Formação Profissional.
Mukherji, Partha, Jacop Aikara, and Chandan Sengupta. 1998. *Sociology in South Asia: Heritage and Challenges*. Madrid: International Sociological Association.
Müller-Jentsch, Walther, ed.,1999. *Konfliktpartnerschaft: Akteure und Institutionen der industriellen Beziehungen*, 3rd ed. München: Hampp.
Neumann, László. 1997. "Circumventing Trade Unions in Hungary: Old and New Channels of Wage Bargaining." *European Journal of Industrial Relations* 3(2):181–200.
Parcel, Toby. 1999. *Research in the Sociology of Work: Vol. 7. Work and Family*. Greenwich, CT: JAI Press.
Parcel, Toby, and Daniel B. Cornfield, eds. 2000. *Work and Family: Research Informing Policy*. Thousand Oaks, CA: Sage.
Proudhon, Pierre-Joseph. 1969. *Selected Writings of Pierre-Joseph Proudhon*. London: Macmillan.
Rinehart, James W. (with the assistance of Seymour Faber). 1975. *The Tyranny of Work*. Don Mills, Ontario: Academic Press.
Schwartzman, Helen B. 1993. *Ethnography in Organizations*. Qualitative Research Methods Series, No. 27. Newbury Park, CA: Sage.
Seidman, Gay. 1994. *Manufacturing Militance: Workers Movements in Brazil and South Africa, 1970–1985*. Berkeley: University of California Press.
Song, Ho-gùn. 1991. *Han'guk ùi nodong chòngch'i wa sijang* [Labor Politics and Markets in Korea]. Sòul: Nanam.
Song, Ho-gùn. 1994. *Yòllin sijang, tach'in chòngch'i* [Open Market, Closed Politics]. Sòul: Nanam.

Standing, Guy, J. Sender and J. Weeks. 1996. *Restructuring the Labour Market: The South African Challenge*. Geneva: International Labour Office.

Streeck, Wolfgang. 1998. "Industrielle Beziehungen in einer internationalisierten Wirtschaft." Pp. 169–202 in *Politik der Globalisierung*, edited by Ulrich Beck. Frankfurt: Suhrkamp.

Sztompka, Piotr. 1998. *Building Open Society and Perspectives of Sociology in East-Central Europe*. Madrid: International Sociological Association.

Thompson, Paul, and Chris Warhurst, eds., 1998. *Workplaces of the Future*. Basingstoke: Macmillan.

Touraine, Alain. [1969] 1971. *The Post-Industrial Society*. New York: Random House.

Wajcman, Judy. 1998. *Managing Like a Man*. Cambridge: Polity.

Wallerstein, Immanuel. 1998. "Is Sociology a World Discipline?" *Contemporary Sociology* 27(4):325–326.

Webster, Eddie. 1996. "Changing Workplace Relations in South Africa." In *Sawubona Africa: Embracing Four Worlds in South African Management*, edited by R. Lessem and B. Nussbaum. Sandton: Zebra.

Womack, J.P. 1990. *The Machine that Changed the World*. New York: McGraw-Hill.

Zghal, Abdelkader, and Ahmed Iadh Ouaderni. 1998. *Questions from Arab Societies*. Madrid: International Sociological Association.

II

The Americas

The sociology of work has developed distinctively in each of the four American nations covered in this book—Brazil, Canada, Mexico, and the United States. In each nation, sociologists of work have pursued a widening array of research themes during the last few decades. Coterminous with the broadening of the research agendas within each of these nations, research themes have increasingly overlapped among these four nations.

The sociology of work has distinct intellectual origins in the four American nations. In Brazil, the emergence of the sociology of work in the 1960s was closely linked to the emergence of an urban–industrial working class and addressed the problems and prospects of trade unionism among workers and in relation to the state. In English and French Canada, the early focus on the study of occupations gave way—in the 1960s and 1970s—to an emerging nationalistic, critical, and feminist sociology of work. The sociology of work in Mexico shifted from an earlier emphasis of historiographic research on trade unionism and structural labor market and labor process research in the 1970s toward an integrative body of research in the "new labor studies" in the 1980s and 1990s. In the United States, the early focus on factory worker attitudes and behavior during the early 20th century widened to include themes about work organization, labor market careers, segmentation and stratification, and workplace restructuring.

Despite the distinctive national paths taken by the sociology of work in the Americas, several common research themes have been addressed by sociologists in the Americas in recent years. Among these themes are the development and consequences of gender inequality in the workplace; description and assessment of the consequences of workplace restructuring, including post-Fordist/Taylorist organizational forms, interorganizational relations, and production chains; worker involvement in decision making; and the growth, decline, and revitalization of trade unionism.

2

Brazil

Nadya Araujo Guimarães and Marcia de Paula Leite

INITIAL CHALLENGES

Two main challenges in the 1960's laid the foundations for a modern Sociology of Industrial Labor in Brazil: one historical and the other institutional. The first drove the attention of Brazilian intellectuals to explain the nature and attitudes of a new social group—a native urban working class, a product of an industrial order in process of consolidation. The second flowed from the need to institutionalize a mode of thought, that is, to formally consolidate and socially legitimize a disciplinary domain for Social Science.

The emergence of a native working class was part of a process that claimed for itself a more precise explanation: a new sociopolitical reality combining intense urban growth, intensified industrialization (since the second half of the 1950s), and strong populist appeal to these urban workers. The challenge laid, then, in understanding this native proletariat, explaining its constitution as a distinct social group in the context of new forms of sociability in large

This chapter was translated from the Portuguese by Elisa Nascimento.

Nadya Araujo Guimarães • Department of Sociology, University of Sao Paulo, 05.508-900 São Paulo, Brazil.   **Marcia de Paula Leite** • Department of Social Sciences and Education, University of Campinas, Campinas-SP-Brazil-CEP 13083-970.

Worlds of Work: Building an International Sociology of Work, edited by Daniel B. Cornfield and Randy Hodson. Kluwer Academic/Plenum Publishers, New York, 2002.

23

Brazilian cities, especially São Paulo, the industrial heart of the Brazilian economy.

An important intellectual effort at that time was establishing the parameters of the future the Sociology of Work in Brazil. Two main issues were included in this effort. On the one hand, there were studies that sought to investigate the political and professional attitudes of workers in their relations with labor unions. For these authors, the cultural and regional origins of the native working class would provide the first explanation of their forms of expression in Brazil (Cardoso, 1962; Lopes, 1965; Pereira, 1965; Rodrigues, 1970). On the other hand, there were those who raised questions about the structural linkages between populist unionism and the State, evaluating the consequences of tutelage to the performance of labor unions in their role as builders of labor consciousness (L. Rodrigues, 1966; J. Rodrigues, 1968; Simão, 1966).

Explanations acquired academic rigor and disciplinary style, both in methodological and theoretical terms; and a point of no return was established regarding the earlier tradition, characterized by analyses with a political-ideological or political-programmatic bent (Telles, 1962; Linhares, 1962; Miglioli, 1963; Dias, 1962).

These pioneer studies brought to the fore three basic questions to the understanding of unionism and industrial relations in Brazil, which are still relevant (Vianna, 1978; Guimarães and Castro, 1987). First, how did proposals for emancipation of the working class formulated on the level of political parties find expression in union politics? Second, what effects did the nature of labor union structure exert on the struggles of workers seeking their emancipation? Third, how did the cultural background of these workers and their situation in the labor market limit the possibilities for emergence of a strong and autonomous trade union movement?

The second challenge had an institutional nature and dealt with the consolidation of Sociology and the legitimacy of its practitioners. Sociologists had a main role in this process of institutionalizing Social Science in Brazil, and sought to make its analytical discourse prevail. To achieve this goal, their analysis should be capable of unveiling what was emerging in the new competitive order, impregnating Brazilian society, and consolidating that society as a nation. Responses were expected to urgent questions: What was the nature of the process of change witnessed in the 1950s and 1960s? Who were its workers, where did they come from, and what kind of aspirations did they have? How was the industrial bourgeoisie formed and what could we say on its ideas about the economic development? Which are the structural correlates to the industrialization process? What kind of value system structured social relations in urban environments and how did this new social order share the scene with the values of an archaic Brazil (supposed to be under effect of a structural crisis)?

Facing this kind of questions, sociologists, in those years, dared to run the risk of formulating a theory on the nature of Brazilian society, challenging the ethnocentrism of sociological theories of modernization (Lopes, 1967) and laying the foundations for reflections that later on would give way to the studies on social structure and social classes in situations of dependent development (Cardoso, 1964; Ianni, 1967; Cardoso and Faletto, 1970). Studies on labor and industrial workers played a strategic role on the construction of interpretations among these pioneers. By carrying them out, Brazilian sociology of work demonstrated its capacity for dialogue with different interpretations about modern industrial society, whether articulated from the starting point of United States academic thought on industrial relations (as Dunlop and Kerr), or from the vantage point of European thought on the nature of labor and working class consciousness (as Friedmann, Naville, and Touraine).[1]

THE "NEW UNIONISM" AND THE NEW SOCIOLOGY OF INDUSTRIAL LABOR

An important theoretical inflection marked the sociology of industrial labor in Brazil toward the end of the 1970s, inaugurating a new wave of studies. This inflection came on the heels of two processes. On the one hand, the resurgence of the trade union movement in 1978, renewed in its agenda and organizational forms—the so-called "new unionism"—after many years of absence from the public scene. This resurgence took place in a new context, which was no longer grounded on a populist ideology, but was marked by the echoes of an "economic miracle" (1967–1973) nurtured under the authoritarian leadership of military governments.

On the other hand were the repercussions in the Brazilian intellectual milieu of the new tendencies in the Sociology of Work: the analysis of actors' social practices drove scientific interest to the observation of daily life in the factories, emphasizing subjective construction of experiences as the main avenue to understanding individual and collective behavior at work. This also implied a methodological divide: qualitative rather than quantitative analysis, sustained in depth interviews and observation of labor process organization, tended to prevail as the most important research strategies. In Brazil, as indeed in the greater part of Latin America, Marxist thought was experiencing an unparalleled academic diffusion and success at this moment. In the area of labor studies, at least two currents fed this intellectual supremacy. On the one hand, the reinterpretation of Marxian theory proposed by Braverman, strongly anchored in the heuristic value of labor process analysis, set off, in Brazil,

---

[1]The relevance of this dialogue can be documented by its repercussions in France: the prestigious journal *Sociologie du Travail* dedicated one of its issues (4, 1961) to diffuse the new studies on the Brazilian working class.

what Littler, with the Anglo-Saxon world in mind, dubbed "Bravermania." On the other hand, there was the vigor of Marxist-inspired English social history (Thompson and Hobsbawn), which was renewing and challenging narrow structuralism and placing value on the dimension of the work experience.[2]

This inflection led early macro analysis on political parties and unions, as well as its reflections on the working class formation process, to lose prominence to another style of micro analysis, that of the so-called "labor processes studies." They sought to understand the "way in which capital organizes the productive consumption of the workforce" (Sorj, 1983: 3) and the political forms of resistance developed by workers in the course of their daily production activities at the shop-floors (Maroni, 1982).

One of the most important trademarks of this new interpretative vein was the critique of the theoretical position that had prevailed until then, especially the view of the working class as passive and lacking consciousness (Pereira, 1979; Fischer, 1985). Directing their gaze to what was happening on factory floors, case studies within corporations revealed multiple and heterogeneous workers' collectives that developed complex strategies of resistance to domination (Le Ven, 1983). As Sader and Paoli effectively expressed it, "the social science researchers of the 1980s found themselves looking at a political moment marked by various movements of struggle against different forms of oppression, a process that removed the attributes of 'alienation' and heteronomy traditionally attributed to the workers from the scene." In reality, according to Sader and Paoli, the emerging movements had "the effect of sanctioning new interpretations and images that were being produced," demonstrating the "perception of a noncoincidence between prevailing representations and the social experience of reality" (1986: 60). Attentive to the political dimensions and the subjective forms of expression that came through in the discourse of this "new unionism," sociologists began to confront the challenge of rebuilding a sociological interpretation of the work experience, recovering through it the meaning of the perspective of *multiple subjects* weaving the experience together (Lobo, 1991).

The dynamics of empirical research itself progressively broadened interest in the direction of new themes, little explored until that time: capitalist

[2]Some analyses, developing even before the emergence of strikes in the heart of Brazilian industry in 1978 and 1979, anticipated the new direction the working class movement in Brazil would take. In particular, the writings of Weffort (1972, 1978, and 1979) were precursors; he was concerned with understanding not only the social and subjective construction of a new social group (as had been done in the 1950s and 1960s) but also with explaining the emergence of this group as an important actor on the institutional scene. Studying the modality of political inclusion of urban wage earners in the populist state, he laid the analytical foundations for future discussions of the interests and forms of representation and negotiation placed on the table, after 1978, by this "new unionism."

strategies of labor organization and workforce management, labor market segmentation, sexual and social division of labor, and effects of technology on work, skills and resistance to managerial strategies of domination and control. In this process, the study of strikes and social conflicts shifted its focus: the performance and orientation of union leadership, a central issue in the 1960s and 1970s, gave way to the need to throw light on the relation between workers' demands and the labor process; attention was diverted to the new social practices that emerged on the factory floor.

As noticed by Abreu (1985:3) broadening of the scope of analysis also meant, for Brazilian Sociology, the challenge to incorporate the contribution of other areas of knowledge, earlier already familiar with the study of the workplaces, such as: production engineering, business administration, the psychology of labor, as well as studies of occupational health, particularly ergonometrics, and the psychopathology of work.

GENDER AND LABOR PROCESS PERSPECTIVE: A CROSS-FERTILIZATION

This dialogue between the Sociology of Work and correlated areas in the field of the Social Sciences sharpened the acuity of this new generation of interpreters, rendering more valuable, in their eyes, the analysis of relationships between factory life and life outside the factory. They emphasized, especially, the nexus between the social practices and representations built in other institutional contexts (like the family, the domestic unit, the school, the neighborhood, etc.) and their expression in the workplace.

Perhaps the interfaces between the Sociology of Work and Gender Studies constitute a suitable example of virtuous emulation among thematic fields within the domain of Brazilian social science. In fact, the interest in women's participation in the industrial labor force made its mark on the history of analyses of the female condition in Brazil, constituting, as Bruschini suggests (1993: 2), "the port of entry into women's studies in the Brazilian academy" (Blay, 1978; Madeira e Singer, 1975; Saffioti, 1969). Indeed, until the 1970s, analyses in vogue (even the most impressive ones), dedicated to the study of industrialization by import substitution and to the structure of the working class in Brazil, had remained impermeable to what Lobo (1991) expressed as their "sexed composition," which left questions of gender invisible to the mainstream of Brazilian academic production. The insistence with which feminist studies began to point out the "occupational ghettoes" existing in a labor market described as strongly segmented (Saffioti, 1981; Bruschini, 1985) sparked off another area of interest, which became, in the 1970s and 1980s, an important interpretative challenge for the Sociology of Work in Brazil.

This challenge was based on changes in the occupational structure that were already becoming evident. On one hand, the sectorial composition of female employment became more complex with the increasing integration of women in the sectors labeled "dynamic," particularly in segments of manufacturing like mechanical industry or in the production of electrical and electronic equipment (Humphrey, 1984; Hirata, 1988; Gitahy, Hirata, Lobo e Moysés, 1982; Moura et al., 1984; Moysés, 1985; Spindel, 1987[a]; Liedke, 1989). On the other hand, the 1981-1983 economic crisis, far from doing away with their recently created opportunities (Spindel, 1987b), made evident the need to associate the study of inequality of access to the *labor market* with the analysis of forms of segregation in the *labor process* (Hirata and Humphrey, 1988).

Sociology of Industrial Labor and Sociology of the Family and Gender Relations were, then, as related fields, nourished reciprocally with notable intensity during the 1980s in Brazil. As a result of this cross-fertilization new research designs emerged on the study of the sexual division of labor and gender roles: case studies in corporations, eminently qualitative, oriented to observing the organization and administration of social relations of gender within concrete labor processes. Daily factory life became, then, the key analytical instance for responding to the question of why Brazilian women, despite their ability to penetrate the industrial labor market, and even in the dynamic industries, found themselves there confined to the most subordinate, worst paid, and least qualified positions (Abreu, 1979 e 1981; Acero, 1980; Spindel, 1980; Caulliraux, 1981; Moysés, 1985; Moura et al, 1984; Neves, 1990, Liedke, 1989).

In this sense, the concept of "division of labor" itself began to be seen as more than a simple division of tasks; it also implied asymmetrical distribution of control, hierarchy, skills, career, and wage or salary. Gender was revealed to be a determining variable in the building of this asymmetry, and the studies turned to the ingredients of labor culture on which this determinant was grounded. These asymmetries expressed traditions and hierarchies—that is, *symbolic* components—socially constructed and experienced (Lobo and Soares, 1985; Humphrey and Hirata, 1984; Moura et. al., 1984; Moysés, 1985; Abreu, 1986; Rodrigues, A., 1978). It's interpretation required understanding not only the concrete and microcosmic forms of producing consent and reproducing domination, but also the construction of resistance and collective action.

In this way, shop-floor observation made from the perspective of gendered labor processes revealed the existence of various job situations that put into effect social differences among workers constructed *outside* the production process and *existing previously to* the economic insertion of individuals; differences that, once created or produced, could be appropriated without even being perceived by those subject to them (Rodrigues, A., 1978). Thus, when "work is no longer a physical operation that involves a workforce *but becomes a communicative practice,* neither gestures nor the language of administration or of working women and men can be generalized" (Lobo, 1991: 261). The theoretical formulation of Brazilian Sociology acquired, then, the necessary complexity and turned its attention to other experiences just as symbiotically allied as gender to the experience of being a worker: for example, ethnicity/ race or age (Castro, 1989; Morel e Pessanha, 1991; Castro e Guimarães, 1993; Silva, 1993; Agier, 1994; Sansone, 1994).

CLASS FORMATION AND EMERGENT IDENTITIES: UNIONISM AND SOCIAL MOVEMENTS

During the late 1970s and early 1980s there also flowered a new line of studies starting from socioanthropological and historiographical researches that cast their eyes on various moments of working class formation in Brazil, with influential results on the way sociologists conceived their methodologies and interpretations to deal with issues like discipline and control at work, or collective action and workers political autonomy under authoritarian regimes (Alvim, 1985; Blass, 1986; Hardmann, 1983; Hardmann e Leonardi, 1982; Paoli, 1987; Leite Lopes, 1976 e 1988; Rizek, 1988: Minayo, 1986; Morel, 1989; Ramalho, 1986).

Sociology, in particular, found its attention attracted to the innovative nature of the emerging demands and practices of the so-called "new unionism," although workers and unions submission to severe repression under military governments. For some authors, the impressive metal workers strikes and its related social movements (as women's, or catholic activists) the took place by the end of the 1970s were challenged to demonstrate what their contribution was to be, meaning whether or not they merely expressed the aspirations of a workers' elite in the modern industrial sectors, aspirations characterized by their special working conditions and equally specific demands, which probably would be impertinent to the Brazilian working class as a whole (Almeida, 1978). As Vianna stated (1984: 56), if this kind of interpretation was to be confirmed, "the identity of the 'new unionism' would tend to separate it from the rest of the workers." Nevertheless, for other interpreters, these practices expressed the reaction of a social group which, while enjoying a relatively advantageous wage level, was likewise submitted to oppressive working conditions and for that reason would be capable of assuming the vanguard of a movement contesting the authoritarian forms of administration of the labor force imposed by managers in the context of a dictatorial regime (Humphrey, 1982).

Humphrey's study on the automobile industry became a landmark in this new phase of the Sociology of Industrial Labor in Brazil. One of the most important findings of his study consisted of showing clearly that the workers responsible for implementing the "economic miracle," during the golden economic years of military regime in Brazil, had developed a feeling of "injustice with respect to the ever-shrinking compensation for their efforts toward growth", to which was added "the consciousness that employers did have the resources to offer higher wages and better working conditions" (Humphrey, 1982: 159).

The forcefulness of the workers' protests against the so-called "wage squeeze" ("*arrocho salarial*") imposed by the military dictatorship stimulated some analysts to emphasize the eminently economic foundation of the 1978 metal workers strike (Antunes, 1986). Others, treading the trail blazed by Humphrey, emphasized the experience of injustice to which workers were submitted in the workplace as a fundamental element in explaining the impetus of this struggle. These authors underlined the need to integrate into the analysis the question of worker subjectivity, a dimension that would show itself to be of undeniable heuristic value (Abramo, 1986).

Humphrey's findings, quite well explored by the bibliography that followed, were enriched by an important complementation in the work of Sader (1988). Conjugating the analysis of the "new unionism" with that of other social movements that arose in this same context, Sader called attention to the birth of distinct discursive forms by means of which social segments emerging on the political scene thematicized their life situations. Thus, taking up the same empirical field examined before by Humphrey, Sader (1988: 194-5) documented how the São Bernardo do Campo Metal Union began to "thematicize injustices from the angle of the lack of reciprocity between the importance of the work performed, on the one hand, and the remuneration received and the precariousness of working conditions and living conditions on the other." The linkage between working conditions and living conditions, labor union struggles and social movements, opened the way to new studies, which strengthened the ties between the Sociology of Labor and Urban Sociology. Thus, the understanding was construed that the "new unionism"—by confronting the military regime and articulating its critique of factory authoritarianism captained by management with the critique of authoritarianism in matters of state—sketched out a workers' alternative for the transition to democracy in the country. In this sense, it introduced a new political actor onto the Brazilian public scene (Sader, 1988).

Several other studies evidenced the relationship existing between, on the one hand, forms of organization of the labor process and human resources management predominant in Brazilian industrial plants and, on the other, the characteristics of the emerging trade union movement (Leite, 1985 e 1987; Almeida, 1982). Following the spread of the movement itself, these studies moved to nonfactory settings, like that of workers in the construction and housing industry (Vargas, 1979; Bicalho, 1983), that of bank employees (Segnini, 1988; Blass, 1992; Pereira e Crivellari, 1991; Silva, 1991; Grün, 1986), and other sectors of middle-class wage earners that acquired an important presence in the Brazilian union movement starting in the middle of the 1980s (Rodrigues, L., 1991; Noronha, 1991). What stands out as an element of convergence among these authors' interpretations is the interest in analyzing forms of labor organization and the struggles and demands they stimulated.

(DE)CENTRALIZING WORKERS COLLECTIVE ACTION: REGIONAL AND INSTITUTIONAL SPACES

The paths along which the collective attitudes and practices of the so-called "new unionism" was spreading from core to periphery of industrial Brazil were equally pursued. The idea was to understand how these attitudes and practices were reproduced in "greenfield" sites, other regional contexts of recent industrialization, fruits of the process of productive expansion and industrial decentralization unleashed by the military governments in their effort to complete the process of import substitution and evade from unions militantism. Thus, new industrial poles like Belo Horizonte-Betim, Salvador-Camaçari, Recife, Manaus, Porto Alegre-Canoas-Triunfo attracted the attention of Brazilian researchers who turned to explanation of the process of constituting a modern working class, a process now already in course on a national scale (Spindel, 1987a; Le Ven e Neves, 1985; Le Ven, 1987; Guimarães, 1988 e 1998; Guimarães e Castro, 1988 e 1990; Agier, Castro e Guimarães, 1994; Liedke, 1992; Cattani, 1991; Lima, 1995).

Other analyses sought to unveil the processes by which forms of workers' organization in the workplace were constituted and spread (Silva, R., 1985; Faria, 1986; Keller, 1988; Rodrigues, I., 1990), making clear the different ways in which workers articulated their resistance to authoritarianism with the support of the formal or tacit knowledge they had about the labor process (Maroni, 1982; Grün, Ferro e Zilbovicius, 1987). Equally important were those analyses that traced the diffusion of the practice of collective bargaining. With this practice, the "new unionism" challenged both the countless legal provisions constraining bargaining, but also the employers' resistance to negotiating the conditions under which work was performed (Silva, R., 1990; Almeida, 1981).

The dynamics of the labor union movement in the period were also studied from the point of view of quantitative analyses on strikes (Noronha, 1991; Sandoval, 1994) and the proliferation of unions (Silva, 1992). The first group of studies witnessed a noteworthy process of consolidation in the movement, configured in the increasing number of strike mobilizations during the 1980s. The latter group, on the other hand, pointed to a paradoxical situation: while, in some cases, the increase in the number of unions could signify a strengthening of workers' organization, in others it denoted only the atomization of union organization brought on by the nature of the Brazilian legislation.* Also, the constitution of central union organizations began to challenge analysts who turned to investigating the characteristics of the different national trade union tendencies, their political concepts and practices, as well as the profile of their activists. Brazilian trade unionism was becoming ideologically plural and its dynamics corresponded to the dynamics of the multiple actors in the labor union context, no longer reducible to the earlier difference between "authentic unionists" and "*pelegos*"† (Rodrigues, 1990, 1991 and 1992; Rodrigues and Cardoso, 1993).

The movement's impetus and its capacity to maintain its place on the political scene strengthened the forms of labor organization, making workers important actors in the struggle for the country's redemocratization. The social and political role of the actors from the "new unionism" in the creation of the Workers' Party–PT, in 1979, was also an object of analysis in several studies (Moisés, 1981), fueling, moreover, a new generation of Brazilianists, whose attention was captured by the labor milieu (Keck, 1991; Seidman, 1992; French, 1993; Martin, 1995).[3]

Once the transition to civilian government was complete, sociological reflections went on to inquire about the labor union movement's influence on the building of a new democratic order, expressed initially during the 1988 Constituent Assembly proceedings. For some authors (L. Rodrigues, 1988), this new institutionality ended up strengthening the old union leadership, piled up in the federations and confederations that were opposed to the "new unionism." But others (Leite and Silva, 1988) emphasized the advances brought into being by the new Constitution with respect, for example, to the winning of the right to strike and greater freedom of action for labor unions, while at

---

*In the context of Brazilian labor legislation, the system of trade union organization under state tutelage involved what is called "unicidade sindical" (literally," trade union oneness"), meaning that one union was authorized by the State to advocate the interests of workers in a given sector of industry. Trade unions were financed by a tax collected by the State, and "base unions" (locals) were also granted a monopoly of representation by state authorization. Thus, the choice of union representation was not made by the workers themselves and trade unions independence was limited. (Tranlator's note)

†"Pelegos," meaning saddle cushions, is an expression used to denote leaders of the unions created under state tutelage, who acted essentially as intermediaries between labor and the government bureaucracy charged with implementing labor legislation. "Authentic unionists" refers to union leadership arising organically out of workers' struggles. (Translator's note)

[3]This is another interesting characteristic of this second moment in the constitution of the Sociology of Industrial Labor in Brazil: international interchange was deepened and a new circuit of Brazilianists was consolidated around the field of industrial labor and its organization. The emergence of this "new unionism" replaced Brazil on the agenda of comparative labor studies.

the same time recognizing that certain principles of the old labor union structure (which the "new unionism" fought against) had managed to survive (the principle of single trade unions, compulsory collection of the labor union tax, and the monopoly of representation by the base unions), keeping alive the main elements of an organization that was based on "atomized corporatism" (Silva and Leite, 1987: 38). What increased and grew more profound in this period was reflection about the meaning of labor union legislation, the major traits of which persist even under the new Constitution (Comin, 1994; Boito, 1993) and its effects on the Brazilian model of industrial relations, a "legislated" model, to borrow the idea from one of its interpreters (Noronha, 1999).

In reality, the question of the limits of a new proletarian and labor union movement produced important results for the Sociology of Industrial Labor in Brazil. Almeida (1988) and Noronha (1991), for example, sounded an alert to the lack of synchronization existing between the strength of the labor movement on the social plane and its scant political significance, understood as the capacity to "influence the definition of governmental policies in the social area, including policy on wages and salaries" (Almeida, 1988: 328). Sader also called attention to the fact that the consummation of the democratic transition in 1985 (with the election of the first civilian President since 1962) meant a defeat for the political project implicit in the social movements that emerged at the end of the 1970s. "Led 'precociously' to combat in the political arena, they expressed their immaturity as power alternatives on the level of political representation" (Sader, 1988: 315). In this way, "neither the unions would have been capable of appearing before the State as respectable interlocutors, nor would the political parties have expressed labor union demands in Congress with sufficient strength to force a compromise" (Castro e Guimarães, 1990: 219–221). From this resulted the apparent "paradox of formally conquered, but scarcely implemented, rights" (id.), exemplified by the Constitutional provisions unable to be enforced because their implementing legislation was not enacted.

CRISIS, RESTRUCTURING, AND LABOR: BRAZILIAN SOCIOLOGY OF WORK IN THE 90'S

From the perspective of some interpreters, the 1980s were, for Brazil, simply a "lost decade." This view was sanctioned by the economists, who focused on the performance of economic growth in general and employment in particular. Nevertheless, the transition to democracy, large-scale social mobilizations, the strengthening of the workplace organizations and labor union movements also set the tone of the period; and these are also crucial aspects in a sociological interpretations of this period. This strengthening of the public spheres of expression in civil society occurred at the same time that the country took its first steps toward a new form of global integration with economic opening, state reform and amplified deregulation. How, then, did a work culture carved out on the experience of authoritarianism come to exist side by side with the social appeal for democratization? How did the extension of citizenship to the shop-floors, one of the first-hour banners of the "new unionism," temper new managerial strategies of technological and organizational modernization of Brazilian industry in an international context of increasing competitive integration? How recently achieved rights (under a new Constitution) could be challenged and reverted by a new wave of de-regulation?

The interpretations and analytical paths of the Brazilian Sociology of Work reflect, in great measure, the directions and vicissitudes of the process of industrial restructuring itself. Heterogeneous, it affected in different ways and with various degrees of intensity the distinct industrial sectors, the diverse regions of the country, and the various groups of workers (Abramo, 1990; Leite, 1994b).

In a first and embryonic moment, which covers the first half of the 1980s, innovative proposals were restricted to the adoption of quality control circles, while businesses were not concerned with changing the forms of labor organization in a meaningful way or investing more effectively in new microelectronic equipment. Several studies pointed, then, to the partial and reactive nature of this "Japanization," of doubtful efficacy and quick to perish (Fleury, A., 1985 and 1988; Hirata, 1983; Salerno, 1985; Carvalho, 1987; Castro, 1995; Hirata, 1993).

A second moment began with the reanimation of economic activity in 1984-85 (after the recession that had left its mark on the years of 1981-83), and extended into the last years of the 1980s, characterized by rapid diffusion of basic microelectronic equipment. This confluence of trends stimulated research on the individual and collective (whether organized as unions or not) forms of symbolic and political elaborations about the new technical conditions of daily life at work (Marques, 1986; Neder, 1988; Abramo, 1988; Leite , 1994[a]; Rizek, 1994). Thus, the issues related to the symbolic dimension in the study of labor organization and administration gained ground (Araujo, 1997), and categories like "technical culture" (Valle, 1991) or "enterprise culture" (Fleury, 1986) became important tools of analysis.

While at this time a small group of firms was making an effort to introduce new forms of work organization, studies documented the employers' resistance to broader changes in their strategies of workforce management and in particular to amplifying the margins of workers' participation in decisions relating to the productive process (Leite and Silva, 1991; Hirata et. al., 1992; Humphrey, 1994; Ferro, 1992; Castro e Guimarães, 1991; Castro, 1995; Marx, 1999; Arbix and Zilbovicius, 1998). The paradox of this so-called "conservative modernization" instigated researchers to turn their attention to understanding firm strategies of technical-organizational innovation (often unequal, in their nature and intensity) in the different sectors (Salerno, 1994; Lobo, 1994; Segre e Tavares, 1991; Rizek, 1991; Grün, 1992; Castro 1995; Arbix and Zilbovicius, 1998).

The early 1990s signs the emergence of a new phase. Changes in economic policy (rapid commercial opening in a context of economic growth crisis and retraction of the internal market), together with the redefinition of the form of state intervention (less protection by the ending of various regulatory mechanisms, especially fiscal and financial ones), obliged firms to quickly redirect their goals and strategies. What stands out here are the multiple measures of cost reduction conducive to concentrating enterprise efforts on the renovation of organizational strategies and adoption of new forms of labor management that could render compatible initiatives to reduce the number of employees and to make labor flexible, on the one hand, with, on the other, the need for workers' involvement in the challenges of production in a more competitive context and under the orientation of new (economic and political) ways of regulating unions and firm actions.

These changes, accelerated along with the spread of quality and productivity programs, altered the discourse of entrepreneurs, which now began to address, with insistence, new issues like: improving on labor force skills, simplification of wage and career structures, reduction of hierarchical levels, and promotion of workers' active commitment (Grün, 1999). For this very reason, openly authoritarian policies of relationship at the shop-floors began to be challenged by the need to attract the individual worker, assuring his active commitment, in order to introduce less conflictive forms of labor management under uncertain and more competitive conditions for production (Gitahy e Rabelo, 1991; Humphrey, 1991; Carvalho, 1992; Leite, E., 1993; Leite,M. 1993; Castro, 1993). Interpreters had to face some difficult questions: Could this process be pointing to "incremental cultural changes in the firms" (Fleury, M., 1993)? How do such changes impact on a dispute for hegemony and legitimacy among competitive management discourses within the firm (Grün, 1999)? What are their effects on the negotiation of labor relations?

The Sociology of Industrial Labor in Brazil debated, then, and in a heated manner, the meaning of these changes. For some, they contained the embryo of a possible democratization of labor relations on the shop-floor (Gitahy e Rabelo, 1991). Others, however, underscored their possible limits: authoritarian practices persisted, especially with respect to relations with unions and with labor organizations in the workplace (Leite,M. 1993; Humphrey, 1993; Ruas, 1993 a). Indeed, with very localized exceptions (resulting from workers' efforts to assure arenas in which they could intervene and negotiate changes, as in the automobile industry), the employers predominant position was to marginalize unions and undermine (or eliminate) the viability of workers' organizations within factories (Castro and Dedecca, 1998; Antunes, 1999).

Nevertheless, important novelties took place during this same period. On the one hand, trade unions were displaying the first signs of a programmatic transition that could take them from the old posture of "unconditional resistance" to positions more amenable to negotiation and to contracting the conditions under which innovations were to be introduced (Bresciani, 1991). On the other hand, the union movement had consolidated its own intellectuals and legitimized its own reflection, constructed and propagated out through non-academic institutions.[4] We would risk stating that, for the first time since the end of the 1950s – when Sociology was constituted as the monopolizer of legitimate interpretative discourse, by institutionalizing the rules of a "*metier*" and the training of those who would intervene there –, the field of work and labor studies began to contain more than one producer of legitimate discourse. The institutions and actors of the labor union movement qualified themselves as interpreters; their spokespeople began to interact with academically seated Sociology, finally being recognized by it as part of the same discursive field, and not only as its "objects."

CHALLENGES AND PERSPECTIVES

All these processes, while embryonic, brought to the fore new interpretative challenges, central to our end-of-the-century Sociology of Work. These challenges converge to a new subject – the meaning of current Brazilian society modernization (a term that curiously is coming back to center stage, right where it had been in the fifties and sixties).

The first and theoretical one is not even close to being a local challenge. On the contrary, it had become current in the international debate because it dealt with the horizons of labor society in general and the heuristic value of labor studies for the understanding of contemporary societies in particular (Antunes, 1995 and 1999). In the Brazilian case, this debate took on a local color to the extent that its necessary counterpart was the confrontation of another challenge: the discussion of the crisis of Fordism and the transition toward new paradigms of production. How could this crisis be understood, in a case like Brazil's, when this form of regulation had never taken on the traits

---

[4]Among these institutions, we would emphasize DIEESE—Labor Union Department of Statistics and SocioEconomic Studies, and DESEP—the Social, Economic, and Political Studies Department of the Single Workers' Central Union (CUT). DIEESE, over its long history, evolved from its role of technical support for the negotiations on wages, benefits and workplace conditions to that of a (socially) legitimate and (intellectually) authorized interpreter of the processes in which it was originaly involved as a secondary, supporting actor.

of what Boyer called "genuine Fordism", but on the contrary was understood as a special mode of regulation, a "peripheral Fordism" . This argument was already included in our agenda, as a legacy of the 1970s and 1980s intellectuals, who had to deal with characterizing Brazilian fordist-taylorist factory regimes (Humphrey, 1982; Silva, 1991; Vargas, 1985). But, while it was an important finding, it is clearly insufficient to express the new terms of the debate: had the emergence of the so-called "Japanese model" and its correlate strategies of production and labor management forged a new normative culture, one capable of irresistible imposition and transferability—like every "one best way"? Since the end of the 1980s, the Brazilian Sociology of Work has dedicated much of its effort in empirical analysis (Carvalho, 1993; Zilbovicius, 1999; Marx, 1999; Salerno, 1998; Druck, 1997) and theoretical reflection (Hirata et alli, 1989; Hirata, 1993; Antunes, 1995 and 1999) to confronting and refuting any kind of facile and oversimplifiyingly affirmative answer to this question.

But the response to this first challenge was interlinked with facing a second one. Observing the actors, it seemed that redefinitions of their structural configuration and political expression were underway, in step with this new national and international scenario. Thus, important dimensions of the industrial organization, of the industrial relations and of the labor market became the object of negotiations between actors who recognized each other as legitimate interlocutors. In this sense, the situation in the 1990s was distinct from the experience of the 1970s and the beginning of the 1980s, when a factory regime based on political and market despotism guaranteed the workers' acceptance of goals and modes of organizing production (Humphrey, 1982; Carvalho, 1987; Guimarães, 1988; Silva, 1991; Cardoso e Comin, 1993).

On the other hand, the restructuring that was underway made it imperative to understand the new face of industrial organization in Brazil, as well as the new patterns of interrelationship that began to characterize networks of clients and suppliers, internal or external. It altered the structural profile and the forms of solidarity and hierarchy that had become established among employer sectors, influencing the way in which they were beginning to negotiate working conditions on the factory floor (Gitahy e Rabelo, 1993; Abreu e Ramalho, 1999).

This was undoubtedly a third challenging terrain brought before Brazilian interpreters in the 1990s. To face it, our Sociology of Work once more renewed its focus, redefining the object and style of empirical research: it was necessary to shift the focus away from the single firm (deeply analyzed in qualitative one-case study research designs) and direct it to production chains, combining analysis of the labor process organization and firm strategies with study of the reshaping of the industrial organization, concentrating attention on global inter-firm networks.

In fact, Brazilian experience of subcontracting and formation of production chains has taken shape as an important tendency in the last few years, especially since 1990 when the economy was rapidly opened up to the international market. Subcontracting, not only of activities linked to services supporting production but also of productive areas in themselves, began to be identified by several researches already being carried out in the beginning of the 1990s (Martins and Ramalho, 1994; Gitahy and Rachid, 1995). Some authors (Rabelo, 1989; Gitahy and Rachid, 1995; Leite, E. 1996 e 1997; Gitahy, et. al., 1997) demonstrated that, parallel to the practice of subcontracting, a movement toward qualification of suppliers conducted by contracting firms with a view to guaranteeing the quality of the products supplied, could indicate that an effort was being articulated between large and small firms, like that which the international bibliography was identifying in other countries (Brusco, 1982; Piore and Sabel, 1984).

However, this movement did not spread the employment and working conditions found in the leading companies in the productive process throughout the production chain as a whole. With respect to working conditions, the studies pointed out a process of deterioration, the more visible the further one followed downstream the productive chain. This process of deterioration included the perpetuation of repetitive and unskilled tasks, the acceleration of rhythms, the intensification of supervision control, and the rise in incidence of occupational disease (Martins and Ramalho, 1994, Ruas and Antunes, 1997; Bresciani, 1997, Carleial, 1997; Leite, M. 1999; Leite, M. and Rizek, 1997; Carleial, 1997; Salerno, 1998; Hirata, 1998a). With respect to employment contracting conditions, the works underscored the process of increased precariousness that was unleashed, demonstrating the rise of informality, the shrinking of wages, the increase of the work period, and the loss of benefits (Singer, 1996 and 1999; Pochmann, 1999; Hirata, 1998b). The overlapping of these processes with the sexual division of labor cannot be underestimated; countless studies underscored this tendency, emphasizing the confinement of women to the most degraded positions (Leite, M., 1999; Hirata, 1998[a]) as well as the most precarious job situations (Bruschini, 1997; Segnini, 1996; Posthuma and Lombardi, 1997; Hirata, 1998b).

Faced with the new reality of the 1990s, Brazilian interpreters once more posed the uncomfortable question of the meaning of these changes. The responses have pointed out that these tendencies are not inexorable. On the contrary, some studies have shown that industrial relations have revealed themselves to be an important factor in the definition of the conditions in which the process of subcontracting takes place and therefore of the quality of employment and working conditions that can be assured throughout the production chains. Examples in this vein have been pointed out for different sectors of industry and regions of the country (Leite, M. and Rizek, 1997; Bresciani,

1997; Carleial, 1997; Abreu et. al., 1999; Castro and Dedecca, 1998; Lima, 1998).

Finally, faced with the new reality of the 1990s, studies on the workplace were led to confront a fourth challenge: to intensify their analytical dialogue with the studies that take the labor market as their central focus of observation. Indeed, the Sociology of Work, which at its dawn took up labor market studies as one its privileged themes, little by little, especially in view of the central importance of studies of the labor process, stopped cultivating this focus of observation. The economics of labor was responsible for the best descriptions and analyses developed in the 1980s. The restructuring of forms of labor contracting and use, coeval with the restructuring of the productive structure, made it urgent to return to the labor market as a critical sphere of observation.

In this respect, emphasis on the theme of flexibilization of labor has perhaps been emblematic. In a country like Brazil, where the flexible use of the workforce seems to be a generic given, how can one grant analytical meaning to the category of "flexibility"? The specificity of this process could only have its effects well interpreted if it were analyzed simultaneously from the point of view of intra- *and* extra-factory determinants, which affect the new contractual forms that are expressed in the labor market (Dedecca and Montagner, 1993; Dedecca, Montagner and Brandão, 1993; Mattoso, 1999; Carleal e Valle, 1997). This analysis placed in evidence, once again, important differentials that distinguish the opportunities of various groups of workers, like women, whose intense afflux into the labor market is associated, in the 1990s, with the tendency to increased female unemployment, rising more swiftly than male unemployment (Bruschini, 1998; Lavinas, 1998) or youth, who while sharing with women the tendency to higher and more rapidly attained levels of schooling are subject to acute problems of insertion into the labor market; or black (afro-Brazilian) workers, whose high levels of integration in the market do not find a counterpart in the nature of the positions they occupy within the market nor in the remuneration they receive (Hasenbalg and Silva, 1995; Castro and Sa-Barreto, 1997; Silva, 1995).

Moreover, this intense social selectivity, a corollary to industrial restructuring, reopened the discussion on growth and exclusion. In Brazil, recent sociological studies on poverty and citizenship (Telles, 1992; Lopes and Gottshalk, 1990; Lopes, 1993) enriched the most orthodox tradition of our Industrial Sociology, mainly concerned with the new work environments in industry that would nest the "survivors" of the restructuring process; analysis on poverty and exclusion preserved the focus on the "redundants". The studies on transitions in the labor market also renewed the Brazilian Sociology of Work broadening its research designs by the introduction of quantitative longitudinal approaches applied to macro-social analysis of large secondary data basis (Cardoso, 2000; Caruso and Pero, 1997; Castro, 1998). Interest was re-kindled in occupational mobility, an interest not cultivated since the studies on social stratification of the 1950s and 1960s (Huntington, 1965) or since the vogue in studies on occupational marginality in the 1970s.

Thus, in recent researches on the restructuring of industry in Brazil, comparative and longitudinal strategies of analysis have gained ground, in which the trajectories of firms (or groups of firms), but also the trajectories of workers, are followed over time and from different vantage points. The emergence of comparative and longitudinal studies is doubtlessly a methodological style that demands the formulation of hypotheses with broader explanatory force.

Comparisons, moreover, have become increasingly integrated into the results and interpretations. The multiplication of comparative researches and exchange networks among researchers seems to point to a new "Latin-Americanism" in Brazilian Sociology. From the 1950s to the 1970s, a Latin American Sociology attracted intellectuals all over the Continent, stimulated by the theme of development. We would risk saying that a recreation of this interest took place in the 1990s, with the studies of work as its starting point. [5]

REFERENCES

Abramo, L. (1986). *O Resgate da Dignidade*, Master's Dissertation, USP.
Abramo, L. A. (1990). "Novas tecnologias, difusão setorial, emprego e trabalho no Brasil: Um balanço," *BIB - Boletim Informativo e Bibliográfico de Ciências Sociais*, No. 30, Rio de Janeiro, Vértice/ANPOCS.
Abreu, A. (1985). "Processo de Trabalho e Ciências Sociais: A Contribuição do GT Processo de Trabalho e Reivindicações Sociais," Texts for Discussion in the Master's Program in Social Sciences, Rio de Janeiro, IFCS/UFRJ.
Abreu, A. (1986). *O avesso da moda - trabalho a domicílio na indústria de confecção*. São Paulo, Hucitec, 302 p.
Almeida, M. H. T. (1978). "Desarrollo Capitalista y Acción Sindical, *Revista Mexicana de Sociologia*, XI:XL.
Almeida, M. H. T. (1981). "Tendências Recentes da Negociação Coletiva no Brasil," *Revista Dados*, 24:2.
Almeida, M. H. T. (1982). "Novas Demandas, Novos Direitos," São Paulo, CEBRAP, mimeo.
Almeida, M. H. T. (1988). "Difícil caminho: Sindicatos e política na construção da democracia," in F.W. Reis e G. O'Donnel (Eds.), *A Democracia no Brasil: Dilemas e Perspectivas*, São Paulo, Vértice.

[5]This movement toward "Latin Americanization" of the Sociology of Work has advanced, in the last few years, in the direction of creating its own regional institutions: the Sociology of Work Latin American Association [*Associación Latinoamericana de Sociología del Trabajo* – ALAST] and its journal *Revista Latinoamericana de Estudios del Trabajo*, which has been circulating regularly since 1994.

Alvim, M. (1985). *Constituição da Família e Trabalho Industrial*: Um Estudo sobre Trabalhadores Têxteis numa Fábrica com Vila Operária, Ph.D. Thesis, UFRJ.

Antunes, R. (1986). *A Rebeldia do Trabalho*, São Paulo, Ensaio/Editora da UNICAMP.

Bicalho, N. (1983). *Construtores de Brasília*, Petrópolis, Vozes.

Blass, L. (1989). "A greve: uma festa" in *Ciências Sociais, Hoje - 1989*, São Paulo, ANPOCS/Vértice.

Blass, L. (1992). *Estamos em greve*, São Paulo, Hucitec/Sindicato dos Bancários de São Paulo.

Bresciani, L. P. (1991). *Tecnologia, Organização do Trabalho e Ação Sindical*: Da Resistência à Contratação, Master's Dissertation, São Paulo, Poli/USP.

Cardoso, F. H. (1962). "Proletariado no Brasil: situação e comportamento social." *Revista Brasiliense* 41, May-June, pp. 98–122.

Cardoso, A., & Comin, A. (1993). "Câmaras setoriais, modernização produtiva e democratização nas relações de trabalho no Brasil: a experiência do setor automobilístico," Communication presented at the 1st Latin American Congress of Sociology of Labor, México City, 22–26 de Novembro.

Cardoso, F. H. (1964). *Empresário Industrial e Desenvolvimento Econômico*. São Paulo, Difusão Européia do Livro.

Cardoso, F. H., & Faletto, E. (1970). *Dependência e Desenvolvimento na América Latina– Ensaio de Interpretação Sociológica*. Rio de Janeiro, Zahar Ed.

Carvalho, R. Q. (1987). *Tecnologia e Trabalho Industrial*, Porto Alegre, L&PM Editores.

Carvalho, R. Q. (1992). "Projeto de Primeiro Mundo com Conhecimento e Trabalho de Terceiro?", Campinas, IG/UNICAMP, *Texts for Discussion*, n.12.

Castro. M. G. (1988). *Gender, Family and Work*, Ph.D. Thesis, University of Florida, Gainesville.

Castro, N. (1993). "Modernização e Trabalho no Complexo Automotivo Brasileiro: Reestruturação Industrial ou Japanização de Ocasião?," *Novos Estudos CEBRAP* 37, November, pp. 155–173.

Castro, N., & Guimarães, A. (1990). "Trabalho, Sindicalismo e Reconversão Industrial no Brasil nos Anos 90," *Lua Nova* 22, São Paulo, CEDEC.

Dedecca, C., & Montagner, P. (1993). "Flexibilidade Produtiva e das Relações de Trabalho: Considerações sobre o Caso Brasileiro," São Paulo, 26 pp.

Dias, E. (1962). *História das Lutas Sociais no Brasil*. São Paulo, EDAGLIT, 329 p.

Faria, H. (1986). *A Experiência Operária nos Anos de Resistência*: A Oposição Sindical Metalúrgica de São Paulo e a dinâmica do Movimento Operário, Master's Dissertation, PUC/SP.

Ferro, J. (1992). "A produção enxuta no Brasil", in Womack, Jones e Roos, *A Máquina que Mudou o Mundo*, Rio de Janeiro, Campus, Apêndice B.

Fischer, R. (1985). "`Pondo os pingos nos is` sobre as relações do trabalho e políticas de administração de recursos humanos," in M. T. Fleury & R. Fischer (Eds.), *Processo e Relações do Trabalho no Brasil*, São Paulo, Atlas.

Fleury, A. (1985). "Organização do trabalho na indústria: Recolocando a questão nos anos 80", in M.T.Fleury e R.Fischer (Eds.), *Processo e Relações do Trabalho no Brasil*, São Paulo, Atlas.

Fleury, A. (1988). "Análise a nível da empresa dos impactos da microeletrônica sobre a organização da produção e do trabalho," São Paulo, USP/DEP, mimeo.

Fleury, M. (1993). "The culture of quality and the management of human resources," *IDS Bulletin* 24:2, April 1993.

Gitahy, L., & Rabelo, F. (1991). "Educação e desenvolvimento tecnológico: O caso da indústria de autopeças", Campinas, DPCT/IG/UNICAMP, *Texts For Discussion*, 11.

Gitahy, L., & Rabelo, F. (1993).

Grun, R. (1986). "Taylorismo e fordismo no trabalho bancário" in *Revista Brasileira de Ciências Sociais*, n. 2, v. 1.

Guimarães, A. (1988). *Factory Regime and Class Formation: the Petrochemical Workers in Brazil*, Ph.D. Thesis, Univ. Wisconsin-Madison.

Guimarães, A., & Castro, N. (1987). "Movimento sindical e formação de classe," *Caderno CRH* 5.

Guimarães, A., & Castro, N. (1988). "Espaços regionais de construção da identidade: a classe trabalhadora no Brasil pós-77", in: *Ciências Sociais, Hoje - 1988*, ANPOCS/ Vértice, São Paulo.

Guimarães, A., & Castro, N. (1990). "Classes, regimes fabris e mudança social no Nordeste Brasileiro," L. Valadares e E. Preteceille (Eds.) *Reestruturação Urbana: Tendências e Desafios*, Rio de Janeiro, Nobel.

Guimarães, A., Agier, M., & Castro, N. (1995). *Imagens e Identidades do Trabalho*. S.Paulo, HUCITEC.

Hardmann, F. (1983). *Nem Pátria, Nem Patrão*, São Paulo, Brasiliense.

Hirata, H. et al. (1992). "Alternativas sueca, italiana e japonesa ao paradigma fordista: Elementos para uma discussão do caso brasileiro," in *Gestão da Qualidade, Tecnologia e Participação* (Cadernos Codeplan 1), Brasília.

Hirata, H. (1983). "Receitas japonesas, realidade brasileira," *Novos Estudos CEBRAP*, 2.

Humphrey, J. (1982). *Fazendo o "Milagre,"* São Paulo, Vozes/CEBRAP.

Humphrey, J. (1990). "Adapting the 'Japanese Model' to Brazil," Communication presented at the International Seminar "Autour du Modele Japonais," Paris.

Humphrey, J. (1991). "Japanese methods and the changing position of direct production workers: Evidence from Latin America," IDS, University of Sussex, Falmer, Brighton, England.

Humphrey, J. (1992). "The management of labour and the move towards leaner production in the Third World: The case of Brazil," Communication presented to the International Institute for Labour Studies Forum, Geneva, November.

Humphrey, J. (1993). "The impact of 'Japanese' management techniques on labour in Brazilian manufacture," Sussex, IDS.

Humphrey, J., & Hirata, H. (1984). "Hidden inequalities: women and men in the labour process", in: *Anais*, IV National Encounter, Vol.1, Brazilian Association of Population Studies, São Paulo, pp. 271–300.

Ianni, O. (1967). *O Colapso do Populismo no Brasil*. Rio de Janeiro, Ed. Civilização Brasileira.

Keck, M. (1991). *PT: A Lógica da Diferença*, São Paulo, Ática.

Keller, W. (1986). "Os Processos de Negociação Coletiva e a Difusão das Comissões de Empresa no Setor Metalmecânico Paulista", São Paulo, CEBRAP, Research Report.

Leite Lopes, J. S. (1976). *O Vapor do Diabo - O Trabalho dos Operários do Açúcar*, Rio de Janeiro, Paz e Terra.

Leite Lopes, J. S. (1988). *A Tecelagem dos Conflitos de Classe na "Cidade das Chaminés,"* São Paulo, Marco Zero.

Le Ven, M. (1983). "Processo de Trabalho e Classe Trabalhadora," Paper presented at the VII Annual Encounter of ANPOCS, São Paulo.

Le Ven, M., & Neves, M. (1985). "A crise da indústria automobilística: automação e trabalho na FIAT", in *Ciências Sociais, Hoje - 1985* São Paulo, ANPOCS/Cortez.

Leite, E. (1993). "Uma escola em cada empresa?" Paper presented at the Seminar "Reestruturação Produtiva, Reorganização do Trabalho e Relações Industriais," São Paulo, CEBRAP, July.

Leite, M. (1985). "Reivindicações Sociais dos Metalúrgicos," in M.T. Fleury; R. Fischer (Eds.). *Processo e Relações do Trabalho no Brasil*, São Paulo, Atlas.

Leite, M. (1985a). "A Classe Operária e a Questão Sindical," in M.T. Fleury; R. Fischer (Eds.). *Processo e Relações do Trabalho no Brasil*, São Paulo, Atlas.

Leite, M. (1987). "Três Anos de Greve em São Paulo: 1983/1985," in *São Paulo em Perspectiva*, July/September.

Leite, M. (1993). "Inovación tecnológica, organización del trabajo y relaciones industriales en el Brasil," *Nueva Sociedad*, 124, Caracas, Editorial Nueva Sociedad.

Leite, M. e Silva, R. (1988). "Os Trabalhadores na Constituinte," *Documento de Trabalho*, 1, São Paulo, ILDES.

Leite, M., & Silva, R. et al. (1991). *Modernização Tecnológica, Relações de Trabalho e Práticas de Resistência*, São Paulo, Iglu/ILDES/LABOR.

Linhares, H. (1962). *Contribuição à História das Lutas Operárias no Brasil*. Rio de Janeiro.

Lobo, E., & Soares, V. (1985). "Masculino e feminino na linha de montagem," Paper presented to the Working Group "Labor Process and Social Demands," IX Annual Meeting of ANPOCS, São Paulo. In: E. Lobo. *A Classe Operária tem Dois Sexos*, São Paulo, Brasiliense, 1991.

Lopes, J. (1965). *Sociedade Industrial no Brasil*. Rio de Janeiro.

Lopes, J. (1967). *A Crise do Brasil Arcaico*. São Paulo, Difusão Européia do Livro.

Lopes, J., & Gottschalk, A. (1990). "Recessão, Pobreza e Família: a Década mais que Perdida", *São Paulo em Perspectiva*, SEADE 4: 2, April-June, pp. 32–36.

Maroni, A. (1982). *A Estratégia da Recusa*, São Paulo, Brasiliense.

Miglioli, J. (1963). "Como são feitas as greves no Brasil." *Cadernos do Povo* 13. Rio de Janeiro, Civilização Brasileira.

Minayo, M. (1986). *Os Homens de Ferro—Estudo sobre os trabalhadores da Vale do Rio Doce em Itabira*, Rio de Janeiro, Dois Pontos.

Moisés, J. (1981). "A Estratégia do Novo Sindicalismo," *Revista de Cultura e Política*, São Paulo, CEDEC, 5/6

Moysés, R. (1985). "O processo e a divisão sexual do trabalho nas indústrias farmacêutica e de cosméticos", Paper presented to the Working Group "Women in the Labor Force," IX Annual Meeting of ANPOCS, São Paulo.

Morel, R. (1989). *A Ferro e Fogo* - Construção e Crise da Família Siderúrgica: O Caso de Volta Redonda, Ph.D. Thesis, FFLCH/USP.

Moura, E. et al. (1984). "A utilização do trabalho feminino nas indústrias de Belém e Manaus," *Anais do IV Encontro*, 1, ABEP, São Paulo.

Noronha, E. (1991). "A Explosão das Greves na Década de 80," in A. Boito Jr. (Ed.), *O Sindicalismo Brasileiro nos Anos 80*, São Paulo, Paz e Terra.

Paoli, M. (1987). "Os trabalhadores urbanos na fala dos outros - Tempo, espaço e classe na história operária brasileira," in José Sérgio Leite Lopes (Ed.), *Cultura e Identidade Operária*, Rio de Janeiro, Marco Zero/PROED/UFRJ-Museu Nacional.

Pereira, L. (1965). *Trabalho e Desenvolvimento no Brasil*. São Paulo, Difusão Européia do Livro.

Pereira, V. (1979). *O Coração da Fábrica*, Rio de Janeiro, Campus.

Ramalho, J. R. (1986). *Estado Patrão e Luta Operária* - Conflitos de Classe na Fábrica Nacional de Motores, Ph.D. Thesis, USP.

Rizek, C. (1988). *Osasco: 1968–A Experiência de um Movimento*, Master's Dissertation, FFLCH/USP.

Rodrigues, A. (1978). *Operário, Operária*, São Paulo, Ed. Símbolo.

Rodrigues, I. J. (1990). *Comissão de Fábrica e Trabalhadores na Indústria*, São Paulo, Cortez/Fase.

Rodrigues, J. A.(1968). *Sindicato e Desenvolvimento no Brasil*. São Paulo, DIFEL.

Rodrigues, L. M. (1966). *Conflito Industrial e Sindicalismo no Brasil*. São Paulo, Difusão Européia do Livro.

Rodrigues, L. M. (1970). *Industrialização e Atitudes Operárias*. São Paulo, Brasiliense.

Rodrigues, L. M. (1974). *Trabalhadores, Sindicatos e Industrialização*, São Paulo, Brasiliense.

Rodrigues, L. M. (1988). "Os Sindicatos na Nova Constituição." *Jornal da Tarde*, March 14th.

Rodrigues, L. M. (1990). *CUT: Os Militantes e a Ideologia*, São Paulo, Paz e Terra.

Rodrigues, L. M. (1991). "As Tendências Políticas na Formação das Centrais," in A. Boito Jr. (Ed.), *O Sindicalismo Brasileiro nos Anos 80*, São Paulo, Paz e Terra.

Rodrigues, L. M. (1992). "Os sindicatos na Nova Constituição," *Jornal da Tarde*, 14/3/88.

Rodrigues, L. M., & Cardoso, A. (1993). *Força Sindical: Uma Análise Sócio-Política*, Rio de Janeiro, Paz e Terra.

Sader, E. (1988). *Quando novos personagens entraram em cena*, São Paulo, Paz e Terra.

Sader, E., & Paoli, M. C. (1986). "Sobre 'Classes Populares' no Pensamento Sociológico Brasileiro," in R. Cardoso (ed.). A *Aventurar Antropológica*. Rio de Janeiro, Paz e Terra.

Salerno, M. (1985). "Produção, trabalho e participação: CCq e kamban numa nova imigração japonesa", in *Processo e Relações do Trabalho no Brasil*, op. cit.

Segnini, L. (1988). *A Liturgia do Poder*, São Paulo, EDUC/São Paulo Bank Workers' Union.

Silva, E. (1991). *Refazendo a Fábrica Fordista*, São Paulo, HUCITEC.

Silva, R. (1985). "Comissões de Fábrica e Autonomia dos Trabalhadores," in Fleury, M.; Fischer, R. (Eds.). *Processo e Relações do Trabalho no Brasil*, São Paulo, Atlas.

Silva, R. (1990). "As Negociações Coletivas no Brasil e o Sistema de Relações de Trabalho," XVI Annual Meeting of ANPOCS, published in Abramo and Cuevas (Eds.) *El sindicalismo Latinoamericano en los 90* II , Santiago de Chile, ISCOS/CISL/CLACSO, 1992.

Silva, R. (1992). "Representatividade e Renovação no Sindicalismo Brasileiro," *Cadernos do CESIT* 10, UNICAMP, July.

Simão, A. (1966). *O Sindicato e o Estado*: suas relações na formação do proletariado de São Paulo. São Paulo, Dominus.

Sorj, B. (1983). "O Processo de Trabalho na Indústria: Tendências de Pesquisa," *BIB - Boletim Informativo Bibliográfico de Ciências Sociais* 15, Rio de Janeiro, 1st semester 1983.

Spindel, C. (1987). "A formação de um novo proletariado: as operárias do Distrito Industrial de Manaus," São Paulo, IDESP, Research Report.

Telles, J. (1962). *O Movimento Sindical no Brasil*. Rio de Janeiro, Vitória.

Telles, V. (1992). *A Cidadania Inexistente*: incivilidade e pobreza. Um estudo sobre trabalho e família na Grande São Paulo, Ph.D. Thesis, USP.

Vargas, N. (1979). *Organização do Trablho e Capital: Um Estudo da Construção Habitacional*, Master's Dissertation, UFRJ.

Vargas, N. (1985). "Gênese e difusão do taylorismo no Brisil" in ANPOCS. *Ciência Sociais Hoje*, São Paulo, Cortez, pp. 155–191.

Vianna, L. W. (1978). "Estudos sobre sindicalismo e movimento operário: resenha de algumas tendências." *BIB - Boletim Informativo e Bibliográfico de Ciências Sociais* 3, Rio de Janeiro.

Vianna, L. W. (1984). "Atualizando uma Bibliografia: 'Novo Sindicalismo', Cidadania e Fábrica, *BIB - Boletim Informativo e Bibliográfico de Ciências Sociais* 17, Rio de Janeiro, 1st semester 1984.

Weffort, F. (1972). *Participação e Conflito Industrial*. Caderno 6, São Paulo, CEBRAP.

Weffort, F. (1978). "Os sindicatos na política (Brasil: 1955-1964)." *Ensaios Opinião*, 2-5.

Weffort, F. (1979). "Democracia e movimento operário: algumas questões para a história do período 1945-1964." Parts 1 and 2, *Revista da Cultura Contemporânea*, 1 and 2. Part 3, *Revista de Cultura Política* 1.

APPENDIX: CONTACT INFORMATION

Scholarly Associations

ABET—Associação Brasileira de Estudos do Trabalho (Brazilian Association on Labor and Work Studies)
E-mail: abet@pucminas.br
Website: www.race.nuca.ie.ufrj.br/abet

ANPOCS—Associação Nacional de Pós-Graduação e Pesquisa em Ciências Sociais (Brazilian Social Sciences Association)
E-mail: anpocs@org.usp.br
Website: http://www.anpocs.org.br
The Association supports two working groups on *"Work and Society"* E-mail: acardoso@iuperj.br
Website: http://www.iuperj.bre/Portugues/Associacao/anpocs/Trabalho and *"Labor and Politics"*: msantan@bridge.com.br

ANPED—Associação Nacional de Pesquisa e Pós-Graduação em Educação (Brazilian Association on Education Studies): Working Group on "Work and Education"
E-mail: lsmachad@net.em.com.br

Publications

Revista Brasileira de Ciências Sociais
anpocs@org.usp.br

Dados
iuperj@iuperj.br

Novos Estudos CEBRAP
www.cebrap.org.br

Trabalho e Educação
lsmachad@net.em.com.br

Educação e Sociedade
revista@cedes.unicamp.br

Boletim Eletrônico GT "Sindicalismo e Política"
boletimgt@bridge.com.br

Estudos Feministas
clcosta@floripa.com.br

3

Canada

Anthony Giles and Jacques Bélanger

Prior to the 1970s, a review of Canadian research on the sociology of work would have made very quick reading indeed. Despite a smattering of fascinating studies of the world of work, some as early as the late 19th century, it was not until the rapid expansion of Canadian universities in the 1960s and 1970s that a substantial body of sociological research focusing on work began to accumulate. Since then, the amount of published research, as well as its level of theoretical and methodological sophistication, has grown in leaps and bounds.

Yet for all this growth, it is impossible to identify a unified "Canadian sociology of work." Indeed, one of the distinctive characteristics of the field is its heterogeneous nature, embracing as it does not only researchers with an institutional affiliation to sociology but also those in other fields such as industrial relations, labor studies, political economy, and feminist studies who approach work from a sociological angle. Even within sociology itself, relatively few researchers specialize exclusively in the sociology of work, though many more have made important contributions. Finally, cutting across this diversity is an even deeper fault line—the political, economic, and cultural

Anthony Giles and Jacques Bélanger • Department of Industrial Relations, Université Laval, Quebec, Canada G1K 7P4.

Worlds of Work: Building an International Sociology of Work, edited by Daniel B. Cornfield and Randy Hodson. Kluwer Academic/Plenum Publishers, New York, 2002.

divisions between "English Canada" and "French Canada," which have produced two distinctly separate sociologies of work.

Over and above these divisions, however, the sociological study of work
in Canada is characterized by a number of recurring themes that spring from
distinctive characteristics of the Canadian political economy—late industrialization, a labor force built up through massive waves of immigration, a long-
standing economic development strategy focused on natural resources, and a
high level of economic dependence on a succession of larger countries. This
material context has had a marked influence on research, in terms of both its
enduring themes—such as the interrelationships between work and ethnicity,
or the longstanding preoccupation with the natural resources sector—and its
shifting attention over time, as the evolution of Canadian and world capitalism has reshaped work and the social issues connected to work.

In grappling with these issues, Canadian sociologists of work—especially
those working at the micro level—have frequently imported their theoretical
and methodological tools from abroad. In some cases, this orientation to foreign theories and methods has verged on intellectual dependence, though in
others it has produced a rather distinctive synthesis that contributes in its
own right to the wider field.

These, then, are the themes that inform this interpretive analysis of the
development and current condition of the Canadian sociology—or sociologies—
of work.[1] In the first part of this chapter, we trace the evolution of the central
themes in the sociology of work in Canada through three phases: the origins
and establishment of the field, up to the early 1970s; the emergence of a critical, nationalist, and feminist sociology of work, from the early 1970s through
to the late 1980s; and recent research trends in the context of the far-reaching
restructuring of work that has been occurring over the last 10 to 15 years. In
the second part, we describe the institutional context of the sociology of work.
The chapter concludes with a brief assessment of the accomplishments of the
Canadian sociology of work and the challenges facing it at the beginning of a
new century and millennium.

THEMES IN THE SOCIOLOGY OF WORK IN CANADA

Although a handful of departments of sociology were founded relatively
early, sociology, *qua* academic discipline, only became firmly established in

---

[1]There are few reviews in the literature devoted to the Canadian sociology of work, none of
which cover the field in the exact way we have chosen to define it. Among those upon which
we draw are Rocher (1962), White (1984), Storey (1991), and Legendre (1997). An excellent
introduction to the field is by Krahn and Lowe (1998).

Canadian universities in the 1960s (Forcese, 1990). Nevertheless, sociologically inspired studies of work have a much longer history—as do the themes that have preoccupied sociologists. Accordingly, we begin our analysis with a brief look at some of the origins and early traditions of the sociology of work.

Origins and Establishment

The few sociologically oriented studies of work prior to the 1930s, although sometimes making use of methods such as the social survey or participant observation, were conducted outside the university setting by social reformers or academic-practitioners concerned with bringing the plight of workers, and especially immigrant workers, to public attention (Campbell, 1983). Even the occasional academic study, such as Edmund Bradwin's (1928) first hand account of the "contract system" and the exploitation of immigrants in frontier work camps, was no less inspired by the necessity of reform, even if it also served as his Ph.D. thesis in sociology at Columbia.

The involvement of university-based researchers dates from the 1930s. At McGill University, where the Chicago School was influential, Everett Hughes played a key role (Shore 1987). Although Hughes's most significant contribution to Canadian sociology was his classic study of the impact of industrialization on the social structure of a small town, *French Canada in Transition*, those who followed in his footsteps developed a tradition of mico-level studies of occupations and professions that focused on issues such as occupational socialization, role adaptation, professional hierarchies, and other aspects of the interior life of work. Thus, from the 1940s through the 1960s, sociologists explored a variety of occupations and professions, including doctors, nurses, dentists, lawyers, and the military (e.g., Hall, 1946; Ross, 1961; Solomon, 1954; Wipper, 1994), generally using an ethnographic approach.

This was perhaps the least distinctively "Canadian" area of the sociology of work during these years, being almost entirely inspired by theories and methodologies borrowed from the United States. Indeed, the introduction to the section on "Work" in the major sociology reader of the time commented that "the research in this section clearly reveals that the sociological characteristics of work in Canada are very similar to those in the United States. On this evidence, there is no social organization of work which is distinctively Canadian" (Blishen et al., 1961:232). The one distinctive Canadian characteristic to which these sociologists paid attention was the problem of English–French relations (e.g., Beattie and Spencer, 1971; Hall, 1971).

The first stirrings of a different approach, one more concerned to explore the distinctive characteristics of work in Canada and its connection to broader patterns of class inequality, and in the tradition of the early studies of the social reformers, were also felt in the 1930s. Here too, McGill played a key role when it hired London School of Economics-trained Leonard Marsh to develop and coordinate an interdisciplinary social–science research program on problems of employment and unemployment. Besides economic studies, the program also included investigations into the adaptation of immigrants, English–French relations and "women's work," as well as detailed studies of railway workers, the agricultural labor market, and Marsh's own classic, *Canadians In and Out of Work* (1940), a sweeping analysis of occupations, inequality, unemployment, and the class structure.

Although McGill's research program did not continue after the war, interest in the occupational structure and its connection to social stratification soon came to occupy a central place in Canadian sociology. Methodologically inspired by similar studies in other countries, particularly the United States, this more macro-level focus inevitably raised questions about the specificity of Canadian society, leading Forcese to call it "the first truly distinctive Anglo–Canadian sociology" (1990:46).

One element of this wider analysis was a growing interest in dissecting the occupational structure. Blishen (1958), for example, used 1951 census data on incomes and education to rank occupations according to their status, whereas others tackled the same task by using prestige ratings. More important, however, was the pathbreaking work of John Porter, culminating in *The Vertical Mosaic* (1965), which founded a Canadian tradition of sociological inquiry into the connection between occupational aspirations and outcomes on the one hand, and the structures and processes of social mobility and relations of power and privilege on the other. In terms of the sociology of work, Porter's work had two important consequences: First, it was guided by a concern to demonstrate the persistent patterns of inequality produced, in part at least, through labor market institutions; and second, it revived interest in advancing the understanding of Canada per se. Although Porter's findings were later to come under critical scrutiny (Brym 1989), his legacy is a vibrant and critical school of macrosociological research on the wider setting of work in Canada.

Strikingly absent from this early research were two of the central figures of industrial society—the blue-collar worker in the industrial firm and the lower-echelon white-collar employee—as well as their unions. Nevertheless, as the 1960s began to draw to their explosive close, some sociologists began to rediscover the industrial workplace. Westley and Westley (1971), for example, explored the theme of the "mass consumption society" and the orientations of young, urbanized, more educated, and affluent workers; others began to inquire into the area of job satisfaction of industrial workers (e.g., Meissner, 1971) and the linkages between production technologies and workers' integration (e.g., Fullan, 1971). Interestingly, research into the crucial resource production sector seems to have declined during these years (but see Lucas, 1971), though in retrospect this proved only to be a hiatus.

As in English Canada, the origins of French–Canadian sociology go back to the late 19th century, but the discipline only began to put down institutional roots in Francophone universities in the 1940s and 1950s. And although some of the sociologists hired in the early years had been trained in industrial sociology, the research of this period focused more on rural and urban community studies than on work per se (Rocher, 1962). When Francophone sociologists finally did begin to look at work in the late 1950s and early 1960s (Legendre, 1997), the themes they took up sometimes paralleled those examined by their English-speaking colleagues, but they also diverged in important ways. First, the belated yet fast-paced industrialization and urbanization of Quebec led to a greater emphasis on social change. Second, at the beginning of the 1960s, Quebec entered a period of rapid and far-reaching political and cultural change—the *Révolution tranquille*—that saw the themes of modernization and nationalism take center stage in intellectual life. Third, these developments prompted Francophone sociologists of work to pay attention to the primary "ethnic" division in Quebec society, the English–French divide.

It is therefore not surprising that statistical studies of occupations and occupational mobility focused on the transition from a rural society to an urban, industrialized society, as well as on the different occupational patterns of French and English Quebeckers (De Jocas and Rocher, 1957; Dofny and Garon-Audy, 1969). Occupational mobility and rapid economic change also lay at the heart of a major research project conducted by researchers at Université Laval. Combining ethnographic observation with careful statistical analysis, this "milestone in industrial sociology in Quebec" (Rocher, 1962:183) looked at the transformation of the work of lumberjacks in rural Quebec from a seasonal occupation filled by farmers to a year-round industry characterized by rapid mechanization and rigid company policies, and then at the wider changes in the occupational structure, mobility patterns, and social structure of traditional rural communities (e.g., Fortin, 1961).

Francophone sociologists also began to look at industrial workers, unions, and the question of the affluent society in these years (Dofny and David, 1965), and in so doing began slowly to shift from American to French sociological theory in their choice of concepts and debates, and to choose themes that were in tune with the social changes then sweeping through Quebec, such as the developing nationalism of the province's unions (e.g., Dofny and Bernard, 1968).

Although sociologists in Quebec and English Canada only began to take an interest in unions and the institutions of collective work relations at the very end of the period, the postwar years saw the emergence of a strong tradition of industrial relations (IR) research that partially filled the gap. Although much of the IR research of this period was more strongly influenced by law and economics than by sociology (Giles and Murray, 1988), there were some notable exceptions. For example, in the late 1940s, the University of Toronto's Institute of Industrial Relations initiated a series of plant-level studies to examine the effects of technological change on shop floor social relations; another researcher associated with the Institute, the anthropologist C. W. M. Hart (1949), dissected the power structure of Windsor, Ontario and traced the expanding role of unions in this center of automobile production and union town. In Quebec, the influence of sociology on IR was more pronounced, fostering a tradition of collaboration between the two fields that was perhaps best reflected in *La Grève de l'amiante*, a collection of articles about the 1949 strike in the asbestos industry that, in challenging the structure of political and economic authority in the province, was a key turning point in the social and labor history of Quebec.

Thus, by the early 1970s, the sociology of work had become established in Canada. It was, however, already marked by a range of approaches and perspectives. One fissure ran between English- and French-speaking researchers, and a second line divided professional sociologists from those scholars in other fields, such as industrial relations, whose work, although contributing to the sociological understanding of work and employment, tended to be conducted separately. And a third line of division was evident within English–Canadian sociology. On the one side were those sociologists whose chief concern was to analyze the specifically Canadian character of work relations. On the other side were those such as the microsociologists interested in the professions and occupations, for whom Canada constituted little more than a laboratory in which to explore more universal themes and issues, generally borrowed with little modification from the dominant schools of American sociology.

Yet across these divisions it is still possible to discern broad themes that were shaped by the specific character of the Canadian political economy: a focus on ethnicity and its connections to work; a concern for work on the frontier and in the hinterland; and interest in the social changes produced by industrialization, especially in Quebec. Alongside these enduring themes, the concerns of researchers were also modified over time by the evolving material context: the early focus on the harsh and exploitive working conditions and worries about the "labor question" in the early stages of industrialization; the burgeoning of interest in employment and unemployment in the 1930s; and the post-World War II preoccupation with identifying (and promoting) mechanisms of social stability and integration, both in workplaces and in the world of labor–management relations.

Revolt

Between the early 1970s and the late 1980s, Canadian sociology underwent profound change, a triple "revolt" against orthodoxy. The first transformation was rising nationalism in society at large and across academe. In English Canada, nationalism led to efforts to "Canadianize" sociology and, on the theoretical terrain, the rediscovery of the Canadian political economy tradition that had long emphasized the distinctive character of Canadian economic, social, and political development, and, notably, the role of staple exports in shaping those developments (Brym, 1989). French-language sociologists were caught up in a rather different species of nationalism—the growing drive in Quebec to affirm its distinct "national" identity and give meaning to that identity through the creation of a independent nation.

The second, and in some ways more profound, transformation was the radicalization of sociology. As in many other countries, the social and industrial turbulence of the late 1960s and early 1970s saw a revival of Marxist and other currents of radical thought in explicit opposition to orthodox paradigms. Following hard on the heels of radicalization came the third—and probably the most lasting—revolt: the rise of the feminist movement and the advent of gender analysis. Thus, although colored by different brands of nationalism, Anglophone and Francophone sociology both "developed a common political-economy/neo-Marxian commitment to the analysis of class and other social inequalities and, somewhat later, [an infusion of] feminist thought" (Forcese, 1990:43; see also Legendre, 1997). Nonetheless, these common shifts occurred largely in parallel, for the two sociologies continued their long-established pattern of drawing on different international literatures, as well as their almost total ignorance of research conducted by each other.

Taken together, this triple transformation had profound implications for the sociology of work in Canada. First, radical interest in the working class and feminist interest in employment inequality conspired to raise the stature of the sociology of work in terms of published research, its coverage in textbooks, special issues of journals, and the publication of the first textbooks devoted to the sociology of work (e.g., Chen and Reagan, 1985; Lundy and Warme, 1981).

Second, the established traditions in the Canadian sociology of work were often given a new focus. For example, research into occupational status continued, with researchers updating earlier socioeconomic status scales and occupational prestige ratings (e.g., Blishen, Carroll, and Moore, 1987), as did research into occupational mobility, aided by nationwide surveys in 1973 and 1986 (Wanner, 1993). In this research, some of the original themes of the 1950s and 1960s continued to be explored, such as English–French comparisons and the comparison of Canadian occupational mobility patterns with those of the United States; increasingly, however, it took on a more critical edge as neo-Marxist and feminist scholars shifted the focus toward the structural factors that accounted for the broader pattern of stratification. The revival of interest in Canadian political economy in general, and the concern in Quebec to understand the emergence of a francophone business class, also changed the conceptual prism. An example here is the difference between the original elite studies by Porter and the update conducted by Wallace Clement (1975). Although applying the same techniques as Porter, Clement sought to explain the pattern of elite dominance not in terms of values, but in terms of the structure of power in the political economy and its pattern of dependent industrialization.

One area, however, remained relatively immune to these changes: the study of occupations and professions continued apace in the 1970s and 1980s, typically focusing on socialization in occupations and professions (e.g., Haas and Shaffir, 1986, Vincent, 1979), or on career structures in particular occupations (e.g., House, 1975).

The third consequence of the triple revolt was the initiation of several new themes that departed in more significant ways from orthodoxy. Thus, the radical current renewed interest in the workplace itself, particularly the blue-collar workplace (Storey, 1991). Although harbingers of this theme began to appear in the early 1970s, a more significant milestone was James Rinehart's *The Tyranny of Work* (1975), a sweeping analysis of alienation at work, managerial de-skilling efforts, and growing worker unrest. Looking back at Rinehart's book, it is possible to detect the beginnings of two new key themes in work research in Canada. The first was the attempt by radical sociologists to show that, despite its many material achievements, capitalism still fostered alienation in the workplace and some semblance of class consciousness in the sociopolitical sphere. Research in this area was explicitly counterposed to more traditional research on job satisfaction (itself growing in the period; e.g., Bunstein et al., 1975). The second theme was the analysis of the labor process, with a particular emphasis on managerial control strategies, technological change, and skills. Indeed, in the space of some 15 years, Canadian research in this area expanded enormously (e.g., Heron and Storey, 1986).

Although the Canadian labor process literature drew heavily on theories and debates originating outside Canada—on Braverman and other American and British authors in English Canada, and on the work of Alain Touraine and Serge Mallet in Quebec—the rise of English–Canadian nationalism stamped this research with a particular cast, notably, the focus of researchers on the resource extraction industries that had long been so central to Canadian economic development (e.g., Clement, 1981, 1986; Marchak, 1979; Sacouman, 1980), and on the more general connections between distinctive features of the Canadian political economy and the world of work (Smucker, 1980).

A significant exception to this preoccupation with the resource extraction and manufacturing sectors were studies in the emergent feminist tradition. Lowe (1987), for example, traced the feminization of office and clerical work in the 20th century; Steedman (1986) examined the relationship between skill and gender in the clothing industry; Reiter (1986) looked at managerial control in the fast-food industry; and, in Quebec, there was a pronounced emphasis on the tertiary sector, especially the impact of technological change on women.

Alongside the new interest in alienation and the labor process, other new themes emerged. Feminism stirred interest in the general place of women in the world of work (e.g., Armstrong and Armstrong, 1978) and also gave rise to a rich stream of studies of domestic labor and its connection to the world of paid employment (e.g., Luxton, 1980). Critical research also expanded in the area of occupational health and safety, with a particular focus on issues of power and control (e.g., Reasons, Ross, and Paterson, 1981). Power and control were also central to sociologists' new interest in the role of the state in shaping work. Here the radical–nationalist synthesis was particularly clear, for this literature sprang from the intersection of the international debate over the role of the capitalist state, with a concern to understand the contours of power in Canadian society (e.g., Huxley, 1979). Last, the swelling of industrial unrest in the late 1960s and early 1970s also reawakened sociological interest in unions. At first, reflecting the rise of nationalism in English Canada, attention was directed to the branch plant character of many unions operating in Canada (e.g., White, 1975). Second, the emerging radical paradigm broadened the critique to the institution of unionism in general, drawing attention to its role in mediating and containing expression of class conflict. Third, feminist scholars began to point out the myriad ways in which unions reinforced gender inequality and created obstacles to women's participation in unions (e.g., Gagnon, 1974). But as sharp as these critiques were, unions remained one of the last institutional expressions of working-class identity. Thus, for researchers interested in the state and working politics, unions and their links to social democratic political parties became a matter of interest (e.g., Johnston and Ornstein, 1982).

In summary, then, the sociology of work in Canada went through a period of vigorous expansion between the early 1970s and the late 1980s. The explosion of social and industrial unrest in the late 1960s and early 1970s, coupled with the rising tide of nationalism in Quebec and English Canada, played a critical role in fostering both the general growth and the specific intellectual direction taken by the field, namely, the triple revolt of nationalism, radicalism, and feminism.

Recent Themes

In retrospect, it is somewhat ironic that at the very moment when the generation of critical scholars began their assault on orthodoxy in the mid-1970s, the system that they were so trenchantly dissecting was beginning to come unstuck. Indeed, by the late 1980s, it had become clear that changes in the organization of production and work, patterns of employment, labor market structures, and labor–management relations reflected not just a tinkering with the system but a deeper restructuring. Thus, recent Canadian research in the sociology of work has been dominated by—and, to a greater degree than in the past, united in—an effort to decipher the profound changes that have been occurring in the world of work, an enterprise that has been shaped by a mixture of traditional and new themes, established and emerging conceptual tools.

The first continuity with the past is the continuing prominence of the broadly "critical" paradigm that emerged in the 1970s. Thus, even though the focus and tone of research has shifted, the sociology of work remains a distinctly progressive enterprise, conducted in the main by scholars (and their students) whose theoretical orientations were forged by the debates and issues that took center stage in the 1970s and early 1980s. Of particular importance is the feminist current, which has continued to produce a steady stream of research into gendered work relations (e.g., Livingston and Luxton, 1989), the uneasy relationship between women and unions (Creese, 1995), women's segregation within the professions (Armstrong and Armstrong, 1992) and gender inequality in the occupational and mobility structure (Davies, Mosher, and O'Grady, 1996).

A second continuity is the persistence of a number of time-honored research themes. For example, occupational mobility continues to attract attention, especially as it is connected to gender (e.g., Manley, 1995) and in Quebec (De Sève, Bouchard, and Hamel, 1999), as does the impact of ethnicity on work. The traditional focus on the primary and secondary sectors has also continued, evidenced by a considerable body of case study research in pulp and paper, aluminum, automobiles, steel, mining, fishing, and similar areas. Although research into the services sector is growing, it has not kept pace with the changing structure of the labor market.

A third parallel with earlier periods is the continuing fragmentation of the field. Thus, although English- and French-speaking sociologists of work have increasingly focused on similar issues, there is still little dialogue between them. On the other hand, it is possible to detect something of a rapprochement between sociologists of work and industrial relations scholars. More generally, all of the schools that make up the Canadian sociology of work continue to be strongly influenced by theoretical trends in the international literature.

Beyond these underlying continuities, however, the search to understand the rapidly changing landscape of work and employment has produced some significant changes in orientation, a growth of interest in a number of particular topics, and a decline in some others.

The most general shift is one of perspective and emphasis. Whereas in the previous period researchers tended to view the social relations of work and employment primarily in terms of the endemic structural influences of capitalist relations of production, current research is focused on how capitalism is changing and successfully absorbing challenges from below. To be sure, few sociologists of work in Canada subscribe to a simplistic "post-capitalism" thesis, but the structural continuities of capitalism have receded to the status of background assumptions, and there has been an increasing acceptance that the recent wave of change, although open-ended in many respects, is fundamental and likely to be long-lasting.

In association with this general change in perspective, there have been discernible changes in the topics that have absorbed the energies of sociologists of work. For example, the changing structure and dynamics of the labor market have become a central concern (see Krahn and Lowe, 1998), including studies of the rise of contingent work (e.g., Mercure, 1996), the nature of joblessness and its consequences for workers, youth unemployment and the linkages between the education system and the labor market (Anisef and Axelrod, 1993). Similarly, research on new technology has continued to expand, especially in the areas of "employability" and job security (Bernier, 1999). Broader issues regarding public policies in matters of training and labor market policy have also been added to the agenda (Johnson, McBride, and Smith, 1994).

Alongside the transformation of labor markets, the nature of changes within the workplace has also come under increased scrutiny. Although research into the organization and management of work developed strongly in the 1970s and 1980s, it has been given a new impetus by management efforts to foster various forms of direct worker participation and more efficient way of managing production. By and large, research on this theme has relied on detailed case studies and has stressed the tensions associated with the definition of new systems of work rules. In Quebec, a key emphasis has been the analysis of the articulation between new organizational arrangements and the set of institutions developed in the postwar decades (Bélanger and Dumas, 1998). In English-speaking Canada, sociologists have been particularly critical of workplace innovation, as two recent studies illustrate. On the basis of a longitudinal study of CAMI, a Suzuki–General Motors auto transplant in Ontario, Rinehart, Huxley and Robertson (1997) have shown how union members and their leaders soon lost their illusions regarding the effects of worker commitment under lean production. Similarly, on the basis of field research in potash and uranium mining, Russell argues that "post-Fordism is not quite the reality that it first set out. . . . About the empowerment of workers, households, and communities, it is not. About the creation of more participative, skilful labour processes, it is, at best, tangential. Rather, the emerging economy is, first and foremost, about doing more with less and for less" (1999:199).

The focus on the impact of changes in production and employment is also clear in research on unionism, which is probably as lively in Canada as anywhere else. Among IR academics, there appears to have been a move away from traditional studies of unions as institutional actors in the collective bargaining system and toward an assessment of how unions are adapting in order to preserve or regain their strength as a collective actor in a context of globalization and economic restructuring. For example, a recent special issue of *Sociologie et sociétés* (1999) addressed the question of the social and subjective attachment of workers to their unions in the new economic environment. Similarly, research on unions and restructuring has documented the tensions that unions are encountering as they seek to redefine their role in the context of workplace change (e.g., Wells, 1997).

In tandem with rising interest in topics such as training and education, work reorganization, technological change, and unionism, there has been a decline in some others. For instance, there has been a movement away from broader issues of class structure, social movements, and political conflict, toward a more micro-level focus on organizational questions. This shift is particularly clear in Quebec, where the labor movement's long-standing hostility to new forms of work organization has given way to a more positive view of the potential benefits of post-Taylorism, sparking a wave of research into what is occurring in unionized workplaces (e.g., Lapointe, 1998). In English Canada, the same shift away from broad issues is also evident. For example, while the issue of state and class politics has not entirely vanished, it has taken a backseat to the newer issues, or has been fragmented into discrete policy areas that are studied alone (such as occupational health and safety, family policy, etc.). More broadly, there has been a marked decline in the emphasis on the distinctive character of the Canadian political economy and its influence on work in Canada. Indeed, one of the striking aspects of current research is the way that current trends are treated as global, with Canada as one of many laboratories that, although distinctive in some respects, is undergoing changes in work that are more universal in character.

Finally, the sociology of work in Canada has taken on a more pronounced, comparative flavor in the past decade or so, both at the macro (Clement and Myles, 1994; Kettler, Struthers, and Huxley, 1990) and the micro level (e.g., Smith et al., 1997). In Quebec, for example, there has been much discussion of whether it is possible to distinguish a distinct "Quebec model" (for a critique, see Gagnon, 1995). In contrast, there seems to be little debate in English–Canadian sociology about a possible "Canadian model," though IR scholars have studied the diverging patterns of unionization in Canada and the United States.

In addition to the ebb and flow of different research themes and topics, it is also important to underline developments on the theoretical front. Perhaps most striking in this respect is the influence that recent trends in the sociology of work in France have had on research in Quebec. In particular, the emergence of a wider "sociology of the firm" has been taken up by a number of Quebec sociologists (e.g., Bélanger, Grant, and Lévesque, 1994; Dupuis and Kuzminski, 1998). In association with the influence of the more general vogue in France for social action theory, this has meant that research in Quebec has focused strongly on the complexity of the innovation process itself (e.g., Harrisson and Carrière, 1997). In contrast, English-language sociologists have tended to draw on American and British literature emphasizing the more objective conditions that structure work and work reorganization. Moreover, these differences are related to a growing ideological divergence: Whereas in English Canada most sociologists, because of their attachment to class analysis, are critical of workplace innovation, Francophone sociologists have proved more (guardedly) optimistic.

The 1990s also saw a partial lowering of the barriers between the sociology of work and the field of industrial relations, the result of two factors. First, over the past decade or so, IR researchers in North America have become increasingly interested in the issue of workplace and labor market change, a movement that has aligned them more closely with the interests of sociologists (e.g., Betcherman and Lowe, 1997). Second, although mainstream IR research still tends to be guided more by a preoccupation with the economic dimensions of workplace change and less with the impact of such changes on workers and the social organization of work, a number of IR researchers, many trained outside the dominant tradition of institutionalism in North America, have begun to introduce a more sociological perspective to IR research (e.g., Godard, 1994; Lévesque and Côté, 1999).

In summary, then, research in the sociology of work in Canada has concentrated in recent years on the profound changes sweeping through labor markets and the workplace. In this endeavor, it has continued to emphasize themes and approaches developed in earlier periods, but it has also evolved in important ways. We return to these themes in the conclusion of this chapter.

THE INSTITUTIONAL CONTEXT

Most Canadian sociological studies of work are conducted by academics located in university departments of sociology or industrial relations, in business schools, or in specialized centers for teaching and research in IR or labor studies. This research is typically independent, although funding is often provided by government through a competitive peer review process. Nevertheless, governments and their funding agencies have sometimes sought to influence research by providing funding for themes considered to be relevant to public policy. At the national level, for example, recent "strategic themes" include "Women and Change," "Challenges and Opportunities of a Knowledge-Based Economy," and "Exploring Social Cohesion in a Globalizing Era." In recent years, funding agencies have also supported interuniversity and interdisciplinary research groups such as the five Strategic Research Networks in Education and Training, several of which are coordinated by sociologists or have a major sociological component. In addition, Human Resources Development Canada supports the Canadian Workplace Research Network, whose mandate is to promote research on workplace change and innovation; linkages among researchers, practitioners, and policymakers; and the dissemination of research.

Besides its funding of academic research, the state also plays a role through the efforts of its own agencies and by commissioning research into specific topics. Statistics Canada, for example, collects a wide variety of data that is useful to sociologists of work, including regular surveys (e.g., the monthly Labour Force Survey) and periodic surveys (such as the recently launched Longitudinal Workplace and Employee Survey). Additionally, public inquiry commissions have occasionally sponsored research by sociologists on various aspects of work, and individual government departments sometimes award research contracts to academics to investigate specific issues.

Outside the university–government nexus, some work research is conducted under the auspices of a handful of independent research institutes. The most significant of these is probably Canadian Policy Research Networks Inc.'s (CPRN) Work Network, which has conducted research into training in the new economy, human resources in government, work in the nonprofit sector, and the changing employment relationship. In addition, a major focus of the CPRN's Family Network is the interrelationships between changes in family structures and the labor market. Mention should also be made of the Canadian Centre for Policy Alternatives, a progressive think tank founded in 1980 with the support of the trade union movement. The labor movement, although often skeptical about the academic trappings and purpose of university-based research (see Reiter, 1992), has also been involved in specific research projects conducted by sociologists (e.g., Lévesque and Murray, 1998; Lowe and Northcott, 1986; Rinehart, Huxley, and Robertson, 1997). Links to the business community, however, appear to be even more episodic.

Although there are no Canadian scholarly journals devoted exclusively to the sociology of work, five major sociological journals frequently publish research in the field of work: *Recherches sociographiques*; the *Canadian Review of Sociology and Anthropology* (the official journal of the Canadian Sociology and Anthropology Association); *Sociologie et sociétés*; the *Canadian Journal of Sociology*; and *Cahiers de recherche sociologique*. Outside the field of sociology, the most important medium for publishing research on the sociology of work remains *Relations industrielles/Industrial Relations*. Other important journals include *Labour/Le travail* (primarily for labor historians), *Studies in Political Economy*, *Recherches féministes*, *Atlantis*, and the *Journal of Canadian Studies*. Outside academe, Statistics Canada's monthly *Perspectives on Labour and Income* publishes articles written by in-house researchers, as well as academics, on a wide range of subjects of interest to sociologists of work.

The state therefore plays a considerable—and growing—role in shaping, directly or indirectly, Canadian research in the sociology of work. It is the major source of research funding; it subsidizes journals and other publications in the field; its own agencies define and collect much of the data used by sociologists; and is increasingly seeking to define research themes. Thus, alarm bells have been rung about both the "steering effect of financial agencies" (Forcese, 1990:45) and the growing tendency of these agencies to stress the development of "partnerships" with organizations outside the university. However, while it is true that research agendas are shaped by the priorities of governments (as well as by the need to tailor research proposals so that they appeal to the corporations and unions to which researchers are seeking access), social scientists are, in our experience, adept at fashioning their proposals in such a way as to conform—superficially at least—to the priorities of those who guard the purse strings and gates. Certainly the continued critical edge of much research in the sociology of work suggests that, while they have not been immune to the strictures and lures put in their way, they have hardly become mere handmaidens of dominant interests.

CONCLUSION

Although the first half of the 20th century saw only a few sociological investigations of work and employment, the second half, and especially the last quarter, saw a sustained expansion. The story we have tried to tell, however, is not one of simple linear growth, but rather of shifting themes and approaches. From the early studies of industrialization, urbanization, and immigration, to the concern for employment and unemployment in the depression, to the stability of the postwar years, on to the swelling of unrest at the end of the postwar boom, and now in the midst of a period of far-reaching restructuring, the Canadian sociology of work has been guided above all by the evolving condition and experience of work itself. Yet change has not been absolute, for a number of aspects of the Canadian reality have recurred in sociologists' attempts to understand work. The existence of two founding peoples has intertwined with patterns of work and employment, not to mention issues of power, authority, and opportunity, providing fertile ground for sociological research. The huge waves of immigration that stocked the labor market have added to this cultural complexity, making Canadian sociologists especially sensitive to the interplay of ethnicity, employment, and work relations. And the traditional pattern of Canadian economic development, rooted in the extraction and export of natural resources, has also led to an expertise in work outside the urban industrial core.

We have also seen that the Canadian sociology of work is something of a mosaic. Instead of a single, cohesive body of work focused on the study of narrowly defined industrial or occupational sociology, a wider and looser community of scholars is engaged in the task of understanding the social aspects of work. Like any mosaic, that community is composed of a range of separate elements that are simultaneously distinct yet part of a larger pattern. Some of the joints between the separate pieces, such as the enduring division between the sociology of work in English Canada and the *sociologie du travail* of Francophone Quebec, undermine the potential unity of the whole, whereas others, such as the increasing cross-fertilization between industrial relations, labor studies, and sociology, work in the other direction.

We have also emphasized how the Canadian sociology of work reflects the broader reality of a society struggling with its sense of uniqueness and its dependence on larger economies. Within the sociology of work, this tension is reproduced in the division between those who lean heavily on the theories and debates originating in the countries that dominate the social sciences and those who, by melding these approaches with an understanding of Canadian and Quebec distinctiveness, have created a mosaic more closely resembling the genetic sense of the term.

As the Canadian sociology of work enters a new century and millenium, its key challenge is to preserve and strengthen its mosaic-like qualities: to find a way to better cement the diverse pieces together, without trying to fuse them into an indistinguishable mass. Thus, English- and French-speaking sociologists of work should continue to study their different societies, but they also need to learn more from and about each other; scholars from the many fields that make up the broad church of the sociology of work should remain faithful to their respective traditions but at the same time might profit from a stronger dose of interdenominationalism; and, finally, it will be essential, especially in an age of globalization, to remain open to international influences without losing sight of the way work relations are irretrievably embedded in the social relations of distinct societies.

ACKNOWLEDGMENTS: We would like to thank Graham Lowe, Hélène David, William Buxton, Daniel Mercure, Gregor Murray, and the editors of this volume for their useful and generous comments. Jean-Noël Grenier provided valuable research assistance.

REFERENCES

Anisef, Paul, and Paul Axelrod, eds. 1993. *Transitions: Schooling and Employment in Canada.* Toronto: Thompson Educational Publishing.

Armstrong, Pat, and Hugh Armstrong. 1978. *The Double Ghetto.* Toronto: McClelland and Stewart.

Armstrong, Pat, and Hugh Armstrong. 1992. "Sex and the Professions in Canada." *Journal of Canadian Studies* 27(1):118–35.

Beattie, Christopher, and Byron G. Spencer. 1971. "Career Attainment in Canadian Bureaucracies: Unscrambling the Effects of Age, Seniority, Education and Ethnolinguistic Factors on Salary." *American Journal of Sociology* 7:472–90.

Bélanger, Jacques, and Martin Dumas. 1998. "Teamwork and Internal Labour Markets: A Study of a Canadian Aluminum Smelter." *Economic and Industrial Democracy* 19:417–442.

Bélanger, Paul R., Michel Grant, and Benoît Lévesque, eds. 1994. *La modernisation sociale des entreprises.* Montreal: Les Presses de l'Université de Montréal.

Bernier, Colette. 1999. "Mutations du travail et nouveau mode de qualification/formation." *Relations industrielles* 54:51–79.

Betcherman, Gordon, and Graham S. Lowe. 1997. *The Future of Work in Canada: A Synthesis Report.* Ottawa: Canadian Research Policy Networks, Inc.

Blishen, Bernard R. 1958. "The Construction and Use of an Occupational Class Scale." *Canadian Journal of Economics and Political Science* 24:521–531.

Blishen, Bernard, Frank E. Jones, Kaspar D. Naegele, and John Porter, eds. 1961. *Canadian Society.* Toronto: Macmillan Company of Canada.

Blishen, Bernard R., W. K. Carroll, and C. Moore. 1987. "The 1981 Socioeconomic index for occupations in Canada." *Canadian Review of Sociology and Anthropology* 24:465–488.

Bradwin, Edmund. [1928] 1972. *The Bunkhouse Man.* Toronto: University of Toronto Press.

Burnstein, M., N. Tienharra, P. Hewson, and B. Warrander. 1975. *Canadian Work Values.* Ottawa: Information Canada.

Brym, Robert J., with Bonnie J. Fox. 1989. *From Culture to Power: The Sociology of English Canada.* Toronto: Oxford University Press.

Campbell, Douglas F. 1983. *Beginnings: Essays on the History of Canadian Sociology.* Port Credit: Scribblers' Press.

Chen, Mervin Y.T. and Thomas G. Regan. 1985. *Work in the Changing Canadian Society.* Toronto: Butterworths.

Clement, Wallace. 1975. *The Canadian Corporate Elite.* Ottawa: McClelland and Stewart.

Clement, Wallace. 1981. *Hardrock Mining: Industrial Relations and Technological Changes at INCO.* Toronto: McClelland and Stewart.

Clement, Wallace. 1986. *The Struggle to Organize: Resistance in Canada's Fisheries.* Toronto: McClelland and Stewart.

Clement, Wallace, and John Myles. 1994. *Relations of Ruling.* Montreal: McGill–Queen's University Press.

Creese, Gillian. 1995. "Gender Equity or Masculine Privilege? Union Strategies and Economic Restructuring in a White Collar Union." *Canadian Journal of Sociology* 20:143–166.

Davies, Scott, Clayton Mosher, and Bill O'Grady. 1996. "Educating Women: Gender Inequalities among Canadian University Graduates." *Canadian Review of Sociology and Anthropology* 33: 125–142.

De Jocas, Yves, and Guy Rocher. 1957. "Inter-Generation Occupational Mobility in the Province of Quebec." *Canadian Journal of Economics and Political Science* 23:57–68.

De Sève, Michel, Gérard Bouchard, and Martin Hamel. 1999. "Un siècle de mobilité professionnelle: Un aperçu régional." *Recherches Sociographes* 40:55–81.

Dofny, J., and P. Bernard. 1968. *Le syndicalisme au Québec*. Task Force on Labour Relations, Study No. 9. Ottawa: Queen's Printer.

Dofny, Jacques, and Hélène David. 1965. "Les aspirations des travailleurs de la métallurgie à Montréal." *Recherches sociographiques* 6:61–85.

Dofny, Jacques, and Muriel Garon-Audy. 1969. "Mobilités professionnelles au Québec." *Sociologie et Sociétés* 1:277–301.

Dupuis, Jean-Pierre and André Kuzminski, eds. 1998. *Sociologie de l'économie, du travail et de l'entreprise*. Montreal: Gaëtan Morin.

Forcese, Dennis P. 1990. "Sociology in Canada: A View from the Eighties." *International Journal of Canadian Studies* 1(2):35–53.

Fortin, Gérald. 1961. "Les changements socio-culturels dans une paroisse agricole." *Recherches Sociographiques* 2:151–170.

Fullan, Michael. 1971. "Industrial Technology and Worker Integration in the Organization." *American Sociological Review* 35:1028-1-39.

Gagnon, Mona-Josée. 1974. "Les femmes dans le mouvement syndical québécois." *Sociologie et Sociétés* 6:17–36.

Gagnon, Mona-Josée. 1995. "Le nouveau modèle de relations du travail au Québec et le syndicalisme." *Revues d'Études Canadiennes* 30(1):30–40.

Giles, Anthony, and Gregor Murray. 1988. "Towards an Historical Understanding of Industrial Relations Theory in Canada." *Relations Industrielles* 43:780–811.

Godard, John. 1994. *Industrial Relations, the Economy and Society*. Toronto: McGraw-Hill Ryerson.

Haas, Jack, and William Shaffir. 1986. "Taking on the Role of Doctor: A Dramaturgical Analysis of Professionalization." Pp. 330–349 in *Work in the Canadian Context*, edited by K. L. P. Lundy and B. Warme. Toronto: Butterworth.

Hall, Oswald. 1946. "The Informal Organization of the Medical Profession." *Canadian Journal of Economics and Political Science* 12:30–44.

Hall, Oswald. 1971. "The Canadian Division of Labour Revisited." Pp. 89–99 in *Canadian Society*, edited by R. J. Ossenberg. Scarborough: Prentice-Hall.

Harrisson, Denis, and Jules Carrière. 1997. "Cheminement de l'innovation dans l'entreprise: jeux d'acteurs, organisation et institution." *Recherches Sociographiques* 38:9–33.

Hart, C. W. M. 1949. "Industrial Relations Research and Social Theory." *Canadian Journal of Economics and Political Science* 15:53–73.

Heron, Craig, and Robert Storey, eds. 1986. *On the Job: Confronting the Labour Process in Canada*. Montreal: McGill–Queen's University Press.

House, J. D. 1975. "Organization without formalization: The Case of a Real Estate Agency." *Canadian Journal of Sociology* 1:19–32.

Huxley, Christopher. 1979. "The State, Collective Bargaining and the Shape of Strikes in Canada." *Canadian Journal of Sociology* 4:223–240.

Johnson, Andrew F., Stephen McBride, and Patrick J. Smith, eds. 1994. *Continuities and Discontinuities: The Political Economy of Social Welfare and Labour Market Policy in Canada*. Toronto: University of Toronto Press.

Johnston, William, and Michael D. Ornstein. 1982. "Class, Work, and Politics." *Canadian Review of Sociology and Anthropology* 19:196–214.

Kettler, David, James Struthers, and Christopher Huxley. 1990. "Unionization and Labour regimes in the Canada and the United States." *Labour/Le Travail* 25:161–187.

Krahn, Harvey J., and Graham S. Lowe. 1998. *Work, Industry, and Canadian Society*, 3rd ed. Toronto: ITP Nelson Canada.

Lapointe, Paul-André. 1998. "Identités ouvrières et syndicales: Fusion, distanciation et recomposition." *Sociologie et sociétés* 30:189–212.

Legendre, Camille. 1997. "Institutionnalisation et professionnalisation de la sociologie du travail au Québec: Un aperçu." *Recherches Sociographiques* 38:51–88.

Lévesque, Christian, and Pascale Côté. 1999. "Le travail en équipe dans un univers de production allégée." *Relations Industrielles* 54:80–110.

Lévesque, Christian and Gregor Murray. 1998. "La régulation paritaire du changement à l'épreuve de la mondialisation." *Relations industrielles* 53:90–122.

Livingston, D. W., and Meg Luxton. 1989. "Gender Consciousness at Work: Modification of the Male Breadwinner Norm among Steelworkers and Their Spouses." *Canadian Review of Sociology and Anthropology* 26:240–275.

Lowe, Graham S. 1987. *Women in the Administrative Revolution*. Toronto: University of Toronto Press.

Lowe, Graham S., and Herbert C. Northcott. 1986. *Under Pressure: A Study of Job Stress*. Toronto: Garamond.

Lucas, Rex A. 1971. *Minetown, Milltown, Railtown*. Toronto: University of Toronto Press.

Lundy, Katherina L.P., and Barbara Warme, eds. 1981. *Work in the Canadian Context*. Toronto: Butterworths.

Luxton, Meg. 1980. *More Than a Labour of Love*. Toronto: Women's Press.

Manley, Michael C. 1995. "The Intragenerational Occupational Task Mobility of Men and Women." *Canadian Journal of Sociology* 20:1–30.

Marchak, Patricia. 1979. "Labour in a Staples Economy." *Studies in Political Economy* 2:7–35.

Marsh, Leonard C. 1940. *Canadians In and Out of Work*. Toronto: Oxford University Press.

Meissner, Martin. 1971. "The Long Arm of the Job: A Study of Work and Leisure." *Industrial Relations* 10:239–260.

Mercure, Daniel. 1996. *Le travail déraciné*. Montreal: Boréal.

Porter, John. 1965. *The Vertical Mosaic*. Toronto: University of Toronto Press.

Reasons, Charles E., Lois L. Ross, and Craig Paterson. 1981. *Assault on the Worker.* Toronto: Butterworths.

Reiter, Esther. 1986. "Life in a Fast-Food Factory." Pp. 309–326 in *On the Job*, edited by C. Heron and R. Storey. Kingston and Montreal: McGill–Queen's University Press.

Reiter, Esther. 1992. "The Price of Legitimacy: Academics and the Labour Movement." Pp. 349–362 in *Fragile Truths*, edited by W. K. Carroll, L. Christiansen-Ruffman, R. F. Currie, and D. Harrison. Ottawa: Carleton University Press.

Rinehart, James W. (with the assistance of Seymour Faber). 1975. *The Tyranny of Work.* Don Mills: Academic Press.

Rinehart, James, Christopher Huxley, and David Robertson. 1997. *Just Another Car Factory?*. Ithaca, NY: ILR Press.

Rocher, Guy. 1962. "Les recherches sur les occupations et la stratification sociale." *Recherches Sociographiques* 3:173–184.

Ross, Aileen D. 1961. *Becoming a Nurse.* Toronto: Macmillan.

Russell, Bob. 1999. *More with Less: Work Reorganization in the Canadian Mining Industry.* Toronto: University of Toronto Press.

Sacouman, James R. 1980. "Semi-Proletarianzation and Rural Underdevelopment in the Martimes." *Canadian Review of Sociology and Anthropology* 17:232–245.

Shore, Marlene. 1987. *The Science of Social Redemption.* Toronto: University of Toronto Press.

Smith, Michael R., Anthony C. Masi, Axel van den Berg, and Joseph Smucker. 1997. "Insecurity, Labour Relations, and Flexibility in Two Process Industries: A Canada/Sweden Comparaison." *Canadian Journal of Sociology* 22:31–63.

Smucker, Joseph. 1980. *Industrialization in Canada.* Scarborough: Prentice-Hall.

Solomon, David. 1954. "Civilian to Soldier: Three Sociological Studies of Infantry Recruit Training." *Canadian Journal of Psychology* 8:87–94.

Steedman, Mercedes. 1986. "Skill and Gender in the Canadian Clothing Industry, 1890–1940." Pp. 152–176 in *On the Job*, edited by C. Heron and R. Storey. Kingston and Montreal: McGill-Queen's University Press.

Storey, Robert. 1991. "Studying Work in Canada." *Canadian Journal of Sociology* 16:241–264.

Vincent, Claude L. 1979. *Policeman.* Toronto: Gage.

Wanner, Richard A. 1993. "Patterns and trends in occupational mobility." In *Social Inequality in Canada*, 2d ed., edited by J. Curtis, E. Grabb and N. Guppy. Scarborough: Prentice-Hall.

Wells, Donald M. 1997. "When Push Comes to Shove: Competitiveness, Job Insecurity and Labour-Management Cooperation in Canada." *Economic and Industrial Democracy* 18:167–200.

Westley, William A., and Margaret W. Westley. 1971. *The Emerging Worker: Equality and Conflict in the Mass Consumption Society.* Montreal: McGill–Queen's University Press.

White, Terrence H. 1975. "Canadian Labour and International Unions in the Seventies." Pp. 288–306 in *Prophecy and Protest*, edited by S. D. Clark, J. P. Grayson, and L. M. Grayson. Toronto: Gage Educational Publishing.

White, Terrence H. 1984. "Industrial, Work, and Organizational Sociology in Canada." Pp. 175–210 in *Models and Myths in Canadian Sociology*, edited by S.D. Berkowitz. Toronto: Butterworths.

Wipper, Audrey, ed. 1994. *The Sociology of Work in Canada: Papers in Honour of Oswald Hall*, rev. ed. Ottawa: Carleton University Press.

APPENDIX: CONTACT INFORMATION

Scholarly Associations

Canadian Sociology and Anthropology Association
http://alcor.concordia.ca/~csaa1/

Association canadienne des sociologues et anthropologues de langue française
acsalf@Inrs-culture.uquebec.ca

Canadian Industrial Relations Association
http//www.cira-acri.ca/

Research Centers, Institutes and Networks

Canadian Policy Research Networks Inc.
http://www.cprn.org

Canadian Centre for Policy Alternatives
http://www.policyalternatives.ca

Centre for Research on Work and Society
http://www.yorku.ca/crws/

Strategic Research Networks in Education and Training
http://socserv2.mcmaster.ca/srnet/srnet.htm

Publications

Canadian Review of Sociology and Anthropology
Contact Canadian Sociology and Anthropology Association

Relations industrielles/Industrial Relations
http://www.rlt.ulaval.ca/ri-ir/

Recherches sociographiques
http://www.soc.ulaval.ca/rechsoc/

Sociologie et sociétés
http://www.pum.umontreal.ca/revues/sociolog/

Canadian Journal of Sociology
http://www.arts.ualberta.ca/cjscopy/

Labour/Le travail
http://www.mun.ca/cclh/

Studies in Political Economy
http://www.carleton.ca/spe

Journal of Canadian Studies
http://www.trentu.ca/publications/jcs/

Recherches féministes
http://www.fss.ulaval.ca/lef/Revue/index.htm

Atlantis
http://www.msvu.ca/atlantis/

Perspectives on Labour and Income
rogebru@statcan.ca

4

Mexico

Enrique de la Garza Toledo

INTRODUCTION

Labor studies in Mexico have passed through three stages (de la Garza, 1986). The first consisted of writings of political and union activists up to the 1930s. Some of the important union leaders from the beginning of the century wrote politically oriented chronicles of important events of the workers' movement. Second, from the 1940s up to 1968, studies of labor law and apologetic writings concerning relations between the labor movement and State predominated. Third, from 1968 to the present, the current round of labor studies appeared, which were more academic and diversified in terms of subject matter.

In this latest period, three research styles have been developed: historiographic, structuralist, and labor process styles. By style, I mean the combination of a way in which to define the object of study, with its theoretical and methodological orientation, and the preference for certain investigative techniques. Labor sociology in Mexico has not had a very long history; it was started by the 1970s and initially reduced to the history of the labor movement. From the end of the 1980s, labor sociology has been an important and developed field of sociology in Mexico.

Enrique de la Garza Toledo • Department of Sociology, Metropolitan University of Mexico–Iztapalapa 09340 Mexico, D.F., Mexico.

Worlds of Work: Building an International Sociology of Work, edited by Daniel B. Cornfield and Randy Hodson. Kluwer Academic/Plenum Publishers, New York, 2002.

The Historiographic Style

This is the style that was most developed in the 1970s. In those years, it was the main current in research. The 1970s were marked by a radicalization of the world of university academia, with Marxism exercising a very strong influence, and professor and student activists emerging on the scene. In this sense, in labor research, the collective action of the workers was given priority, particularly in investigations into present day phenomena, although historiographic studies soon reached into the past, mainly to the period following the Mexican revolution. In the 1970s, the favorite topics dealt with in labor studies concerned trade union independence from the state, union democracy, corporativism, and labor' s participation in the elections. The basic problem was the relation between unions and the state (Cordoba, 1978), discussed from a perspective critical of corporativism and an analytical perspective characteristic of the political sciences (Woldenberg, 1980b). In those years, the Center for Historical and Social Studies of the Workers Movement (CEHSMO), an agency tied to the Labor Ministry, and its magazine *Historia Obrera*, played a very important role in encouraging and disseminating these types of studies.

Within the historiographic current, a form of analysis termed *chronologist* predominated. It consisted of elaborating a chronicle of present or past movements, centered on the action and ideology of the union, political party, government, or business leaders involved. Most of these studies were about the question of trade union democracy and independence, to the extent that the cases given priority were those in which the workers questioned their corporativist leaders. Behind this was a simplified version of Marxism—from *What is to be done?* by Lenin—according to which workers are unable on their own to acquire *class consciousness* and require the presence of party intellectuals who bring in such consciousness from the outside. The chronicles of these movements also prioritized the use of journalist sources. This current declined as the independent labor movement proved itself impotent when faced with the state's turn to neoliberalism and the productive restructuring that began in the 1980s (Aguilar, 1990).

Structuralism in Labor Studies

In the 1970s, a critical, although not activist academic current emerged, beginning as studies on population and labor force. Initially, it adopted the perspective of the segmented currents in the labor market, sometimes combined with Marxist political economy. These sociodemographic studies diversified toward an analysis of migratory patterns, manpower mobility within sectors of the economy, sociodemographic characteristics of the workforce, and wages (Muñoz and de Oliveira, 1977). Soon the current reneged on segmentation, discovering that there was a very strong mobility among the supposed segments of the labor market. This approach led it to prioritize the domestic unit as capable of articulating the various segments of the labor market, for example, formal with informal employment (de Oliveira, 1989a). Due to the importance of women in the domestic unit and the informal tasks involved in the reproduction of the workforce, these studies eventually led to gender studies (de Oliveira, 1989b) and research on the informal sector of the economy (Cortés, 1990). A specific structuralist current in labor studies has tried to link such variables as union affiliation, wages, and collective bargaining with conflicts and strikes (Zazueta and de la Peña, 1981; Reyna and Zapata, 1974; Bortz, 1979).

This current's main problem is common to all structuralism, reducing action and subjectivity to positions in the structures of the labor market or domestic units, and an emphasis on quantification. The techniques that were prioritized for gathering information have relied on government statistics concerning the workforce and surveys using closed questionnaires. This current, contrary to the historiographic approach, has continued to develop, incorporating more subjective elements with qualitative techniques.

The "Labor Process" Current

This current began in the same period as the other two, under the influence of the labor and student movements of the 1970s. Although it developed was on a lesser scale than the historiographic current, these currents competed with one another in trying to explain the labor movement. As opposed to the historiographic current, whose starting point was the relations between the top union leadership and the state, the "labor process" current analyzed the common workers in their work life, work conditions, and transformation. In the emergence of this current, anthropologists played a very important role in conducting two major investigations, one in the nascent automotive industry in Ciudad Sahagun (Novelo and Urteaga, 1979) and the other among the shoemakers of the Leon, Guanajuato area (Nieto, 1986). The theoretical inspiration of this current came from the Italian *Operaist* tendencies (Panzieri and Negri) and from an *Operaist* reading of the first Touraine (Sariego and Santana, 1982), when Touraine approved, until 1970, the centrality of work in the whole of social relations. Based on this reading, workers' collective action would be mainly the result of contradictions in the work processes (Sánchez, 1980). In particular, the technological changes would have consequences on workplace organization and this, in turn, on skills. Braverman's (1972) conception concerning tendencies toward skills reduction was also adopted. The concept of skilled labor would be central to explain, as Mallet (1970) does, the forms of worker consciousness, and the different forms of action and organization adopted by the workers (Bizberg, 1982; Quiroz, 1980). The structuralism of the labor process was present despite attempts to differentiate forms of worker consciousness. This latter point was more deduced than directly investigated. This current was the first to undertake interesting descriptions of work processes, technologies, and organizations, but during a period in Mexico in which Taylorism and Fordism were the big novelties. The most frequently used research techniques were observation of productive processes, interviews with qualified workers, and some surveys of workers in production departments. In 1980 and 1981, this current organized two important seminars in the National Autonomous University of Mexico on "Crisis, New Technologies, and Labor Processes" and found outlets in which to publish their contributions in influential magazines of the time, such as *Cuadernos Politicos* (Editorial ERA publishing house) and *Coyoacan* (an independent magazine with a Trotskyist orientation). However, this activist "labor process" current, like historiography, entered into decline following the June 1984 strikes, the last massive attempt of the trade union movement to halt the advent of nascent neoliberalism in state policies. The deception and the intellectuals' disbelief at the changes at the beginning of the 1980s, mainly the conceptualization concerning neoliberalism in relation to the previous Keynesian and welfare state, and the productive restructuring that began with characteristics different than those associated with Taylorism, led to the breakup of the study groups researching the labor process. Their participants either changed topics or accepted posts in the public administration.

The sociodemographic current, on the other hand, continued its academic studies, although without the influence that the two former currents had in their time. Under these conditions, there emerged a new generation of academics that, as students in the 1970s, had experienced the influences of the currents in labor studies dominant in that decade. But contrary to the previous generation of specialists, they were neither members of political organizations nor did they feel that their investigations should be aimed at denouncing injustices or raising workers' consciousness. On the other hand, they were better equipped in social, methodological, and technical theories of investigation than their predecessors, and were especially familiar with the main international theoretical currents in the social sciences. This new generation of the 1980s was to be the main protagonist of the *new labor studies* in Mexico, which would be centered on productive restructuring. In this sense, it is the heir to the labor process current but projects its vision from that field toward the labor market, to the spheres of reproduction and industrial relations.

NEW LABOR STUDIES IN MEXICO

The new labor studies in Mexico adopted broad theoretical guidelines from the beginning. First, the French theory of regulation, created by Aglietta and Lipietz, underscored the modes of regulation between production and consumption. This theory was brought to Mexico by students of Boyer and Lipietz, who, at the beginning of the 1980s, sought to substitute this theory for the theory of dependence, which, in decline at the time, had dominated the horizon in the 1970s in Latin America (Gutierrez, 1988). There followed theories about Toyotism and lean production, with less impact that the previously mentioned theory. Then came Kern, and Schuman's (1998) *new concepts of production* (which meant the emergence of anthropocentric concepts in work organization), brought by German academics who conducted empirical research in Latin America. Later on, the *flexible specialization* of Piore and Sabel made its debut in a search for industrial districts for research purposes, and very recently, the theory of *industrial governance* (the emergence of new institution of governance of the market and of the economic system; Dussel and Ruiz, 1997), which in the 1990s gave rise to research on productive chains (de la Garza, 1993a).

Independent of other important individual efforts, the central formative nucleus in the theories of productive restructuring emerged as a result of a theoretical seminar held at the National University of Mexico in the mid-1980s and lasted 2 years. Participating in this seminar were researchers and postgraduate-level students from different educational institutions, some of whom became the main exponents of the new type of labor research being conducted in the Northern Border College, the Autonomous Metropolitan University, the National Autonomous University of Mexico, and the Latin American Faculty of Social Sciences. The most important topics covered by these new labor studies are as follows.

Technological Change and Workplace Organization

Studies in this field began in the 1970s as part of the labor process tradition and continued in the new labor studies, with other theoretical frameworks and problems linked to the third technological revolution characterized by the introduction of information technology and computing in the productive processes, and Toyotism. Researchers soon realized that, in Mexico, new forms of workplace organization were more relevant for productive restructuring than the new technologies and that the local processes of adaptation implied mixtures of Taylorism and Toyotism as dominant forms in the new relations (Carrillo, 1993). The sectors most studied have been the terminal automotive industry, the *maquiladoras*, modern services such as telecommunications (de la Garza, 1986) and banks, as well as the state-run companies, be they privatized or not (aviation, steel, oil, electric power generation, railroads) (Barbosa, 1992; Leyva, 1988; Melgoza, 1992). The empirical conclusions weigh in favor of partial applications of total quality and Just In Time (JIT) concepts, especially statistical control of the process, JIT, and quality circles (Mertens, 1990). For workers, these concepts translate into an increase in workplace tasks, speed up, and change of skills but not of salaries, which are generally low, independent of whether or not the sector is modernized. In addition, the thesis of the polarization of the productive apparatus is gaining a consensus, that modernization involves a minority of companies, mainly large enterprises, and that the great majority of companies have not introduced technological changes or modified workplace organization. This does not imply stagnated segments, but rather articulations among companies with different levels of modernization: a marked heterogeneity among companies in terms of sociotechnical level (technologies, organization, labor relations, and workforce characteristics) but not among workers. In general, skills are low level in both modern and backward companies, possibly due to a form of workplace organization that separates workers' tasks from those of technicians and engineers. The characteristics of the workforce differ more on a gender and job seniority basis than in relation to job skills, with strong regional differences in this regard. An example of this is the majority presence of women workers in the *maquiladoras*, with a high voluntary turnover in employment; that is, the working class in Mexico is not characterized by having new, high skills, but by being comprised of women and youth, with short, very mobile employment experience and low skill levels, who are paid low wages (de la Garza, 1993b).

Labor Flexibility

This is one of the topics most studied, and on which the best information is available. The current stage of labor flexibility in Mexico began at the beginning of the 1980s with the opening of the terminal automotive plants in the northern border states and the growth of *maquiladoras* in this same period. By the middle of the 1990s, labor flexibility had already become the key word for change in labor relations. Three stages can be identified in the current labor flexibility drive; the first, between 1982 and 1992, when changes were a dominant feature in the collective bargaining agreements in large companies. The changes were one-sided, leaving the unions outside the decision-making process concerning restructuring (Quintero and de la O, 1992; Covarrubias, 1992). Later, between 1992 and December 1994, the government itself sought to in-

duce the transformation of the corporativist unions and make them participants in the modernization of the companies. In this stage, productivity agreements and bonuses were established. The final stage, from 1995 to the present,
coincides with the failure of the policy of granting bonuses as a way of raising
workers' income. The bonuses as a percentage of the base salary were low,
with some exceptions. Nonetheless, the most extensive studies demonstrate,
first, that most of the collective bargaining agreements have not changed, but
when they have, the tendency toward flexibility is the most prevalent feature;
second, that there are very important regional differences in terms of the intensity of the flexibility; and, third, that it is functional flexibility that has
most advanced (Melgoza and De la Garza, 1992).

These studies are supplemented by others that emphasize trade union
strategies with respect to flexibility and productivity. These investigations show
a panorama in which three main union strategies are being implemented: (1)
hard resistance, characteristic of the independent trade unionism of the left
and some sectors of corporativist unionism; (2) "company unionism," that is,
unions subordinated to the company, with functions in the workplace that
normally would correspond to the company personnel department (this is the
case with the so-called *white unions* in Monterrey and it has extended to a
minority of corporativist unions on a company wide level); (3) the strategy of
the unions seeking to act as a go-between with management, without at the
same time strictly submitting to the company but recognizing the changes
that have occurred in the field of collective bargaining negotiations and attempting not to lose power with respect to productive restructurings. This
latter strategy is a minority phenomenon and especially common in unions
that in the past year have left the Congress of Labor or maintain a critical
stance vis-à-vis the official labor confederation. This position also extends to a
minority sector of the independent unions, such as the Authentic Labor Front
(de la Garza, 1993b).

Unions and Productive Restructuring

Historiographic studies centered on the question of union democratization have been replaced by those dealing with the consequences of productive
restructuring for the unions and their strategies in response to this phenomenon. These new studies went through two stages; in the first, the accent was
placed on the trade union defeats of the late 1980s with respect to the question of company restructurings (aviation, steel, railroads, oil, auto, Cerveceria
Modelo brewery, mining) (Leyva, 1995; Bensunsan and García, 1990; Raygadas,
1989); in the second stage, in the 1990s, the emphasis was on the cases of
successful union negotiations. Thus, a different sense was given to the con-

cept of neocorporativism, at variance with that advanced by Schmitter (1993), in terms of a union that, without ceasing to be tied to the State, becomes a *company union* (Telephone Workers Union, Social Security Institute Employees Union). Recently, attention has been placed on the break of some unions with the Congress of Labor and the emergence of organizational alternatives, such as the left-wing May First Inter-Union Coordinating Committee and the National Workers Union, the latter headed by the telephone and social security employees unions. This panorama has very recently led to interest in union democracy, but in connection with possible transformations of structures and trade union dynamics, is now spurred by the modernization of the companies, all viewed through the prism of the problem of reconstructing the union's representativeness, legitimacy, and democratic internal life; that is, union studies, now conducted from a perspective of the sociology of trade unionism and in connection with productive restructuring, are not on the decline but, on the contrary, have been renewed, with new problems and theoretical concepts.

Labor Market

The sociological focus on the labor market has been favored by the low level of development of economic studies on this question. We have previously noted the emergence in the 1970s of the sociodemographic school of the labor market that has directed its focus on the informal sector, the domestic unit also sociological in its orientation, and women. The other school of thought that leads to a consideration of the domestic unit, also sociological in its orientation is the current that in the 1970s studied the rural economy from Chayanov's (1974) perspective. In both cases, it has been the concept of the domestic unit and reproduction that has allowed production to be articulated with reproduction and consumption, under the premise that in the domestic units it is consumption that determines production in family units (de Oliveira, 1989b). However, the most important part of this focus continues to be held hostage to demographic variables. For example, the supply of jobs is a function of variables such as sex, age, and educational level, while the demand for employment is not analyzed as such; therefore, the points of contact with the new labor studies are scarce. There are two exceptions. First are the studies of the labor market conducted by the Western Center for Research and Studies in Social Anthropology, in which survival strategies are linked with employment patterns. These studies allow us to reject the segmentationist thesis by demonstrating the significant capillarity existing between the formal and informal job market (Escobar, 1986; Gabayet, 1988). Second, recent studies on the labor market and migration employ the concepts of social networks combined with labor patterns, which give important weight to the subjective construction of employment expectations in opposition to the neoclassical theories (Pries, 1992).

Labor Culture

This question has been analyzed from three vantage points:

1. The reproduction of the workforce, mentioned in the previous section, in order to analyze the decision to obtain employment.
2. The labor process with two approaches: The first derives culture and consciousness from the workplace situation, such as Bizberg's study of the La Truchas steel plant, and the second tries to analyze this question in its own right, as professional identity, for example, the shoemakers from Leon.
3. Collective action, such as Leyva's studies on the railroad workers (Leyva, 1995) and Angelic Cuellar's (1998) writings on rubber workers, using concepts characteristic of the new theories on social movements.

On this question, one can observe hermeneutic theories on subjectivity coming together with theories that make use of the concept of *agency*, in an attempt to link structures, subjectivities, and collective actions. Again, due to antineoclassical theories, there are practically no labor studies in Mexico from the perspective of rational action; while on the other hand, there are many combinations between major theoretical frameworks (Giddens, Bordieu, Habermas, Touraine) and regional theories of the social movements (Melucci, 1982). The current fascination in this field is centered on the incorporation of the subjectivity of the collective participants in the analyses. In general, the new labor studies focus on active participants who do not blindly respond to pressures of the social structures.

Managerial Strategies of Modernization

These studies are very recent; previously, analyses focused on businessmen as political subjects or studied their capital holdings. Now there are efforts under way to study how businesspeople construct their modernization strategies (Mertens, 1995), under structural pressure, but through a process of making sense of a situation that pits science against subjectivity. This leads to the interest in business culture. The little that is thus far known is that businesspeople faced with identical pressures of the market do not employ the same modernization strategies. There are at least two strategies in Mexico, one based on flexibility, with the involvement of the workforce, and another that seeks cost reduction. In addition, there are important regional differences in business culture that have an impact on modernization strategies. Again, the studies on this topic are critical of the perspective of the rational actor, and they enter into the broader debate on whether there are global tendencies toward the convergence of production models. This polemic is present in neoinstitutionalism, for example, Womack's (1990) considerations on the spread of "lean production."

Productive Chains

These studies, also from the 1990s, have been developed under the direct or indirect influence of M. Piore. Up to now, there have been two important results: first, that locally or regionally, businessmen are establishing new, non-commercial institutions of mutual support; that is, commercial liberalization in any event requires noncommercial institutions; second, that the chains promote modernization, but this occurs with tremendous unevenness in terms of workplace conditions, job security, and wages. In synthesis, the topics approached from a sociological perspective have been broadened and updated in Mexico, but the central problem that escapes many such studies is the change in labor relations. The exception to this trend is the focus employed by the followers of Piore, who have stressed for moving from the sociology of work to the sociology of the company, without considering labor.

THE INSTITUTIONALIZATION OF THE SOCIOLOGY OF WORK

The new labor studies in Mexico, which might well be considered as an expanded sociology of work, have been consolidated mainly due to the existence of informal research networks. One such network began in the previously mentioned seminar held at the National Autonomous University of Mexico (UNAM), which in the 1980s established ties with a commission of the Latin American Council of Social Sciences (a Latin American multigovernmental organization, with headquarters in Buenos Aires, that promotes research in the social sciences). Although it did not provide financing, it did establish important personal contacts in the Southern Cone region. Based on this experience, the Technological Change and Union Response in Mexico project was conducted, which allowed researchers to have a broad vision of how productive restructuring was unfolding in the large companies at the end of the 1980s, and how work and the unions were being affected. The result was a series of books, academic degree theses, and articles on many branches of the economy. Another major project was Models of Industrialization in Mexico, financed by Mexico's National Council of Science and Technology. This study encompassed 14 industrial zones and 60 researchers, through a survey of companies that allowed many regional differences and differences due to company size to be detected in chains, technology, organization, labor relations, and workforce profiles. This was followed by the Business Modernization Strategies project, which worked in five zones with 14 researchers, also financed by the National Council of Science and Technology.

Since the end of the 1980s, university professors have taught courses on new topics in the sociology of work at the Autonomous Metropolitan University Iztapalapa campus (UAMI), Oaxtepec, Guadalajara, Puebla and Tlaxcala, as well as special courses such as those organized by the Veracruzana University and the UAMI. Key in this process of institutionalization were the four Jalapa colloquia, true congresses that since 1987, have presented hundred of papers and debate between proponents of the new labor studies and the historiographic current. In the heat of this intellectual effervescence surrounding the sociology of work, specialized postgraduate degree programs have been created in the field, such as those offered by the UAMI and that of the University of Aguascalientes, and have provided sociology of labor studies programs at the College of Mexico, FLACSO, the UAM Xochimilco campus, the University of Guadalajara, the Northern Border College, and the UNAM. Academic journals and trade union education centers have played an important role. To begin with, articles in the journals *Trabajo* (an independent magazine published by the Center of Labor Analysis, which is tied to the UAMI postgraduate program in social studies) and *Revista Latinoamericana de Estudios del Trabajo* (magazine of the Latin American Association of Sociology of Work, founded in Mexico City, with its headquarters currently located in Argentina), and the presence of sociology of work studies in *Frontera Norte* (Northern Border College), *Perfiles Latinoamericanos* (FLACSO), *Investigacion Economica* (Institute of Economic Research of the UNAM) and other nonspecialized but equally prestigious journals such as the *Revista Mexicana de Sociologia* (Institute of Social Research of the UNAM), *Estudios Sociologicos* (College of Mexico), *Estudios Sociales* (College of Sonora) and *El Cotidiano* (UAM Azcapotzalco campus) culminated in the First Latin American Sociology of Work Congress in Mexico City and the founding of the *Revista Latinoamericana de Estudios del Trabajo* and the Latin American Sociology of Work Association.

The financing agency that has most supported research in the field of the sociology of work in Mexico is the CONACYT (the Mexican government agency that supports scientific investigation), but the institution that has most contributed to disseminating studies on the sociology of work through publications, seminars, and conferences is the F. Ebert Foundation (sponsored by the German social democratic party). The International Labor Organization, which at the beginning of the 1980s held a major international seminar on Technological Revolution and Employment, has undertaken important research but is limited to the personnel employed by this institution. Special mention should be made of the participation by Mexican investigators in international research networks (with Cornell University on telecommunications, with Columbia University on productive chains, with the Paris-based Gerpisa team on the automotive industry, with the University of California at La Jolla on corporativism) that has allowed for fresh exchanges of theoretical perspectives and empirical discoveries. However, this clear process of institutionalization in the academic world has not had its counterpart in the level of companies' interest and only very partially in the trade unions and government institutions. Companies do not finance research in this field except for some consulting services contracted from private universities with a predetermined political agenda. A similar phenomenon occurs in the case of the trade unions except that they have sometimes shown an interest in holding educational courses for their members on new labor issues. At the same time, it should be mentioned that, on this level, the academic institutions compete with other independent centers specifically dedicated to such activities, such as the Institute of Trade Union Studies of the Americas (belonging to the Teachers Union of the Americas), the National Center for Social Promotion (financed by the Konrad Adenauer Foundation of Germany), and the Workers University of Mexico (founded by Vicente Lombardo Toledano). In terms of government institutions, the interesting trajectory of the Labor Ministry (STyPS) in the 1970s, promoting research, publications, and congress on labor history, was suspended as of the 1980s, and information was considered dangerous given labor–management tensions related to workplace flexibility and productive restructuring. This situation remained until 1997, when the panorama seems to have changed, with the STyPS now promoting a magazine, granting awards for research, financing projects, providing scholarships for postgraduate students, and organizing different seminars on labor issues.

Finally, in terms of the relations between the sociology of work and other academic fields, note that there would be a first block of subjects linked to and centered on a sociological focus: economy, anthropology, political science, and part of administration sciences. On the other hand, there are academic disciplinary fields that deal with labor, but without any relation to the sociology of work, such as engineering, psychology, industrial relations, law, and most topics dealt with in administration sciences. This inclusive and hegemonic character of the sociology of work in new labor studies can possibly be attributed to the following:

1. The underdeveloped nature of studies in labor economy, administration, and industrial relations in Mexico on the level of theory and empirical research (the former by omission and the latter two for having developed more as technical sciences and advisory services).
2. The intellectual tradition of interest in economic development, the State, and the labor movement, which has allowed topics to be joined together that in other countries appear as subjects in differentiated academic disciplinary fields (e.g., corporativism with productive re-

structuring, the State with workplace flexibility, and labor culture with trade union and management strategies).

3. The strength of the focus on active participants, which, considered together with interactions, problems of power, and processes of signification, have prevented perspectives such as the theories of rational choice from having any influence on labor studies in Mexico.

CONCLUSIONS

The sociology of work in Mexico is a young science that emerged in the 1970s and still has baggage from the 1980s. Previously there was no probusiness industrial sociology, such as that existing in the United States or Europe; thus, this field of study did not suffer the same type of break in the transition from industrial sociology to the sociology of work. The break was of a different nature, with studies on workers' movements, dominant in the 1970s, that offered great resistance against the nascent science, resistance marked by theoretical and especially political preferences against the current that we have called the labor process and that is the more direct predecessor of the new labor studies. These new labor studies can encompass several academic disciplinary fields, but the sociological focus of active participants has an important weight in them. It is also a focus in which the current polemics negating the importance of work have not had an impact. For example, postmodernism has not permeated these studies, which remain loyal to the idea of totality, in the sense that the starting point for the studies is the productive process and they are articulated with the labor market (migrations, labor patterns, and social networks), with the social reproduction of the workforce and its culture on diverse levels. Such studies include labor and industrial relations, and in that context encompass not only trade unionism and the labor movement but also businesspersons as subjects of labor. This broad and restless Mexican sociology of work will not encounter any problem in extending its range of interest to nonsalaried labor, medium-level management, and engineers, as well as the inclusion of free time, and urban or rural space. The first researches based on this perspective have appeared on the agroindustrial, hotel, formal commercial, and street vendor sectors.

The sociology of work in Mexico, having broad theoretical starting points that are not only sociological but also economic and political, fits into previous intellectual traditions whose concern centered on development, the State, and the social and political subjects, but its focus is now on work-related questions. With this in mind, the concepts of the production and industrialization models seem central to the concerns of this academic discipline. This has had major analytical advantages, because maintaining a sociological focus has allowed academic disciplinary limits to be broken and concepts to be reconstructed that do not always appear together in the developed countries. Thus, new concepts appear based on old terms: the contractual model of the Mexican revolution, neoliberal corporativism, the sociotechnical configuration of the productive processes, and socioeconomic production units. This has been possible because communication has been maintained, with discussion on social theory and methodology taking place internationally. Therefore, the sociology of work's use of the teachings of Bordieu, Habermas, Giddens, and Touraine or the critique of positivism and the hypothetical deductive method, are not at odds with its thrust.

The task of the sociology of work, now institutionalized in the Mexican academic world, is to continue fighting for its recognition in the world of business, labor unions, and government. In this endeavor, it must develop the operative aspects that have a long tradition in the developed countries and which, in Mexico, have been reduced to basic scientific research. This question is very important, not only to broaden the legitimacy of this academic disciplinary field but also to increase the labor market for university graduates who, up to now, have found employment almost exclusively in the university setting of instruction and research.

REFERENCES

Aguilar, J. 1990. *Historia de la CTM: 1936–1990*. Mexico City: Autonomous Metropolitan University–Azcapotzalco.

Barbosa, F. 1992. "La reestructuración de Pemex." *El Cotidiano* 46(March–April) Mexico City: Autonomous Metropolitan University–Azcapotzalco.

Bensunsan, G., and C. García. 1990. "Cambios en las relaciones Laborales : cuatro experiencias en transición." Working Paper 32. Mexico City: Ebert Foundation.

Bizberg, I. 1982. *La Acción Obrera en Las Truchas*. Mexico City: Colmex.

Bortz, J. 1979. "Problemas de la Medición de la Afiliación Sindical en México." Second Regional Colloquium on Labor History. Merida, Yucatan: Center for Historical and Social Studies of the Workers Movement.

Braverman, H. 1972. *Trabajo y Capital Monopolista*. Mexico: Editorial Nuestro Tiempo.

Carrillo, J. (Coordinator) 1993. *Condiciones de Empleo y Capacitación en las Maquiladoras de Exportación en México*. Mexico City: Secretaria del Trabajo y Prevision Social.

Chayanov, A. V. 1974. *La Organización de la Unidad Económica Campesina*. Buenos Aires: Nueva Visión.

Contreras, O. 1987. "Modernización Minera : el caso de Sonora", *El Cotidiano*, 16(March–April) Mexico City: Autonomous Metropolitan University–Azcapotzalco.

Córdoba, A. 1987. *La Política de Masas y el Futuro de la Izquierda en México*. Mexico City: ERA.

Cortés, F. 1990. *Crisis y Reproducción Social: Los comerciantes del sector informal.* Mexico City:. M. A. Porrúa.

Covarrubias, A. 1992. *La Flexibilidad Laboral en Sonora.* Hermosillo: Colegio de Sonora.

Cuellar, A. 1998. "Los Obreros de Tornell frente a dos Procesos Políticos." In *Los Estudios Sobre la Cultura Obrera en México,* edited by E. de la Garza, et. al. Mexico City: Conaculta.

de la Garza, E. 1986. "La investigación sobre la Clase Obrera en México." *Nueva Antropología,* 8(29):20–40.

de la Garza, E. 1986. "¿Quién ganó en Telmex?" *El Cotidiano,* No. 32. Mexico City: UMA.

de la Garza, E. 1993a. "Los Estudios Laborales en México." *Ciencia* 44:1180–1192. Mexico City: Academia de la Investigación Científica.

de la Garza, E. 1993b. *Reestructuración Productiva y Respuesta Sindical en México.* Mexico City: Instituto de Investigaciones Economicas–UNAM.

de Oliveira, O. 1989a. "La Participación Femenina en los Mercados de Trabajo Urbanos en México." *Estudios Demográficos y Urbanos,* 4(3. Sept.–Dec.): Mexico City: El Colegio de México.

de Oliveira, O., et. al. 1989b. *Grupos Domésticos de Trabajo y Reproducción Cotidiana.* Mexico City: Colmex-Porrúa.

Dussel, E., and C. Ruiz. 1997. *Pensar Globalmente y Actuar Regionalmente.* Mexico City: Ebert Foundation–Autonomous Metropolitan University–Azcapotzalco.

Escobar, A. 1986. *Con el Sudor de tu Frente.* Guadalajara: El Colegio de Jalisco–CIESAS.

Gabayet, L. 1988. *Obreros Somos.* Guadalajara: El Colegio de Jalisco–CIESAS.

Gutierrez, E, 1988. *Testimonios de la Crisis.* Mexico City: Siglo XXI.

Leyva, M. A. 1988. "Ferrocarriles, luz verde a la modernidad." *El Cotidiano* 21:10–15. Mexico City: Autonomous Metropolitan University–Azcapotzalco.

Leyva, M. A. 1995. *Poder y Dominación en FFNNM.* Mexico City: Ebert Foundation–Autonomous Metropolitan University–Azcapotzalco.

Mallet, S. 1970. *La Nueva Clase Obrera.* Barcelona: Tusquets.

Melgoza, J. 1992. "Sindicato y Cultura Política en el SME." Master's thesis, Autonomous Metropolitan University–Azcapotzalco, Mexico City.

Melgoza, J., and E. de la Garza. 1992. "Los Sindicatos Frente a la Productividad: Telefonistas y electricistas." *El Cotidiano* 41(May–June): Mexico City: Autonomous Metropolitan University–Azcapotzalco.

Melucci, A. 1982. *Sistema Político, Partiti e Movementi Sociali.* Milano: Feltrinelli.

Mertens, L. 1992. *Crisis Económica y Revolución Tecnológica.* Caracas: ORIT–Nueva Sociedad.

Mertens, L. 1995. *Cambio Tecnológico y Mercados de Trabajo.* Mexico City: OIT.

Muñoz, H., and O. de Oliveira. 1977. *Migración y Marginalidad Social en la Ciudad de México.* Mexico City: El Colegio de México.

Nieto, R. 1986. "El Oficio de Zapatero." *Nueva Antropología* 8(29):30–42.

Novelo, V. y A. Urteaga. 1979. *La Industria en los Magueyales.* Mexico City: Nueva Imagen.

Pries, L. 1992. "Trayectorias Laborales."Pp. 180–195 in *Ajuste Estructural, Mercados Laborales y TLC.* Mexico City: Colmex.

Quintero, C., and M. E. de la O. 1992. "Sindicalismo y Contratación Colectiva en las Maquiladoras Fronterizas." *Frontera Norte*, 4:80–95.
Quiroz, J. O. 1980. "Procesos de Trabajo en la Industria Automotriz." *Cuadernos Políticos* 26:25–40.
Raygadas, L. 1989. "Corporativismo y Reconversión Industrial en la Minería." Master's thesis Facultad de Ciencias Politica y Sociales–UNAM, Mexico City.
Reyna, J. L., and F. Zapata. 1974. *Tres Estudios sobre el Movimiento Obrero en México*. Mexico City: El Colegio de México.
Sánchez, S. 1980. "Los Trabajadores del Calzado en Guanajuato." *Cuadernos Políticos* 24(April–June): Mexico City: ERA.
Sariego, J. L., and R. Santana. 1982. "Transición Tecnológica y Resistencia Obrera en la Minería Mexicana." *Cuadernos Políticos* 30(Jan.–March): Mexico City: ERA.
Schmitter, K. 1993. "Continuamos en el Siglo del Corporativismo?" Pp. 1–35 in *Teoría del Neocorporativismo*. Guadalajara: Universidad de Guadalajara.
Schumann, M. 1998. "New Concepts of Production and Productivity." *Economic and Industrial Democracy* 19(1):60–76.
Street, S. 1992. *Maestros en Movimiento*. Mexico City: Cuadernos de la Casa Chata.
Woldenberg, J. 1980a. "Characteristics of the Studies on the Working Class and the Labor Movement in Mexico: 1970–1978." Memorias del Encuentro sobre Historia del Movimiento Obrero, Vol. 1. Puebla: Universidad Autonoma de Puebla.
Woldenberg, J. 1980b. "Notas sobre la Burocracia Sindical en México." *Azcapotzalco*, Vol. 1. Mexico City: Universidad Autonoma de Puebla.
Womack, J. P. 1990. *The Machine that Changed the World*. New York: McGraw-Hill.
Zazueta, C., and R. de la Peña. 1981. *Estructura Dual y Piramidal del Sindicalismo Mexicano*, Serie Estudios, No. 10. Mexico City: CNIET, Secretaria del Trabajo y Prevision Social.

APPENDIX: IMPORTANT RESEARCH CENTERS ON THE SOCIOLOGY OF LABOR IN MEXICO

Maestría y Doctorado en Estudios Sociales
Universidad Autónoma Metropolitana-Iztapalapa
GT@Xanum.uam.mx

Facultad Lationamericana de Ciencias Sociales
Flacso@flacso.flacso.edu.mx

Instituto de Investigaciones Sociales, UNAM
Sara@servidor.unam.mx

Instituto de Investigaciones Económicas, UNAM
Bouzas@servidor.unam.mx

Centro de Investigaciones Superiores en Antropología Social
Ciejuare@juarez.ciesas.edu.mx

Centro de Estudios Sociológicos, El Colegio de México
Zapata@colmex.mx

Universidad Autónoma de Aguas Calientes
Departamento de Sociología
Mahernan@aqua.uaa.mx

Organización Internacional del Trabajo
Mexico@mex.oit.org.mx

El Colegio de la Frontera Norte
Carrillo@colef.mx

5

The United States

Arne L. Kalleberg and Kevin T. Leicht

INTRODUCTION

Work is a central institution in the United States. The work that Americans do has a major influence on their position within the stratification system in the United States. Work is also the basis on which important social benefits such as health insurance and many pension benefits are distributed. Changes in work in the United States reflect key societal trends such as advances in technology, globalization and internationalization, demographic changes in the population and the labor force, the growth of services, and the differentiation of manufactured goods. Changes in the nature of work, in turn, have a major impact on the number of hours Americans spend working, what they do in their leisure time, their consumption patterns, their attitudes toward success and failure, and a host of other attributes that shape the way they live and interact with each other.

The centrality of work in the United States is mirrored in the prominent position occupied by the study of work within American sociology. From studies

Arne L. Kalleberg · Department of Sociology, University of North Carolina, Chapel Hill, North Carolina 27599. Kevin T. Leicht · Department of Sociology, University of Iowa, Iowa City, Iowa 52242.

Worlds of Work: Building an International Sociology of Work, edited by Daniel B. Cornfield and Randy Hodson. Kluwer Academic/Plenum Publishers, New York, 2002.

of the consequences of Frederick Taylor's scientific management system at the turn of the 20th century, to investigations of the nature of the human relations movement led by Elton Mayo and his colleagues, to studies of occupations by Everett C. Hughes and his students at the University of Chicago, to research by industrial sociologists on unions and labor–management relations in the 1950s, to studies of organizations during the past 30 years, there has been no shortage of issues studied by sociologists of work in the United States.

The prominence of sociology of work in American sociology is due in part to its linkages to other aspects of sociology, such as stratification, the family, the life course, leisure studies, organizations, occupations, and industrial relations. Moreover, the sociology of work is a fertile meeting area for other disciplines, and sociological understandings of work have both contributed to—and been informed by—theoretical debates and research conducted by economists, psychologists, historians, industrial relations scholars, and researchers located in business schools, among others. This breadth reflects the multilevel nature of topics in the sociology of work: these topics span macro (the economy and culture), mezzo (organizations and the industrial relations system), and micro (jobs and teams) levels (Kalleberg and Berg, 1987).

Developments in the study of work in the United States are intimately related to issues and trends taking place throughout the world. Sociologists of work in the United States have always been aware of and receptive to developments in other countries that have influenced Americans' thinking about which theoretical questions are important to study and how to study them. For example, the sociotechnical school in Scandinavia and Japanese management influenced a generation of managers as well as sociologists of work concerned with increasing productivity in the United States. Moreover, discussions of unionization in the United States have used as a baseline the variations in labor–management relations characterized by the corporatist model in Scandinavia, political unionism in France, and company unionism in Japan. Conversely, many work-related developments in the United States have spread to other countries. Thus, the scientific management movement quickly found adherents in the newly founded Russian Republic and elsewhere. Moreover, measures of occupational prestige developed in the United States in the 1930s and 1940s found their way into international prestige scores. In addition, organizational studies have been replicated by French, German, and other researchers anxious to assess the relative roles of structure and culture in shaping the organization of work. And, the relationship of people to their work has been studied comparatively by those concerned with demonstrating the importance of industrial democracy.

In this chapter, we provide an overview of some of the main themes that characterize the sociology of work in the United States. We identify six major enduring themes and, for each theme, summarize some of the main issues, research questions, and research studies related to it. We then identify six additional emergent themes of more recent vintage that reflect important changes taking place in the institution of work in the United States. These emergent themes are likely to become significant issues in the sociology of work in the United States in coming years. Finally, we discuss some aspects of the institutional context that supports the study of work in the United States, including opportunities for research and availability of data sets.

IMPORTANT THEMES IN THE SOCIOLOGY OF WORK IN THE UNITED STATES

Six Enduring Themes

Work Organization and the Labor Process. How and why work is organized the way it is has been a major issue in the United States. Sociological research on this issue has been framed by debates rooted in Emile Durkheim's conception of the division of labor, Karl Marx's view of the labor process as rooted in capitalist control, and by discussions of the efficiencies and dysfunctions of bureaucracy as a way of organizing work that drew upon Max Weber's classic discussions of bureaucracy.

Harry Braverman's *Labor and Monopoly Capital* (1974) focused research and theory on the question of work organization in terms of class struggle and labor control rather than organizational efficiencies. His neo-Marxist analysis maintained that the organizational division of labor resulted from class conflict over the way in which work was organized. Braverman's theory sparked a lively debate, with supporters applauding his critical approach to issues of organizational design and critics charging that he neglected the role of worker agency in shaping the labor process. (Smith, 1994, describes the conceptual transformation that topics related to skill levels and control strategies have undergone in the 20 years since the publication of Braverman's book and identifies the unresolved issues facing this area.) Richard Edwards's *Contested Terrain* (1979) sought to overcome some of these criticisms by describing the evolution of labor control systems in the United States. His discussion integrated a bureaucratic perspective with a neo-Marxist view that the historically contingent nature of the labor process was driven by the dynamics of capitalist development.

Braverman's theory of the organizational, or detailed, division of labor also sparked a lively debate regarding the impact of work organization on changes in skills. He argued that capitalists sought to de-skill workers by creating a detailed division of labor in which labor costs, and therefore workers' power, were minimal. Writers who felt that technology and other drivers of the labor process resulted in increases in skills challenged his view. The debate over whether skills have been upgraded or downgraded as a result of changes in the organization of work and technological change has been extensively reviewed by Spenner (1983) and Form et al. (1988), both of whom concluded that it depended on whether you looked at the entire economy (which yielded evidence for upgrading) or at specific occupations (such as printers, which provided evidence for downgrading). An example of research on skill changes in the U.S. economy is Szafran's (1996) analysis of how changes in the relative size of detailed occupation groups from 1950 through 1990 affected the likelihood that workers would experience various kinds of tasks (e.g., occupations with greater substantive complexity and social interaction, and occupations requiring lower motor skills). A volume edited by Bills (1995) contains a number of studies related to changes in skills.

Labor Markets and Careers. The study of labor markets emerged as an important issue in the sociology of work within the United States in the 1960s. The initial impetus was fueled by radical economists (Bluestone, Harrison, David Gordon) who sought to understand the persistence of the urban poor despite efforts to enhance their labor market competitiveness by increasing their human capital. The resulting explanation was dual labor market theory (Gordon, 1972), which posited that the labor market was divided into two main sectors: the primary market consisting of good jobs and the secondary market comprised of bad jobs. The working poor were concentrated in the secondary market, where lack of opportunity for skill development doomed them to a career of low wages and unemployment. The primary market, by contrast, consisted of good jobs that paid relatively high wages (and had relatively steep wage trajectories), since workers were able to advance their careers by moving up ladders within internal labor markets. These internal labor markets were the main structural characteristics of primary markets (Doeringer and Piore, 1971) and were a major incentive used by the bureaucratic control systems discussed above (Edwards, 1979).

In the early 1970s, sociologists turned to theories of internal and dual labor markets as a way of conceptualizing the structure of opportunities that facilitated or impeded individuals' mobility and advancement. Such a conceptualization of the structure of opportunities, many felt, was missing in Peter Blau and Otis Dudley Duncan's classic study of mobility in the United States, *The American Occupational Structure* (1967). Sociologists quickly expanded the dual labor market theory by elaborating the structure of labor market segmentation and its impacts on labor mobility, careers, and earnings inequality, among other issues (the literature on this topic was reviewed by Kalleberg and Sørensen, 1979). Studies of labor market segmentation included analyses of internal labor markets and promotion processes within firms as well as how barriers within the occupational structure impeded the free mobility of workers from one occupation to another (Althauser and Kalleberg, 1981). These perspectives argued that initial placements in the labor market were critical for predicting further advancement or stagnation in the development of work careers (Rosenbaum, 1984). While empirical results largely failed to support segmented labor market perspectives (Hodson and Kaufman, 1982), this research was part of a larger movement to account for the demand for employees and to explain the preexisting labor market structure in the production of inequality.

Studies have also shown that race and gender matter for organizational career mobility. Baldi and McBrier (1997) found that the determinants of promotion differed systematically for blacks and whites (see also Wilson, Sakura-Lemessy, and West, 1999). Maume (1999) used panel data on individuals (the PSID, or Panel Study of Income Dynamics) to examine the effect of occupational gender segregation on promotions. Maume found that a high percentage of women in the occupation positively affected men's chances of moving to a supervisory position but lowered women's chances of attaining a management position.

Professions as Distinctive Forms of Work Activity. Studies of professions have played a prominent role in the sociology of work in the United States. Professions such as physicians, lawyers, accountants, and scientists are among the elite occupations in the United States and are at the leading edge of social change. These established professions are also characterized by high autonomy and control over the work, thereby providing a useful contrast to organizational control systems.

Sociologists have spent a great deal of time attempting to define professional work. This effort has led to considerable controversy in recent years (Abbott, 1988). Some researchers attempt to define professional work using a series of traits that they believe distinguishes professional work from other types of work activity. Characteristics such as high skills, autonomy and control, professional ethics, institutionalized training, professional associations, and a service ideal are the most prominent traits mentioned (Wilensky, 1964). Others focus on traits such as the ability of professional groups to monopolize specific market niches, define their activities as exclusively legitimate, keep occupational competitors from entering the market, and control the supply of practitioners to ensure relatively high fees and salaries (Derber, Schwartz, and Magrass, 1990). Researchers have directed most of their attention toward the established professions (usually medicine and law) and start their research by asking why these occupational groups are such a powerful force in the U.S. labor market.

Others have sought to answer a more historical question: How do would-be professional groups end up in their dominant positions? To answer this question, researchers usually start at a point in history where the professions lacked the prestige, domination, privilege, and compensation that they currently enjoy, and attempt to follow the sequence of historical events that propelled otherwise unprivileged occupations toward professional status. These researchers often focus on critical interactions with clients, the state, and changing economic conditions to explain the development of the relative power of professional groups (Starr, 1982). Studies in this tradition have generally concluded that the power and prestige of professional work result from a complex interaction between intentional actions on the part of professional incumbents and larger societal changes that increase the demand for professional services.

Another theme with which researchers on the professions in the United States have grappled, especially since World War II, is whether corporate capitalism has compromised professional work through the expansion of control and challenges to traditional professional prerogatives (Larsen, 1977). This group has paid particular attention to new organizational arrangements for delivering professional services (health maintenance organizations in medicine—see Hoff's [1999] study of identity and solidarity among physician managers in a changing health maintenance organization; large corporate law firms and in-house counsel arrangements in law—see Van Hoy, 1997; Epstein et al., 1999; and engineering—see Thomas, 1994) and studied the effects of these arrangements on the organization of professional work (see the review by Leicht and Fennell, 1997). This research is often directly connected to studies of the labor process and primary labor markets (discussed earlier). These changes in the context of professional work are also related to efforts to unionize (see below), as illustrated by Budry's (1997) description of the development of the Union of American Physicians and Dentists (UAPD), the most successful physicians' union to date.

Meaning of Work. Americans have long viewed work as a central life interest, though some workers (e.g., blue-collar workers) are more likely to seek fulfillment in other areas of life (Dubin, 1956). A study by Nancy Morse and Robert Weiss in 1955 showed that work was a central life interest for the vast majority of Americans: 80% of men said that they would continue to work even if they did not have to do so for economic reasons. Since the 1970s, surveys of the American population (the General Social Surveys) have consistently shown that about 70% of Americans say that they would continue to work. Juliet Schor's (1991) statistics on hours worked confirm these results using behavioral data: Americans work more hours than people in any industrial country except Japan.

Another indicator of the meaning of work is what people feel is important in their job. Since 1973, responses to the General Social Survey have revealed that Americans usually rate "intrinsic" aspects of work (i.e., having a job that gives them a feeling of accomplishment) as the job characteristic that they would prefer most, more than "extrinsic" rewards such as promotions and income. That Americans tend to evaluate intrinsic dimensions of jobs as more important than extrinsic dimensions is corroborated by the results from similar surveys of workers (see Committee on Techniques for the Enhancement of Human Performance, 1999). Obtaining intrinsic rewards is especially important for job satisfaction, organizational commitment, and psychological functioning in a country such as the United States, which places a great emphasis on individual autonomy (Lincoln and Kalleberg, 1990). However, these preferences for job characteristics differ for men and women: Tolbert and Moen's (1998) analysis of data from national surveys of workers over a 22-year period showed that there are relatively stable gender differences in preferences for job attributes (e.g., women are more likely to value intrinsic rewards, while men value extrinsic rewards more), and that the gender gap in preferences has widened among younger workers in recent years.

The absence of intrinsic rewards constituted for Marx a form of work alienation, and he was concerned that the detailed division of labor characteristic of the organization of work under capitalism (discussed earlier) would result in workers' inability to derive challenge and feelings of accomplishment from their jobs. Even participative management does not provide workers with the same level of positive and meaningful experiences as found under the craft organization of work, as Hodson's (1996) analysis of organizational ethnographies shows. The same analysis (1999) also found that anomic managerial behavior—such as the lack of trust—decreased citizenship behaviors and increased worker resistance behaviors.

Perceptions of alienation also differ for men and women: Ross and Wright's (1998) analysis—based on a national telephone probability sample—found that women's work is more alienating than men's work. Racial composition also matters: Mueller et al. (1999) found, for example, that white teachers in nonwhite school contexts (but not black teachers in white school contexts) had more negative work attitudes (lower job satisfaction and organizational commitment).

Good collections of papers dealing with issues related to the meaning of work are found in Gamst (1995) and in the special issue of *Work and Occupations* on Attitudes and Emotions at Work (2000).

Unionization and Organized Labor. Sociologists of work in the United States historically have been particularly concerned with issues related to unionization and to the organization of labor more generally. One reason for this research emphasis is that the United States has one of the lowest rates of unionization of any industrialized nation. Research in this area traditionally has focused on three major issues: union organizing activity; resistance to union organizing activity on the part of employers and political actors; and the assets and liabilities of unionization for different groups of workers.

First, research on union organizing activity has gone in two directions, focusing on the historical moments when union-organizing activity was especially successful (e.g., in the 1930s and early 1940s), or on individuals' decisions to join unions and vote for union certification. Historically, union organizing in the United States has been most effective during periods of rapid industrialization (such as in the 1890s) or in severe economic crises such as the depression of the 1930s. It usually has been met with considerable resistance and violence by employers and the state, and this resistance has taken both legal and extralegal avenues. Union organizing in the United States reached a peak shortly after World War II, and unionization rates have been in slow and consistent decline since then. (Less than 14% of the U.S. labor force currently belong to a union.)

A second, related, strand of research has looked at the activities of employers and the state in resisting unionization activity. While much of this work focuses on the same historical moments when union organizing was proceeding rapidly, other researchers have focused on the day-to-day ability of employers to exploit the relatively lax labor laws and enforcement mechanisms provided by the U.S. federal government and most state governments. This research has focused on welfare capitalism, blacklisting, manipulating union organizing elections, and the growing post–World War II wave of organizational consultants that specialize in keeping workplaces union free (Freeman, 1994).

A third thrust of research focuses on the worker as an individual actor in union decision making (Lipset, Trow, and Coleman, 1956). These studies focus on the individual characteristics of workers that promote union organization and commitment (gender, race, education, types of supervision, etc.), the roles that individual workers play in union governance and decision making, and the benefits and liabilities that come from union membership. Cornfield and Kim (1994) found that prounion sentiment is strongest among socially diverse, low-socioeconomic status workers (see also Bronfenbrenner et al., 1998). These studies have found that unionized workers are more productive, and unionized companies have lower within-firm earnings inequality (Freeman and Medoff, 1984). Unionized workers are also more likely to experience layoffs, and there is a considerable and lively debate about whether and how unions contribute to labor market inequalities between organized and unorganized workers (Leicht, 1989; Rubin, 1988; Wallace, Leicht, and Raffalovich, 1999). The relatively lax labor market regulation in the United States has helped to generate these debates.

Workplace Stratification and Inequality. Workplace stratification and inequality have received a great deal of attention from sociologists of work in the United States for two main reasons. First, the United States has one of the highest levels of income and earnings inequality of the industrialized nations, and this inequality has risen considerably since the early 1980s. Second, because of the generally unregulated nature of the U.S. labor market, much of inequality in earnings and income occurs *within* firms, occupations, and jobs rather than between them.

Research on social inequality in the workplace prior to the 1980s focused almost exclusively on individuals' occupational attainment and the structure of labor markets. These studies examined the intergenerational transmission of occupational positions and the ability of schooling and other achieved characteristics to improve or retard high-quality occupational placement. Much of this research was a direct consequence of the 1960s War on Poverty started by the Kennedy and Johnson Administrations. While this research suggested that greater investments in education would overcome the effects of disadvantaged backgrounds, the extensive investments in educational interventions during the War on Poverty failed to produce the desired result of increasing labor market opportunities for underrepresented groups. These puzzles were responsible in part for the development of dual labor market theory and other segmented labor market perspectives, as discussed earlier.

Sociological studies of work and inequality since the 1980s have focused in greater detail on the institutions and organizations that structure labor market opportunities (see the Special Issue of *Work and Occupations* on Social Inequality in the Workplace, 1998). These have been fueled by a growing recognition that workplace inequalities were produced in the specific context of business firms and within the opportunity structures of specific occupations (Baron and Bielby, 1980; DiPrete, 1989). As income inequality grew in the 1980s, there was a growing recognition that firm profitability and market position played a critical role in the production of workplace inequality. This recognition became all the more salient due to reports by researchers and the popular press of growing within-firm earnings inequality between managers and blue-collar workers. This gap, which in the United States was never low, has risen to unprecedented levels and spawned much research activity as an extension of this long-standing theme (Kalleberg and Van Buren, 1996).

Six New Themes of Recent Scholarship in the United States

Deindustrialization and Spatial Diffusion. Studying the causes and consequences of deindustrialization and spatial diffusion of business activity constitutes a major new theme in the sociology of work in the United States over the past 20 years. Deindustrialization refers to the systematic disinvestment in a nation's manufacturing infrastructure (see Bluestone and Harrison, 1982). The unregulated nature of product and labor markets in the United States, combined with a lack of government capacity to implement an industrial policy (see Magaziner and Reich, 1984) and the crisis in profitability among manufacturing firms in the late 1970s and early 1980s, led to widespread plant closings and relocations. In the process, thousands of manufacturing jobs were eliminated and thousands more were moved to other parts of the United States not normally identified with manufacturing activity (the Southeast and West) or to locations in other countries with lower labor costs, more favorable tax treatment, and lax environmental regulations.

Research on the consequences of deindustrialization has taken three directions. First, researchers who have studied the consequences of layoffs and plant closings for individual workers and their communities (Perrucci and Targ, 1993; Wallace and Rothschild, 1988; see also Milkman, 1997) have found that laid off manufacturing workers rarely acquire new jobs with pay and benefits comparable to those they left. Communities are also rarely able to replace thousands of lost tax dollars with new industry or services (Perrucci and Targ, 1993). Second, other researchers have studied the rise of the service sector, paying special attention to the growth of temporary work, unstable work careers, and the labor process involved in service production (Biggart, 1989; Hoschchild, 1983; Rifkin, 1995).

A third emphasis draws on the perspectives of demographers, urban sociologists, and students of social stratification to study spatial mismatches between jobs and workers. Much of this work deals with the plight of the urban poor, left behind by the decline of traditional manufacturing work and the rise of a suburban-based service sector job market (Wilson, 1996; Kasarda, 1990). These researchers point to a growing polarization of economic opportunities in cities, where wealthy residents work at privileged jobs with very high incomes, spatially segregated from a growing unemployed urban poor with incomes far below the poverty line. Low-income residents are at a considerable economic and cultural disadvantage in the new service economy due to the locally dependent nature of services and the reliance on interpersonal skills.

Growth of Labor Force Diversity.   The U.S. civilian labor force grew sharply during the 20th century: from about 30 million people in 1900 (which constituted about 40% of the U.S. population) to about 145–150 million by the year 2000 (about half of the U.S. population). In addition to getting bigger, the U.S. labor force has also become more diverse: It has gotten older, better educated, less white, and more female. Perhaps the most dramatic and far-reaching change has been the growing labor force participation rate of women, which increased from about 1 in 5 to about 3 in 5 between 1890 and the mid-1990s (Committee on Techniques for the Enhancement of Human Performance, 1999).

These changes in the labor force toward greater diversity have made some issues more pressing than they were when the U.S. labor force was predominately male and the typical family consisted of a male breadwinner and a wife who stayed at home with the children. For example, issues of how to combine work and family life now occupy a prominent place on the agenda of managers and sociologists of work, who are both concerned with how to help families cope with the stress of dual careers and increased responsibilities (see below). In addition, women are still paid less than men, and issues of comparable worth are hotly debated. Sex segregation persists in the United States, though women are making inroads into many jobs formerly held by men (Reskin and Roos, 1990). (See also the cross-national analysis of the gender gap in income by Rosenfeld and Kalleberg, 1990.)

The increased representation of nonwhites within the U.S. labor force has raised issues of how to manage diversity and to accommodate persons of different cultures within the same workplace. It has also stimulated debate about the desirable amount of immigration and its impact on the jobs held by nonimmigrants. Moreover, the aging of the population has fueled debates over age discrimination, the preservation of the Social Security system and institutions to encourage lifelong learning, and second (and third and fourth) careers that permit older workers to continue to lead productive lives.

Studies of the nature and consequences of labor force diversity in the United States can be found in the volume on gender and ethnicity/race at work edited by Browne (1999) and in several recent Special Issues of *Work and Occupations* (November, 1992; May, 1998; November, 1999).

Changing Employment Relations and the Increased Emphasis on Flexibility. The image of employment relations and careers that characterized the sociology of work for most of the post–World War II period was one in which people worked full-time for a single employer and advanced steadily up a ladder within an internal labor market until they retired. These "standard" employment relations resulted from a strategy of internalization on the part of employers, who sought to create stability within their workforce. This situation began to change in the United States in the 1980s, as employers became increasingly concerned with having greater flexibility in order to respond to challenges posed by rapid technological change, increased price competition, and the changing labor force described in the previous section. One way that employers sough to achieve this flexibility was by externalizing part of their labor forces through nonstandard work arrangements such as temporary, contract, and part-time work. These efforts to externalize were fueled by an emphasis on downsizing, resulting in greater job insecurity among Americans (*The New York Times*, 1996).

Externalization of employment is a retreat from internalized bureaucratic employment relations to a set of ongoing transactions with the open labor

market (Pfeffer and Baron, 1988) and harkens back to an earlier era in economic organization in the United States, when factory labor was not continu-
ously employed but rather subcontracted from the outside (Williamson, 1985).
Good quantitative evidence on the extent of growth in nonstandard work is
sparse, though it is fairly clear that there has been a secular rise, particularly
in temporary help agency employment in the United States since the mid-
1970s. The nature of the constraints by which employees are bound to their
firms—particularly employment laws and union contracts—differs among countries, though employers' ability to adjust the sizes of their workforces is problematic in all industrial nations, even in the United States, which is characterized by relatively low union power and, at least theoretically, the doctrine of
employment at will (Piore, 1986).

Nonstandard work arrangements affect the quality of jobs. Kalleberg,
Reskin, and Hudson (2000) analyzed data from a large labor force survey (the
February 1995 supplement to the Current Population Survey) and showed
that temporary and part-time jobs in the United States tend to be "bad" in
terms of providing low wages and not providing fringe benefits such as health
insurance and pensions. Other types of nonstandard work—such as contract
work—often pay relatively high wages, though they too provide fewer fringe
benefits than regular full-time jobs.

While some employers have responded to their needs for flexibility by
taking the "low road" of downsizing and externalizing some of their work,
other U.S. organizations have taken the "high road" and sought to increase
their functional flexibility by enhancing the commitment of employees and
their participation in decision making, and providing them with multiple skills
so that they can be redeployed from one task to another (for a review of how
U.S. organizations have adopted each of these two approaches to the problem
of flexibility, see Smith, 1997; for a discussion of the debate about functional
flexibility and "post-Fordism," see Vallas, 1999). Committed, permanent employees are assumed to enhance an organization's efficiency and effectiveness, thereby improving its competitive advantage, performance, and productivity (Pfeffer, 1998). One major way this has been accomplished is by the
creation of self-directed teams that are empowered to make decisions formerly
made by managers and other elements of "high performance" work systems
(Appelbaum et al., 2000).

Networks.   The United States is becoming an increasingly networked
society, and the growing complexity of connections between organizations
and people requires sociologists of work to rethink their assumptions about
key questions, such as how work is organized, and how people and jobs are
matched in labor markets.

Organizational boundaries are becoming blurred by the growth of nonstandard work arrangements (discussed earlier) and the proliferation of alli-

ances and joint ventures among companies. These organizational networks represent in part attempts by employers to reduce their uncertainties and resource dependencies, and otherwise respond to the changes in competition, technology, and the turbulent economic conditions that have characterized the American economy since the 1980s.

The creation of networks among organizations is changing the ways in which sociologists of work study organizations. Organizational networks make it difficult to know where the boundaries of organizations are, and the use of nonstandard work arrangements such as temporaries or subcontractors make definitions of who is an "employee" (and of what organization) increasingly problematic. The growth of alliances that span countries also makes it hard to distinguish American companies from non-American ones, blurring the distinctions made in this volume between work in the United States and in other countries.

Networks among organizations also change the nature of careers, particularly by creating opportunities for workers to move from one organization to another. Joint ventures, supplier–buyer relations, and other organizational networks facilitate the creation of "boundaryless careers" (Arthur and Rousseau, 1996) that span organizations. Tight labor markets in high-skill areas increase opportunities for holders of valued skills who wish to change employers in occupational internal labor markets. These networks underscore the need for sociologists of work to study careers by moving beyond single organizations to take into account the multiplicity of organizations in which careers now unfold.

Networks also play an important role in helping Americans find jobs, as Granovetter (1974) pointed out a quarter of a century ago. These networks are organized along a variety of dimensions, including religion, ethnicity/race and kinship, the latter being especially important for immigrants and other groups that might otherwise be left out of labor markets for good jobs (Bridges and Villemez, 1994).

Work and Family Conflicts.   While modern industrial economies inherently produce conflict between work and home, the United States is especially fraught with public policy conflicts over the interface of work and family. Work and family conflicts are magnified in the United States by three main trends: (1) Female labor force participation has risen to the point that dual-earner couples are the norm; (2) the United States has the highest divorce rate among industrialized countries, which results in the existence of many single-parent families; and (3) the United States has no comprehensive set of social policies to deal with the interface of work and family roles (such as paid family leave and mandatory fringe benefits)(see the collection of articles in Parcel and Cornfield, 2000).

Most of the research on the work–family interface has focused on women, though a growing number of studies have begun paying attention to the impacts on men. Much of this research documents the time binds and cultural barriers created when women (who still do a disproportionate amount of housework and child care, a situation often referred to as the "second shift") enter labor markets where the separation of work and family is taken as the norm and jobs come with the institutional assumption that unpaid caregivers are performing domestic tasks (Nelson and Bridges, 1999). Other researchers look at the availability (or lack thereof) of affordable child care, parental leave, and other "family friendly" policies that are provided or neglected by large employers.

Researchers studying the work and family interface also focus on the consequences for stratification and careers of simultaneously performing work and family roles. Some researchers have documented the long-term income disadvantages for women of performing gender-typed roles in female-dominated occupations (England, 1992; Witkowski and Leicht, 1995). Others study the consequences of the changing organization of work that results when workplaces are reorganized to become more "family friendly." This research often focuses on professional and managerial jobs (Leicht and Fennell, 1997; Pierce, 1996; J. Wallace, 1999). Most of this research actively engages human capital theory and the "new household economics" in an attempt to explain decision making under different resource constraints.

The Plight of the Middle Class.   The changing nature of middle-class roles in the United States is becoming an increasingly important issue for sociologists of work, due in part to many of the themes we have already discussed. The middle class in the United States carries a unique set of cultural baggage. It has been touted as the economic and political backbone of the country (Phillips, 1990, 1993) and is an important carrier of social mobility norms that are a central component of the culture of economic opportunity in the United States (*The New York Times*, 1996). Yet there is considerable evidence that members of the middle class are suffering an economic crisis. Their earnings from work have been stagnant since the early 1970s (while the economic situation of the bottom 20% has declined in recent decades). Traditional middle-class jobs with good pay and benefits, job stability, and steady promotions are among those that are most threatened by corporate restructuring and downsizing. And the political system is widely regarded as "betraying" the middle class through tax policies that favor the unearned income of the wealthy over the earned income of jobholders.

Most research so far on these issues has documented the problems of the middle class without suggesting coherent solutions. The U.S. workplace that the middle class relied on has been drastically reorganized since the mid-1980s. As we have discussed in previous sections, this workplace is now characterized by (1) flatter organizational hierarchies, as new information technologies eliminate the need for most layers of middle management; (2) the growing use of temporary workers employed on an as-needed basis; (3) the extensive use of subcontracting and outsourcing to small firms to produce parts and provide services once provided by relatively permanent employees; (4) massive downsizing of the permanent workforce resulting from these trends, combined with the replacement of skilled workers by machine tenders; (5) a postunion bargaining environment in which unions have no place and no structural ability to gain a foothold for bargaining with employers; and (6) virtual organizations that occupy no fixed structural location but exist as webs of technologically driven interactions. Some researchers have predicted dire consequences as a result of these trends (Massey, 1996; Moore, 1996; *The New York Times*, 1996; Rifkin, 1995). Others are more optimistic about the "post corporate" future (Boyett and Conn, 1992).

Other research combines insights from political and economic sociology to explain the growing political plight of the middle class. Political support for tax cuts, government restructuring, and debt financing have left the middle class out of the political equation in Washington at the national level (Phillips, 1990, 1993). As individual states have jumped on the bandwagon favoring unearned income over earnings from jobs, these governments have also restructured their tax systems to penalize the middle class (Phillips, 1993). Some researchers have identified this shifting government emphasis (and the growing regressiveness of the tax system) as a major fuel behind growing middle-class resentment of the welfare system and the poor (Leicht, 1998).

The Institutional Context of the Sociology of Work in the United States. Sociological research on work in the United States is a lively enterprise. It is spread out over many institutional contexts: academic units of universities (sociology departments, business schools, industrial relations departments and schools) and nonacademic settings (research centers, government agencies, and consulting firms). These research enterprises are funded by a variety of agencies: government foundations (such as the National Science Foundation, Department of Labor, National Institutes of Health) and private foundations, such as the Russell Sage Foundation (which has an ongoing program on the "Future of Work") and the Alfred P. Sloan Foundation (which has funded a great deal of research on specific industries). The appendix to this chapter consists of websites of data and funding sources, professional associations, and serial publications.

Sociological studies of work use diverse methods. As we have discussed in this chapter, there are many large-scale surveys of the labor force as well as of organizations, occupations (e.g., professionals such as physicians, lawyers, and teachers), and industries (e.g., manufacturing, services). Complementing these quantitative surveys are qualitative studies of selected work structures such as particular workplaces, occupations or industries, including hundreds of ethnographies (see Hodson, 2001).

This high degree of activity has resulted in the availability of a large (and growing) number of data sets that are publicly available for secondary analysis. The federal government encourages such dissemination of data through its policy that all data collection efforts sponsored by federal funds must be archived for public use within 1 year after the completion of the project. The major archive is the Inter-University Consortium for Political and Social Research (ICPSR), housed at the University of Michigan at Ann Arbor. Available data sets include cross-sectional surveys of the U.S. labor force (such as the Current Population Survey, the General Social Surveys), panel surveys of the U.S. labor force (e.g., Panel Study of Income Dynamics, the National Longitudinal Surveys of young and older men and women), and organizational surveys (the National Organizations Survey—see Kalleberg et al., 1996).

Sociologists of work in the United States have many outlets in which to publish their research, reflecting the diversity of the field. These include general sociological journals (*American Sociological Review, American Journal of Sociology, Social Forces*) as well as more specialized ones (*Administrative Science Quarterly, Academy of Management Journal, Academy of Management Review, Industrial Relations, Industrial and Labor Relations Review, Work and Occupations*). American sociologists also publish their material in non-U.S. journals, such as *Work, Employment and Society, European Sociological Review, Sociology,* and *Acta Sociologica*. English-language book publishers around the world have been very receptive to research by U.S. sociologists of work, and scores of new titles appear yearly and address new and interesting problems and crises in the U.S. workplace.

CONCLUSIONS

Like almost all research in sociology, the study of work in the United States is driven by the problems that sociologists see in their immediate environment. The U.S. context is distinctive in many ways that make the study of work especially challenging and interesting. Some of the dominant features of the U.S. context include an overriding commitment to free product and labor markets; great ideological emphasis on individualism and negotiation; low government capacity to intervene in the labor market, combined with fragmented governmental jurisdictions; low employee bargaining power and few institutionalized employment guarantees; no history of electoral socialism or military intervention in political affairs; permeable national boundaries for capital and people; and high levels of racial and ethnic diversity.

The institutional support for the sociology of work in the United States is similarly fragmented but widely available to most serious scholars. A relatively extensive list of government agencies, private foundations, private research firms, and "think tanks" fund and conduct research. Data that others have collected are widely available and cheaply disseminated. Much like the people they study, American sociologists of work have to negotiate individually a maze of agency names, data sources, and policy initiatives to conduct their research. Many of the wide variety of settings in which U.S. sociologists work are also subject to the same waves of workplace change that they study in their own research. In this sense, life imitates social science and the relationship between theory, research, and everyday life is always interesting.

While the sociology of work in America traces its roots to classical European social theorists, the subject matter and problems addressed are directly affected by this unique national context. Studies of work organization and the labor process are especially interesting because our employers have had an unusually free hand to determine the organization of work. Our labor markets produce large varieties of jobs of varying skill, stability, desirability, and compensation. The organization of the professions is fragmented across diverse work settings and payment systems. Traditional ideologies of individualism and the Protestant Ethic come in conflict with modern (and postmodern) consumer and leisure cultures that affect individual commitment to work and careers. Organized labor battles constantly with employers and an often indifferent and unprotected workforce. Social inequality has increased drastically, and tax systems increasingly favor the rich and those who collect unearned income. There are many cases of deindustrialization, downsizing, outsourcing, and the other individually unnerving characteristics of the "post-bureaucratic" workplace to study in the United States because there are few (if any) institutional barriers to stop them. These problems and issues constitute important topics for sociologists of work to study in the future.

REFERENCES

Abbott, Andrew. 1988. *The System of Professions: An Essay on the Division of Expert Labor.* Chicago: University of Chicago Press.

Althauser, Robert P., and Arne L. Kalleberg. 1981. "Firms, Occupations and the Structure of Labor Markets: A Conceptual Analysis." Pp. 119–149 in *Sociological Perspectives on Labor Markets* edited by Ivar Berg. New York: Academic Press.

Appelbaum, Eileen, Thomas Bailey, Peter Berg, and Arne L. Kalleberg. 2000. *Manufacturing Advantage: Why High-Performance Work Systems Pay Off.* Ithaca, NY: ILR Press.

Arthur, M. B., and Denise M. Rousseau. 1996. *The Boundaryless Career: A New Employment Principle for a New Organizational Era.* New York: Oxford University Press.

Baldi, Stephanie, and Debra Branch McBrier. 1997. "Do the Determinants of Promotion Differ for Blacks and Whites?" *Work and Occupations* 24:478–497.

Baron, James N., and William T. Bielby. 1980. "Bringing the Firms Back In: Stratification, Segmentation, and the Organization of Work." *American Sociological Review* 45:737–765.

Biggart, Nicole Woolsey. 1989. *Charismatic Capitalism: Direct Selling Organizations in America.* Chicago: University of Chicago Press.

Bills, David B., ed. 1995. *The New Modern Times: Factors Reshaping the World of Work.* Albany, NY: State University of New York Press.

Blau, Peter, and Otis Dudley Duncan. 1967. *The American Occupational Structure.* New York: Wiley.

Bluestone, Barry, and Bennett Harrison 1982. *The Deindustrialization of America.* New York: Basic Books.

Boyett, Joseph H., and Henry P. Conn. 1992. *Workplace 2000: The Revolution Shaping American Business.* New York: Plume.

Braverman, Harry. 1974. *Labor and Monopoly Capital: The Degradation of Work in the Twentieth Century.* New York: Monthly Review Press.

Bridges, William P., and Wayne J. Villemez. 1994. *The Employment Relationship: Causes and Consequences of Modern Personnel Administration.* New York: Plenum Press.

Bronfenbrenner, Kate, Sheldon Friedman, Richard W. Hurd, Rudolph A. Oswald, and Ronald L. Sieber, eds. 1998. *Organizing to Win: New Research on Union Strategies.* Ithaca, NY: ILR Press.

Browne, Irene, ed. 1999. *Latinas and African American Women at Work: Race, Gender, and Economic Inequality.* New York: Russell Sage Foundation.

Budry, Grace. 1997. *When Doctors Join Unions.* Ithaca, NY: Cornell University Press.

Committee on Techniques for the Enhancement of Human Performance, Commission on Behavioral and Social Sciences and Education, National Research Council. 1999. *The Changing Nature of Work: Implications for Occupational Analysis.* Washington, DC: National Academy Press.

Cornfield, Daniel B., and Hyunhee Kim. 1994. "Socioeconomic Status and Unionization Attitudes in the United States." *Social Forces* 73:521–532.

Derber, Charles, William A. Schwartz, and Yale Magrass. 1990. *Power in the Highest Degree: Professionals and the Rise of the New Mandarin Order.* New York: Oxford University Press.

DiPrete, Thomas A. 1989. *The Bureaucratic Labor Market: The Case of the Federal Civil Service.* New York: Plenum Press

Doeringer, Peter B., and Michael J. Piore. 1971. *Internal Labor Markets and Manpower Analysis.* Lexington, MA: Heath.

Dubin, Robert. 1956. "Industrial Workers' Worlds: A Study of the Central Life Interests of Industrial Workers." *Social Problems* 3:131–142.

Edwards, Richard. 1979. *Contested Terrain.* New York: Basic Books.

England, Paula. 1992. *Comparable Worth: Theories and Evidence.* New York: Aldine De Gruyter.

Epstein, Cynthia Fuchs, Carroll Seron, Bonnie Oglensky, and Robert Saute. 1999. *The Part-Time Paradox: Time Norms, Professional Lives, Family, and Gender.* New York: Routledge.

Form, William, Robert L. Kaufman, Toby L. Parcel, and Michael Wallace. 1988. "The Impact of Technology on Work Organization and Work Outcomes: A Conceptual Framework and Research Agenda." Pp. 303–328 in *Industries, Firms, and Jobs:*

Sociological and Economic Approaches, edited by George Farkas and Paula England. New York: Plenum Press.

Freeman, Richard B. 1994. *Work Under Different Rules.* New York: Russell Sage Foundation.

Freeman, Richard B., and James L. Medoff. 1984. *What Do Unions Do?* New York: Free Press.

Gamst, Frederick C.,ed. 1995. *Meanings of Work: Considerations for the Twenty-first Century.* Albany : State University of New York Press.

Gordon, David M. 1972. *Theories of Poverty and Underemployment.* Lexington, MA: Heath.

Granovetter, Mark. 1974. *Getting a Job: A Study of Contacts and Careers.* Cambridge, MA: Harvard University Press.

Hodson, Randy. 1996. "Dignity in the Workplace Under Participative Management: Alienation and Freedom Revisited." *American Sociological Review* 61:719–738.

Hodson, Randy. 1999. "Organizational Anomie and Worker Consent." *Work and Occupations* 26:292–323.

Hodson, Randy. 2001. *Work with Dignity.* New York: Cambridge University Press.

Hodson, Randy, and Robert L. Kaufman. 1982. "Economic Dualism: A Critical Review." *American Sociological Review* 43:534–541.

Hoff, Timothy J. 1999. "The Social Organization of Physician–Managers in a Changing HMO." *Work and Occupations* 26: 324–351.

Hoschchild, Arlie Russell. 1983. *The Managed Heart: Commercialization of Human Feeling.* Berkeley: University of California Press.

Kalleberg, Arne L., and Ivar Berg. 1987. *Work and Industry: Structures, Markets and Processes.* New York: Plenum Press.

Kalleberg, Arne L., David Knoke, Peter V. Marsden, and Joe L. Spaeth. 1996. *Organizations in America: Analyzing their Structures and Human Resource Practices.* Thousand Oaks, CA: Sage.

Kalleberg, Arne L., Barbara F. Reskin, and Ken Hudson. 2000. "Bad Jobs in America: Standard and Nonstandard Employment Relations and Job Quality in the United States." *American Sociological Review* 65:256–278.

Kalleberg, Arne L., and Aage B. Sorensen. 1979. "The Sociology of Labor Markets." *Annual Review of Sociology* 5:351–379.

Kalleberg, Arne L., and Mark E. Van Buren. 1996. "The Structure of Organizational Earnings Inequality." Pp. 214–31 in *Organizations in America: Analyzing their Structures and Human Resource Practices* edited by Arne L., Kalleberg, David Knoke, Peter V. Marsden, and Joe L. Spaeth.. Thousand Oaks, CA: Sage.

Kasarda, John D., ed. 1990. *Jobs, Earnings and Employment Growth Policies in the United States.* Boston: Kluwer Academic Publishing.

Larsen, Magali S. 1977. *The Rise of Professionalism.* Berkeley: University of California Press.

Leicht, Kevin T. 1989. "On the Estimation of Union Threat Effects." *American Sociological Review* 54:1035–1047.

Leicht, Kevin T. 1998. "Work (If You Can Get It) and Occupations (If There Are Any)? What Social Scientists Can Learn from Predictions of the End of Work and Radical Workplace Change." *Work and Occupations* 25:36-48.

Leicht, Kevin T., and Mary L. Fennell. 1997. "The Changing Organizational Context of Professional Work." *Annual Review of Sociology* 23:215–231.

Lincoln, James R., and Arne L. Kalleberg. 1990. *Culture, Control and Commitment: A Study of Work Organization and Work Attitudes in the United States and Japan*. Cambridge, UK: Cambridge University Press.

Lipset, Seymour M., Martin Trow, and James S. Coleman. 1956. *Union Democracy*. New York: Free Press.

Magaziner, Ira C., and Robert B. Reich. 1984. *Minding America's Business: The Decline and Rise of the American Economy*. New York: Vintage.

Massey, Douglas 1996. "Inequality in the Age of Extremes." *Demography* 33:1–20.

Maume, David J., Jr. 1999. "Glass Ceilings and Glass Escalators: Occupational Segregation and Race and Sex Differences in Managerial Promotions." *Work and Occupations* 26:483–509.

Milkman, Ruth. 1997. *Farewell to the Factory : Auto Workers in the Late Twentieth Century*. Berkeley: University of California Press.

Moore, Thomas S. 1996. *The Disposable Workforce: Worker Displacement and Employment Instability in America*. New York: Aldine de Gruyter.

Morse, Nancy C., and Robert Weiss. 1955. "The Meaning and Function of Work and the Job." *American Sociological Review* 20:191–198.

Mueller, Charles W., Ashley Finley, Roderick D. Iverson, and James L. Price. 1999. "The Effects of Group Racial Composition on Job Satisfaction, Organizational Commitment, and Career Commitment: The Case of Teachers." *Work and Occupations* 26:187–219.

Nelson, Robert L., and William P. Bridges. 1999. *Legalizing Gender Inequality: Courts, Markets and Unequal Pay for Women in the United States*. Cambridge, UK: Cambridge University Press.

The New York Times. 1996. *The Downsizing of America*. New York: Times Books.

Parcel, Toby L., and Daniel B. Cornfield, ed. 2000. *Work and Family*. Thousand Oaks, CA: Sage.

Perrucci, Robert, and Michael Targ. 1993. *Plant Closings: International Contexts and Social Costs*. New York: Littlefield.

Pfeffer, Jeffrey. 1998. *The Human Equation: Building Profits by Putting People First*. Boston: Harvard University Press.

Pfeffer, Jeffrey, and James N. Baron. 1988. "Taking the Workers Back Out: Recent trends in the structuring of employment." *Research in Organizational Behavior* 10:257–303.

Phillips, Kevin. 1990. *The Politics of Rich and Poor: Wealth and the American Electorate in the Reagan Aftermath*. New York: HarperPerennial.

Phillips, Kevin. 1993. *Boiling Point: Democrats, Republicans and the Decline of Middle Class Prosperity*. New York: HarperPerennial.

Pierce, Jennifer L. 1996. *Gender Trials: Emotional Lives in Corporate Law Firms*. Berkeley: University of California Press.

Piore, Michael J. 1986. "Perspectives on Labor Market Flexibility." *Industrial Relations* 25:146–166.

Reskin, Barbara F., and Patricia A. Roos. 1990. *Job Queues, Gender Queues: Explaining Women's Inroads into Male Occupations*. Philadelphia: Temple University Press.

Rifkin, Jeremy. 1995. *The End of Work: The Decline of the Global Labor Force and the Dawn of the Post-Market Era*. New York: Putnam.

Rosenbaum, James E. 1984. *Career Mobility in a Corporate Hierarchy.* Orlando, FL: Academic Press.

Rosenfeld, Rachel A.. and Arne L. Kalleberg. 1990. "A Cross-national comparison of the Gender Gap in Income." *American Journal of Sociology* 96:69–106.

Ross, Catherine, and Marylyn P. Wright. 1998. "Women's Work, Men's Work, and the Sense of Control." *Work and Occupations* 25:333–355.

Rubin, Beth A. 1988. "Inequality in the Working Class: The Unanticipated Consequences of Union Organizing and Strikes." *Industrial and Labor Relations Review* 41:553–556.

Schor, Juliet. 1991. *The Overworked American: The Unexpected Decline in Leisure.* New York: Basic Books.

Smith, Vicki. 1994. "Braverman's Legacy: The Labor Process Tradition at 20." *Work and Occupations* 21:403–421.

Smith, Vicki. 1997. "New Forms of Work Organization." *Annual Review of Sociology* 23:315–39.

Spenner, Kenneth I. 1983. "Temporal Changes in the Skill Level of Work." *American Sociological Review* 48:824–837.

Starr, Paul E. 1982. *The Social Transformation of American Medicine.* New York: Basic Books.

Szafran, Robert F. 1996. "The Effect of Occupational Growth on Labor Force Task Characteristics." *Work and Occupations* 23:54–86.

Thomas, Robert J. 1994. *What Machines Can't Do: Politics and Technology in the Industrial Enterprise.* Berkeley: University of California Press.

Tolbert, Pamela S., and Phyllis Moen. 1998. "Men's and Women's Definitions of 'Good' Jobs: Similarities and Differences by Age and Across Time." *Work and Occupations* 25:168–194.

Vallas, Steven P. 1999. "Rethinking Post-Fordism: The Meaning of Workplace Flexibility." *Sociological Theory* 17:68–101.

Van Hoy, Jerry. 1997. *Franchise Law Firms and the Transformation of Personal Legal Services.* Westport, CT: Quorum.

Wallace, Jean E. 1999. "Work-to-Nonwork Conflict among Married Male and Female Attorneys." *Journal of Organizational Behavior* 20:797–816.

Wallace, Michael, Kevin T. Leicht, and Lawrence E. Raffalovich. 1999. "Unions, Strikes and Labor's Share of Income: A Quarterly Analysis of the United States, 1949–1992." *Social Science Research* 28:265–288.

Wallace, Michael, and Joyce Rothschild. 1988. "Plant Closings, Capital Flight, and Worker Dislocation: The Long Shadow of Deindustrialization." *Research in Politics and Society* 3:1–35.

Wilensky, Harold L. 1964. "The Professionalization of Everyone?" *American Journal of Sociology* 70:137–158.

Williamson, O. E. 1985. *The Economic Institutions of Capitalism.* New York: Free Press.

Wilson, William J. 1996. *When Work Disappears: The World of the New Urban Poor.* New York: Knopf.

Wilson, George, Ian Sakura-Lemessy, and Jonathan P. West. 1999. "Reaching the Top: Racial Differences in Mobility Paths to Upper-Tier Occupations." *Work and Occupations* 26:165–186.

Witkowski, Kristine, and Kevin T. Leicht. 1995. "The Effects of Gender Segregation,

Labor Force Participation and Family Roles on the Earnings of Young Adult Workers." *Work and Occupations* 22:48–72.

Work and Occupations. 1992. Special Issue on "Sex Segregation and Gender Stratification" edited by Jerry A. Jacobs. Vol. 19(4, November).

Work and Occupations. 1998. Special Issue on "Gendered Work and Workplaces." Vol. 25(2, May).

Work and Occupations. 1998. Special Issue on "Social Inequality in the Workplace." Vol. 25(4, November).

Work and Occupations. 1999. Special Issue on "Ethnicity, Race, and Gender in the Workplace, edited by Jennifer L. Glass. Vol. 26(4, November).

Work and Occupations. 2000. Special Issue on "Attitudes and Emotions at Work." Vol. 27(2, February).

APPENDIX: WEBSITES OF RESEARCH RESOURCES

Data Sources

Bureau of National Affairs, Inc.
http://www.bna.com/

Gallup Organization
http://www.gallup.com/

General Social Survey
http://www.ropercenter.uconn.edu/gss98.html
http://www.icpsr.umich.edu/GSS99/index.html

Inter-university Consortium for Political and Social Research
http://www.icpsr.umich.edu/

Panel Study of Income Dynamics
http://www.isr.umich.edu/src/psid/

The Work–Family Research Literature Database
http://cwf.bc.edu/literature/searchmain.html

U.S. Bureau of Economic Analysis
http://www.bea.doc.gov/

U.S. Bureau of Labor Statistics
http://www.bls.gov/

U.S. Bureau of the Census
http://www.census.gov/

Funding Sources

Alfred P. Sloan Foundation
http://www.sloan.org/main.htm

National Institutes of Health
http://www.nih.gov/

National Science Foundation
http://nsf.gov/sbe/ses/sociol/start.htm

Russell Sage Foundation
http://russellsage.org/

U.S. Department of Health and Human Services
http://www.os.dhhs.gov/

Professional Associations

Academy of Management
http://www.aom.pace.edu/

American Sociological Association (ASA)
http://www.asanet.org/

ASA Section on Economic Sociology
http://www.asanet.org/sections/economic.html

ASA Section (in formation) on Labor and Labor Movements
http://www.bgsu.edu/departments/soc/prof/mason/ASA/index.html

ASA Section on Organizations, Occupations, and Work
http://www.campus.northpark.edu/sociology/oow/

Industrial Relations Research Association
http://www.irra.uiuc.edu/

Society for the Study of Social Problems
http://itc.utk.edu/sssp/

Serial Publications

Academy of Management Journal
http://www.aom.pace.edu/amj/

Academy of Management Review
http://www.aom.pace.edu/amr/

Administrative Science Quarterly
http://www.cornell.edu/ASQ/

Industrial and Labor Relations Review
http://www.ilr.cornell.edu/depts/ILRrev/

Industrial Relations
http://socrates.berkeley.edu/~iir/indrel/indrel.shtml

Labor Studies Journal
http://www.irc.csom.umn.edu/LES/lsj.htm

Research in the Sociology of Work
http://www.sociology.ohio-state.edu/work/

Work and Occupations
http://www.sagepub.com/ (click on "journals listing")

III

Asia, Africa, and the Pacific

The paths taken in the development of the sociology of work have varied across the profound societal transformations in the four nations of this region are covered—Australia, India, Korea, and South Africa. As the range of research themes broadened within each of the nations in recent decades, however, common research themes emerged as well.

Major societal transformations strongly influenced the trajectory of the sociology of work within each of these four nations. In Australia, the national system of industrial relations was deregulated and decentralized in favor of enterprise bargaining during the 1980s. With these changes, the sociology of work in Australia addressed a growing array of themes about changes in industrial relations, work attitude formation, flexibility, outwork and the redefinition of employment relations, and gender and racial/ethnic inequality in the workplace.

The sociology of work in India has addressed themes associated with independence in 1947 and subsequent industrialization. Among these themes are the salience of caste and class in rural and urban India, working-class formation and trade union solidarity, new forms of work organization and technological change, and gender inequality in the workplace.

In South Africa, changes in the sociology of work are associated with the democratization, economic globalization, and end of apartheid. Among the research themes pursued in South Africa are de-skilling, racism in the workplace, and the development of racial Fordism. Working-class formation and the role of trade unionism are issues that have endured after the end of apartheid.

The end of authoritarian rule in 1987 increased the range of research themes pursued in the sociology of work in Korea. Important research themes include the development of labor market inequality, changing technology and employment systems, and working-class formation through trade unionism.

Some of the key themes in Asia, Africa, and the Pacific are the growth, decline, and the revitalization and the role of labor movements in profound societal transformations; new forms of work organization; and racial/ethnic and gender relations in the workplace.

6

Australia

Sandra Harding and Richard Sappey

INTRODUCTION AND SCENE–SETTING

The overwhelming feature of the literature reporting Australian perspectives on the sociology of work is that it is relatively underdeveloped. For the most part, theoretical perspectives employed to explain work in Australia derive from European, particularly U.K., and U.S. traditions. Yet the study of work, particularly work relationships, does feature strongly in the Australian literature. Such work is largely undertaken within an industrial relations framework, complementing a long, national tradition of institutionalized industrial relations in Australia.

Understanding something about the institutional context of work in Australia helps make sense of the themes that have emerged around the sociology of work and explain the particular contribution to the field from Australia. The larger historical story of the Australian nation may be located in any number of published histories. Here, we provide an overview of this history as an important contextual setting for our review.

At the outset, it is important to remember that Australia began as a dump-

Sandra Harding   ·   Faculty of Business, Queensland University of Technology, Brisbane, Australia Qld 4001.   Richard Sappey   ·   Lecturer in Industrial Relations, Griffith University, Brisbane, Australia.

Worlds of Work: Building an International Sociology of Work, edited by Daniel B. Cornfield and Randy Hodson. Kluwer Academic/Plenum Publishers, New York, 2002.

ing ground for British miscreants. Colonial outposts on the mainland continent and the small southern island of Tasmania united in 1901 to become the federated nation-state of Australia with a new Constitution that permitted strong, central control of industrial relations and finance. The worldwide depression of the 1890s that had jolted the nation was accompanied by great industrial unrest. This recent experience unscored the felt need for a centralist approach to both economic development and industrial relations in the fledgling nation. As a result, the State took an active role in economic development, particularly in providing the infrastructure for a vast but sparsely populated continent.

The great wealth provided by natural resources meant that a historic compromise could be achieved between the urban working class, what was at the time uncompetitive manufacturing capital, and the State (Rowse, 1984). This compromise featured the protection of competing import industries; State-organized arbitration, with centralized wage fixing and resolution of industrial disputes through a web of industrial tribunals; and an expansive welfare safety net and the "White Australia Policy" that served to preserve well-paid jobs in a congenial industrial environment for those of Western European, preferably British, origin (Harding, 1995). While permanent unions were a part of the industrial landscape at this time, they pursued economic prosperity, and better wages and conditions on behalf of members, rather than a more radical agenda (Frenkel, 1986). In other words, the specific historical circumstances of the establishment of the Australian nation meant that relations at work were structured and stabilized to minimize disruption. This is not to suggest an absence of industrial disputation. Fierce disputes arose post–World War I and during, and in the aftermath, of the Great Depression. However, these were dealt with in what had become routinized ways, by and through the State.

This centralized system persisted until relatively recently. In the 1980s, the then Labor Government led by Prime Minister Robert Hawke created neocorporatist "Accords," agreements among government, peak employer bodies, and the peak union body, the Australian Council of Trade Unions (ACTU). These agreements set Australian industrial relations on a different path, so that today, labor markets have been deregulated and enterprise-based bargaining is becoming the norm, with a vestigial role played by the industrial relations tribunals, particularly the Australian Industrial Relations Commission. In very recent times, new, aggressive industrial relations legislation initiated by the conservative, current Federal government, comprising a coalition of the Liberal and National parties, takes Australian workplaces further down the path of deregulation. In the near term, work and industrial relations in Australia are likely to become more contested and ripe for analysis.

The other part of this contextual tale relies on an understanding of sociology as a discipline in Australia. The current location of sociology as a discipline is, in part, explained by the elimination of advocates of sociology from universities in Australia during the early 1920s (Mitropoulous, 1999). This purge centered around the anticommunist hysteria of the period. The quite anticommunist sociology of the day was linked to Marxism in the minds of many. Consequently, there were few sociology departments in Australian universities; with most scholars interested in aspects of work were housed in faculties of commerce and/or economics. Labor economists dealt with many of the same concerns as their sociologist counterparts in the United States and the United Kingdom, but without the same overt acknowledgment of the potential insights of sociological–theoretical perspectives. Later, we examine the current location of sociology of work in Australian universities, and it is clear that little has changed. For the moment, it is important to return to the key task at hand, an exploration of the key themes in the sociology of work in Australia.

KEY THEMES

One of the significant challenges we faced in identifying key themes concerned timing. How far back should we go in seeking to establish the facts about the sociology of work in Australia?

Our initial foray into the literature appeared to provide a neat solution. We thought that we would restrict our exploration in time and commence our review of the literature from 1974, the year that Braverman published his watershed work. We started with the key sociology journal for this region, the *Australian and New Zealand Journal of Sociology*, now retitled the *Journal of Sociology*, and found that this publication had, indeed, taken up the challenge posed by Braverman's work. In 1981, in response to Braverman (1974), the journal published papers drawn from a symposium held to examine the sociology of work and industry in Australia. We expected that this symposium would feature a coherent statement on the status of the subdiscipline at the time and provide a rallying point for the articulation of a new research agenda. Neither of these expectations were met. Instead, the published papers canvassed a number of discrete issues. Papers explored New Zealand waterfront workers and proletarians (Kerr Inkson, Gidlow, and Gidlow, 1981), an ethnography of New Zealand office workers (Perry, 1981), ethnic segregation in the Australian labor market (Lever-Tracy, 1981), the effect of structural changes in the Australian economy on young working-class people (P. Dwyer and Wilson, 1981), the effect of de-skilling on the relations between skilled and unskilled Australian metal workers (Maxwell, 1981) and the development of a sociological model of industrial accidents (T. Dwyer, 1981).

While these papers were interesting, they did not provide a big picture of the subdiscipline, as we had hoped. However, after further review of the literature, we came to the conclusion that the products of the symposium represented well the fragmented nature of work undertaken in this field in Australia. A symposium that captured the challenges and key ideas of the time in this field would have provided evidence of a coherent, subdisciplinary engagement. Instead, divergent topics were addressed, implying the intellectual fragmentation of the subdiscipline. As we discuss later, this intellectual fragmentation is matched by an institutional fragmentation, in which the location of the sociology of work in Australian academe occurs more frequently in faculties of commerce or economics than in departments of sociology. Both types of fragmentation are still in evidence today.

Our review of the literature resulted in the identification of three key areas of activity. The first and most significant thematic area concerns industrial relations. The second key thematic area examines various aspects of inequality at work, including labor markets and studies of occupation, gender segregation and race/ethnicity at work. Finally, we found a range of publications focusing on the emerging theme of outwork as a key issue. We explore each of these themes in turn, and note enduring and emergent issues for each.

Industrial Relations and the Sociology of Work

While industrial relations literature features a huge range of contributions from many scholars, we have identified four broad, overlapping subthemes in the more sociological literature in this tradition. The first three subthemes are enduring in nature. The fourth, the flexibility debate, is emergent and plays out classical concerns at the point of production.

The first subtheme comprises studies of job satisfaction. Such studies are common, with more recent studies working within a sociotechnical systems approach. Studies of satisfaction have broadened out into organizational analyses. Dunphy and Griffiths (1998) provide a short history of such analyses. While some insights are drawn from sociological perspectives, sociological approaches have been swamped by other theoretical traditions, particularly industrial psychology and human resource management, dealing with practical approaches, schemes, and systems.

The second subtheme of work in the industrial relations tradition focuses on the influence of technology on work and work relationships. This issue received significant attention during the 1970s and 1980s. Such work has tended to focus on the relationships between technological change and employment (e.g., Deery, 1982; Groenewegen, 1970; Lansbury, 1980) and technological change and job satisfaction (e.g., Scott, 1974).

The third subtheme consists of case studies in industrial relations that focus on how industrial relations is played out in particular settings at the organizational or sectoral level. For example, Clegg (1975) explored the building industry, Kreigler (1980) the steel industry, Maconachie (1993) the public sector, and van den Broek (1997) a service-based company. These studies, as well as published collections of case studies (e.g., Williams, 1988), have been influenced by labor process theory. Within them, work and workplace relationships are pursued in ways that add rich data to often-neglected areas of analysis.

The fourth subtheme in this tradition began as a debate about flexibility, focusing on the adoption of so-called "new production concepts" (e.g., Badham and Matthews, 1989; Gahan, 1991). The pursuit of "flexible" employment relationships has become a key issue for Australia. The rhetoric surrounding this issue constructs flexibility as an necessary enhancement of the labor market, breaking free of a centralized industrial relations system that is not responsive to particular conditions facing particular organizations and favoring more responsive, enterprised-based arrangements. The price, however, is more contingent work, greater casualization of the workforce and, potentially, attenuated pay and conditions (Burgess, 1996). This work focuses attention on the costs imposed on workers, providing ammunition for the development of public policy that harks back to classic themes of job security and worker control.

To a great extent, these subthemes are related to the institutional nature of Australia's industrial relations systems. Almost always, there is a close fit between scholars' published work and the public policy and political environment. For example, the debate over new, post-Fordist production relationships was stimulated by the neocorporatist Accord period of the 1980s and complementary policy development. Similarly, the issue of linking technological change to redundancy was processed through the institutional system, establishing a minimum set of conditions for retrenched workers. The Australian union movement, through its centralized peak organization, the Australian Council of Trade Unions, as the labour partner in the Accord, used the institutional system to make working arrangements more flexible, provide greater access to training and skills formation, and improve job satisfaction and productivity (Curtain and Matthews, 1990). Emergent issues in the literature have been reflected in contextual changes, and these changes have sparked scholars' interests.

Inequality

Inequality at work is the second key theme in the Australian literature. Indeed, studies of inequality lie at the heart of much work in the subdiscipline as a whole. Three inequality subthemes are evident in the literature: labour market demographics, gender segregation, and racial/ethnic segregation. Each is important and reflects classical areas of inquiry, particularly economic inequality. All subthemes are of particular contemporary relevance in Australia and each is examined in turn.

Much work has been undertaken to establish the demographics of the Australian labour market, focusing on wage inequality, as well as occupational status and prestige differentials. Certainly, since the early to mid-1970s, when the unemployment rate in Australia first rose to the most alarming proportions since the end of World War II, earnings inequality has remained an area of keen interest for scholars. Early work by scholars such as Congalton (1963), Boreham and Dow (1980), and Daniel (1983) has set the scene for more recent, comparative work (see, e.g., Blau and Kahn, 1992; Kelley and Evans, 1993). Godbout (1993) pursued this subtheme, comparing employment change and sectorial distribution in 10 countries, including Australia, from 1970–1990. Hunter (1995) demonstrated increasing employment inequality in Australia, with "low status" geographical areas bearing the brunt of falls in employment levels. Borland and Wilkins (1996) examined change in the distribution of earnings for men and women in Australia. Preston (1997) relied on human capital theory to explain wage determination in Australia, but finds that this perspective is not equal to the task of explaining persistent wage inequality. Woldring (1995) pursued an emergent line of inquiry in light of the growing, popular interest in Australian executives' remuneration. He focused on the ethics of the growing differential between the salaries of Australian executives and workers, particularly in the light of poor company performance and a persistently high unemployment rate, often in excess of 10% of the Australian workforce.

Alongside this work, sociologists have explored occupational prestige and status hierarchies. The work of Frank Jones (1989) has been very important, with others taking up this theme (Daniel, 1983; Zagorski, 1988). The Australian Class Project has also involved a focus on Australians at work (Baxter et al., 1989).

While much work undertaken within this theme has focused on the big picture of economic inequality in general terms, two important subthemes focus on further social stratifications: gender and racial/ethnic inequality at work in Australia.

While gender at work studies have often focused on earnings inequality (Kidd and Shannon, 1996; Maclachlan, 1990; Vella 1991), the position of women in organizational life has also been investigated in a more comprehensive way. For example, the Hearn et al. (1990) edited monograph deals with the sexuality of organization, focusing on the production and reproduction of organizations and organizational life in Australia, Canada, the United Kingdom, and the United States. Judy Wajcman (1991) made an important contribution through her exploration of the link between technology and patriarchial relations at work, and gender and the management task (1998). Cordery (1997) examined sex-linked differences in commitment at work. Amanda Sinclair (1994) focused on the chilly climate that exists for women executives in Australia. Savage and Witz (1992) looked at gender and bureaucracy in Australia, and Probert and Wilson (1993) examined gendered work as part of "the pink collar blues." Studies of work and family run alongside this subtheme, with a focus on the effects of Equal Employment Opportunity and Affirmative Action legislation, and "family-friendly" policies at work (Smith, 1992; Wolcott, 1998).

Our brief review cannot do justice to the rich vein of Australian scholarly work relative to issues of gender relations and gender inequality at work. Much of this work is undertaken from a sociological perspective, though some is informed by a more management-oriented view of the world that emanates from business schools.

Similarly, racial/ethnic inequality at work is an important subtheme of sociology of work in Australia. This emphasis is hardly surprising given Australia's history. The first piece of legislation passed by the new Federal government of 1901 heralded the introduction of the White Australia Policy. This legislation served to limit immigration from non-Western European, particularly non-British, source nations and contributed to the marginalization of indigenous peoples in Australia (Harding, 1995). However, since the end of World War II, Australia has experienced massive immigration, first from Eastern Europe, and then from elsewhere in the world, including more recent waves of immigration from Asia. This change has set the scene for a range of studies exploring the position of new migrants, as well as their progeny, compared to native-born Australians. These studies look at wage inequality and migrants' broader socioeconomic status (Kelley and Evans, 1991; Shu, 1996). Other work has begun to focus on the position of indigenous Australians at work (Daly, 1995; Taylor, 1994), with a recent comparison between the positions of indigenous men of Australia and the United States (Gregory and Daly, 1997). Moreover, a range of Federal government publications canvass issues associated with immigrant labor (Flatau, 1991; Vanden Heuval, 1996) and racial/ethnic relations at work (Hawthorne, 1994; Human Rights and Equal Opportunity Commission, 1992).

Race/ethnicity at work is likely to continue to receive scholarly and popular attention in Australia. White Australian sympathies have reemerged, gaining some measure of popular support through the policy prescriptions advocated by a new, radical political party, Pauline Hanson's One Nation Party. Pauline Hanson was elected to Federal Parliament in 1996 as a Queensland independent, advocating simple fixes for persistent unemployment in poorer urban areas, including her electorate of Oxley, west of Brisbane, and the bush. Among her prescriptions were policies limiting immigration, particularly from Asia, both to "protect" Australia's British-ness and to preserve jobs for native-born Australians. While her perspectives were ascendent for a short period, with 11 One Nation members elected to the Queensland State Parliament in mid-1997 and a Senator from Queensland elected to Federal Parliament in 1998, her political party has imploded. All 11 One Nation Party members of the Queensland State Parliament have severed ties with the party amid claims and counterclaims of financial misconduct and despotic governance. While it is not likely to be a long-lived phenomenon, at least in the guise of the One Nation Party, this experience reveals a degree of underlying and persistent racism in the Australian community.

Outwork

Outwork is the third, and emergent, theme in the sociology of work in Australia. While there is not a great deal of sociological work published in this regard as yet (see the Lafferty et al. 1997, study on home-based work), this development has received attention from government, unions, and the press.

Outwork represents recent trends for work to become deinstitutionalized, as least as far as place of work is concerned. Early work in this area has focused on workers in the textile/clothing industries in Australia (Delaney, 1994, 1996). Of course, many of these outworkers are women, more particularly, women from non-English speaking backgrounds, and there have been many allegations about sweated labor and exploitation. A 1995 study undertaken by the Textile, Clothing and Footwear Union of Australia provided evidence of this exploitation, a matter picked up by the popular press. With current trends toward increased use of telecommuting and further deregulation of Australia's industrial environment, the area of outwork is likely to generate increasing interest. Couple this with the development of virtual corporations, the growing use of electronic business, remote management control, an increasingly global environment, and the fact that much sociology of work in Australia emanates from business schools, and this area appears ripe for scholarly attention.

Conclusion

These three key themes of sociology of work in Australia center attention on the subdiscipline. Industrial relations is likely to see a resurgence of scholarly interest in the future, as the industrial environment in Australia becomes more contested. Critical sociological perspectives are likely to yield significant insights into this development. The interest in labor process theory within this theme appears to be considerable, yet relatively little has been published in this theoretical tradition. Much of this work is tucked away in unpublished, higher-degree research, in working paper and discussion paper series, perhaps heralding an increased interest in sociology of work issues among newer scholars.

Inequality, particularly gender and racial/ethnic inequality will continue to be of interest to scholars and public policymakers alike, particularly in the current political environment. Outwork is likely to become an area of burgeoning interest for Australian sociologists and management scholars.

While Braverman's work has influenced theory development, research, and teaching in industrial relations in Australia (e.g., Deery and Plowman, 1991; Dufty and Fells, 1989; Keenoy and Kelly, 1998), the impact of his work has not been as great in Australia as in the United Kingdom, in particular, where collective bargaining has a longer history.

This observation brings us back to the central importance of the institutional context of work in Australia to explain enduring and emergent themes. Renewed interest in sociology of work issues, and in the subdiscipline itself, is likely to be driven by the decline of institutional industrial relations in Australia. Decentralization has meant a move away from an industry-level approach to industrial relations, where "awards" are made defining pay and conditions for whole groups of workers in a particular industry, in favor of workplace-level agreements. While these agreements are processed through a weakened tribunal system and union membership continues to decline (see Peetz, 1998), industrial relations are likely to become more contested across the nation and this, in turn, is likely to drive scholarly research and theorizing to the workplace level. Already, recent surveys reveal changing patterns of work, particularly work intensification, the emergence of a variety of control systems, labor market segmentation, and workplace health and safety (see, e.g., Hopkins, 1988; Willis, 1989), sparking new interest in the subdiscipline.

METHODOLOGY

The history and present landscape of the study of the sociology of work in Australia is largely a reflection of traditional sociological methods. Most researchers in the field have employed a variety of methods, including surveys, interviews, and observations ranging from structured to unstructured interviews, participant to nonparticipant observation, and organizational, sectoral, or national surveys. In many cases, data gathered in these ways are supplemented by reference to various types of historical records and documentation, such as job descriptions, union records, and reports.

Most large studies conducted in Australia in recent years have drawn upon industrial relations surveys undertaken in the United Kingdom (e.g., the Workplace Industrial Relations Survey, WIRS). Such comparative studies are usually funded by the Australian Research Council. The Australian Workplace Industrial Relations Surveys (AWIRS; Callus et al., 1991; Morehead et al., 1997) have provided the most comprehensive data on work in Australia. While these surveys tend to have an industrial relations focus, they have also explored the employment relationship, working conditions, and aspects of work related to the labor process, such as skills formation and control. They also provide insight into the activities and attitudes of some occupational groups, particularly general managers, and human resource and industrial relations managers. The University of Sydney's Australian Centre for Industrial Relations Research and Training (ACIIRT) used the AWIRS survey in its publication, *Australians at Work*, to discuss the conditions under which Australians are working, and the deficiencies and inequalities of contemporary production and distribution systems. More specific studies have provided additional data on particular industries, occupations, or dimensions of work, such as managerial strategy (e.g., Deery and Purcell, 1989).

Smaller studies, particularly surveys of specific groups of interest, are also funded privately. Sources of private funding include centralized union (Australian Council of Trade Unions) and peak employer organizations (e.g., Business Council of Australia; Australian Industry Group and Australian Council of Commerce and Industry) and individual unions, employer associations, and not-for-profit organizations.

A current project, the Australian National Organisation Survey (AusNOS), led by Sandra Harding and Donald Tomaskovic Devey, promises to yield significant insights into work and organization in Australia. The study aims to produce a map of corporate Australia, focusing on formalization, decision making, and structural issues, as well as conditions for enterprise development in Australia. Survey became available during 2000. The project was funded by an Australian Research Council Strategic Partnerships with Industry grant. In addition, the current iteration of the International Social Science Survey Australia (ISSSA) includes several pages of questions that focus on work, working conditions, and remuneration.

Some comparative cross-industry (Kitay and Lansbury, 1997) and individual workplace studies (e.g., Lansbury and Macdonald, 1992; Patrickson, Bamber, and Bamber, 1995) have used more qualitative methodologies, including interviews that either provide background information or flesh out details in survey data.

Finally, the ethnographic tradition has not assumed a strong position in the sociology of work in Australia. Some notable studies (Clegg, 1975; Kreigler, 1980) have made use of observations (participant and nonparticipant) to explore particular issues. However, it is our impression that a good deal of this style of research has been conducted by students as part of their research degree programs, but this is rarely published.

Much of what we know about work in Australia comes to us through industrial relations studies, including analyses of unions explaining what their members do at work. Some studies have concentrated on the work of specific groups (e.g., Aboriginal cattle station workers in Stevens, 1974; immigrant workers in Lever-Tracey, 1981; Lever-Tracy and Quinlan, 1988). The most detailed accounts also arise from industry or workplace industrial relations studies, often linked to labor process theory (e.g., Boreham et al., 1996, on hospitality; Deery and Mahoney, 1994, on retail; Barry, Bowden, and Brosnan, 1998, on coal). Such research usually employs a variety of methodologies.

All this leaves us with relatively little raw knowledge of work itself but a good deal of insight into the employment relationship surrounding it. Again, this is a reflection of the enduring institutional dominance of industrial relations focused research work in Australia.

THE INSTITUTIONAL CONTEXT OF THE SOCIOLOGY OF WORK

Most research funding for studies of work comes from the State, particularly the Australian Research Council, in the form of research grants for particular projects based in universities alone or operating in conjunction with other organizations. In general, such projects incorporate sociology of work research into broader studies, with a specific research agenda or question at the core. These projects tend to have particular policy outcomes as the objective.

Sociological research is conducted within, or for, organizations such as government departments, corporations, and agencies (as part of the State bureaucracy) that primarily administer legislation in relation to employment, industrial relations, regional and industry-specific development, education, and social welfare. Trade unions and not-for-profit organizations are other key sources of research funding.

Industrial sociology, the sociology of work, and organizational sociology have become integrated with, or at least connected to, other disciplines. In Australia, sociology of work has traditionally been located in departments of industrial relations or economics. However, in more recent times, the subdiscipline has been located in departments and schools of management and human resource management. It is also clear that labor historians, as part of studies of occupations and unions, and labor economists, as they investigate labor market segmentation, increasingly draw upon sociological insights to inform their research and theory development.

We undertook an examination of Australian universities' websites in order to enhance our understanding of teaching and research in the sociology of work. Of the 39 universities, 30 housed faculties, schools, or departments that were responsible for sociological teaching and research. By comparison, 75 distinct organizational units within Australian universities were involved in management, business, and industrial relations. Growth in business-related areas has occurred as a result of increased funding to those units as a result of increased student enrollments. However, while many business-related schools or departments, particularly those specializing in management, human resource management, and/or industrial relations, possess a capacity and a rationale for teaching the sociology of work, our impression is that little such teaching occurs outside departments of sociology.

Working further down this thread, we examined the websites of schools and departments of sociology. While websites do not necessarily provide a comprehensive picture, we note that 12 universities teach subjects that directly concern sociology of work, yet "Sociology of Work" as a subject title is almost nonexistent. Most subject titles embrace gender or technology. Others cite globalization, leisure, culture, working lives and time. Subjects bearing titles that explicitly cite sociology of work or its key concerns appear to be isolated and elective. Unless attached to industrial relations or management curriculums, sociology of work, industrial sociology, and organizational sociology cannot be considered prominent in any program of study in Australia. We found no sociology of work–industrial sociology major as such.

It may be that this absence of sociology of work from study programs is explained by the vocational focus of many Australian tertiary education study programs. Graduates with relatively ill-defined or nonvocational emphases to their studies, as may be seen to be the case with a focus on the sociology of work, may be limited in their employment prospects. Sociology of work appears to be, at best, an adjunct to more vocationally focused studies in industrial relations or management. Similarly, sociology of work as a subdiscipline is interpeted as an adjunct to the main study program in business or management. This particular location in the academy does not augur well for the future of the subdiscipline. Indeed, its marginalization appears likely to be reproduced over time.

Apart from the main sociological journals (see Table 1), the main publication outlets in Australia for those who research and theorize about the sociology of work are the *Journal of Industrial Relation, Labour and Industry,* and the *International Journal of Employment Studies.* To a lesser extent the *Economic and Labour Relations Review; Policy, Organisation and Society; Prometheus,* and the *Asia–Pacific Journal of Human Resource Management* all feature sociological work. Of course, much sociological work is published outside of the key sociology journals. Indeed, much work of interest by Australian scholars is published in U.K. and U.S.-based publications. Perusal of the sources of articles cited in

Table 1. The Main Sociological Journals

Discipline	Journal
Sociology	*Journal of Sociology: The Journal of the Australian Sociological Association* *Journal of Australian Studies* *Prometheus* *The Australian Journal of Social Issues*
Business/ Management	*Asia Pacific Journal of Human Resources* *Australian Journal of Management* *Australian Journal of Management and Organisational Behaviour* *Australasian Marketing Journal* *Bond Management Review* *International Journal of Organisational Behaviour* *Journal of the Australian and New Zealand Academy of Management* *New Zealand Journal of Business* *Small Enterprise Research: The Journal of SEAANZ*
Industrial relations	*Australian Journal of Labour Economics* *International Journal of Employment Studies* *Labour and Industry* *New Zealand Journal of Industrial Relations* *The Economic And Labour Relations Review* *The Journal of Industrial Relations*

this work reveals its broad publications base. The main conference that accepts sociology of work papers is the Association of Industrial Relations Academics of Australia and New Zealand (AIRAANZ). Such work is also featured to a lesser extent at the annual meeting of the key sociological scholarly association, the Australian Sociological Association (ASA). Some useful contacts points in the field of sociology of work are also shown in Table 1.

CONCLUSION

While it is possible to identify key enduring and emergent themes in the sociology of work in Australia, much of this work is undertaken by scholars who are not located in sociology departments. Indeed, much of this work is not published in journals of sociology. Instead, most of the work in this area is undertaken by industrial relations scholars and located in business, management, or commerce faculties, schools, and departments.

While some contributions have been important, this is not a strong area of interest for Australian sociologists. On the one hand, the lack of coherent, unabashedly sociology of work study programs at Australian universities does not augur well for the future of the subdiscipline at a time when certain themes are ripe for exploration and analysis. Instead, the subdiscipline is fragmented in its location in Australian academe, with little prospect of renewal or revitalization in the face of this fragmentation.

On the other hand, to the extent that sociological perspectives and approaches become incorporated in the work of scholars trained in other disciplines, prospects do not appear quite so bleak. The challenge will be to ensure that such scholars understand both the sociological context of their own work, most particularly the implications of the theoretical perspectives they employ, so that new insights can be developed and applied to explain work, organization and industry, both in Australia and elsewhere.

REFERENCES

Australian Centre for Industrial Relations Research and Training. 1999. *Australia at Work. Just Managing?* Sydney: Prentice-Hall.
Badham, R. a,nd J. Matthews. 1989. "The New Systems Production Debate." *Labour and Industry* 2(2):194–246.
Barry, M., Bowden, B., and P. Brosnan. 1998. *The Fallacy of Flexibility: Workplace Reform in the Queensland Open Cut Coal Industry.* Sydney: Allen and Unwin.
Baxter, J. H., P. Boreham, S. Clegg, J. Emmison, D. Gibson, G. Marks, J. Western, and M. Western. 1989. "The Australian Class Structure: Some Preliminary Results from the Australian Class Project." *Australian and New Zealand Journal of Sociology* 25(1).
Blau, F., and L. Kahn. 1992. "The Gender Earnings Gap: Learning from International Comparisons." *AEA Papers and Proceedings* 82(2):533–538.
Boreham, P., and G. Dow. 1980. *Work and Inequality.* South Melbourne: Macmillan.
Boreham, P., Lafferty, G., Roan, J., and G. Whitehouse. 1996. "Training, Careers and Numerical Flexibility: Equity Implications in Hospitality and Retailing." *Journal of Industrial Relations* 38(1):3–21.
Borland, J., and R. Wilkins. 1996. "Earnings Inequality in Australia." *The Economic Record* 72(216):7–23.
Braverman, H. 1974. *Labor and Monopoly Capital.* New York: Monthly Review Press.
Burgess, J. 1996. "Workforce Casualisation in Australia." *International Employment Relations Review* 2(1):33–53.
Callus, R., Morehead, A., Cully, M., and J. Buchanan. 1991. *Industrial Relations at Work: The Australian Workplace Industrial Relations Survey.* Canberra: Australian Government Publishing Service.
Clegg, S. R. 1975. *Power, Rule and Domination: A Critical and Empirical Understanding of Power in Sociological Theory and Organizational Life.* London: Routledge and Kegan Paul.
Congalton, A. 1963. "Occupational Status in Australia." Studies in Sociology No. 3. Sydney: University of New South Wales.
Cordery, J. 1997. "Sex-Linked Differences in Affective Organizational Commitment: The Interaction of Organizational Level and Gender." Organisational and Labour Studies Discussion Paper No. 2. Crawley: University of Western Australia.

Curtain, R., and J. Matthews. 1990. "Two Models of Award Restructuring in Australia." *Labour and Industry* 3(1):58–75.

Daly, A. 1995. "The Determinants of Income for Employed Indigenous Australians." *International Journal of Manpower* 16(4):11–28.

Daniel, A. 1983. *Power, Privilege and Prestige: Occupations in Australia.* Melbourne: Longman Cheshire.

Deery, S. 1982. "Trade Unions, Technological Change and Redundancy Protection in Australia." *Journal of Industrial Relations* 24(2):155–175.

Deery, S., and D. Plowman. 1991. *Australian Industrial Relations*, 3rd ed. Sydney: McGraw-Hill.

Deery, S., and A. Mahoney. 1994. "Temporal Flexibility: Management Strategies and Employee Preferences in the Retail Industry." *Journal of Industrial Relations.* 36(3):332–352.

Deery, S., and J. Purcell. 1989. "Strategic Choices in the Management of Industrial Relations in Large Organisations." *Journal of Industrial Relations* 31(4):459–477.

Delaney, A. 1994. "Outworking in Australia: an Examination of the Use of Immigrant Women as Sweated Labour in the Clothing Industry in the 1990s." *Migration Action* 16(2–3):15–21.

Delaney, A. 1996. "My Home is My Haven, My Home is My Workplace." *Alternative Law Journal* 21(5):217–219, 222.

Dufty, N., and N. Fells. 1989. *Dynamics of Industrial Relations in Australia.* Sydney: Prentice-Hall.

Dunphy, D., and A. Griffiths. 1998. *The Sustainable Corporation.* Sydney: Allen and Unwin.

Dwyer, P., and B. Wilson. 1981. "Structural Change: Job Prospects and Working Class Responses." *Australian and New Zealand Journal of Sociology* 17(2):31–40.

Dwyer, T. 1981. "The Production of Industrial Accidents: A Sociological Approach." *Australian and New Zealand Journal of Sociology* 17(2):59–65.

Economic and Labour Relations Review. 1995. Special Issue, Vol.6(1).

Flatau, P. 1991. "Labour Market Experience, Education and Training of Young Immigrants in Australia: An Intergenerational Study." Canberra: Australian Government Publishing Service.

Frenkel, S. 1986. "Industrial Sociology and Workplace Relations in Advanced Capitalist Societies." *International Journal of Comparative Sociology.* 27(1–2):69–86.

Frenkel, S., and C. Royal. 1997. "Globalization and Employment Relations." *Research in Sociology of Work* 6:3–41.

Gahan, P. 1991. "Forward to the Past: The Case of "New Production Concepts." *Journal of Industrial Relations* 33(2):155–77.

Godbout, T. 1993. "Employment Change and Sectoral Distribution in 10 Countries, 1970–90." *Monthly Labor Review.*

Gregory, R., and A. Daly. 1997. "Welfare and Economic Progress of Indigenous Men of Australia and the US, 1980–1990." *The Economic Record* 73(221):101–119.

Groenewegen, P. D. 1970. "Employment and Machinery: Two Classical Debates on the Effects of Automation." *Journal of Industrial Relations* 12(3):348–359.

Harding, S. 1995. "Multiculturalism in Australia: Moving Race/Ethnic Relations from Extermination to Celebration?" *Race, Gender and Class* 3(1):7–26.

Hawthorne, L. 1994. "Labour Market Barriers for Immigrant Engineers in Australia." Bureau of Immigration and Population Research. Canberra: Australian Government Publishing Service.

Hearn, J., D. Sheppard, P. Tancred-Sheriff, and G. Burrell, eds. 1990. *The Sexuality of Organization*. London: Sage.

Hopkins, A. 1988. "Deskilling, Job Control and Safety: Why Miners Violate Safety Regulations." *Labour and Industry* 1(2):322–334.

Human Rights and Equal Opportunity Commission. 1992. "Race Relations in the Workplace: A Report on Pilot Projects Undertaken in Industry." Sydney: Author.

Hunter, B. 1995. "The Social Structure of the Australian Urban Labour Market: 1976–1991." *The Australian Economic Review* 110:65–79.

Jones, F. 1989. "Occupational Prestige in Australia: A New Scale." *Australian and New Zealand Journal of Sociology* 25(2):187–199.

Keenoy, T., and D. Kelly. 1998. *The Employment Relationship in Australia,* 2nd ed. Sydney: Harcourt Brace.

Kelley, J., and M. Evans. 1991. "Prejudice, Discrimination and Labour Market Attainments of Immigrants in Australia." *American Journal of Sociology* 97(3):721–759.

Kelley, J., and M. Evans. 1993. "The Legitimation of Inequality: Occupational Earnings in Nine Nations." *American Journal of Sociology.* 99(1):75–125.

Kerr Inkson, J., and B. Gidlow. 1981. "Waterfront Workers as Traditional Proletarians: A New Zealand Study." *Australian and New Zealand Journal of Sociology* 17(2):10–20.

Kidd, M., and M. Shannon. 1996. "The Gender Wage Gap: A Comparison of Australia and Canada." *Industrial & Labor Relations Review* 49(4):729–746.

Kitay, J., and R. D. Lansbury. 1997. *Changing Employment Relations in Australia*. Oxford, UK: Oxford University Press.

Kriegler, R. J. 1980. *Working for the Company: Work and Control in the Whyalla Shipyard*. Melbourne: Oxford University Press.

Lafferty, G., R. Hall, W. Harley, and G. Whitehouse. 1997. "Homeworking in Australia: An Assessment of Current Trends." *Australian Bulletin of Labour* 23(2):143–156.

Lansbury, R. D. 1980. "New Technology and Industrial Relations in the Retail Grocery Industry." *Journal of Industrial Relations* 22(3):275–292.

Lansbury, R. D., and D. Macdonald. 1992. *Workplace Industrial Relations*. Oxford, UK: Oxford University Press.

Lever Tracey, C. 1981. "Labour Market Segmentation and Diverging Migrant Incomes." *Australian and New Zealand Journal of Sociology* 17(2):21–30.

Lever-Tracy, C., and M. Quinlan. 1988. *A Divided Working Class: Ethnic Separation and Industrial Conflict in Australia*. London: Routledge and Kegan Paul.

Maclachlan, M. 1990. "Occupational Segregation: The Extent of Gender Segregation in Victoria and Australia." Women's Employment Branch, Department of Labour.

Maconachie, G. 1993. "From Bureaucrat to Professional: Skill and Work in the Commonwealth Employment Service." *Journal of Industrial Relations.* 35 (2): 221-241.

Maxwell, V. 1981. "Status Relations of Australian Metal Workers." *Australian and New Zealand Journal of Sociology* 17(2):50–58.

McCormack, D. 1992. "The Labour Market Experience of Migrant and Australian Born Youth." Economics and Commerce Discussion Paper No. 27. Melbourne: La Trobe University.

Miller, P. 1989. "Gender Wage Discrimination in Australia: A Reassessment." Discussion Paper, Crawley: University of Western Australia.

Miller, P. 1994. "Gender Discrimination in Training: An Australian Perspective." *British Journal of Industrial Relations* 32(4):539–565.

Mitropoulous, A. 1999. " Discipline and Labour: Sociology, Class Formation and Money in Australia at the Beginning of the Twentieth Century." *Journal of Sociology* 35(1):77–91.

Morehead, A., M. Steele, M. Alexander, K. Stephen, and L. Duffin. 1997. *Changes at Work: The 1995 Australian Workplace Industrial Relations Survey*. Melbourne: Longman.

Patrickson, M., V. Bamber, and G. J. Bamber,eds. 1995. *Organisational Change Strategies*. South Melbourne: Longman.

Peetz, D. 1998. *Unions in a Contrary World*. Oxford, UK: Oxford University Press.

Perry, N. 1981. "Progressive Emancipation and the Negotiation of Disenchantment: An Ethnography of New Zealand Office Workers." *Australian and New Zealand Journal of Sociology* 17(2):41–49.

Preston, A. 1997. "Where are we now with Human Capital Theory in Australia?" *The Economic Record* 73(220):51–78.

Probert, B., and G. Wilson. 1993. "Gendered Work." In *Pink Collar Blues: Work, Gender and Technology*. Melbourne: University of Melbourne Press.

Rowse, T. 1984. "Surrendering Australia." *Meanjin Quarterly* 43(3):379–384.

Savage, M., and A. Witz. 1992. *Gender and Bureaucracy*. Oxford, UK: Blackwell.

Scott, W. H. 1974. "Orientation of Specialists in a Continuous Process Plant." *Journal of Industrial Relations* 16(3):223–229.

Shu, J. 1996. "Labour Force Status in Australia of Newly Arrived Immigrants from Asia." *Asian Migrant* 9(2):47–54.

Sinclair, A. 1994. "Trials at the Top." Melbourne: The Australian Centre, University of Melbourne.

Smith, C. 1992. "Trends and Directions in Dual-Career Family Research." *Women in Management Review* 7(1):23–28.

Stevens, F. 1974. *Aborigines in the Northern Territory Cattle Industry*. Canberra: Australian National University Press.

Taylor, J. 1994. "Measuring the Occupational Segregation of Australia's Indigenous Workforce: A Census-Based Analysis." *Social Indicators Research* 31(2):175–204.

Textile, Clothing and Footwear Union of Australia. 1995. *The Hidden Cost of Fashion*. Sydney: TCFUA.

Van den Broek, D. 1997. "Human Resource Management, Culture Control and Union Avoidance: an Australian Case Study." *Journal of Industrial Relations* 39(3):332–348.

Vanden Heuval, A. 1996. "Non-English-Speaking-Background Immigrant Women and Part-time Work." Canberra: Australian Government Publishing Service.

Vella, F. 1991. "Gender Roles, Occupational Choice and Gender Wage Differentials." Economics and Econometrics. Working Paper No. 235. Canberra: Australian National University.

Wajcman, J. 1991. "Patriarchy, Technology, and Conceptions of Skill." *Work and Occupations* 18(1):29–45.

Wajcman, J. 1998. *Managing Like a Man: Women and Men in Corporate Management.* Sydney: Allen and Unwin.

Williams, C. 1988. *Blue, White and Pink Collar Workers in Australia.* Sydney: Allen and Unwin.

Willis, E., ed. 1989. *Technology and the Labour Process: Australasian Case Studies.* Sydney: Allen and Unwin.

Wolcott, I. 1998. *Work and Family.* Canberra: Australian Government Publishing Service.

Woldring, K. 1995. "The Ethics of Australian Executive Remuneration Packages." *Journal of Business Ethics* 14:937–947.

APPENDIX: CONTACTS

Association of Industrial Relations Academics of Australia and New Zealand
www.mngt.waikato.ac.nz/depts/sml/airaanz/

Australian Centre for Industrial Relations Research and Training
www.econ.usyd.edu.au/acirrt

Australian Industrial Relations Commission
www.airc.gov.au

Australian National Organisation Survey
s.harding@qut.edu.au

Centre for Economic Policy Research, Australian National University
http://cepr.anu.edu.au

Department of Employment, Workplace Relations and Small Business
www.dewrsb.gov.au

International Social Science Survey Australia (ISSSA)
www.international-survey.org

Melbourne Institute of Applied Economic and Social Research
www.ecom.unimelb.edu.au/iaesrwww

Research School of Social Science, Australian National University
http://rsss.anu.edu.au

The Australian Sociological Association (with links to a range of useful sites)
www.newcastle.edu.au/department/so/tasa

7

India

Sharit K. Bhowmik

This chapter attempts to examine the development of sociology of work in India. It stresses current research and tries to assess the discipline's position in academia and other fields. A brief background on the nature of Indian society, the process of industrialization in India, and the subsequent emergence of studies relating to work help in understanding the changing nature of the studies. This chapter concentrates mainly on research related to the urban–industrial sector.

NATURE OF THE LABOR FORCE

India is the second largest country in the world in terms of population and has recently crossed the one billion mark. The last census, in 1991, showed that around 25% of the population resided in urban areas and the rest in rural areas. The labor force in the country numbered 317 million in 1991. Of this, a mere 8.5% (27 million) were engaged in the formal sector, while 270 million were engaged in the informal sector. Women constituted one-third of those engaged in the informal sector and one-seventh of those employed in the for-

Sharit K. Bhowmik • Department of Sociology, University of Mumbai, Vidyanagari, Santacruz (East) Mumbai, India.

Worlds of Work: Building an International Sociology of Work, edited by Daniel B. Cornfield and Randy Hodson. Kluwer Academic/Plenum Publishers, New York, 2002.

mal sector. Around 185 million workers were engaged in the rural–informal sector. The urban–informal sector comprised around 95 million workers.

The distinction between the formal and informal sectors is crucial for understanding employment relationship. Workers in the formal sector are engaged in factories, and commercial and service establishments. Around 70% of the workers in this sector are employed in government, quasi-government, and public sector enterprises. The private sector provides employment to only 30% of the labor force in the formal sector. The wages of workers in the formal sector are substantially higher than those engaged in the urban–informal sector. Moreover, a range of labor laws, guaranteeing permanence of employment and provision for retirement benefits, protect their jobs.

Though in principle labor laws in India are expected to apply to all sections of industrial labor, there are built-in provisions in these laws that exclude large sections of the labor force. The most important law regulating work in industries is the Factories Act. All other laws, such as the Employees State Insurance Act, the Workmen's Compensation Act, the Provident Fund and Family Pension Act, and the Payment of Gratuity Act, apply only to establishments covered by the Factories Act, which is applicable only to manufacturing units that employ a minimum of 10 workers and use power in manufacturing, and a minimum of 20 workers if the unit does not use power. Hence, a large section of industrial workers employed in small industries do not have legal protection in their work. We can thus see that the composition of the labor force in India shows wide contrasts.

FEATURES OF SOCIETY IN INDIA

A brief description of the nature of Indian society is necessary before we proceed further. India is a land comprising ethnic, religious, and linguistic differences. These identities at times cause strain to the integrity of the country. Indeed, one of the main problems of the State is to integrate these various differences into the democratic fabric of the nation. A more important divide among the people is the specific nature of social hierarchy, known as the caste system. Caste, as a form of social hierarchy, is peculiar to Indian society. The gradation of castes is based on the degree of ritual purity a caste has in comparison to others. At the upper end of the system are the Brahmins, the scholars of the religious texts or priests. At the lowest end are those castes performing manual labor and activities regarded as unclean (scavenging, cremation of the dead, tanning and leather work, etc.). These castes are regarded as untouchables.

The practice of untouchability is not very prevalent, because the Constitution of India has banned it. Moreover, the Constitution grants positive discrimination to protect the interests of the former untouchable castes. These include special provision for education and reservation of jobs in the government and public sector undertakings. Nonetheless other forms of caste discrimination persist.

INDUSTRIALIZATION IN INDIA

Factory production started in India in the early part of the 1850s. The objective then was to export manufactured goods to markets in Britain. These factories were thus established in the port towns of Calcutta and Bombay (now known as Mumbai) to facilitate export. Cotton textile mills were established in Bombay and jute mills in Calcutta. Later, factories were established in Madras (now known as Chennai), another port town. One of the reasons for setting up industries was that costs of production were much lower in India because labor was available at very cheap rates. A couple of decades earlier, in 1839, tea plantations came up in the northeastern province of Assam. The tea produced was, again, for consumption in Britain.

Cheap labor existed mainly for two reasons. First, the indigenous economy had been devastated with the introduction of colonial rule of the East India Company a hundred years earlier. During this period, the local crafts were replaced by cheaper imports of factory-produced goods from Britain. This led to the gradual rout of the rural artisans in the country. The peasants were no better off, for in many parts of the country, in the place of food crops, they were forced to cultivate cash crops, which were needed as raw materials for factories in Britain. Besides, the cultivators paid higher taxes due to the new types of land settlements and land revenue imposed by the colonial rulers. As a result, there was a general impoverishment of the rural population. These people served as pools of cheap labor when the factories were built.

The other reason for labor being cheap was that during the initial stages of industrialization, the colonial government did not regulate work or wages. The workers were unorganized and the industrialists were able to make them work for long hours at low wages. Women and children were most affected in this system, for their wages were even lower.

The industrial base in India remained narrow during the initial years. The 1911 census showed that there were around 800,000 laborers engaged in the secondary and tertiary sectors. Of these, 524,000 were employed in factories and plantations. In fact, the jute industry and tea plantations employed 400,000 workers, namely, half the total labor force. The situation improved with the onset of World War I in 1914. The war created a need for industrial goods, and the colonial government sought to meet this by expanding the engineering goods sector in India. During this period, the first steel mill was set up in Bihar, in northern India. This region has an abundance of mineral wealth. The railways, introduced in 1860s primarily to carry raw materials to the cotton textile mills in Mumbai and the jute mills in Calcutta, increased its network (Gadgil 1982). These features led to the expansion of the working class. Moreover, this created an opportunity for the existing factory workers to be promoted to the ranks of skilled workers and supervisors, positions formerly held by Europeans (Mukherjee 1945:240). Hence, changes occurred in the composition of the working class, which until then was composed mainly of unskilled workers. The inclusion of skilled and literate workers provided conditions for starting trade unions.

STUDIES ON WORK IN COLONIAL INDIA

Studies on the early phase of industrialization were carried out mainly by economic historians. A significant study on the working class in Mumbai was conducted by M. D. Morris (1965). Morris described the nature of work from the mills inception until the time of independence (i.e., 1947) from the various records of the employers associations and the government. His findings show that the Factories Acts of 1881 and 1891 were ineffective in regulating the work of women and children, who remained the most exploited workers in the workforce.

Workers were drawn from different castes and formed themselves into clusters of similar status groups. Morris found that caste divisions among the workers were not exclusive and did not prevent members of different castes from working side by side with one another. In other words, recruitment to the workforce was neither inhibited by the traditional divisions of caste in the countryside nor did this affect the functioning of the mill.

At the same time, Morris's study shows that the attitudes of the other castes toward the untouchable castes were radically different. Workers belonging to the untouchable castes were systematically excluded from the spinning section of the mill because neither Hindu nor Muslim workers were willing to work with them, the reason being that the worker has to wet the thread with his spit before threading it in the spindle. A worker belonging to an untouchable caste would pollute the cloth and no other worker would be willing to touch it. Morris, however, notes that there may be other reasons for this practice. Workers in the weaving section were paid the highest wages and wanted to consolidate this preserve for their kinfolk or caste members. The inclusion of untouchable castes in this section would upset this monopoly. Hence, they raised the issue of untouchability to exclude these people. Another of Morris's major findings is that during the initial phase, untouchables did not migrate to the mills. The shops with higher wages in the factories were dominated by the other castes. This also disproves Max Weber's suggestion that the labor force in India comprised "declassed and pariah castes" of the countryside.

A later study by Rajnarain Chandavarkar (1994) is equally significant. Chandavarkar covered the period 1900–1940, but the scope of his study is broader than that of Morris. Though his focus is on the textile industry he also covers the small-scale manufacturing enterprises that mushroomed due to the growth of the large factories, the docks, and the railways. Moreover, Morris dealt mainly with the conditions of industrial workers and industrial relations within the factory, whereas Chandavarkar included the living conditions, housing, and settlement patterns in the working-class areas of the city in his study. These two studies complement each other in several ways. Whereas Morris dealt with the issue of caste in the workplace, Chandavarkar's study placed considerable stress on the housing pattern of the different castes, though the residences were similar in size. These were one-room tenements in large buildings called *chawls* in local parlance. Chandavarkar's study showed that the different caste groups preferred to cluster in common buildings. This limited social intercourse among workers of different castes outside their workplace.

Historical studies on jute workers in Calcutta do not have the same sociological depth as these two studies on Mumbai. The more important studies have concentrated on the working class movement in the early 20th century, when labor unrest was particularly high. A comprehensive study on the formation of the working class by Ranajit Dasgupta (1994) dealt extensively with labor struggles and the trade union movement in the industry.

A significant but controversial work on this aspect by Dipesh Chakravarty (1989) is identified with the subaltern school of Indian history, which ostensibly based its analysis on Antonio Gramsci's work on the role of subalterns. However, this concept was used to counter the conventional Marxist approach of analyzing conflicts through class categories, with an emphasis on political consciousness and collective action. The subaltern historians have tried to use an ideology based on Marxist thought (Gramsci) to counter traditional Marxist analysis. Marxist historians have used the materialist conception of history, stressing class struggle in relation to the socioeconomic formation. The subaltern historians placed greater stress on cultural factors in analyzing struggles of the marginalized. They also tended to stress more the specific nature of local events, while minimizing the role of collective action on a larger plane.

The subaltern historians concentrated mainly on analyzing peasant movements, but Chakravarty was the first among them to extend this to the working class. In analyzing consciousness of the subaltern groups in the jute factories, he stressed on the role of religion (of the workers), caste affiliations, and cultural practices. A strong criticism of the subaltern approach can be found in a volume edited by Samita Sen and Arjan de Haan (1999). This volume, containing papers relating to the social history of labor in the jute industry, has an excellent introduction on the need for studying labor history. It stresses the fact that merely studying cultural processes, without giving sufficient importance to the socioeconomic formation, can lead to one-dimensional and misleading research. Ranajit Dasgupta's chapter in the volume points out several wrong conclusions in Dipesh Chakravarty's work, in which he tended to misunderstand the cultural processes on which he based his study. The editors stress that besides the peasantry, the urban working class also played a decisive role in shaping the nature of politics expressed in the struggle for freedom from colonial rule.

This proposition is in fact an important issue in social sciences in the country. It can be seen that a majority of works in contemporary history, sociology and politics concentrate on India's rural society. Studies on the urban–industrial sector are comparatively fewer. In sociology particularly, as we will see, one finds very few significant studies on the industrial sector. Whereas, in reality, though social problems in rural society affect urban society, it is equally true that industrialization, however scanty and diffuse it may be, has had a greater effect in transforming society in India. I discuss this aspect in more details in the section on contemporary issues.

An important section of the labor force in colonial India worked in plantations and mines. The laborers in these industries were different from those in urban–industrial areas, because they belonged to the more impoverished sections of the peasantry. The work was strenuous and took place under difficult natural conditions. Bhowmik's (1981) study of tea plantation workers in northeastern India (Assam and the northern districts of West Bengal) shows that these workers were largely drawn from tribal communities in Central India. Assam, the largest and oldest tea-growing area in the country, used indentured labor in the early phase. In West Bengal, the indenture system was not prevalent but, once recruited, laborers were not free to leave the plantations. Wages were low and the living and working conditions poor. A tea plantation worker was paid half the wage of a textile worker.

Janaki Nair's (1998) study of workers in the Kolar Gold Fields, the only gold mine in the country, elaborates on living and working conditions of mine workers. A large section of the workers were drawn from the untouchable communities in the region. These people initially saw work in the mines as an alternative to their exploited existence in the villages. However, after working in the mines, they were unable to leave because of several mechanisms that tied them down. The most common of these was indebtedness to the moneylenders, who charged exorbitant interests. The employers did nothing to ease this situation as indebtedness ensured that the workers would continue to work until the debt was repaid. Nair also explores the role of caste in union formation. The socially conscious, lower castes insisted that issues of untouchability should be tackled by the trade unions along with other problems concerning work.

During the colonial rule, Jamshedpur, a town in the north Indian state of Bihar, gained importance as an industrial center when a large steel plant was established there in the early 20th century. The is mineral-rich region and has iron ore and coal mines. Two recent studies on this area (Bahal, 1995, Simeon, 1995) detail different aspects of the labor movement. Bahal's study is a scholarly documentation of labor recruitment policies and the growth of unionization. Simeon's study is similar but places greater stress on trade unions and nationalist politics.

THE POSTCOLONIAL SITUATION

After India attained independence on August 15, 1947, changes occurred in the industrial policy. India adopted a socialist model of development, and accordingly, tried to restrict the growth of industries to those sectors that would lead to a growth of the country's infrastructure. India also adopted the idea of central planning from the Soviet Union and placed emphasis on heavy industries. This led to the growth of the public sector as the new, large industries were initiated through the government and, in most cases, with foreign collaboration. After 1956, large-scale industries for the manufacture of steel and heavy electrical equipment were established through the public sector. Mining, especially coal, iron ore, and mica, was expanded. These were expected to give a boost to other industries.

Major changes in industrial policies have taken place since 1985. The Prime Minister then was Rajeev Gandhi, the son of Indira Gandhi and the grandson of Jawarharlal Nehru. Soon after assuming office, he announced that India had to "march to the twenty-first century" and advocated radical changes in the industrial policy. The first measure was to reduce bureaucratic controls on expansion of industries in the private sector. Restrictions on foreign collaborations in private enterprise were reduced. The culmination of this approach occurred on July 21, 1991 (after the assassination of Rajeev Gandhi), when the new government laid before Parliament set its Industrial Policy Statement, which was a major departure from the past policies of earlier governments. This marked the beginning of structural adjustment and liberalization of the economy.

STUDIES ON WORK AFTER INDEPENDENCE

During the first decade or so after independence, there were hardly any sociological studies on industry or labor. Sociologists, Indian and foreign, concentrated more on studying villages. It was only in the late 1950s that a few sociologists turned their attention to the study of industrial labor. During the same time, the issue of labor commitment was raised by some American sociologists. It was believed that the growth of industrialization in developing countries was hampered by a labor force that was unaccustomed to an industrial way of life. Two major publications, one edited by Moore and Feldman (1960) and the other by Kerr, Mayers, and Dunlop (1960), put forth this view. These writers argued that nonindustrialized countries such as India had features in their social structure that impeded commitment of labor to industry. These features include a closed system of stratification, emphasis on primordial loyalties, religious values, strong attachment to land, and so on. Moore and Feldman (1960) noted that "commitment involves both performance and acceptance of the behavior appropriate to an industrial way of life" (p. 1). Kerr et al. observed that a committed worker is one who stays on the job and has severed major connections with land. These studies tried to compare the situation in developing countries with those of the developed industrialized countries, using the features of the labor force in the latter as the model.

These propositions were general observations and not specifically related to the labor force in India. They could apply as well to countries in Africa, Indonesia, or any other industrializing country. The implications were quite clear: Labor in developing countries was not committed to industry because it had strong attachment to agriculture, and because there existed social institutions that were particularistic and not universalistic.

A number of studies carried out in the 1960s, mainly by sociologists and social anthropologists, proved the contrary. These were all microstudies that provided intensive, qualitative data on the subjects studied. Richard D. Lambert (1963) studied workers in five factories in Poona (now known as Pune) in western India. While studying the general situation in Poona, he found that workers employed in small factories, where wages were low and there was hardly any social security, were apt to change their jobs. When these workers secured employment in large factories, where employment was secure and wages were higher, they seldom left their jobs. For these workers, factory employment implied lifetime commitment. In fact, the workers were overcommitted. At the same time, they showed no signs of transforming their attitudes and social relations. They viewed their jobs in the same way that they viewed their traditional caste occupations in which the specialist (the worker in this case) serves the patron (the industrialist). Lambert thus found that traditional culture was consistent with industrialization.

A study by N. R. Sheth (1958) of a factory in the early 1960s is regarded as an important contribution to industrial sociology in India. This anthropological work viewed the factory as a composite (functional) unit. Sheth's findings, based on observation, were that, rather than impede commitment, traditional culture could in fact promote commitment. Recruitment of the labor force was based on particularistic norms of obligation to caste and kin that were bound by ties of personal obligation. Workers accepted obligation to their supervisors as religious duty. Sheth also found that the functional stability of the system was reinforced by the caste system. He concluded that there was no contradiction between traditional values and industrialism.

Other studies explained the problem differently. Mark Holmstrom (1976), in his study of workers in three factories in Bangalore, argued that the attitudes of factory workers in India were not very different from those of workers in developed countries. Overcommitment can be interpreted as a result of the general insecurity of getting permanent employment outside the formal sector rather than a carryover of traditional attitudes. M. D. Morris (1965), in his historical study of textile workers cited earlier, had found that the turnover in the factories was very high, indicating an unstable labor force. However, he noted that this instability was mainly due to the better wages offered in some of the mills, and other employment opportunities in the city, and not due to the pull of the countryside. Charles A. Mayers (1958) suggested that managerial policies were equally responsible for promoting or impeding labor commitment. When management adopted short-term policies of increasing profits through low wages and exploitation at work, labor turnover was high. His study of a cotton mill in South India showed that labor turn over and absenteeism dropped sharply after management introduced welfare measures. B. R. Sharma's (1971) study of an automobile factory in Mumbai found that workers engaged in monotonous, short-cycle work were less committed, whereas skilled workers engaged in maintenance and toolmaking showed greater commitment to their work. In either case, traditional culture was not a barrier to commitment.

The studies dealing with the problem of labor commitment were important contributions to understanding the attitudes of workers toward work. Most of these studies became important texts for students in management institutes and industrial sociologogists in the country. Another important contribution to the sociology of work was the study of trade unions and industrial relations, which I shall discuss in the following section.

STUDIES ON TRADE UNIONS AND INDUSTRIAL RELATIONS

Though factory production started in 1850s, trade unions made their appearance at a much later stage—in 1918, after World War I. The first federation of trade unions was founded on October 31, 1920, and was called the All India Trade Union Congress (AITUC). After its formation, the colonial government became more cautious in dealing with labor and attempted to grant some concessions. The government passed the fourth Factories Act in 1922, which reduced the work day to 10 hours, and in 1926, passed the Trade Union

Act, which provided for registration of trade unions. Until the time of independence the divisions in the movement were mainly concerned with their role in the freedom struggle.

After independence, the movement started splitting on ideological, particularly political, lines. Almost all trade unions in the country were linked with political parties. When the political parties split, their trade union fronts were also split, thus fragmenting them further. There are at present seven recognized national trade union federations. A federation gains recognition as a national federation if its constituent units have a collective membership of 500,000 or more, and this membership is spread over at least four states and in four industries. Each of these seven national federations, with the exception of one—Hind Mazdur Sabha (Indian Workers' Council)—is linked with a national political party. Besides, there are several other federations, numbering over a hundred, that operate at the national and regional (state) levels or in specific industries. Multiplicity of trade unions and involvement of political parties in the union are considered the two main weaknesses of the trade union movement in India. Another significant feature of trade unions is that the members of leadership (namely, the important office bearers) are not workers. In most cases, they are wholetime activists of the political party to which the union is aligned. This is an advantage in the sense that the outside leader cannot be victimized by management in the same manner as can an internal leader. At the same time, the disadvantage is that these leaders may not be able to assess the real problems of the workers.

Two major publications by Chaman Revri (1958) and Sukomal Sen (1979) on the growth of trade unions are well researched and can be regarded as important starting points for studies on trade unions. Earlier studies had linked trade unions with the problems of industrialization and industrial relations in independent India. One such endeavor by Oscar Ornati (1955) was a comprehensive study of labor and industrial relations that included an analysis of the framework of industrial relations and wage legislation, among other issues. Three studies on trade unions are regarded as important contributions. These are by V. B. Karnik (1966), who was a trade union leader belonging to the Hind Mazdur Sabba (HMS), V. D. Kennedy (1966), and H. Crouch (1966). The latter two were Fulbright scholars from the United States. All three works, published the same year by the same publisher (which no longer exists), stressed the need for independent trade unions. Independence, in this case, referred to political parties. These studies argued that involvement of political leaders (especially from the Communist Party) were diverting trade unions from their original goals of defending workers' interests. Instead, political leaders manipulated workers to back their political ambitions. These studies provided insights into the working of trade unions, their involvement in politics, and their relations with government.

These studies on trade unions and industrial relations were mainly based on secondary sources or surveys, and were conducted by labor economists. E. A. Ramaswamy's (1977) work on the textile industry in Coimbatore was a pioneering study in sociology. An in-depth analysis on the functioning of trade unions, and based on intensive fieldwork, it explored the relations between the trade union and its members, and contradicted some of the current beliefs on trade unions.

Ramaswamy found that trade union unity cuts across caste loyalties. In times of industrial conflict, workers supported their trade union even in factories, where the majority of the workers belonged to the same caste as their employers. This was different from N. R. Sheth's position, noted earlier; as he found that caste was an important factor in maintaining stability. Another important finding related to trade unions and political parties. Ramaswamy found that the influence of the political party on the trade union was restricted to the general elections, where the supporters of the trade union were expected to vote for their political candidate. Political influence was not felt in the day-to-day functioning of the trade union, especially while tackling work-related issues. The union leaders adopted a pragmatic stance in tackling problems between workers and the management. The political affiliation of the union leader did not influence his decisions. Mark Holmstrom's (1976) study of workers in Bangalore, quoted earlier, though not focused on trade unions, found that workers' loyalties to their union was stronger than their caste ties. Both studies used a social anthropological method of observation for data collection.

Ramaswamy's (1986) contribution to the sociology of work is not restricted to trade unions. He later conducted a study on industrial relations by analyzing two major strikes in Madras and found that the power exercised by the state overrides objectivity in industrial relations. He noted that though the State has tried to protect the interests of labor through a series of legislations, in times of conflict between labor and capital, the State invariably supports capital.

This view is reinforced in the case of the Bombay Textile Strike in 1982–1983. In this strike, over 250,000 textile workers in the metropolis struck work for 18 months, creating the longest strike, involving the largest number of workers. It ended in failure mainly because the State firmly backed the textile mill owners. This strike has been documented by Rajani Bakshi (1987) and H. van Wersch (1992). The former, a journalist, reported extensively on the strike for a Calcutta-based newspaper, and the latter, is a social anthropologist, collected his data through observation, by living among the workers.

One of the major problems of the trade unions is that they are unable, or unwilling, to expand their base to sectors outside the formal sector. For example, within the formal sector, there is an informal sector comprising casual and contract labor that is not covered by the laws granting protection and job security to workers. A study conducted in 1992 (Davala, 1993) found that in eight major industries in the country, the casual and contract laborers outnumbered the permanent workers. Yet, in most cases, these workers were not unionized. In fact, in some cases, the trade unions viewed these workers with suspicion and as potential threats, because management could manipulate them easily and counteract work stoppages through them.

The trade unions affiliated to the national federations do not appear to be interested in unionizing workers in the informal sector. A study by Davala (1995) based on data from secondary sources, showed that workers in the informal sector constituted less than 1% of the total membership of the seven national federations, despite the fact that employment in the informal sector had been growing, while declining in the formal sector due to the strategies adopted by large firms. Most of these firms used the putting-out system to save costs. Instead of manufacturing the entire product in their own factories, these firms preferred to farm out products to the informal sector.

Mark Holmstrom (1986), in a detailed analysis of the links between the two sectors, saw this as a complementary division of labor between the large- and small-scale industries. The small-scale sector finds its market within the large-scale sector. Labor and factory laws are not applicable to the small-scale sector, which reduces costs of production. Labor productivity in the small enterprises is low, but costs are reduced due to the low level of wages. The larger firms are thus able to procure their products cheaply.

Since the 1960s, the growth of heavy industries with higher level of technology created a new section of workers who were in many ways different from workers in the traditional industries such as textiles, jute, plantations, and mines. Their higher levels of skills were acquired through technical institutes, their wages were higher and they did not come from traditional working-class backgrounds. A study of workers in the Bokaro Steel Plant, a large public sector enterprise, showed that the workers were drawn from the rural middle classes (Bhowmik, 1991). These workers were fairly involved in trade union activities at their workplace but showed a totally different attitude toward another section of the working class, namely, agricultural workers. They were opposed to increasing wages or benefits for agricultural workers because they were landholders in their respective villages and required the services of agricultural labor. The trade union leaders also did not try to overcome this barrier.

An interesting case of trade unions not being able to understand the aspirations of these technical workers can be seen in a case study of a strike in Bangalore in 1978 (Subramaniam, 1980). These workers were from the Mico Bosch factory, a multinational company manufacturing spark plugs. Introduction of new technology had increased the pace of work, and the workers demanded that they be given relief. Another grievance of the workers was poor transport from the city to the factory. The trade union declared a strike on these issues. The union insisted that a fatigue allowance be given because the workload had increased. The workers, on the other hand, were well paid and wanted a reduction in the workload, not more allowances as compensation. Similarly, the workers wanted the company to provide their transport from their homes to the factory and back, but the union negotiated for a higher transport allowance. The strike was a failure, and the union leaders could not understand why the workers were not interested in higher allowances.

Similar cases can be found in E. A. Ramaswamy's study of a spinning mill in Coimbatore (Ramaswamy 1994). He studied this unit for two decades and was able to note the changing attitudes of the management, the workers and the unions. In this case, too, the aspirations of the workers, especially during the later stage of the study, when wages had increased substantially, and the actions of the unions were mismatched.

One of the major weaknesses of trade unions is that they have not been able to change their strategies to counter the manipulations of employers (Bhowmik, 1998; Sherlock, 1996). The problem has become more acute since the liberalization program. Traditional means of redress such as strikes and other forms of work stoppage are ineffective. The unions need to develop new methods of intervention, such as demand for industrial democracy, or even, provide support to new types of ownership, such as worker cooperatives and employees' stock options. These aspects have been dealt in detail in two issues of the journal *Seminar* (1995 and 1997).

WORK AND TECHNOLOGY

We have seen in an earlier section that sociologists were preoccupied in the 1950s and 1960s with exploring the relationship between traditional cultural practices and work in the factory. The more recent problems in this context revolve around the role of changing technology and work. The studies on this subject cover different aspects of the consequences of changing technology on work. The more important studies are on worker response to new technology and the impact of technology on women workers. The subject of flexible specialization has also drawn some attention.

The impact of technology on work has been dealt with in case studies presented in a book edited by Amiya Bagchi (1994). Unfortunately, most of the studies in this book take a critical look at different industries using microelectronics in their production process; they do not necessarily deal with the response of the workers. There are a few significant studies in this book. One of them, by Bagaram Tulpule and R. C. Datta, examine the textile industry, where air-jet looms have been introduced. The authors find that as the cost of implementing new technology is relatively higher in this industry, labor cost is lower. Hence, new technology does not really help the management in cutting costs. Another paper by Datta (1999) on the use of new technology in the textile industry shows that management does not make substantive gains in reducing costs through new technology. Efficiency is also not increased substantially. Hence, in some industries, management does not adopt new technology, since it does not necessarily improve quality or increase profits.

Worker response to new technology is discussed in a study by Lakshmi Nadkarni (1998), who has studied a few factories in Pune and interviewed the workers extensively. She finds that workers in general are not opposed to the introduction of new technology, since they know that this is one of the means of improving the products. The workers felt that they should be trained so that they could cope with technological change. These responses are different from those of the trade unions that oppose new technology because it might displace labor. The impact of technological change on locomotive drivers in the railways has been examined by M. S. Kitchlu (1999) in a dissertation that examines the changes in the family life, health, and involvement in trade unions of these workers in a divisional office. He has tried to examine how workers and their families cope with the changed situation.

The issue of flexible specialization was first raised by Mark Holmstrom (1993), who argued that the Italian experience of small industries using microelectronic machinery could be the future for India's industries. He studied the electronics industry in Bangalore (which came to be known as India's Silicone Valley) and found that it has the potential of emerging as the "high road" to flexible specialization. The small industries used computerized numerically controlled (CNC) machines and computer-aided design (CAD) to manufacture high-precision equipment. They employed highly skilled laborers, like those in the large industries. Other studies (Laurisden cited in Bagchi, 1994; Das and Panayiotopoulis, 1996) showed that most small industries used the "low road" of flexible specialization, which comprises low technology and low-skilled, low-paid labor.

The impact of new technology on women workers has been studied by some social scientists. Fernandes (1997) has discussed the problem in the jute industry in Calcutta. Traditional industries such as jute, cotton textiles, and mines had more than 20% women in their workforce until the 1920s. This has been reduced to less than 4% at present. These women occupy the lowest levels of unskilled labor. Several factors are responsible for the decline in employment of women in the formal sector. It can be seen that as wages increase, and job security and social security measures are granted, employment of women decreases. At the same time, employment of women in the informal sector has increased. As mentioned earlier, according to the 1991 census, only one out of seven workers in the formal sector was a woman, whereas in the informal sector, one-third of the workers were women. The studies of Uma Kalpagam (1994) and Nirmala Bannerji (1991) in this field are noteworthy. Yet it is a fact that not much research has been done on women and work in the formal sector; much more needs to be done.

INSTITUTIONAL DEVELOPMENT OF THE DISCIPLINE

There are a number of research institutes that deal with the problems of work. In this section I briefly note the type of work done by some of them and the journals that deal with the subject. At the national level, the V. V. Giri National Labor Institute, run by the Labor Ministry of the Government of India, is the apex institute for labor studies. It has a strong research component and has undertaken significant studies on child labor, women workers, and workers in the informal sector. Anther important institute in Delhi is the Sriram Institute of Human Resource Development, which conducts research on various aspects of industrial relations. It also publishes a journal, the *Indian Journal of Industrial Relations*, that is the only one of its kind in the country. The Centre for Education and Documentation (CED) is a Non-Government Organisation (NGO) that is engaged in research on labor problems. It publishes a monthly journal, *Labour File*, that deals with a specific aspect of labor in each issue. The Department of Personnel Management and Industrial Relations and the Centre for Labour Studies at the Tata Institute of Social Sciences, Mumbai, is also known for its contribution to work and technology.

There are a few regional labor institutes that concentrate on their respective states or regions. Two prominent institutes of this type are the Maharashtra Institute of Labour Studies, Parel, Mumbai, and the Mahatma Gandhi Labour Institute, Ahmedabad. The former has built up a formidable reputation in labor research in western India, while the latter is regarded as the premier institute of its kind in the state of Gujarat. Both institutes are run by their respective state governments.

Some of the national trade union federations have research institutes that have undertaken useful studies. The most prominent is Maniben Kara Institute of Labour Studies. This institute, run by the HMS, has done significant research on wages, port- and dockworkers, railway workers, and workers in the informal sector. The Ambekar Institute of Labour Studies is run by the Rashtriya Mill Mazdur Sangh (National Mill Workers' Organisation), which at present is the representative trade union of the textile industry in Mumbai. It has undertaken research on the textile industry and garment manufacturing units. The contribution of the India office of the Friedrich Ebert Stiftung, Delhi, has been very useful in the promotion of labor studies. This organization has supported several research and training programs for labor. Most of its publications (some of which have been quoted in this chapter) have high academic content but are written in a simple style, so, that is easily understood by trade union activists.

Besides the journals mentioned earlier, two more journals need to be mentioned for their contribution: the *Indian Journal of Labour Economics* and *Economic and Political Weekly*. The former is published by the Indian Society of Labour Economics, and the latter is the most widely read academic journal of social sciences in India. It has a biannual supplement, *Review of Labour*, in which five or more research articles are published, and also publishers research articles and commentaries on labor in its regular issues.

Labor researchers, academics, and practitioners have started their own professional organization known as the Indian Society of Industrial Relations. This organization publishes a bulletin for its members and hosts conferences and seminars on issues relating to managerial and labor problems.

CONCLUDING OBSERVATIONS

As a discipline, industrial sociology, which includes sociology of work, has a lot of potential in India. It is offered either as a compulsory or elective course in nearly all the universities where sociology is taught. Besides, most institutes of management studies, especially those specializing in human resource development and personnel management, include industrial sociology in their curriculum. There are, however, areas that have not been researched adequately. Two major, identifiable areas are work and technology, and work in the services sector, both extremely relevant areas in the present situation of economic liberalization and structural adjustment. The paucity of studies on the impact of changing technology on work and work organization is felt by anyone teaching industrial sociology or sociology of organizations, since one has to rely on studies conducted in the countries of the north, which may not always be ideal for interpreting the situation in India. Hence, there is a need to study the changes taking place in production organizations that have introduced new technology. A number of the conflicts between management and labor are caused due to these changes, which not only affect the nature of work but also social relations outside the realm of work. Studies of these situations could help create smoother adaptation to technological change.

In recent times, the large-scale manufacturing sector has declined as production is carried out in the small-scale sector through a system of outsourcing. Former industrial metropolises such as Mumbai and Calcutta no longer provide jobs in the industrial sector. There is a shift instead to the services sector and to white-collar employment in these cities. India has at present 28 million plus cities and this number will increase in the future. With few exceptions, these cities provide employment largely in the services sector. The problems of this sector has not been adequately studied by sociologists. In fact, studies on work in the services sector could well provide insights into the general problems of urbanization in the country. For example, religious, caste, and ethnic tensions have increased in urban areas. In most cases, certain political, communal, or caste groups cause these conflicts. However, studies on the changes in occupations, nature of work, and working conditions due to a shift from the production sector to the services sector may provide a better understanding of the causes of urban unrest. Sociology of work could thus become a relevant tool for understanding not only the internal structure of organizations but also the rapidly changing social processes in the urban context.

REFERENCES

Bagchi, Amiya K., ed. 1994. *New Technology and the Workers' Response: Microelectronics, Labor and Society,* Delhi: Sage.

Bahal, Vinay. 1995. *The Making of the Indian Working Class: The Case of Tata Iron and Steel Company 1880–1946.* Delhi: Oxford University Press.

Bakshi, Rajani. 1987. *The Long Haul: Bombay Textile Strike*, Mumbai: BUILD Documentation Centre.

Bannerji, Nirmala. 1991. *Women in a Changing Industrial Scenario.* Delhi: Sage.

Bhowmik, Sharit. 1981. *Class Formation in the Plantation System.* Delhi: People's Publishing House.

Bhowmik, Sharit. 1991. "Rural–Urban Links of Industrial Workers: A Study in the Bokaro Steel Plant." Pp. 157–170 in *Rural Urban Nexus*, edited by K. L. Sharma and Dipankar Gupta. Jaipur: Rawat Publications.

Bhowmik, Sharit, V. Xaxa, and M. Kalam. 1996. *Tea Plantation Labor in India.* Delhi: Friedrich Ebert Stiftung.

Bhowmik, Sharit. 1998. "The Labour Movement in India: Present Problems and Future Prospects." *Indian Journal of Social Work* 59(1):147–156.

Chakravarty, Dipesh. 1989. *Rethinking Working Class History: Bengal 1890–1940.* Delhi: Oxford University Press.

Chandavarkar, Rajnarain. 1994. *The Origins of Industrial Capitalism in India: Business Strategies and the Working Class in Bombay 1900–1940.* Cambridge: Cambridge University Press.

Chatterji, R. H. 1980. *Unions, Politics the State in India.* Delhi: South Asian Publishers.

Crouch, Harold. 1966. *Trade Unions and Politics in India.* Bombay: Manaktalas.

Das, Subesh K., and P. Panayiotopoulis. 1996. "Flexible Specialisation: New Paradim for Industrialisation for Developing Countries?" *Economic and Political Weekly (Review of Labour)* 31(52):L57–L61.

Dasgupta, Ranajit. 1994. *Labor and Working Class in Eastern India: Studies in Colonial History.* Calcutta: K. P. Bagchi and Company.

Datt, Rudder, ed. 1997. *Organising the Unorganised Labor*. Delhi: Vikas Publishing House.

Datta, R. C. 1999. "New Technology and Textile Workers." *Economic and Political Weekly* (*Review of Labour*) 34(39):L41–L44.

Davala, Sarath, ed. 1993. *Employment and Unionisation in Indian Industry*. Delhi: Friedrich Ebert Stiftung.

Devala, Sarath, ed. 1995. *Unprotected Labour in India*. Delhi: Friedrich Ebert Stiftung.

Fernandes, Leela. 1997. *Producing Workers: The Politics of Gender, Class and Culture in the Calcutta Jute Mills*. Philadelphia: University of Pennsylvania Press.

Gadgil, D. R. 1982. *Industrial Evolution of India in Recent Times, 1860–1939* (new edition). Delhi: Oxford University Press.

Holmstrom, Mark. 1976. *South Indian Factory Workers: Their Life and Their Work*. Cambridge: Cambridge University Press and Delhi: Allied Publishers (1978).

Holmstrom, Mark. 1986. *Industry and Inequality: The Social Anthropology of Indian Labour*. Cambridge: Cambridge University Press.

Holmstrom, Mark. 1993. "Flexible Specialisation in India?" *Economic and Political Weekly* 29(31).

Kalpagam, Uma. 1994. *Gender and Labour*. Delhi: Sage Publications.

Karnik, V. B. 1966. *Indian Trade Unions: A Survey*. Bombay: Manaktalas.

Kerr, Clarke, C. A. Mayers, and J. Dunlop. 1960. *Industrialism and Industrial Man*. Harmondsworth: Penguin.

Kitchlu, M. S. 1999. *Sociological Study of Railway Workers in a Town in South India*. Unpublished Ph.D. dissertation, Jawaharlal Nehru Library, University of Mumbai, Mumbai, India.

Lambert, Richard D. 1963. *Workers, Factories and Social Change in India*. Princeton, NJ: Princeton University Press and Bombay: Asia Publishing House.

Mayers, C. A. 1958. *Labor Problems in the Industrialization of India*. Cambridge: Cambridge University Press.

Moore, W. E., and A. S. Feldman, eds. 1960. *Labor Commitment and Social Change in Developing Areas*. New York: Social Science Research Center.

Morris, Morris D. 1965. *The Emergence of an Industrial Labor Force in India: A Study of the Bombay Cotton Mills, 1854–1947*. Berkeley: University of California Press and Bombay: Oxford University Press.

Mukherjee, R. K. 1945, *The Indian Working Class*, Bombay: Popular Prakashan.

Nadkarni, Lakshmi. 1998. *Sociology of Industrial Worker* (sic). Jaipur: Rawat Publications.

Nair, Janaki. 1998. *Miners and Millhands: Work, Culture and Politics in Princely Mysore*. Delhi: Sage.

Ramaswamy, E. A. 1977. *The Worker and His Union*. Delhi: Allied Publishers.

Ramaswamy, E. A. 1986. *Power and Justice*. Delhi: Oxford University Press.

Ramaswamy, E. A. 1987. *Worker Consciousness and Trade Union Response*. Delhi: Oxford University Press.

Ramaswamy, E. A. 1994. *The Rayon Spinners: Strategic Management of Industrial Relations*. Delhi: Oxford University Press.

Ramaswamy, E. A. 2000. *Managing Human Resources*. Delhi: Oxford University Press.

Revri, Chaman. 1958. *Trade Union Movement in India*. Hyderabad: Orient Longman.

Seminar. 1995. "Globalisation and the Unions," Vol. 429.

Seminar. 1997. "Workers and Unions," Vol. 452.

Sen, Samita, and Arjan de Haan, eds. 1999. *A Case for Labor History: The Jute Industry in Eastern India.* Calcutta; K. P. Bagchi and Company.

Sen, Sukomal. 1979. *Trade Union Movement in India.* Calcutta: K. P. Bagchi and Company.

Sharma, B. R. 1971. *Indian Industrial Worker: Issues in Perspective.* Delhi: Vikas.

Sherlock, Stephen. 1996. "Class Reformation in Mumbai: Has Organised Labour Risen to the Challenge?" *Economic and Political Weekly* (*Review of Labour*) 31(52):L31–L38.

Sheth, N. R. 1958. *The Social Framework of an Indian Factory.* Manchester, UK: Manchester University Press and Delhi: Hindustan (1984).

Simeon, Dilip. 1995. *The Politics of Labor under late Colonialism: Unions and the State in Chota Nagpur.* Delhi: Manohar.

Subramaniam, Dilip. 1980. "The Mico Strike." *Economic and Political Weekly* (*Review of Management*) 15(22):M59–M68.

van Wersh, H. 1992. *The Bombay Textile Strike 1982–83.* Mumbai: Oxford University Press.

Venkata Ratnam C. S., ed. 1997. *Challenge of Change: Industrial Relations in Indian Industry.* Delhi: Allied Publishers.

Venkata Ratnam, C. S., G. Botterweck, and Pravin Sinha, eds. 1994. *Labour and Unions in a Period of Transition.* Delhi: Friedrich Ebert Stiftung.

APPENDIX: CONTACTS

List of Major Institutes

V. V. Giri National Labour Institute
P.O. Box 68, Sector 24
Gautam Buddha Magau, U.P., 201301
Contact person: The Director.
Phone: 91-118-91-4535168
Fax: 91-118-91-4532978.
E-mail: vvgnl@vsnl.com

Sriram Institute of Industrial Relations and Human Resources Development
4 Safdar Hashmi Marg
New Delhi 110001
Contact person: Mr. J. S. Sodhi, Executive Director.
Phone: 91-11-3352410
Fax: 91-11-3351953.

Centre for Education and Communication
173 A Khirki Village
Malaviya Nagar, New Delhi 110017

Contact person: Mr. J. John, Director.
Phone: 91-11-6232755.
Fax: 91-11-6286842.
E-mail: edit@labourfile.org
Website: www.labourfile.org

Indian Society of Labour Economics
c/o IIAMR Building
Mahatma Gandhi Road, I. P. Estate
New Delhi 110002
Contact person: Dr. Alakh Sharma
Phone: 91-11-3358166
Fax: 91-11-3319909
E-mail: ihdisid@del3.vsnl.net.in

Indian Industrial Relations Association
c/o International Management Institute
B 30/31 Qutab Institutional Area
New Delhi 110016
Contact person: Dr. C. S. Venkata Ratnam.
Phone: 91-11-6863701
Fax: 91-11-6867539
E-mail: imi@gisd1o1.vsnl.net.in

Friedrich Ebert Stiftung
K-70B Hauz Khas Enclave
New Delhi 110 016
Contact person: Dr. Pravin Sinha
Phone: 91-11-6561361
Fax: 91-11-6564691
E-mail: pravinsinha@fesindia.org

Participatory Development Unit
B5 Oberoi Apartments
2 Sham Nath Marg
Delhi 110 054
Contact person: Ms. Pritikusum, Executive Secretary.
Phone: 91-11-3957732
E-mail: pdu@mantraonline.com

Maharashtra Institute of Labour Studies
Dada Chamarbaughwala Road
Parel, Mumbai 400 012, Maharashtra.
Contact person: Dr. S. T. Sawant, Director
Phone: 91-22-4135332, 4133798
Fax: 91-22-4133085
E-mail: mils@bom3.vsnl.net.in

Mahatma Gandhi Labour Institute
Thaltej, Drive-in Road
Ahmedabad 380052, Gujarat
Contact person: Director General
Phone: 91-79-443890

Maniben Kara Institute of Labour Studies, Shram Sadhana
57 D. V. Pradhan Road, Hindu Colony, Dadar (East)
Mumbai 400 014 Maharashtra
Contact Person: Mr. Vasant Gupte, Director
Phone: 91-22-4144336
Fax: 91-22-4102759
E-mail: mki@vsnl.com

Ambekar Institute of Labour Studies
Mazdoor Manzil, G. D. Ambekar Marg
Bhoiwada, Mumbai 400 012, Maharashtra
Contact person: Mr. G. B. Gowde, Chief Administrator.
Phone: 91-22-4146861
Fax: 91-22.4151664
E-mail: assa@bom3.vsnl.net.in

Department of Personnel Management and Industrial Relations
Tata Institute of Social Sciences
Deonar, Soin Trombay Road
Mumbai 400 080, Maharashtra
Contact Person: Dr. R. C. Datta, Head of the Department.
Phone: 91-22-5563290
E-mail: rcd@tiss.edu

Journals

Indian Journal of Industrial Relations
Indian Journal of Labour Economics
Economic and Political Weekly
E-mail: epw@vsnl.com
Website: www.epw.org.in

Labour File
Website: labourfile.org

8

Korea

Ho-Keun Song and Doowon Suh

The sociology of work in South Korea (henceforth, Korea) attracts broad attention from the sociological community for its extensive research topics and theoretical implications. Merely a small subfield of sociology decades ago, it soon became the most attractive field of study as Korea's industrialization deepened and the importance of work grew in a rapidly changing society.[1] The sociology of work currently occupies a central place not only in sociological research and debate but also in the practical discourse of policymaking. Of about six hundred Korean sociologists, 60% of whom are university professors, approximately one hundred are working in this field, either directly or indirectly. The field brings together diverse research topics, traditional and modern, embracing industrial sociology, and the sociology of occupation/stratification, development and social change, labor markets, and industrial relations.

Prior to the collapse of long-standing authoritarian rule in 1987, the nature and meaning of work was hotly contested. Social scientists, including

---

[1]The first sociology department was established at Seoul National University in 1946, one year after liberation from Japan.

Ho-Kuen Song • Department of Sociology, Seoul National University, Seoul, South Korea 151-742. **Doowon Suh** • Graduate School of International Studies, Korea University, Seoul, South Korea.

Worlds of Work: Building an International Sociology of Work, edited by Daniel B. Cornfield and Randy Hodson. Kluwer Academic/Plenum Publishers, New York, 2002.

sociologists, looked to democracy for many decades in their attempts to solve the labor problems bequeathed by authoritarian repression. Even research in traditional fields, such as industrial sociology and the sociology of occupations, frequently featured practical and challenging arguments to authoritarian rules and practices regulating work and employment. However, the terms *work* and *worker*, once ideological weapons of social scientists in their struggle against authoritarianism, have assumed a more balanced and neutral meaning under incipient democratization.

Main research themes and paradigms have clearly differed by decade. Although work was a central topic in the sociology of stratification/occupations and industrial sociology, and sporadically touched upon in other subfields in the 1960s and 1970s, only one department offered a course under the title of the Sociology of Work. That offering derived from discussion of the classic *Homo Faber*, but did not scrutinize the empirical world of work and workers. Not until the mid-1980s did most sociology departments provide courses on work as an independent subfield under the title Sociology of Work or Work and Organization.

In their efforts over the last several decades to explain Third-World underdevelopment, scholars have adjusted and transformed imported paradigms. The *modernization paradigm*, dominant in the 1970s, waned as the authoritarian regime delegitimized its optimistic premise in the early 1980s. The "revolutionary era" in Korean sociology of the 1980s represented an attempt to explore a new perspective—the *revolutionary paradigm*—far different from mainstream sociology *à la* America, but it also retreated when socialist visions were dashed. Research interest finally diversified under the *democratization paradigm* of the 1990s.

This chapter examines the evolution of the sociology of work in Korea, reviewing research themes, methods, and achievements of the1960s through the 1990s, according to the transition from the modernization to the revolutionary, and to the democratization paradigm. Since the sociology of work is practical and applied in nature, economic and political backgrounds are stressed to explain the rise and fall of each research approach. A brief review of institutional contexts helps illuminate the basis of main research currents, ideological orientations, conflict and cooperation among diverse research institutes and scholar groups, and outlets for publications.

WORKER MOBILIZATION AND LABOR PROBLEMS OF THE 1960S AND 1970S

It is well known that the military government of 1961 triggered the "industrial revolution" in Korea. It impelled high-speed growth over nearly three decades, attracting worldwide attention to Korea's "economic miracle." Rapid social change and fundamental transformation proceeded until the end of the 1970s, when the Yushin regime had laid the foundation for heavy-chemical industrialization. Demographics, for example, changed dramatically. More than 60% of the economically active population in the early 1960s worked in agriculture or fishery, while industry employed less than 20%. By the mid-1970s, workers in mining and manufacturing were the most numerous. From the outset, this reversal drew workers from rural areas, and labor problems became apparent as industrialization deepened in the 1970s.

Worker mobility and rights became main areas of research interest. Demographers investigated the causes and trajectories of urban migration, while sociologists examined characteristics and working conditions of available jobs. Initially, most research, however, was heavily influenced by the modernization paradigm. This research evaluated how successfully rural migrants could adapt to their new industrial environment. Following Inkeles's (1983) neo-classical definition of modernity, many sociologists attempted to measure their values, attitudes, and human capital in order to discern requisites to improve their adaptability (H. Im, 1986; K. Kim, 1992). They asked: How can enough jobs for migrants be created? How can they be trained for modern factories? How can they escape from poverty despite low wages? Although these questions did not exactly constitute a sociology of work, they laid a foundation for later, more substantive research on working conditions and labor practice. It must be recalled, after all, that only about 30 sociologists held Ph.D.'s in the 1960s.

At the end of the 1960s and the early 1970s, sociologists turned to workers' rights when the state became relentlessly authoritarian. The state amended labor laws in ways that empowered employers in managing workers and curtailed workers' ability to demand better pay and treatment. Miners mounted violent strikes in opposition to the government edict to end coal consumption, and garment workers exploded in downtown Seoul street rallies in rebellion against employers' brutality. The self-immolation of a garment worker in the Peace Market in Seoul, in 1970, precipitated public concern for working conditions and worker rights. [2] Accordingly, repressive state control and unprotected workers' rights became central in the sociology of work in the second phase of industrialization. Major researches repeatedly concluded that repressive state policy was the most decisive factor in the proletarianization of industrial workers and their miserable workplace conditions, contradicting government political propaganda that economic growth heralded improved living standards and the end of poverty.

---

[2]Chŏn T'ae-il's story was published in a book in 1983 and finally made a movie in the mid-1990s.

Labor problems regarding exploitation and unfair labor practice mushroomed with the deepening of heavy-chemical industrialization. Income inequality between "good" and "bad" jobs widened. Most production workers in export manufacturing endured long working hours, low wages, and cruel treatment. However, the authoritarian regime quelled public debate on these issues, as a challenge to its legitimacy. Most social scientists eschewed research on these issues because of strict and ubiquitous government surveillance. Nevertheless, some took the risk and studied, for instance, the impact of state economic policy on the occupational division of labor (K. Kim, 1992), state labor control (Ch'oe, 1988), wage policy, and labor supply (Pae, 1980). Some scholars observed labor practices and the division of labor inside the sweatshops in and around metropolitan Seoul, concluding that they were nothing but labor camps without legal and institutional protection (T. Yi, 1982).

Research methods at that time, constrained by a lack of analytical techniques and a shortage of research funds, were far from advanced. A questionnaire survey method was introduced in the latter half of the 1970s, but the required official police permission for its use in industrial districts[3] drove some scholars to risk participant observation to assess working conditions and industrial workers' consciousness.[4] Ready statistics, available primarily only from the government, were profoundly distorted in the areas of labor and industry.[5] Researchers therefore employed more qualitative than quantitative methods to analyze working conditions and consciousness, utilizing workers' diaries, manuscripts, strike pamphlets, household books, interviews, and so forth. Though characteristically unsystematic, these studies raised questions and agendas indisputably fundamental to subsequent research. Although scholars of this period agreed that the progress of modernity could resolve labor problems, it was not long before that consensus wavered.

THE WORKER AS A REVOLUTIONARY WEAPON IN THE 1980S

The brief hope of democracy raised among civilians and intellectuals by the collapse of the Yushin regime in 1979 evaporated with the inauguration of a still stronger military regime in 1980. Frustration culminated in the May 1980 Kwangju Massacre. Political unrest continued but met violent and coercive government reprisal that, according to some estimates, killed or fatally

---

[3]Over one hundred small and large industrial parks were established in the 1970s nationwide. Survey of industrial parks was not banned, but procedures to obtain permission were tricky.
[4]Police and intelligence agencies dispatched officers to supervise important industrial districts.
[5]Korea can currently boast of accurate and extensive official statistics. The National Statistical Office annually publishes diverse statistics, such as *Social Indicators in Korea.*

wounded over five hundred civilians. Despite underlying political turmoil, the Korean economy advanced without interruption. No sign of economic downturn appeared except one short-lived recession in the early 1980s. Massive, well-planned investment in heavy-chemical industries facilitated a technology-intensive phase of industrialization and raised Korea into the company of middle-income countries. The ranks of white-collar workers and managers with higher education and high occupational aspirations swelled.

Market competition for better jobs and pay greatly intensified. The rise of conglomerate capital—the Korean *chaebŏl* that is analogous to the Japanese *zaibatsu*—that virtually ran all kinds of businesses by patrimonial family ownership under unconditional government subsidy, subjected most white-collar employees to a set of job regulations particular to their firm. Internal labor markets (henceforth, ILMs) developed along the collar line and industrial gradation. While differences between white- and blue-collar workers reflected social status distinctions, labor market segmentation by industry was the outcome of a state strategy that pursued the economy of scale. Workers in subcontracting firms clearly differed from employees in *chaebŏl* firms in terms of working conditions, job security, and socioeconomic reward. Although ILMs were not completely consolidated in the early 1980s, workers, especially those in subcontracting and large exporting firms, were extremely discontent with growing inequality and deterioration of working conditions. A few researchers warned that widening socioeconomic gaps within factories would breed class antagonisms conducive to political class confrontation (S. Kim, 1985). This warning was realized in severe political turmoil and labor insurgency in 1987, when authoritarianism collapsed and industrial workers rebelled against both the state and the bourgeoisie.

The 1980s hosted antagonisms on multiple fronts. The more the economy flourished, the greater the confrontation between civil society and the authoritarian state, workers and capitalists, and blue- and white-collar workers, as well as *chaebŏls* and small-to-medium-sized firms. In a state-led industrializing society such as Korea, social scientists tended to attribute growing socioeconomic inequality and political instability to the authoritarian state, often considered a common enemy by all persons with grievances or pessimistic evaluations. This popular antipathy to hardcore authoritarianism brought the revolutionary paradigm to the fore in the social sciences. The sociology of work played a leading role in cultivating radical approaches and debunking the optimistic premise of modernization theories. Consequently, the 1980s were the heyday of Marxist theories that enshrined workers as a revolutionary weapon.

Analytic focus shifted from how successfully and steadily Korea mimicked advanced industrial societies of the West to how Korea differed in terms of the trajectory of capitalist development and its impacts on working conditions and worker consciousness. The concept of "work and workers" easily blended with the practical implications of dependency theory and a Marxist view of Third-World revolution (Amin, 1976; Cardoso and Faletto, 1979; Frank, 1967). Most sociologists were involved, directly and indirectly, in debate on "social formation," exploring the peculiarities of Korean capitalist development and possibilities of breaking the pauperizing grip of dependent development on the working class (see Pak and Cho, 1989a, 1989b, 1991). Theories claimed work was the locus of analysis to illuminate the consequences of unequal exchange and the penetration of foreign capital into domestic markets, and cast the working class as a revolutionary army to destroy the core–periphery nexus. The sociology of work developed key arguments and theoretical concepts pertinent to this agenda and disseminated them to other subfields of sociology.

Sociologists, especially of the younger generation, drew on their bitter experience of incessant political strike in the early 1980s to publish papers in public journals of social criticism. They highlighted the exploitive nature of capitalist underdevelopment and promoted worker resistance. However, this became an ideological bias that significantly limited research scopes and agendas. Frequent themes in major research were, for instance, labor process and labor market under monopoly capital (S. Pak, 1988; K. Yi, 1983); worker exploitation both in large firms and subcontractors (Pak, 1985; Cho, 1984); state wage policy (Ch'oe, 1988); and working-class formation and worker consciousness in dependent development (Kim and Im, 1987). Theories with radical implications—theories about, for instance, de-skilling (Braverman, 1974), a dual labor market (Doeringer and Piore, 1971), labor market segmentation and bureaucratic control (Edwards, 1979), and the politics of production (Burawoy, 1985)—were put forward to explain deterioration of working conditions and repressive labor practices. The "urban poor" was an important topic for sociologists of work, for it reflected the marginalization of the lower classes in dependent development—useful evidence for the Marxist's reserve army thesis (H. Cho, 1985; Hŏ, 1991).

Studies of industrial relations and labor movements also proliferated because of their democratic implications and practical utility. Progressive research mostly concerned how economically oppressed and inhumanely treated industrial workers could become insurgents against authoritarianism and dependence. Political resistance invoked class antagonism and solidarity among opposition groups. However, as some researchers asserted, enterprise unionism in Korea hindered the formation of working-class consciousness (Y. Im, 1985). Industrial unionism was thus pursued as a precondition for promoting workers' common interests and solidarity across firm and enterprise boundaries. Some ascribed the weakness of labor opposition to state corporatism, since it deprived the working class of collective political leverage by legal and institutional control and ideological indoctrination (Ch'oe, 1988). It successfully enforced political exclusion of workers in exchange for their economic inclusion, relying on corporatist theory's assumption that workers were less tolerant of poverty than oppression. Korea's employment system was characterized as authoritarian paternalism for its repressive, violent, and discretionary practices. Numerous studies focused on revealing the brutality of production workers' supervision, their meager wages, and their exclusion from company welfare benefits (U. Cho, 1985).

Despite such apparent single-mindedness, the widely accepted critique that research from the revolutionary paradigm lacked empirical evidence and was mostly speculative and ideological underestimates actual achievements. Clearly, research suffered serious shortcomings in empirical and theoretical validity. But it is unfair to forget the efforts to explore historical data and to derive concrete evidence and impartial interpretation through questionnaire surveys. Such surveys were widely employed by sociologists of work when they attempted to understand working conditions and worker consciousness inside and outside factories. Private and public research institutes, including universities, conducted various social surveys and created valuable data sets; however, public access to them was entirely blocked, which often threw their data analysis into doubt.

Worker manuscripts, union files and newspapers, and other material collected by college students temporarily employed at factories, with their academic agenda disguised, were also used in analysis. Not uncommonly, student activists sympathetic with labor movements observed various aspects of labor relations and working conditions, and conveyed them to academia to encourage linkage and cooperation between students and organized labor.[6] In the absence of large and prestigious research centers on work and labor movements, these materials and reports were never centrally gathered or organized but scattered to individual researchers.

The heyday of Marxism in Korea's social sciences did not establish a revolution but contributed to worker insurrection in 1987. Contrary to the revolutionary paradigm's aspirations, insurgents won the peaceful retreat of hardcore authoritarianism through a new regime, which offered democracy through reform rather than rupture. The revolutionary paradigm lost its attraction and theoretical adequacy as democratization proceeded, easing political repression and expanding worker rights. The common enemy, that is, the state, had been transformed to support worker demands.

---

[6]Reportedly, approximately one thousand student activists participated in a worker action in and around metropolitan Seoul in the labor disputes of 1987.

DEMOCRATIZATION AND DIVERSIFIED INTERESTS OF THE 1990S

Since the late 1980s, Korea has experienced significant social change. The June 1987 Democratic Struggle toppled the authoritarian regime in place since liberation from the Japanese colonialism in 1945. Democratization unfolded, reinforced by the sudden demise of socialism in the West. Events had finally come to a head in the spring of 1987, when Catholic priests divulged that the government had concealed the police's fatal torture of a university student activist in a previous year. People were outraged and numerous antigovernment civilian organizations formed and aligned to oppose state despotism in an unprecedented challenge to the authoritarian regime's legitimacy. The dam burst in a radical and popular revolt on June 10, when President Chun Doo Hwan appointed Roh Tae Woo as the ruling party's presidential candidate.[7] The uprising swiftly expanded nationwide and anarchy ensued, driven by millions of civilians day and night, until Roh acceded on June 29 to the demand to resume direct presidential election.

Shortly after this concession, nonetheless, worker discontent exploded in massive and violent insurrection, rapidly expanding blue- and white-collar organized workers' bases. Labor law before 1987 strictly limited each union to activities within its particular firm. The government and capitalists regarded labor movements as a menace to political stability and economic development. However, the state was forced to relax its repressive control to placate the 1.3 million workers who mounted massive, violent labor disputes. Widely expanded political opportunity structures precipitated new unionization and increased union membership strikingly in 1988 and 1989. Union density increased to 23.3% in 1989, unprecedented in the history of labor movements in Korea. The number of trade unions and union members almost doubled and tripled, respectively, between 1986 and 1989. Militant labor movements and nationwide, rapid unionization notably improved organized workers' socioeconomic welfare. During 1988 and 1989, for instance, nominal wage increase rates were 15.5% and 21.1%, respectively, and real wages rose by 7.8% and by 14.5% (Han'guk, 1997).

The role of labor movements in democratization still awaits systematic scholarly analysis, but two positive effects are evident. First, labor activism enhanced economic justice by narrowing wage gaps between workers and higher-paid groups. For instance, administrative and managerial workers were paid 190% more than production workers in 1987, a superiority reduced to 141% in 1990 (Han'guk, 1997). Second, new insurgent labor movements in-

---

[7]He was Chun's lifelong friend, comrade in the military and the Kwangju Massacre in 1980, and fellow top-ranking officer in the Chun administration, who, despite the revolt, was elected president in December 1987.

creased labor's political autonomy. The authoritarian government had pursued a divide-and-conquer strategy to regulate labor movements. Union leaders at the national center—the Federation of Korean Trade Unions (FKTU)—were co-opted by the government's corporatist control, while grassroots activities were brutally repressed, without protection or support from their umbrella organization (Ch'oe, 1988). In opposition to the FKTU's passive and progovernmental stance, progressive groups of organized labor formed an alternative national center—the Korean Confederation of Trade Unions (Minnochong)—in 1995, embracing both blue- and white-collar unions to ensure labor autonomy and to foster the unity and coalition.

Incipient democratization and ensuing labor activism diversified scholarly interest into various topics concerning wages, company welfare, job security, productivity, and employment systems. Analysis of labor relations transferred in focus from state labor control to tripartite negotiations between government, capital, and organized labor. Foreign-educated Ph.D.'s, mostly young and liberal, returned to Korea to introduce advanced methodologies into sociology of work. Enhanced political freedom and enriched research produced enormous strides in the sociology of work, expanding research agendas to worker mobility, industrial relations, union activities, and labor market segmentation and its consequences on worker solidarity and inequality. Publications multiplied and contending views proliferated.

First, concerning labor relations, scholars' assessment of the Roh administration's (1987–1992) new labor regime varied. One view construed relaxation of repressive control as a harbinger of democratic industrial relations; already, new labor laws provided state welfare to workers and encouraged employers to provide large wage increases (No, 1995). In contrast, detractors charged that labor relations remained unchanged, mainly because the 1987 amendment of labor laws was partial, and, above all, ruling groups' antilabor ideology continued. The amendments could not actualize democratic labor relations: Prohibition of third-party intervention in locals' disputes and of unions' political participation remained intact; public officials and teachers still had no right to organize; new industrial federations were not recognized by the government (Chun Kim, 1989).[8]

Second, researchers' views varied regarding the characterization of firms' internal labor markets (FILMs). In the transition to democracy, employers had to devise managerial strategies to cope with worker demand for higher wages and welfare benefits in the midst of increasing competition in the world market. Working conditions and wages diverged by industry and firm size, dividing labor markets in multiple ways. FILMs emerged, especially in conglomer-

---

[8]Most federations of white-collar unions were approved by the government when the first civilian Kim Young Sam administration assumed political power in 1993.

ate enterprises. Researchers began to examine institutional rules and principles regulating ILMs or FILMs through participants observation and questionnaire surveys. One perspective argued that FILMs increased worker competition inside firms and thus decreased solidarity (Nam, 1990). Another contended that they increased heterogeneity of labor forces across firms but enhanced homogeneity within in terms of wages, job security, and promotion opportunity (I-hwan Chŏng, 1992). In any event, FILMs supported a divide-and-conquer managerial strategy in Korea, which Edwards (1979) identified as an essential goal of bureaucratic control (C. Pak, 1992).

Third, sociologists considered the many significant changes in the employment system. Employees in large firms enjoyed longer-term employment than those in small- and medium-size firms. Such security tended to grow as a union developed power to negotiate. However, the advantage of size in terms of job security diminished when a "flexibility" strategy was introduced into production, remuneration, and promotion at large and competitive firms, in order to cope with prolonged economic recession despite strong union opposition. Sociologists found that temporary and daily workers increased dramatically in number in most large firms and the proportion of workers concerned about job security grew, as many case studies of automobile and electronics factories revealed (Hyŏng-je Cho, 1993).

Fourth, factory and office automation altered job characteristics, occupational structures, and job performance evaluation, bringing sociologists to reexamine such traditional themes as de-skilling/up-skilling of work, embourgeoisiement/proletarianization of the working class, upward/downward mobility, job satisfaction/alienation, and homogenization/diversification of the work force (Chae-hun Kim, 1996; Kim and Sim, 1995; H. Pak, 1991; Chin-yŏng Kim, 1994). Unlike mass production facilities, automated factories drove employers to devise labor controls that intensified worker competition. Debate occurred as to whether new production systems for higher productivity—for instance, "just-in-time" technology—improved job autonomy and satisfaction. Some argued that such systems significantly increased productivity and profits but decreased working conditions, the will to work, and job satisfaction (Cho and Yi, 1989; C. Pak, 1992).

A fifth area of new interest to sociologists concerned labor market fragmentation, a critical issue in economic inequality and work solidarity. According to some, the rapid technological progress and consolidation of FILMs increased heterogeneity of the workforce within firms and jobs (Nam, 1990). Moreover, growth of union activism induced labor market segmentation by expanding wage differentials between organized and unorganized sectors when state intervention in industrial relations diminished. A trade union has two functions: "monopoly" and "collective voice" (Freeman and Medoff, 1984). Although the collective-voice function did not disappear, the monopoly function became gradually more conspicuous among organized firms in heavy-chemical industries. Some unions were publicly criticized for their excessive demands for wage increases and welfare benefits. Inquiry into union wage premiums found that the unionized sector enjoyed a 10% advantage, lower than in the United States or Japan but apparently a factor in labor market segmentation and income inequality (In-su Chŏng, 1991; Pae, 1991; Pak and Pak, 1989; Song, 1991, 1994). Wide consensus held that the working-class labor market showed little fragmentation prior to 1987 under strong state control of institutional factors, including unions' relative wage effects (Hwang, 1985; H. Kim, 1988). Such a unified market structure of manual workers enhanced solidarity in the struggle against repressive state control. As repression retreated in the process of liberalization and democratization, diverse economic and institutional factors influenced workers' socioeconomic well-being. Worker solidarity declined and income inequality grew as the labor market increasingly segmented (Song, 1991).

Sixth, when labor law amendments in 1987 lifted the legal restriction of union structure to enterprise unionism, many expected that trade unionism would easily end the labor segmentation ensured by enterprise unionism and transform into industrial unionism to enhance labor collectivity. Most sectors, however, showed minimal progress. Scholars showed that removal of the legal enforcement of enterprise unionism did not eliminate the firm grip of enterprise union consciousness on union members: They still eschewed coalition movements and lacked class consciousness that reached beyond firm boundaries (T. Kim, 1995). A class alliance between blue- and white-collar unions rarely developed under highly segmented and competitive labor markets. This failure was attributed to the absence of party–union linkages, the lack of voluntary and participatory union experience, and most importantly, manipulative government tactics to reproduce regional cleavages in union movements (Ch'oe, 1993). Also, while withdrawal of direct government interference in industrial relations in the late 1980s provided autonomous realms for collective bargaining with employers, it simultaneously deprived independent enterprise unions of a common movement agenda—antigovernmental political struggle—that might foster coalition among them. Some unions were content with enterprisewide collective bargaining, because it won them increased material benefits through enhanced bargaining power, and saw no need to overcome labor segmentation. However, incipient interunion cooperation occurred among selected industrial sectors. It became the focus of some research to understand the inner mechanisms by which union members affiliated with different enterprise unions could develop a strong sense of interunion solidarity through coalition movements, precipitating transformation from the isolation of enterprise unionism into one, consolidated industrial union (Suh, 1998).

Finally, among the many issues the insurgency of democratic trade union-ism raised for research on work, heated scholarly debate centered on the main reason for the decline in union density and degeneration of labor movements that was apparent after 1990. There is no doubt that democratization loos-ened government labor control. Yet this did not proceed invariably. Between 1987 and 1989, the government abstained from direct intervention in indus-trial relations, but the intensified and radicalized labor militancy of that pe-riod brought renewed harsh repression in 1990. With that, union density gradu-ally declined and labor insurgency moderated. Density peaked in 1989 at 23.3% but plummeted to 15.3% by 1995 (Han'guk, 1997). In January of 1990, re-sumption of government crackdowns coincided with formation of the Korea Trade Union Congress (KTUC), predecessor of the Minnochong, established in 1995 to compete with the FKTU. Some scholars imputed decreasing union density and sinking union activism to the KTUC's "maximalist" principles advocating the logic of "revolutionary mass organization" (Ch'oe, 1993): Im-prudent radical strategies unnecessarily provoked fierce government reprisal, precipitating union movements' deterioration and hampering democratiza-tion. Others hypothesized that working-class militancy attenuated due to con-glomerate capital's sophisticated reformist strategies: Concessions sufficient to satisfy union members' basic needs and ensure their relative economic ad-vantage over unorganized workers mollified collective defiance (Chun Kim, 1989; Pak, 1989; Ch'a, 1989).

In addition to these new and renewed areas of research, with the 1990s came changes in methodologies and agents of research. Due to wide circula-tion of personal computers and development of statistical methods, the soci-ology of work in the 1990s leaned more toward quantitative than qualitative analysis. Advanced analytical methods, such as network analysis, the struc-tural hierarchical model, and event history, were vigorously employed to high-light the interconnection of firms, job trajectory, and market structure. These techniques illuminated hidden aspects of market transaction and interaction, depicting labor and product markets visually in diagrams and graphs (Yi, Song, and Kwŏn, 1995). Network analysis was also applied to the previously unex-plored theme of interunion relations and associational structures between civil and labor movements in terms of information exchange and affiliation (Kim and Song, 1997).

It is notable that many research institutes, private and public, formed in this period, conducting diverse studies and creating rich survey data. For in-stance, the Korean Credit Evaluation Company collected a valuable data set of financial and organizational information on firms in the stock market. When the data set is combined with labor market survey data such as the *Occupa-tional Wage Survey*, conducted annually by the Ministry of Labor, an invalu-able resource emerges, embracing firms' organizational and human capital variables. In addition to questionnaire surveys, sociologists of the 1990s conducted in-depth interviews and participant observation to capture, for instance, internal dynamics of firms and unions, and worker consciousness concerning politics and society. The government and large enterprises occasionally assigned large-scale projects to sociologists of work to assay industrial workers' opinions regarding Korean society in general and the government's social reform and employers' managerial innovation in particular.

THE INTERNATIONAL MONETARY FUND CRISIS AND PROSPECTS FOR FUTURE RESEARCH

The devastating impact in Korea of the recent foreign debt crisis on product and labor markets begs thorough sociological analysis. This unprecedented financial and economic debacle hit in December 1997, when the government officially requested bailout financing from the International Monetary Fund (IMF) when its holdings of foreign currency were virtually drained. The main debtor was not the government but the private sector, including banks, investment firms, and conglomerates. The IMF tied bailout funding to austere state restructuring of the national economy. Among the many fundamental consequences was skyrocketing mass unemployment, a radical reversal of Korea's experience during the high-speed growth era. Almost one million jobs vanished within 3 months after the bailout. The unemployment typhoon has struck the entire national economy regardless of industry, firm size, generation, and occupation, and is expected to strike deeper.

Economic readjustment and restructuring will eventually alter the organizational structure of *chaebŏl* firms and their employment system. Among predictable outcomes, first, FILMs will change significantly as conglomerates introduce new rules and managerial strategies for survival. In fact, changes in pay and promotion systems are already evident in large firms. Second, job security will diminish for both white- and blue-collar workers due to innovative flexibility strategies. These processes will replace long-term employment with an entirely new set of work relations. Contract employment and tenure on the basis of merit and contribution will apply even to top managers. Occupational segmentation, as well as other types of market fragmentation, will proceed from outgrowths of the tripartite negotiations between the government, capital, and labor, which legalized the layoff in February of 1998. In short, Korea's employment relations will bear increasing similarity to those of the free and open market of the United States.

This nexus of eventualities raises two important research issues. First, sociologists of work should assess empirically how successfully large firms carry out structural adjustment. An ideal opportunity for study derives from the recent announcement by five large conglomerates of a restructuring plan to drop subsidiaries with financial deficits and low productivity, sell some prosperous firms to improve financial status, and downsize through mass lay-offs. Innovation of organization and employment relations will be inevitable and serve as a precedent for other large firms' consideration. The contribution of systematic sociological inquiry will be invaluable. Second, these changes will bring pressure on national labor markets. The government and private firms share a common interest in policies for the structural adjustment—for example, flexibility in labor markets—that organized labor strongly opposes. Tension and conflict accordingly mount in both public and private sectors over the degree of downsizing and extent of layoffs. The pressure of growing labor market flexibility places organized labor on the defensive regarding job security and socioeconomic stability. This raises interrelated questions as to whether the firm-centered employment system will persist; to what extent managers and white-collar employees will be exposed to layoff and their traditional occupational privileges will be affected; and how organized labor will oppose restructuring and flexibility schemes and how much it will influence them.

INSTITUTIONAL CONTEXTS

After the labor disputes of 1987, the government and large business belatedly realized the importance of research concerning labor and workers' interests. Foreign pressure to open markets increased the urgent need for research centers to study labor problems and managerial strategies. As a result, numerous institutions, private and public, formed, providing manifold job opportunities for sociologists of work. The government established the Korea Labor Institute in 1988, to study labor issues when most factories, large and small, were severely damaged by militant labor disputes. It became one of the largest and the most productive labor research center in Korea. Conglomerates assigned a special section within their research institutes to deal with labor problems of concern to company business, developing materials and policy alternatives for chief executive officers (CEOs). This marked the first time that large business enterprises employed sociologists of work with higher degrees in their research centers.

Prior to these venues, universities were the most important institutions for research on these topics and for sociologists of work. Of one hundred universities in Korea, only 40 featured a sociology department in the late 1990s, in contrast to the universal presence of a department of economics. As this might betray, sociology was regarded as a radical field by the public in general and government policymakers in particular, so universities, old and new, could not easily obtain Ministry of Education permission to form a department. Nevertheless, sociology departments played a leading role in sociology of work research and education. A few universities even sponsored research institutes dealing with labor issues, which developed valuable materials and information for faculty and students alike, as well as research agendas and opportunities through conferences and workshops.

Besides universities and large enterprises, formal and informal research groups enriched and primed public interest in the sociology of work, formerly, especially under the authoritarian regime, in close affiliation with religious and civil movement organizations. Two centers were conspicuous in the church: the Urban Industrial Mission and the Christian Academy's Research Institute. They pioneered exploration of industrial problems and the predicaments of workers and occasionally provided education programs for young union leaders and activists under the protection of religious organizations. Numerous informal study groups emerged in industrial districts in close connection with union organizations in the 1980s, publishing papers and pamphlets and compiling materials on worker grievances and unfair labor practices. These were led by laid-off workers and student activists and provided opportunities for union leaders to discuss broad union movement issues. After relaxation of labor repression in 1987, some of these groups became small research centers led by university professors or former labor activists.

As labor problems diversified during democratization in the 1990s, research institutes developed multiple interconnections, but a notable fissure formed in terms of ideology and policy orientation. University institutes and institutes run by former labor activists were more likely to champion worker interests, while research centers in large business and the Korean Employers' Federation pursued capitalist concerns. The Korea Labor Institute attempted a balanced, neutral approach through abundance of data and careful analysis. Despite these divisions, all of these institutes recently expressed consensus that under IMF tutelage, it was desirable to avoid confrontation and to establish positive-sum, cooperative industrial relations between labor and capital through negotiation and concession.

The Ministry of Education's Korea Foundation of Research Promotion became a primary funding organization for sociologists of work.[9] Prior to the 1987 uprising, external funds were rarely available except for isolated, highly regarded scholars. Business enterprises did not need to invest in scientific and systematic studies of labor and management because the state had charge of industrial disputes and problems. Most research institutes, including university affiliates, had to procure any external finances independently through

[9]Like the National Science Foundation in the United States, it evaluated research proposals from university professors and affiliates and granted a limited amount of research funds to selected scholars.

aid and donations. This atmosphere changed in the first half of the 1990s as the government and private firms moved to sponsor not only research institutes of their own but also individual sociologists of work to improve labor relations.

Although interdisciplinary work has increased recently, it remains nascent. Universities and the Korea Foundation of Research Promotion encouraged joint projects among scholars with different educational background and methodologies, but their collaboration barely breached departmental boundaries. Among the conflicts and cleavages splintering scholarly groups and their research interests, the intellectual bifurcation between domestic- and foreign-educated scholars was conspicuous: The former were relatively progressive, radical, and sometimes highly speculative, while the latter were liberal in ideological orientation and stressed empirical evidence for theoretical arguments; the former criticized the latter as blind empiricists, rarely attentive to sociopolitical peculiarities of Korean society, whereas the latter reproached the former as unscientific and ideologically biased. Mistrust that was serious enough to require separate study groups in the past has recently eased.

The *Korean Journal of Sociology*, first issued in 1964 and published quarterly by the Korean Sociological Association, organized in 1957, is the most prestigious general journal of sociology. In addition to it, sociologists of work now have numerous additional publishing opportunities, more than scholars in other sociological subfields, due to the presence and proliferation of non-academic journals for public readers interested in labor issues. In the 1980s, when labor movements rapidly became the most important force for political change, various groups of sociologists issued semiacademic journals, such as *Economy and Society* (first published in 1988) and *Industrial Society Review* (1985), dealing with work and labor problems. Recently, the *Korea Journal of Labor Studies* (1995) was launched by an interdisciplinary research group comprising sociologists, economists, and political scientists. An English-language journal unique in this field, the *Korea Journal of Population and Development* (1972), specializes in social and economic development and extends to related topics.[10] Its publisher is the Institute for Social Development and Policy Research, run by the Seoul National University sociology department.

SUMMARY AND CONCLUSION

The foregoing discussion has reviewed the socioeconomic and political bases for paradigmatic change in major research themes and interests in Korea's sociology of work. In the 1960s and 1970s, the modernization paradigm guided analysis of work, workers, and possible factors for improving the effects of

[10]The journal title changed to *Development and Society* in 1998.

modernity on rural migrants. Simultaneously, some sociologists of work attended to the shadow side of high-speed socioeconomic growth under authoritarian repression and detected deteriorating working conditions, industrial worker proletarianization, and growing economic inequality. In view of political frustration in the early 1980s, sociologists turned to the revolutionary paradigm as a theoretical and practical rationale for considering the working class to be a revolutionary weapon. This induced heated debate on theoretical implications of work and worker consciousness in relation to social formation, and, concurrently, on organized labor's political strategies for expediting independent, autonomous capitalist development. The sociology of work played a leading role in shaping social scientific inquiries and ideological disputes. Academic achievements in this period are frequently unfairly denigrated as negligible. However, research undertook the difficult challenge to conceptualize and concretize democratic aspirations. The winding journey to a democratic world of labor entered its first stage in the wake of democratization in the late 1980s. What sociologists of work witnessed in the transition to democracy was complicated as well as intriguing. Interests and research agendas diversified, for while traditional labor problems remained, new issues emerged due to the rapid influx of new information technology and overall changes in economic and sociopolitical situations.

The current economic and financial crises and extensive industrial restructuring will shape the character of Korea's sociology of work in the forthcoming decades and are drawing increasing attention from sociologists in other subfields as well as scholars in other disciplines. Theoretical perspectives can be expected to continue to diversify and research methodologies develop to accommodate new and copious study themes. Institutional bases are likely to proliferate to provide sociologists of work with more tangible and intangible resources for research as their contributions are recognized. These developments will energize interdisciplinary collaboration to compensate for the respective weaknesses of engaged disciplines. We trust that sociology of work in Korea has a bright future, with its heyday yet to come.

REFERENCES

Amin, Samir. 1976. *Unequal Development*. London: Harvester.

Braverman, Harry. 1974. *Labor and Monopoly Capital: The Degradation of Work in the Twentieth Century*. New York: Monthly Review Press.

Burawoy, Michael. 1985. *The Politics of Production: Factory Regimes under Capitalism and Socialism*. London: Verso.

Cardoso, Fernando Henrique, and Enzo Faletto. 1979. *Dependency and Development in Latin America*. Berkeley: University of California Press.

Ch'a, Sŏng-su. 1989. "Kukkwa kwŏnryŏk kwa chabonùi nodong t'ongje [State Power and Labor Control of Capital]." *Sahoe wa sasang* 9:271–283.

Cho, Hi-yŏn. 1985. "Chongsokchòk sanòphwa wa pigongsik pumun [Dependent Industrialization and the Informal Sector]." In *Han'guk chabonjuùi wa nodong munje* [*Capitalism in Korea and Labor Problems*], edited by Hyŏn-ch'ae Pak and Hyŏng-gi Kim. Sŏul: Tolbegae.

Cho, Hyŏng. 1984. "Han'guk ŭi tosi pigongsik pumun kwa pin'gon [The Urban Informal Sector and Poverty in Korea]." Pp. 389–418 in *Han'guk sahoe ŭi chaeinsik 1* [Reconsideration of Korean Society 1], edited by Hyŏng-yun Pyŏn. Sŏul: Hanul.

Cho, Hyŏng-je. 1993. *Han'guk chadongch'a sanŏp ŭi chŏllyak kwa sŏnt'aek* [*Strategy and Choice of Automobile Industry in Korea*]. Sŏul: Paeksan sŏdang.

Cho, Sun-gyŏng, and Yong-suk Yi. 1989. "Sinnodong kwajŏng kwa han'guk ŭi chadongch'a sanŏp [New Labor Process and Automobile Industry in Korea]." *Han'guk sahoehak* 23:73–94.

Cho, U-hyŏn. 1985. "Imgŭm, nodong saengsansŏng, mul'ga mit nodongja ŭi saenghwal [Income, Labor Productivity, Price, and Worker's Life]." In *Han'guk chabonjuùi wa nodong munje* [*Capitalism in Korea and Labor Problems*], edited by Hyŏn-ch'ae Pak and Hyŏng-gi Kim. Sŏul: Tolbegae.

Ch'oe, Chang-jip. 1988. *Han'guk ŭi nodong undong kwa kukka* [*Labor Movements and the State in Korea*]. Sŏul: Yŏlŭmsa.

Ch'oe, Chang-jip. 1993. *Han'guk minjujuùi ŭi iron* [Theory of Korean Democracy]. Sŏul: Han'gilsa.

Chŏng, I-hwan. 1992. "Chejoŏp naebu nodong sijang ŭi pyŏnhwa wa nosa kwan'gye [*Change in the Internal Labor Market of Manufacturing Firms and Industrial Relations*]." Unpublished Ph.D. dissertation. Sŏul: Sŏul Taehakkyo.

Chŏng, In-su. 1991. *Han'guk ŭi imgùm kucho* [*Wage Structure in Korea*]. Sŏul: Han'guk nodong yŏn'guwŏn.

Doeringer, Peter B., and Michael J. Piore. 1971. *Internal Labor Markets and Manpower Analysis*. Lexington: Heath.

Edwards, Richard. 1979. *Contested Terrain: The Transformation of the Workplace in the Twentieth Century*. New York: Basic Books.

Frank. Andre Gunder. 1967. *Capitalism and Underdevelopment in Latin America*. New York: Monthly Review Press.

Freeman, Richard B., and James L. Medoff. 1984. *What Do Unions Do?* New York: Basic Books.

Han'guk nodong yŏn'guwŏn [Korea Labor Institute]. 1997. *1997nyŏn KLI nodong t'onggye* [*KLI Labor Statistics, 1997*]. Sòul: Han'guk nodongyŏn'guwŏn.

Hò, Sŏk-ryŏl. 1991. "Tosi pinminch'ŭng ŭi hyŏngsŏng kwa chaesaengsan [Formation and Reproduction of the Urban Poor]." In *Saheo kyech'ŭng* [*Social Stratification*], edited by Sŏul Taehakkyo sahoehak yŏn'guhoe. Sŏul: Tasan.

Hwang, Han-sik. 1985. "Han'guk nodong sijang ŭi kujo [Labor Market Structure in Korea]." In *Han'guk chabonjuùi wa nodong munje* [*Capitalism and Labor Problems in Korea*], edited by Hyŏn-ch'ae Pak and Hyŏng-gi Kim. Sŏul: Tolbegae.

Im, Hi-sŏp. 1986. *Saheo pyŏndong kwa kach'ikwan* [*Social Change and Values*]. Sŏul: Chŏngumsa.

Im, Yŏng-il. 1985. "Nodongja ŭi chonje chogŏn kwa ŭisik [Workers' Subsistence Condition and Consciousness]." In *Han'guk chabonjuùi wa nodong munje* [Capitalism *and Labor Problems in Korea*], editied by Hyŏn-ch'ae Pak and Hyŏng-gi Kim. Sŏul: Tolbegae.

Inkeles, Alex. 1983. *Exploring Individual Modernity*. New York: Columbia University Press.

Kim, Chae-hun. 1996. "Han'guk pandoch'e kiŏp ŭi tonghyŏnghwa e taehan yŏn'gu [Study of Isomorphism of Korean Semiconductor Corporations]." Unpublished Ph.D. dissertation, Sŏul Taehakkyo, Sŏul.

Kim, Chin-gyun, and Yŏng-il Im. 1987. "Nodongja ŭi ŭisik kwa haengdong [Workers' Consciousness and Action]." In *Hyòndae chabonjuùi wa kongdongch'e iron [Theory of Modern Capitalism and Collectivity]*, edited by Sŏul taehakkyo sahoehak yŏn'guhoe. Sŏul: Han'gilsa.

Kim, Chin-yŏng. 1994. *Chòngbo kisul kwa hwait'ŭ k'alla nodong [Information Technology and White-Collar Labor]*. Sŏul: Hanul.

Kim, Chun. 1989. "Che 6konghwaguk ŭi nodong t'ongje chŏngch'aek [Labor Control Policies of the Sixth Republic]." *Kyŏngje wa sahoe* 3:17–41.

Kim, Hyŏng-gi. 1988. *Han'guk ŭi tokchŏm chabon kwa imnodong [Korea's Monopoly Capital and Wage Labor]*. Sŏul: Kkach'i.

Kim, Kyŏng-dong. 1992. *Han'gugin ŭi kach'igwan kwa sahoe uisik [Korean Values and Social Consciousness]*. Sŏul: Pagyòngsa.

Kim, Kyŏng-dong, and Yun-jong Sim, eds. 1995. *Sin'gisul kwa sinnosakwan'gye [New Technology and New Industrial Relations]*. Sŏul: Hanul.

Kim, Sŏng-guk. 1985. "Sanòphwa wa nosagaldŭng [Industrialization and Industrial Conflict]." In *Han'guk sahoe wa kaldùng ui yŏn'gu [Korean Society and Conflict Analysis]*, edited by Han'guk sahoe hakhoe. Sŏul: Hyŏndae sahoe yŏn'guso.

Kim, Tong-ch'un. 1995. *Han'guk sahoe nodongja yŏn'gu [Study of the Working Class in Korea]*. Sŏul: Yŏksa wa pip'yŏngsa.

Kim, Yong-hak, and Ho-gùn Song. 1997. *Nodong chohap ŭi yŏn'gyŏlmang yŏn'gu [Analysis of Trade Union Networks]*. Sŏul: Noch'ong chungang yŏn'guwon.

Nam, Ch'un-ho. 1990. "Chojik pumun p'igoyongja ŭi imgŭm kyŏlchŏng mohyŏng yŏn'gu [The Wage Determination Model of Organized Workers]." In *Nodong kwa pulp'yŏngdŭng [Labor and Inequality]*, edited by Ho-gŭn Song. Sŏul: Nanam.

No, Chung-gi. 1995. "Kukka ŭi nodong t'ongje chŏllyak e kwanhan yŏn'gu: 1987–1992 [A Study of Labor Control Strategies of the State, 1987–1992]." Unpublished Ph.D. dissertation, Sŏul Taehakkyo, Sŏul.

Pae, Mu-gi. 1980. "Han'guk ŭi nodong sijang kujo [Labor Market Structure in Korea]." In *Han'guk ŭi nodong kyònje [Labor Economics in Korea]*, edited by Chong-ch'ŏl Im and Mu-gi Pae. Sŏul: Munhak kwa chisŏngsa.

Pae, Mu-gi. 1991. *Han'guk ŭi nosa kwan'gye wa koyong [Industrial Relations and Employment in Korea]*. Sŏul: Kyŏngmunsa.

Pak, Chun-sik. 1992. *Han'guk ŭi taegiòp nosa kwan'gye yŏn'gu [Study of Industrial Relations in Korean Large Enterprise]*. Sŏul: Paeksan Sodang.

Pak, Hwŏn-gu, and Yŏng-bŏm Pak. 1989. *Tanch'e kyosŏp kwa imgŭm insang [Collective Bargaining and Wage Increases]*. Sŏul: Han'guk nodong yŏn'guwŏn.

Pak, Hyŏn-ch'ae, and Hi-yŏn Cho. 1989a. *Han'guk sahoe kusŏngch'e nonjaeng (I) [Debate on Social Formation in Korea, Vol. 1]*. Sŏul: Chuksan.

Pak, Hyŏn-ch'ae. 1989b. *Han'guk sahoe kusŏngch'e nonjaeng (II) [Debate on Social Formation in Korea, Vol. 2]*. Sŏul: Chuksan.

Pak, Hyŏn-ch'ae. 1991. *Han'guk sahoe kusŏngch'e nonjaeng (III) [Debate on Social Forma-

tion in Korea, Vol. 3]. Sŏul: Chuksan.

Pak, Hyŏng-jun. 1989. "Tokchŏm chabonjuŭi wa nodong undong [Monopoly Capitalism and Labor Movements]." In *Han'guk sahoe nodongja yŏn'gu* [*Study of Korean Workers*], edited by Han'guk sahoe yŏn'guso. Sŏul: Paeksan Sŏdang.

Pak, Hyŏng-jun. 1991. *Hyŏndae nodong kwajŏngron* [*Theory of Modern Labor Process*]. Sŏul: Paeksan sŏdang.

Pak, Sŭng-hi. 1988. "Taegiŏp ilgwan chagŏpchang ŭi nodong t'ongje e kwanhan sarye yŏn'gu [Case Study of Assembly-Line Labor Control in Large Enterprise]." Unpublished Ph.D. dissertation, Sŏnggyun'gwan Taehakkyo, Sŏul.

Pak, Tŏk-che. 1985. "Nomu kwalli wa nosa kwan'gye [Labor Management and Industrial Relations]." In *Han'guk chabonjuui wa nodong munje* [*Capitalism and Labor Problems in Korea*], edited by Hyŏn-ch'e Pak and Hyŏng-gi Kim. Sŏul: Tolbegae.

Song, Ho-gŭn. 1991. *Han'guk ŭi nodong chŏngch'i wa sijang* [*Labor Politics and Markets in Korea*]. Sŏul: Nanam.

Song, Ho-gŭn. 1994. *Yŏllin sijang, tach'in chŏngch'i* [*Open Market, Closed Politics*]. Sŏul: Naman.

Suh, Doowon. 1998. "From Individual Welfare to Social Change: The Expanding Goals of Korean White-Collar Labor Unions, 1987-1995." Unpublished Ph.D. dissertation. Chicago: University of Chicago.

Yi, Ch'ae-yŏl, Ho-gŭn Song, and Hyŏn-ji Kwŏn. 1995. "Saengsanmul sijang ŭi kujo wa taegiŏp ŭi imgŭm chŏngch'aek [Product Market Structure and Large Company's Income Policy]." *Han'guk sahoehak*: 29:69–104.

Yi, Kak-pŏm. 1983. "Sanŏp palchŏn kwa nodong sijang ŭi pyŏndong [Industrial Growth and Labor Market Change]." In *Han'guk sahoe ŏdiro kago Inna?* [*Where is Korean Society Going?*], edited by Han'guk sahoe hakhoe. Sŏul: Hyŏndae sahoe yŏn'guso.

Yi, T'ae-ho. 1982. *70nyŏndae ŭi hyŏnjang* [*The Scene of the '70s*]. Sŏul: Tolbegae.

APPENDIX: CONTACTS

Research Institutes for Work in South Korea

Kyŏnggi pukpu nodong jŏngch'aek yŏn'guso
[Kyonggi Bukbu Labor Institute]
Kyŏnggi ŭijŏngbu-si
ŭijŏngbu 4-dong 230-16
Phone: (351) 846-8066
Fax: (351) 848-4674
E-mail: DLSR@chollian.net

Nodongkwa kŏn'gang yŏn'guhoe
[Korea Worker's Health and Safety Research Association]
Sŏul Mapo-gu

*English titles with an asterisk are the authors' translations. Others are official English names of research institutes.

Sin'gongdŏk-dong 4-13
Phone: (2)3273-6076
Fax: (2)3273-6079
E-mail: KWHSA@chollian.net

Nodong in'gwŏn hoegwan [Labor Human Rights Center]
Sŏul Yongsan-gu
Namyŏng-dong 127-1
Phone: (2)749-8975
E-mail: LHCC@hitel.net

Nodongjarŭl wihan yŏndae [Federation for Workers]
Pusan Pusanjin-gu
Chŏnp'o 4-dong 660-13
Phone: (51)803-8746
Fax: (51)803-4417
E-mail: nodan@chollian.net

Nodong chŏngch'aek yŏn'guso
[Korea Research Institute for Worker's Human Rights and Justice]
Sŏul Yongsan-gu
Namyŏng-dong 127-1
Phone: (2)749-6052
Fax: (2)749-6055
E-mail: a0011@chollian.net

Nodong chohap Kiŏpkyŏŏngyŏng yŏn'guso
[Worker's Institute for Management Analysis]
Sŏul Kwanak-gu Sillim
5-dong 1410-3
Phone: (2)882-0634
Fax: (2)882-0636
E-mail: wima@chollian.net

Taegu nodong chŏngch'aek yŏn'guso
[Taegu Research Institute for Labor Policy*]
Taegu Sŏ-gu Pisan 2-dong 550-4
Phone: (53)555-4087
Fax: (53)564-0434
E-mail: NODONG@chollian.net

Pusan oegugin nodongja in'gwŏnŭl wihan moim
[Association for Foreign Worker's Human Rights in Pusan]
Pusan Pusanjin-gu
Chŏnp'o 2-dong 193-9
Phone: (51)802-3438
Fax: (51)809-4722
E-mail: NOJA@chollian.net

Puch'ŏn nodong munhwa sent'ŏ
[Pucheon Labor Culture Center]
Kyŏnggi Puch'ŏn-si
Wŏnmi-gu Simgok-dong 87-11
Phone: (32)665-9471
Fax: (32)613-6420
E-mail: NBSMS@chollian.net

Puch'ŏn nodongja hoegwan
[Pucheon Labor Center]
Kyŏnggi Puch'ŏn-si
Wŏnmi-gu Ch'unŭI-dong 136-1
Phone: (32)671-8518
Fax: (32)671-8519
E-mail: BCLC1217@chollian.net

Puch'ŏn han'gil nodong yŏn'guso
[Puch'chŏn Hangil Labor Institute*]
Kyŏnggi Puch'ŏn-si
Wŏnmi-gu Ch'unùI-dong 211-1
Phone: (32)613-3715
Fax: (32)613-3715
E-mail: HGL@chollian.net

Saebyŏgŭl yŏnùn nodong munje yŏn'guso
Chŏnnam Sunch'ŏn-si
Maegok-dong 124-17
Phone: (661)755-5032
Fax: (661)755-5053
E-mail: NO5033@chollian.net

Sŏkt'ap nodong yŏn'guwŏn
[Sokt'ap Labor Institute*]
Sŏul Sŏdaemun-gu
Ch'angch'ŏn-dong 114-9
Phone: (2)324-4141
Fax: (2)325-8780

Yŏndaewa silch'ŏnŭl wihan yŏngnam nodong munje yŏn'guso
[Research Center for Youngnam Labor Movements]
Pusan Pusanjin-gu
Pujŏn 1-dong 264-12
Phone: (51)809-0162
Fax: (51)809-0163
E-mail: Yong94@chollian.net

Inch'ŏn nodong yŏn'guso
[Incheon Labor Institute]
Inch'ŏn Pup'yŏng-gu
Sipchŏng-dong 407
Phone: (32)439-8176
E-mail: ICYWW@chollian.net

Chŏnt'aeil kinyŏm saŏphoe
[Jun Tae Il Memorial Society]
Sŏul Chongno-gu
Ch'angsin 2-dong 131-106
Phone: (2)3672-4138
Fax: (2)3672-4139

Han'guk nodong sahoe yŏn'guso
[Korean Labour & Society Institute]
Sŏul Chung-gu
Hoehyŏn-dong 1-ga 100-49
Phone: (2)778-4225
Fax: (2)776-4444
E-mail: KLSI21@chollian.net

Han'guk nodong iron chŏngch'aek yŏn'guso
[Korean Institute for Labor Studies & Policy]
Sŏul Kwanak-gu
Pongch'ŏn 8-dong 930-41
Phone: (2)874-2933
Fax: (2)874-2935
E-mail: LABOR95@chollian.net

Han'guk Nodong chŏngch'aek chŏngbo sent'ŏ
[Korea Labor Policy & Information Center]
Sŏul Map'o-gu
Sŏgyo-dong 332-4
Phone: (2)326-0710
Fax: (2)323-3275
E-mail: klpic@chollian.net

Han'guk nodong yŏn'guwŏn
[Korea Labor Institute]
Sŏul Yŏngdŭngp'o-gu
Yŏŭido-dong 16-2
Phone: (2)782-0141
Fax: (2)782-0311
E-mail: http://ns.kli.re.kr

Koryŏ taehakkyo nodong munje yŏn'guso
[Labor Education & Research Institute of Korea University]
Sŏul Sŏngbuk-gu
Anam-dong 5-ga 1
Phone: (2)3290-1634
Fax: (2)928-1381

Sŏul taehakkyo kyŏngyŏng taehak nosa kwan'gye yŏn'guso
[Institute for Industrial Relations, College of Business Administration, Seoul National
    University]
Sŏul Kwanak-gu
Sillim-dong San 56-1
Phone: (2)880-6913
Fax: (2)872-2206

Han'guk sanŏp sahoe hakhoe
[The Association of Korean Researchers on Industrial Society]
Sŏul Chongno-gu
Sinmunno 1-ga 173
Phone: (2)720-4725
Fax: (2)735-1208
E-mail: sansahak@ppp.kornet21.net

Han'guk sahoe kwahak yŏn'guso
[Korea Social Science Institute]
Sŏul Chongno-gu
Sinmunno 1-ga 173
Phone: (2)739-2091
Fax: (2)739-2091

Nodong kyŏngje yŏn'guwon
[Labor Economics Institute]
Sŏul Map'o-gu
Taehŭng-dong 276-1
Phone: (2)3270-7317
Fax: (2)3270-7387

Han'guk noch'ong chungang yŏn'guwon
[Research Center of the Federation of Korean Trade Unions]
Sŏul Yŏngdŭngp'o-gu
Yŏŭido-dong 35
Phone: (2)761-4526
E-mail: unitied@chollian.net

9
South Africa

Edward C. Webster

FROM MAYO TO MARX

The sociological study of work emerged as a specialized field within general sociology in South African universities in the late 1960s.[1] This was a logical development, since South Africa was becoming a modern industrial economy. The concerns of management and the views of Elton Mayo's Human Relations School dictated much of the syllabus, focusing on factors affecting productivity, such as high labor turnover, morale, and monotony in industry (Jubber, 1979). The emergence of strong shop-floor-based unions in the 1970s among black workers led to a growing interest in universities in sociological research into the workplace (Webster, 1981:95–102). This included anthropological research on informal work groups, as well as a growing interest in the history of labor among a group of activist scholars sympathetic to the emerging trade unions (Alverson, 1975; Gordon, 1978; Webster, 1978).

[1]In this paper, I have not included the large number of studies on trade unions. Instead I have concentrated on studies of the workplace, defining work broadly rather than confining it to employment.

Edward C. Webster • Sociology of Work Unit, University of the Witwatersrand, Wits 2050 South Africa.

Worlds of Work: Building an International Sociology of Work, edited by Daniel B. Cornfield and Randy Hodson. Kluwer Academic/Plenum Publishers, New York, 2002.

The result was something of a bifurcation between the traditional industrial sociology of work taught largely in the proapartheid Afrikaans-speaking
universities, and the presentation of courses on the "labour process" in antiapartheid, English-speaking universities. "The subjects studied by these two
groups, the theoretical frameworks within which the discipline was taught,
and the methodological approaches employed, were all subject to this political
dividing line. The separation extended as far as two separate sociological associations, separate sociological congresses, and even different academic journals in which sociologists could publish their research" (van der Merwe, 1995).

The labor process approach was strongly influenced by Harry Braverman's
attempt to reinstate Marx's theory of the labor process (Braverman, 1974).
Fueled by the growth of militant industrial unions, the labor process approach
rapidly overtook the traditional industrial sociological perspective in the growing number of industrial sociology programes that emerged in the late 1970s
and early 1980s in South African universities (Lever, 1982). The labor process
approach, with its notion of the inherently antagonistic character of capitalist
production relations and its stress on coercion in the workplace, captured the
despotic nature of the apartheid workplace and generated widespread interest
in the labor process among industrial sociologists.[2] This approach was reinforced by the emergence of a neo-Marxist class paradigm among a group of ex-
iled and expatriate scholars. These "revisionist" scholars attempted to show,
through the use of class analysis, that apartheid aided capitalist development
by providing employers with cheap, rightless black labor (Bozzoli and Delius,
1990).

As resistance to apartheid deepened during the 1980s, the workplace
became a contested terrain and studies of the workplace were overtaken by
studies on the relationship between the trade union movement and national
liberation (Adler and Webster, 1995). The achievement of democracy and exposure of the South African workplace to global competition in the 1990s
revitalized the sociological study of work. It has led to debates between sociologists on whether, and how, a more flexible system of production can be
introduced in South Africa. It has also opened up opportunities for a widening range of research activities and has generated new research partnerships
between the universities and various outside stakeholders.

It is argued in this chapter that a new research program emerged in industrial sociology in South Africa in the 1970s and 1980s that had at its core
Marx's theory of the capitalist labor process. This program generated a number of substantial studies of the labor process that were to transform the so-

[2]One commentator concluded a review of South African labor process studies with the following comment: "One senses in some of the products of South African labour process studies a
premature closure to the complexity of research findings induced by an unremitting exposure
to Braverman and followers" (Lever, 1982).

ciological study of work in South Africa. New concepts such as racial despotism and racial Fordism were developed to understand the nature of work
relations in South Africa. Researchers drew on new currents in Marxist theory,
such as regulation theory, in an attempt to understand the South African
workplace. The question raised by this research is whether to abandon it or
try to protect the theory by build auxiliary hypotheses (Burawoy, 1990).

By and large, South African industrial sociologists have responded to this
challenge by avoiding theoretical debates and have concentrated instead on
concrete studies of the workplace and the struggles that have taken place
within it. The result is a rich body of empirical and ethnographic detail on the
one hand and, more recently, a range of policy-oriented interventions on the
restructuring of work and the new corporatist style institutions on the other.[3]
Where this will lead to, theoretically, is not yet clear; but it is clear that the
workplace has reemerged as a crucial area of research and policy debate.

In this chapter, the enduring research themes that shape the sociology of
work in South Africa, as well as the new themes of recent scholarship in the
sociology of work, are identified. The institutional context through which teaching and research on work are conducted is then described. This chapter does
not cover the substantial body of research on the origins and nature of the
labor movement—what could be described as trade union studies—but instead
concentrates more narrowly on the sociology of work. In the conclusion, we
suggest that the sociological study of work is emerging as an arena of sharp
intellectual and ideological contestation over the impact of globalization on
the world of work.

ENDURING THEMES: OLD AND NEW FORMS
OF CONTROL AT WORK

De-skilling, racism in the workplace, and the nature of Fordism in South
Africa emerged as the three main areas of debate in South African studies on
the sociology of work.

Skill, De-skilling and Skills Enhancement

The first theme began as a debate on the degree to which skills had been
transformed and eroded through capitalist development and whether this could
be described as a "degradation of labour." Research led to a critique of

---

[3]This shift in research agenda has led to sharp criticism from members of the far left, who have
described this policy research as a slavish following of the agenda of the labor movement and
an abandonment of any semblance of critical engagement (Desai, 1997).

Braverman's deskilling thesis, focusing on worker resistance, the subjective experience of work, and tacit skills. Researchers concluded that labor process theory was too restrictive and that a new approach to skills formation, one that recognized the need for constant skills acquisition, career progression, and the importance of informal knowledge, needed to be developed (Webster and Leger, 1992).[4] These studies suggested that capitalist development had not created a single mass of homogenous labor, but a complex, internally differentiated labor market containing an uneven variety of formal and informal skills.

Early research was largely historical and showed how craft workers resisted the process of de-skilling and retained considerable control over the supply of labor (Ewart, 1990; Lewis, 1984; Webster, 1985). Such resistance was quite successful in retaining levels of skill, with the key role being played by the craft union through the mechanism of social exclusion. In particular, by methods of labor market closure, limiting recruitment to an occupation to whites only, and demanding lengthy training, craft workers were able to protect established interests. The result was the survival of a higher number of "craft" jobs than the de-skilling thesis would appear to indicate. By acting defensively to protect their skills through the job color bar, craft workers consolidated their position as a white labor aristocracy at an early stage in the history of industrialization in South Africa (Davies, 1979; Johnstone, 1976; Katz, 1976).[5]

The new bargaining power conferred on "unskilled" and semiskilled workers when mechanization replaced craft skill, emerged as a research interest in the 1980s. In general terms, mechanization undermines the marketplace bargaining power (as embodied in the skills of craft workers) while simultaneously enhancing labors' workplace bargaining power by making capital vulnerable to workers' direct action at the point of production. This, as has been argued elsewhere, provided the conditions for the rapid growth of militant shop-floor-based industrial unionism in the Unites States in the 1930s, after the World War II in Europe, and in semi-industrialized countries such as Brazil, South Korea, and South Africa in the 1970s and 1980s (Arrighi and Silver, 1984; Edwards, 1979).

Research into this link between the transformation of work under monopoly capitalism and the rapid growth of militant shop-floor industrial unions was to dominate research into the sociology of work in South Africa through-

---

[4]This new approach to skills formation has been incorporated into the government's educational policy of "lifelong learning" and a White Paper. It became law during the 1998 session of Parliament.

[5]These results confirm the findings of a number of similar post-Braverman studies that have attempted to rectify this neglect of worker resistance in Braverman's work (see P. Penn, 1982). What is distinctive in the South African context is the racial form taken by resistance and craft workers.

out the 1980s (Adler, 1994; Innes, 1983; Lewis, 1985; Maree, 1985; Sitas, 1984; Southall, 1985. Webster, 1985). It also led to comparisons with militant labor movements in other semi-industrialized countries, such as Brazil, that had undergone a similar pattern of rapid transformation of the labor process, a despotic system of labor control, a lack of a social infrastructure in the community, and restricted access to political power (Seidman. 1994).

In trying to determine why workers were joining the new industrial unions in large numbers, industrial sociologists were drawn beyond the workplace, to an examination of working-class cultural formations. Sitas (1984) called these cultural formations "defensive combinations"; these informal social networks were to provide the basis for collective mobilization of migrant workers. This new direction brought the subjective experience of work into industrial sociology, generating a number of studies that analyzed culture and working life, as well as the relationship of unions to the new social movements (Bonin, 1987).

While evidence of worker resistance to de-skilling qualified Braverman's thesis, it did not challenge his central assumption that "skills" had been removed from modern work. Leger's (1992) research among black underground mine-workers showed that even so-called "unskilled" workers exercised a range of tacit skills, tricks of the trade essential to production, but received no formal acknowledgment.[6] This detailed examination of underground mining found that formal training played a minor role in imparting tacit skills, which were largely learned from "unskilled" black miners. The term *unskilled* grossly underrates the working knowledge required and the skills exercised in these occupations. "There is no such thing as unskilled work and . . . the term is humiliating to the workers so labelled" (Leger, 1992:13). Leger concluded that the absolute divorce of conception from execution, as Taylorism proposed, is an impossibility and Taylorism cannot successfully reduce workers to robots.

In elaborating the concept of tacit skills, Leger argued that the labor process is always a dual process of conflict and cooperation, in which management never gains absolute control over production. It follows that a de-skilled fragmented workforce is not needed by capital to maintain control. The road to productivity enhancement also includes skills enhancement and cooperative relations with trade unions (Adler, 1993:45–49, 58–60). Research on the impact of the new microelectronic technology on metalworkers and clerical workers found that de-skilling was not taking place (Glenn, 1992; Kraak, 1987).

---

[6]The identification of tacit knowledge arose out of research on underground safety, in which Leger found that black miners had knowledge of a range of precursors to rockfalls and an ability to recognize conditions that are potentially hazardous. Following the terminology of British colliers, he used the term "pit sense" to describe the miners' tacit skills about rockfall accidents.

In fact, the opposite occurred: clerical staff found their jobs more stimulating and exciting rather than routinized (Glenn, 1992).

Indeed many companies, under the influence of Japanese-style Green Areas, have begun to tap into workers' tacit skills (Maller, 1992:137). Access to tacit knowledge, Kraak argues, is vital for the continuous innovations required in the global information economy. "The fundamental challenge of the informational economy is to create a dynamic synergy between formalised knowledge as practiced by scientists in the universities on the one hand, and tacit knowledge as practiced by professional and skilled workers in the workplace, on the other. It is in the interaction of these two great knowledge forms . . . [that] new commercial applications best occur" (Kraak, 1997:59).

RACE AND WORK

The second enduring theme began as a debate over the system of labor control in the workplace, a system characterized in South Africa by coercion and racism. Two quite different concepts emerged—racial despotism and racial Fordism—to analyze the South African workplace. Based on quite different intellectual approaches, they have taken the debate in two different directions: the first in the direction of workplace industrial relations, the second in the direction of post-Fordism. However, both approaches are preoccupied with the possibilities of transition toward more orderly, equitable, participatory and productive workplaces.

The concept of racial despotism captures the notion that in apartheid South Africa, work was characterized by coercion rather than consent, and by the domination of one racial group by another (Burawoy, 1985). At the core of this system of total control was the compound in which large numbers of black workers were housed separately from the rest of society but often located within the premises of the workplace. It has been argued that the compound was one of the most effective forms of labor control ever invented (Rex, 1974).

Formally, everyday power in the compound was exercised by the white compound manager, assisted by black *indunas*—management-appointed supervisors. In the workplace, control was exercised by white foremen assisted by black "boss-boys." Although this system of control was to decline in the 1960s with the emergence of modern personnel departments and, later, the rise of shop stewards in the workplace, crucial features of this system persist in the modern workplace (Nzimande, 1991:166–199). African personnel practitioners are reluctant partners of capitalism because racial discrimination has produced a situation in which members of the African middle classes share many of the humiliating conditions with black workers (Nzimande, 1986:49–58).[7]

Initial research focused on the transition from a despotic form of management to an industrial relations system based on trade union rights and collective bargaining (Webster, 1985). The growing rate of unionization of black workers, and the realization that the capitalist system was at risk in the long term because of its association with apartheid, prompted management to introduce participatory schemes in the workplace.

Research on these schemes revealed that employers preferred Japanese-style task-oriented forms of participation such as Green Areas and Quality Circles (Maller, 1992). Research has shown that workers are generally suspicious of management-initiated participation schemes (Barchiesi, 1997; Buhlungu, 1997). The one exception that emerged from Maller's study, was the Volkswagen assembly plant, was potentially a new "kind of workplace democracy" (Maller, 1992:249). Maller concluded that the union was pioneering a new form of unionism that fused oppositional and participative relations in joint union–management forums (Maller, 1994:253).[8]

In the early 1990s, a number of companies established similar joint forums with unions, within which information sharing, consultation and, in some ad hoc cases, joint decision making occurred (Webster, 1996). The result was that industrial relations was no longer confined to collective bargaining but became integrated into human resources management, corporate strategy, and even production issues (Webster, 1996:165). These forums were given statutory form in 1996, when an institutionalized form of worker representation, supported by a defined set of powers, was introduced in the new Labour Relations Act. To date, only eight of these structures—called *workplace forums*—have been established (Sociology of Work Unit, 1997).

In a rich ethnographic study of the changing lives and struggles of black workers in South Africa's gold mines, Moodie (1994:110) argues that relations between management and migrant workers constituted a kind of order, governed by both formal contracts and unwritten *imiteto* or "implicit contracts" between managers and workers, and among workers, which he calls a "moral economy." The arrival of the union in the 1980s challenged managerial despo-

---

[7]Nzimande draws on Wright's concept of contradictory class location to analyze the predicament of the black manager. It should be noted that this article was written in the 1980s, under apartheid, and before any significant program of black advancement.

[8]In a review of the study, von Holdt argues that there is very little evidence of this "new unionism" at Volkswagen and that productivity has not improved. The study suggests, von Holdt argues, "a relatively unstable industrial relations system as well as a degree of instability within union structures. Institutionalisation seems to be limited, there are numerous flashpoints, racism is a prominent grievance, and industrial action has a political dimension" (1996:7–8).

tism as the union sought a transition from the old despotic order to a new, negotiated order. However, a new order was not established; both management and traditional migrants contest this. Thus "this period of transition which still continues today, has been chaotic."

The contested nature of the transition from racial despotism in the workplace is the theme of von Holdt's detailed case study of the trade union struggles in the 1980s and 1990s in Steelco (von Holdt, 1996; von Holdt, 2000). This contest, von Holdt argues, leads to ungovernability, "because the parties are seeking to defend or establish radically incompatible social structures" (von Holdt, 1996: 20). In the 1980s, black workers responded to white racism by creating unions committed to "militant abstentionism": a refusal to identify with any of the goals of the enterprise or the concerns of management. This "culture of resistance" merged with the insurrectionary political climate at the time, creating conditions of "ungovernability" in the workplace.

In spite of a concerted effort by the union in 1990 to shift away from "social movement unionism" toward strategic unionism, the tradition of "ungovernability" at Steelco reemerged in 1994. However, militant actions now appear to be directed against the union and the shop stewards as much as management (von Holdt, forthcoming). Von Holdt attributes the persistence of ungovernability to the fact that the workplace culture has barely changed. "While politically speaking apartheid is no more, in the workplace its legacy continues in low pay, racist differentials, authoritarian management and racism" (Von Holdt, 2000).

FROM RACIAL FORDISM TO NEO-FORDISM

While debates over the concept of racial despotism led to new perspectives on workplace industrial relations, a third area of debate emerged around the nature of Fordism in South Africa.[9] The debate began when it was argued that the kind of Fordist mode of regulation that emerged after 1945 was not aimed at mass production of goods for the whole population. Instead, blacks were excluded from the mass consumption "norms" that applied to whites and, at a later stage, began to apply to Indian and colored groups. In addition, whites monopolized the skilled and supervisory positions in the workplace. Gelb (1987) described this fordist caricature as "racial fordism."

The concept of "racial Fordism" generated a lively debate on the nature of work in South Africa (Bethlehem, 1994; Maller and Dwolatsky, 1993). Some researchers even questioned the usefulness of the concept of "Fordism" given the low volume of South African production. "An assembly line in metropoli-

[9]This formulation of Fordism is drawn from the French Regulation school (Gelb. 1992).

tan plants," Adler writes, "may be producing as many vehicles in an hour as a South African line produces in a day" (1993:43–44). However, the most common question raised was whether a transition from racial Fordism to post-Fordism is taking place in South Africa.

Current research suggests that there is a transition away from racial Fordism inasmuch as the number of black skilled, supervisory, technical, semi-professional, and white-collar workers is increasing and black–white inequality in the workplace is decreasing (Crankshaw, 1997). Indeed, Crankshaw suggests that inequality in South Africa will be driven increasingly by class rather than racial divisions.[10] However, this shift away from racial Fordism is not, researchers conclude, a transition towards post-Fordism. New forms of flexible production are being introduced in a piecemeal, ad hoc way. These shifts mount to a shift in the direction of neo-Fordism rather than post-Fordism (Duncan and Payne, 1993; Ewart, 1992; Kraak, 1996). The most useful contribution to this debate has been Kraak's conclusion that "a hybrid typology of labour processes is emerging comprising existing racial Fordist, jobbing and familial labour processes coexisting alongside recently emerged neo-Fordist applications of the new technologies and managerial techniques" (Kraak, 1996:53).

While the concept of racial Fordism was introduced to analyze the nature of the economic crisis, this research effort shifted in 1990 to "develop an industrial policy that could address the poor performance of South African manufacturing" (Joffe et al., 1995:xi).[11] In their final report, the authors introduce the concept of Intelligent Production, which embraces three interlinked post-Fordist principles: constant skillS acquisition; reorganiZing work along team lines; and cooperation and democracy in the workplace (Joffe et al., 1995:87, 205; Rosenthal and Joffe, 1996).

A range of difficulties in introducing this new work paradigm in South Africa has been identified (Kraak, 1996:53–63; Lloyd, 1994). "However, the real danger of the new South African industrial paradigm is that it will lead to

---

[10]Affirmative Action has been an ongoing issue in management since the late 1970s. For an overview of Affirmative Action see Makhanya (1995) and Innes and Davies (1996). Since 1994, it has been one of the priority issues in the Department of Labour's policy program. In 1996, a Green Paper on Employment Equity was published. In 1997, a Draft Bill was tabled on Employment Equity. The Bill became law during 1998. In terms of the law, all enterprises with more than 50 employees are required to negotiate targets (not quotas) with their employees indicating how they intend to make their workforce representative of the population by a specified period of time. Importantly, "representivity" includes gender and disability.

[11]This shift was led by the Industrial Strategy Project, designed to develop a new industrial policy for South Africa. It was influenced by the works of Michael Piore and Charles Sabel (1984), Michael Porter (1990) and Michael Best (1990), not regulation theory, which no longer seems influential among South African sociologists.

increasing social class differentiation, pitting privileged core workers against increasingly deprived peripheral workers" (Kraak, 1996:70). The negative effect that labor market flexibility could have on workers has emerged as a major theme in recent scholarship in the sociology of work.[12]

NEW THEMES OF RECENT SCHOLARSHIP
IN THE SOCIOLOGY OF WORK

Three new themes of recent scholarship in the sociology of work emerged in the 1990s: labor market flexibility, the "new" economic sociology, and organizational sociology.

Research on the labor market suggests that South African firms are moving in the same direction as their counterparts elsewhere in the world in turning toward greater use of flexible workers, through casual labor, contract labor, subcontracting to smaller firms, homeworkers and other "outworkers," and agency workers (Standing, Sender, and Weeks, 1996:337). However, the precise nature of this trend is a matter of fierce scholarly and public debate. The findings of the first large-scale research of labor market flexibility practices in enterprises, the South African Enterprise Labour Flexibility Survey, showed that the actual number of employees engaged in atypical employment is relatively low (Crankshaw and Macun, 1997). But detailed case studies confirm that atypical employment is growing (Bezuidenhout, 1996; Bezuidenhout and Kenny, 1998; Horwitz, 1995; Kenny and Webster, 1998; Klerk, 1994; Mahone, 1996; Rees, 1997; Theron, 1996). One result is longer working hours, with attendant health problems, increased risk of injury, limited engagement with family members, and heavy burdens for women who have to organize child care during long absences from home (National Labour, Education, and Development Institute, 1997). Research on which workers are confronted by "flexibilization" of their jobs, and how households cope with the implications of these changes, was begun by Kenny (1997). The organizational forms emerging to represent the poor and the unemployed in the city of Durban were identified in a study by Sitas (1998).

The second new theme on social institutions and economic performance draws on the new economic sociology or socioeconomics.[13] Research on this

---

[12]Raphael Kaplinsky, one of the co-authors of the Industrial Strategy Project, has reacted to criticism of the negative effects of greater flexibility by stating that their approach favors "labour friendly approaches to flexibility" as opposed to "labour unfriendly" approaches (Kaplinsky, 1994:535). A similar point is made by those who draw a distinction between "value-added" and "cost-based" strategies. See Bezuidenhout (1997) for a critical discussion of this distinction.

[13]The new economic sociology emerged as a critique of the narrow focus of neoclassical economics on the market and has sought to introduce social explanations of economic

theme arises from a concern with how economic enterprises in South Africa can enhance workers' performance to ensure their survival and growth in the face of increasing international competition and at the same time ensure meaningful worker participation.[14] The transition to democracy has led to new forms of interest mediation between capital and labor at all levels of society (workplace forums), to sector-level institutional arrangements, and at the societal level, to the National Economic Development and Labour Council (NEDLAC) and the Commission for Conciliation, Mediation and Arbitration (CCMA). Through the process of "bargained liberalization," these institutional innovations have the potential, it is argued, to resolve the contradiction between democratization and economic reform (Adler and Webster, 1997).[15]

The creation of new institutions is a protracted process, and it is too early to draw any clear-cut conclusions about whether these social institutions are having an impact on economic performance. Institutional history moves slowly and the workplace remains one of low trust. "Racial identities," it has been argued, "have served to strengthen lateral trust among workers, whilst lowering the potential for vertical trust. Ongoing forms of racism and racial discrimination in the workplace can only serve to reinforce this low trust dynamic" (Macun, 1997:28).

The third area of new research is the emergence of new perspectives on organizational sociology. In spite of intense interest in organizational transformation in South Africa, organizational development (OD) has in the past followed the mainstream literature (van Aardt, 1995). The critical perspectives that have influenced the discipline elsewhere since the 1970s made little impact on South African researchers. However, recently, this has begun to change, with an interest in critical organizational sociology and the impact of African culture on the workplace (Lessem and Nussbaum, 1996). Importantly, this research does not reproduce the "cultural racism" of earlier research that used the concept of black culture as a way of explaining black workers" alleged inadequacies—their high absenteeism, lack of motivation, and low productivity (Fullagar, 1983). Instead, these researchers see African culture, and

decision-making and behavior, primarily the institutional frameworks and methods of governance within which economic action takes place within and outside of firms (Granovetter and Swedberg, 1992; Streeck, 1992).

[14] Debates on economic and industrial policy have been dominated by economists with very little work being done by the new economic sociologists on the limits of economics in understanding these processes. For an attempt to develop an analytical framework for the sociological analysis of the competing economic ideologies in South Africa over the last decade, see Lazar (1996).

[15] The transition to democracy in South Africa generated a widespread use of "transition theory," drawing on the notion of elite pacting developed by Schmitter, Przeworski, and others to understand the democratization process in southern and central Europe and Latin America. For a critique of the uncritical transfer of this notion to the South African transition, see Adler and Webster (1995).

the concept of *ubuntu* (African humanism), as a positive resource for transformation (Lessem and Nussbaum, 1996:13). The theme of organizational change is explored in detail in a study of human resource managers and workplace innovation in Kwazulu-Natal (Sitas, 1995).

INSTITUTIONAL FACTORS SHAPING THE STUDY OF WORK

It has been argued in this chapter that a new approach to industrial sociology emerged in the 1970s. This new, radical industrial sociology emerged as the most popular working group in the Association of South African Sociologists (ASSA) conferences throughout the 1980s. Its focus on the labor movement linked it to the ongoing struggles in the workplace and in society, making the annual ASSA conferences popular events, where academics and academic activists met to engage in what was seen as a shared intellectual and political project.

This new approach to industrial sociology grew in close dialogue with the new industrial unions that emerged in the struggle against apartheid. Research into work became, in a sense, a form of resistance, and research was funded largely by overseas agencies and linked to the agenda of the antiapartheid movement (Webster, 1997). Funding agencies included the Friedrich Ebert Stiftung, a German funding agency linked to the social democratic party, the International Development and Research Center (IDRC) in Canada, the Albert Einstein Institute in Cambridge, Massachusetts, and the International Labour Organisation in Geneva.

As a shift in managerial strategy began to take place in the early 1990s and greater cooperation in the workplace was stressed by business, labor and the new government, funding became more readily available inside the country from both government and the private sector. The emphasis on tripartite cooperation led to renewed interest in productivity and a sponsored study on the workplace by the tripartite body, NEDLAC.

Called the Workplace Change Initiative, this project aims to demonstrate how workplace change can be achieved in order to enhance competitiveness through encouraging enterprises and sectors to enter workplace agreements that guide the parties at a plant level in the process of transforming the workplace. Significantly, the project is managed by Labour Market Alternatives (LMA), a consultancy run largely by graduates of the new industrial sociology. A similar initiative was a study on the labor market sponsored by the International Labour Organisation. The national survey on Enterprise Flexibility was conducted by the only research unit specializing in the sociology of work in the country, the Sociology of Work Unit (SWOP) at the University of Witwatersrand.

In the past, limited funding for studies in the sociology of work was available from the central state funding body, the Human Science Research Council (HSRC). However, until the early 1990s, the HSRC functioned largely as the research arm of the apartheid government. In 1993, the HSRC began a process of transformation and realignment. In 1996, the HSRC decided to focus its external funding on a single research theme, People and Work. It identified employment creation, productivity enhancement, and workplace transformation as the key areas for this research program (HSRC External Project Scheme, 1997–1998). The need to increase productivity in the context of heightened international competition has now become a national research priority, and relatively generous funding for policy-oriented research on the workplace is available. Significantly, one of the main beneficiaries of this new funding strategy by the HSRC was the trade-union-linked research unit, NALEDI, the National Labour and Economic Development Institute, that received funding for a research project on Codetermination and Tripartism from this fund.

In the early 1970s, much of the new sociological study of work was either historical or subordinated to Marxist political economy. With the reemergence of the labor movement in the 1970s and 1980s the sociology of work became closely linked to trade union studies and industrial relations. The close links the labor movement developed with politics also made political science a cognate discipline for the sociology of work. The impact of violence and ethnic mobilization on the workplace has led industrial sociologists in Kwazulu-Natal to explore issues around the construction of identity (Bonin, 1997; Mare, 1992). More recently, economics has become a central discipline in the sociological study of work.

The most interesting interdisciplinary innovation was the creation of the Centre for Industrial, Organisational and Labour Studies at the University of the Natal in 1989. At the core of the innovation was the merger of Industrial Psychology and Industrial Sociology around the study of the world of work. The Centre has generated a rich graduate program with a high proportion of studies on industrial training, organizational culture, and participation and affirmative action (see Table 1).

However, it needs to be stressed that the community of sociologists in South Africa is small, numbering less than 250, many of whom do not have doctorates (South African Sociological Association, 1997).[16] Under these circumstances the possibility of specializing in the sociology of work is limited. Furthermore, the material conditions in teaching sociology have worsened: A rapid growth in student numbers has been accompanied by a significant decline in university resources. There are more than 29,000 sociology students

---

[16]Only four Ph.D.s' in Sociology were awarded at South African Universities in 1996 (South Africa Sociological Association, 1997:3).

Table 1. MA and Ph.D. Dissertations, Centre for Industrial, Organisational and Labour Studies, 1988–1998

Topic	Number	Percentage
Trade Unions, Politics, and Resistance	12	26
Industrial Training	10	22
Organizational Culture and Policies	6	13
Participation and Industrial Democracy	5	11
Affirmative Action	5	11
Gender Studies	4	9
Quality of Working Life (Stress)	3	6
Retrenchment	1	2

Source: Nerita Maharaj, Center for Organisational and Labour Studies, University of Natal, 1998.

in South Africa's 25 universities—a ratio of 1 staff member for every 116 students (South African Sociological Association, 1997).

No specialized journal for the sociology of work exists in South Africa. Most studies are published in local social science journals such as *Transformation, Social Dynamics*, the *South African Sociological Review* (now *South Africa in Transition*), the *African Sociological Review*, the *Industrial Relations Journal of South Africa*, and the *South African Journal of Labour Relations*. The one journal devoted to labor studies—the *South African Labour Bulletin*—is linked to the labor movement and, while it publishes excellent articles that record and analyze struggles in the workplace, it is not an academic journal. Articles are published internationally tend to appear in area studies (such as the *Journal of Southern African Studies*). Occasionally South African scholars publish in international journals that specialise in the sociology of work, such as *Economic and Industrial Democracy*; *Work, Employment and Society*; the *International Labour Review*; and *Labour, Capital and Society*.

CONCLUSION: A WORKPLACE IN TRANSITION

It has been argued in this chapter that globalization is revitalizing the sociological study of work in South Africa, leading to a renewed interest in the field, both in the universities and among policymakers concerned with international competitiveness. Globalization has also led to increasing social polarization in ways not dissimilar to the analysis provided by Marx over a century ago. As Laufer remarked in a leading South African financial newspaper, "So Marx, critical analyst of completely unregulated capitalist development, is again looking like a better economist than he ever was philosopher, developing ideas for a new utopian social order" (Laufer, 1998).

How employers reconcile the strong demands from South Africa's trade union movement with these global pressures for greater efficiency is the central challenge facing the South African workplace. These pressures are creating new demands for reliable social research and policy interventions in the workplace, and demands for an interdisciplinary, problem-solving approach to the study of work, opening up opportunities for a synergy between university-based researchers-practitioners, and policy researchers. This poses exciting possibilities for curriculum reform, the most important being the establishment of interdisciplinary programs aimed at understanding and resolving the complex problems of a workplace within a society in transition.

The challenge facing the South African workplace is one of reconciling the global and the local; greater competitiveness, with employment equity; and greater efficiency, with the demand for more and better jobs. Above all, the transition challenges South African social scientists to locate their study of work in an understanding of the specifics of the South African situation. This must involve a greater recognition of the informal economy and the variety of livelihoods that exist in South Africa. To undertake such a task, sociologists will need to draw on the rich anthropological tradition in South Africa. But for a genuine cross-fertilization to take place, a network of scholars and practitioners needs to be created.

ACKNOWLEDGMENT   I would like to thank Bridget Kenny, a researcher at Sociology of Work United (SWOP), for implementing the survey of South African sociologists that provided me with crucial information for this chapter.

REFERENCES

Adler, G. 1994. "The Factory Belongs to Those Who Work in It." Ph.D. thesis, Columbia University, New York.

Adler, G. 1993. "Skills, Control and Careers at Work: Possibilities for Worker Control in the South African Motor Industry." *South African Sociological Review* 5(2):35–64.

Adler, G., and E. Webster. 1995. "Challenging Transition Theory: The Labour Movement, Radical Reform and Transition to Democracy in South Africa." *Politics and Society* 23(1):75–106.

Adler, G., and E. Webster. 1997. "Bargained Liberalisation: The Labour Movement, Policy making and Transition in Zambia and South Africa." Unpublished paper, Sociology of Work Unit, University of Witwatersrand.

Alverson, H. 1975. "Africans in South African Industry: The Human Dimension." *Contemporary South Africa*, edited by S. Morse and C. Orpen. Cape Town: Juta.

Arrighi, G., and Silver, B. 1984. "Labour Movements and Capital Migration: The United

States and Western Europe in World-Historical Perspective." Pp. 183–216 in *Labour in the Capitalist Economy*, edited by C. Berquist. London: Sage.

Barchiesi, F. 1997. "Flexibility and Changes in Forms of Workplace Subjectivity: A Case Study of the South African Automobile Industry." MA thesis, University of the Witwatersrand.

Best, M. 1990. *The New Competition: Institutions of Industrial Restructuring.* Cambridge, MA: Harvard University Press.

Bethlehem, L. 1994. "Evaluating the Concept of 'Racial Fordism'": A Case-study of the South African Paper Industry." MA thesis, University of Witwatersrand.

Bezuidenhout, A. 1996. "Centralisation through Decentralisation: The Use of Subcontracted Labour in the Light of Intensification of Managerial Control." *South African Journal of Sociology* 27(1).

Bezuidenhout, A. 1997. "Labour Market Flexibility as Friend or Foe: Recasting the Debate." Paper presented to the South African Sociological Association, University of Transkei, Umtata.

Bezuidenhout, A., and C. Bolsman. 1998. "Responding to the Challenges of the New World Order: The State of Sociology of Organisations in South Africa." Paper presented to South African Sociological Association, Johannesburg.

Bezuidenhout, A., and Kenny, B. 1998. "Subcontracting in the Mining Industry." *Innes Labour Brief* 10(1).

Bonin, D. 1987. Class Consciousness and Conflict in the Natal Midlands: The Case of BTR Sameol. Unpublished MA thesis. University of Natal-Duban.

Bonin, D. 1997. "Spatiality in the Construction of Identity: African Women and Political Violence in Kwazulu-Natal." *Society in Transition* 1(1–4):27–42.

Bozzoli, B., and P. Delius. 1990. "Radical History and South African Society." *Radical History Review* 46(7):13–45.

Braverman, H. 1974. *Labour and Monopoly Capital: The Degradation of Work in the Twentieth Century.* New York: Monthly Review Press.

Buhlungu, S. 1997. 'Trade Union Responses to Participative Management: A Case Study." MA thesis, University of the Witwatersrand.

Burawoy, M. 1985. *The Politics of Production.* London: Verso.

Burawoy, M. 1990. "Marxism as Science: Historical Challenges and Conceptual Growth." *American Sociological Review* 55:775–792.

Crankshaw, O. 1997. *Race, Class and the Changing Division of labour Under Apartheid.* London: Routledge.

Crankshaw, O., and I. Macun. 1997. "External Labour Market Flexibility: is there Employment Flexibility in South African Industry?" Unpublished paper, Conference on Labour Markets and Enterprise Performance, Reserve Bank, Pretoria.

Davies, R. 1979. *Capital, State and White Labour in South Africa, 1900–1960.* Brighton: Harvester Press.

Desai, A. 1997. "Race, Class and the Intellectual Left in South Africa"s Democratic Transition." Paper presented at the Conference on Race, Class and Difference, St. Anthony's College, Oxford, UK.

Duncan, D., and B. Payne. 1993. "Just-in-time South Africa: Japanese Systems in the South African Motor Industry." *Capital and Class* 50.

Edwards, R. 1979. *Contested Terrain: The Transformation of the Workplace in the Twentieth Century*. New York: Basic Books.

Ewart, J. 1992. "Restructuring Industry on the Factory Floor: Neo-Fordist Tendencies at Western Cape Firms." *South African Sociological Review* 5(1):1–22.

Ewart, J. W. 1990. "The Political Maintenance of 'Skill': Labour Process Changes and Artisan Domination in the Printing Industry." *Social Dynamics* 16(2):38–55.

Fullagar, C. 1983. "Organisational Behaviour in South Africa: A Historical Overview." In *Behaviour in Organisations: South African Perspectives*, edited by J. Barling. Johannesburg: McGraw-Hill.

Gelb, S. 1987. "Making Sense of the Crisis." *Transformation* 5:33–50.

Gelb, S. 1992. 'The Dynamics of Accumulation: Essays on the Theory of Regulation and Its Application to South Africa." Ph.D. thesis, University of Manitoba, Canada.

Glenn, F. 1992. "A Post-Braverman Analysis of Clerical Workers in the Finance Sector: A Case-Study." *South African Sociological Review* 5(1):23–40.

Gordon, R. 1978. *Mines, Masters and Migrants*. Johannesburg: Ravan.

Granovetter, M., and R. Swedberg, eds. 1992. *The Sociology of Economic Life*. Boulder, CO: Westview Press.

Horwitz, F. 1995. "Flexible Work Practices in South Africa; Economic, Labour Relations and Regulatory Considerations." *South African Industrial Relations Journal* 26(4).

Innes, D. 1983. "Monopoly Capitalism in South Africa." *South Africa Review 1: Same Foundations, New Facades*. Johannesburg: Ravan.

Innes, D., and Davies, R. 1996. "Affirmative Action: A Case Study for Implementation." *Innes Labour Brief* 7(3):5–20.

Joffe, A. et al 1995. *Improving Manufacturing Performance in South Africa*. Cape Town: University of Cape Town Press.

Johnstone, F. 1976. *Class, Race and Gold: A Study of Class Relations and Racial Discrimination in South Africa*. London: Routledge and Kegan Paul.

Jubber, K., ed. 1979. *Industrial Relations and Industrial Sociology*. Cape Town: Juta.

Kaplinsky, R. 1994. Economic Restructuring in South Africa: the Debate Continues. *Journal of Southern African Studies* 20(4).

Katz, E. 1976. *A Trade Union Aristocracy*. Johannesburg: Witwatersrand University Press.

Kenny, B. 1997. "Work, Welfare, and Social Development: 'Flexible" Labour and the Costs of Reproduction." Research project, Sociology of Work Unit, University of the Witwatersrand, Johannesburg.

Kenny, B., and E. Webster. 1998. "Eroding the Core: Flexibility and the Re-Segmentation of the South African Labour Market." Paper presented to the 14th World Congress of Sociology, Montreal, Canada.

Klerk, G. 1994. "Industrial Restructuring and the Casualisation of Labour: A Case Study of Subcontracted Labour in the Process Industries." *South African Sociological Review* 7(1):32–62.

Klerck, G. 1996. "Regulation Theory: Towards a Synthesis in Development Studies." Pp. 113–130 in *Reconstruction, Development and People*, edited by J. Coetzee and J. Graaff. Johannesburg: Thompson.

Kraak, A. 1987. "Uneven Capitalist Development: A Case Study of Deskilling and Reskilling in South Africa's Metal Industry." *Social Dynamics* 13(2):14–31.

Kraak, A. 1997. "Transforming South Africa's Economy: from Racial-Fordism to Neo-Fordism?" *Economic and Industrial Democracy* 17:39–74

Laufer, S. 1998. "Full Marx for Fresh Thinking on Profits." *Business Day*, January 22.

Lazar, D. 1996. "Competing Economic Ideologies in South Africa's Economic Debate." *British Journal of Sociology* 47(4):599–626.

Leger, J. 1992. "'Talking Rocks': An Investigation of the Pit Sense of Rockfall Accidents Amongst Underground Gold Miners." Unpublished Ph.D. thesis , University of Witwatersrand, Johannesburg.

Lessem, R., and Nussbaum. 1996. *Sawubona Africa: Embracing Four Worlds in South African Management.* Sandton: Zebra.

Lever, J. 1982. "Labour Process and the Sociology of Work in South Africa: Preliminary Observations." Unpublished paper, Association of South African Sociologists, University of Western Cape. Belville.

Lewis, J. 1984. *Industrialisation and Trade Union Organisation 1925–1955.* Cambridge University Press.

Lloyd, C. 1994. *Work Organisation and World Class Management: A Critical Guide.* Johannesburg: Red Earth Publications.

Macun, I. 1997. "Cooperation and Trust in South African Industrial Relations: Theory and Evidence." Unpublished paper, Sociology of Work Unit, University of the Witwatersrand.

Maller, J. 1992. *Conflict and Cooperation: Case Studies in Worker Participation.* Johannesburg: Ravan.

Maller, J., and B. Dwolatsky. 1993. "What is Fordism? Restructuring Work in the South African Metal Industry." *Transformation* 22:70–85.

Mahone, G. 1996. *The Informal Sector in Southern Africa.* Harare: Southern African Regional Policy Institute.

Makhanya, M. 1995. "An Overview of affirmative Action in South Africa." Pp. 157–176 in *Industrial Sociology: A South African Perspective,* edited by A. Van Der Merve. Johannesburg: Lexicon.

Mare, G. 1992. *Brothers Born of Warrior Blood: Politics and Ethnicity in South Africa.* Johannesburg, Ravan.

Maree, J. 1985. "The Emergence, Struggles and Achievements of Black Trade Unions in South Africa from 1973 to 1984." *Labour, Capital and Society* 18(2):278–303.

Moodie, D. 1994. *Going for Gold: Men, Mines and Migration.* Berkeley: University of California Press.

National Labour, Education and Development Institute. 1997. *Research Project on Hours of Work and Changing Employment Standards.* Johannesburg.

Nzimande, E. B. 1986. "Managers and the New Middle Class." *Transformation* 1:39–62.

Nzimande, E. B. 1991. "'The Corporate Guerillas': Class Formation and the African Corporate Petty Bourgeoisie in Post-1973 South Africa." Ph.D. thesis, University of Natal, Durban.

Piore, M., and C. Sabel. 1984, *The Second Industrial Divide.* Basic Books.

Penn, P. 1982. "Skilled Manual Workers in the Labour Process, 1856–1864." Pp. 35–

50 in *The Degradation of Work: Skill, Deskilling and the Labour Process*, edited by Stephen Wood. London: Hutchinson.

Porter, M. 1990. *The Competitive Advantage of Nations*. London: Macmillan.

Rees, R. 1997. "Irregular Labour in the Manufacturing, Retail and Construction Sectors." Paper presented at the Department of Labour Workshop on Regulating New Employment Norms, Johannesburg.

Rex, J. 1974. "The Compound, Reserve, and Urban Location-Essential Institutions of Southern African Labour Exploitation." *South African Labour Bulletin* 1(4):4–17.

Rosenthal, T., and A. Joffe. 1996. "Intelligent Production: An Approach to Enterprise Restructuring." *South African Labour Bulletin* 20(4):74–80.

Seidman, G. 1994. *Manufacturing Militance: Workers Movements in Brazil and South Africa, 1970-1985*. Berkeley: University of California Press.

Sitas, A. 1998. "African Worker Responses to Changes in the Metal Industry, 1960–1980." Ph.D. thesis, University of the Wiwatersrand, Johannesburg.

Sitas, A. 1988. "The New Poor and Social Movements in Durban." Unpublished paper, Centre for Industrial, Organisational and Labour Studies, University of Natal, Durban.

Sitas, A. (Project Coordinator). 1995. "Managing Change in Kwazulu-Natal"s Industries." Research Report to the Centre for Science Development,, Centre for Industrial, Organisational, and Labour Studies, University of Natal, Durban.

Sociology of Work Unit. 1997. *Monitoring Workplace Forums*. Johannesburg: University of Witwatersrand Press.

South African Sociological Association 1997. *Directory of Sociology Departments, 1996–1997*. Department of Sociology, University of Stellenbosch.

Southall, R. 1985. "Monopoly Capitalism and Industrial Unionism in South Africa." *Labour, Capital and Society* 18(2):229–235.

Standing, G., J. Sender, and J. Weeks. 1996. *Restructuring the Labour Market: The South African Challenge*. Geneva: International Labour Office.

Streeck, W. 1992. *Social Institutions and Economic Performance*. London: Sage.

Theron, J. 1996. *On Homeworkers*. Institute of Development and Labour, University of Cape Town.

Van Aardt, C. 1995. "An Overview of Organisational Sociology: Perspectives, Themes and Trends." Pp. 236–262 in *Industrial Sociology: A South African Perspective*, edited by A. Van der Merve. Johannesburg: Lexicon.

Van der Merwe, C. 1995. *Industrial Sociology: A South African Perspective*. Johannesburg: Lexicon.

Von Holdt, K. 1996. "The Apartheid Workplace Regime and Ungovernability: Transition in the South African Workplace." Unpublished paper, South African Sociological Association, University of Natal, Durban.

Von Holdt, K. 2000. "From the Politics of resistance to the Politics of Reconstruction: The Union and Ungovernability in the Workplace." Pp. xxx–xxx in *Trade Unions in Transition: Consolidating Democracy in a Liberalising World*, edited by G. Adler and E. Webster. London: Macmillan.

Webster, E. 1978. *Essays in Southern African History*. Johannesburg: Ravan.

Webster, E. 1981. "Servants of Apartheid? A Survey of Social Research Into Industry in South Africa." Pp. 85–113 in *Apartheid and Social Research*, edited by J. Rex. Paris: Unesco Press.

Webster, E. 1985. *Cast in a Racial Mould: Labour Process and Trade Unionism in the Foundries*. Johannesburg: Ravan.

Webster, E., and Leger, J. 1992. "Reconceptualising Skill Formation in South Africa." *Perspectives in Education* 13(2)53–67.

Webster, E. 1996. "Changing Workplace Relations in South Africa." Pp. 35–50 in *Sawubona Africa: Embracing Four worlds in South African management,* edited by R. Lessem and B. Nussbaum. Sandton: Zebra Books.

Wright, E. O. 1978. *Class, Crisis and the State*. London: Verso Books.

APPENDIX: CONTACTS

Major Research Centers concerned with the study of work in South Africa

Centre of Industrial and Labour Studies, University of Natal, Durban
Director: D. Bonin
E-mail: Bonin@nuac.za
Phone: (031) 260-2512

Centre for Social and Development Studies (CSDS), University of Natal, Durban
Director: M. Morris
E-mail: MORRISM@mtb.und.ac.za
Phone: (031) 260-2285

Development Policy Research Unit (DPRU)
University of Cape Town
8001 Old Medical School Building
Hiddingh Campus, 37 Orange Street, Cape Town
Director: D. Kaplan
E-mail: ETISPCPT@UCT.VAX.AC.ZA
Phone: (021) 650- 3987

Industrial Democracy Programme
Faculty of Management
University of Witwatersrand,
PO Box 98
WITS, 2050
Director: L. Douwes-Dekker
E-mail: buwaldad@zeus.mgmp.wits.ac.za
Phone: (011) 488-5591

Industrial Relations Project
Department of Sociology
University of Cape Town
Private Bag

Rondebosch, 7701
Director: J. Maree
E-mail: MAREE@HUMANITIES.VCT.AC.ZA
Phone: (021) 650-3501

Industrial Relations Research Unit
University of Port Elizabeth
PO BOX 1600D, Port Elizabeth
Director: M. Anstey;
E-mail: IRAMMA@UPE.AC.ZA
Phone: (041) 504-2111

International Labour Resource and Information Group (ILRIG)
P.O. Box 213
Salt River, 7924
E-mail: Ilrig@worknet.apc.org
Phone: (021) 476

Labour Market Policy Research Unit
Department of Labour
Private Bag X117
Pretoria. 0001
Director: M. Lesaoana
E-mail: maseka.lesaoana@labour.gov.za
Phone: (011) 309 4145

National Labour and Economic Development Institute (NALEDI)
P.O. Box 5665
Joburg, 2000
Director: R. Naidoo
E-mail: ravi@naledi.wun.apc.org
Phone: (011) 403-2122\3

Sociology of Work Unit (SWOP)
University of the Witwatersrand
Private Bag 3
WITS, 2050
Director: E. C. Webster
E-mail: 029edw@muse.arts.wits.ac.za
Phone: (011) 716-2908

Trade Union Research Project (TURP)
University of Natal
Durban
Director: G. Phillips
E-mail: turp@nu.ac.za
Phone: (031) 260-2438

IV

Europe

The sociology of work emerged along distinctive paths in each of the seven European nations covered in this book—France–Belgium, Germany, Great Britain, Hungary, Portugal, and Sweden. In each nation, the growth of the sociology of work was associated with societal political and economic transformations. These transformations have resulted in the appearance of some common research themes in Europe in recent years.

The sociology of work developed in tandem with political and economic change in Europe. French sociology, including Durkheim's global impact on the discipline, emerged in the late 19th and early 20th centuries with industrialization and urbanization. A more specialized French sociology of work focusing on workers and work organization appeared after World War II, with the reconstruction of a devastated France. In Germany, the global and disciplinewide impact of Marx and Weber continued to unfold across the late 19th and early 20th centuries with continuing industrialization and the ascendance of capitalism. The rebuilding of war-torn Germany generated a more specialized sociology of work beginning in the late 1940s focusing on employment and the organization of workplaces. The sociology of work in Great Britain hails from the early 20th century, with industrialization and a focus on worker attitudes and behavior. In Hungary, the sociology of work originally focused on peasant life in the early 20th century, developed a special focus on informal employment relations under state socialism, and—with economic privatization and marketization during the 1990s—has pursued a variety of themes associated with social inequality, work organization, and efficiency. After the democratic revolution in Portugal during the mid-1970s, the sociology of work emerged with both academic and applied emphases on new models of work organization, the social implications of changing production technology, skills formation, industrial democracy, and enterprise competitiveness in an increasingly diversified economy. In Sweden, the sociology of work has been linked to the birth of the welfare state and the labor movement since the early 20th century and has pursued a variety of themes on workplace humanization and economic democracy.

In recent years, a few common research themes have emerged among the European nations, partly fostered by cross-national exchanges facilitated by the European Union. Among these themes are skills formation and skills-level trends associated with workplace restructuring and changing production technology; gender inequality in wages and employment opportunities; the socioeconomic implications of nonstandard work arrangements; and the growth, decline, and revitalization of labor unions.

10
France–Belgium

Pierre Desmarez

INTRODUCTION

The French-language sociology of work (*sociologie du travail*) in Europe appears as an academic speciality only after World War II and defines itself in opposition to the developments of mainstream industrial sociology in the United States that follow the line traced by the Hawthorne studies and *Management and the Worker*. The manipulative aspects of the "human relations school" are particularly, unanimously stressed by the pioneers of the sociology of work in France.

French-speaking European thinkers of course showed their interest for work and its problems long before sociology of work appeared as a subdiscipline. Industrialization and its consequences were studied during the 19th century and gave birth to important surveys conducted in France and in Belgium. Villermé, Quételet, Le Play, and Ducpétiaux were the promotors of the most important of those studies, which revealed the conditions of life and work of the working class and sometimes provoked the enforcement of new

Pierre Desmarez • Center for the Sociology of Work, Employment, and Organization, Free University of Brussels, 1050 Brussels, Belgium.

Worlds of Work: Building an International Sociology of Work, edited by Daniel B. Cornfield and Randy Hodson. Kluwer Academic/Plenum Publishers, New York, 2002.

regulations (on working hours or children's work), as Villermé's *Tableau de l'état physique et moral des ouvriers employés dans les manufactures de coton, de laine et de soie*, published in 1840.

In a more philosophical vein, Saint-Simon, Cabet, Blanc, Fourier, Comte, and Proudhon also showed interest in the problems of an industrializing society. Some of them are the authors of famous utopies. Besides Paul Lafargue's (1907) quite original *The Right to Be Lazy* (first published in 1883), which questions the proletariat's adhesion to the myth of work, the writings of Proudhon have been of particular importance for the sociology of work. For Pierre-Joseph Proudhon (1969), work is a fundamental feature of human nature, its *raison d'être*. Work is an activity that should be executed on a voluntary basis in a community of complementary craft workers. The fragmentation of tasks in the modern factory made the creation of that kind of community impossible. However, Proudhon believed that the development of sophisticated machines could make possible the recomposition of fragmented tasks and hence transform the worker into a "complete worker" and also foster the elimination of the entrepreneur by recreating a coherent craft community, the *mutualité*, an association of workers guided by general interest. Proudhon's nostalgia for craft industry was considered by Marx as suggesting changes in the capitalist system that would not be able to produce a new society in which workers' exploitation would disappear. This discussion between Proudhon and Marx has had a lasting influence in the sociology of work.

During the first decades of the 20th century, noticeable developments also occurred in economic sociology, sociology of social classes, and sociology of the firm (in Switzerland). In France, most of these developments were in the sociological tradition inaugurated by Emile Durkheim, whose *Division of Social Labor* (1893) contained important insights into the analysis of the way society separated and allocated tasks. One of Durkheim's followers, Maurice Halbwachs, tried to link working and life conditions with social representations, in the first thesis on the working class at the Sorbonne (in 1912).

Although these early developments of the French-language sociology of work in Europe are not only worth mentioning but also require longer comments, the remainder of this chapter focuses on the developments that occurred in *sociologie du travail* as a subdiscipline. This implies that little will be said here about research into industrial relations and sociology of organizations, even if the boundaries between those specialities and sociology of work are unclear.

IMPORTANT THEMES

Shaping perspectives[1]

After World War II, in the socioeconomic context of France, social sciences were considered potentially useful in understanding change and helping the State to adapt to it. The acceleration of industrialization, the preoccupations of the State, and the technical developments rendered sociological studies in industry attractive to young intellectuals. Georges Friedmann's *Industrial Society* (1955), first published in 1946, had a seminal effect. Sociology of work "formed the largest specialist branch of sociological enquiry until around 1960 [. . .]; many, if not the majority, of the most important figures in French Sociology as a whole in the sixties were, or had been, *sociologues du travail*" (Rose, 1979:25).

At that time, many surveys were conducted in various industries and administrations and many researchers devoted a considerable amount of time to the development of this new speciality. A synthesis of this perspective, though not as homogeneous as sometimes claimed, can be found in the famous *Traité de sociologie du travail* edited by Friedmann and Pierre Naville (1961–1962).[2] As it appears clearly in the introductions to the *Traité*, the new speciality was supposed to deal with all aspects of work, as well as the relationships between work and society, including the fact that individuals belonged to different social groups that contributed to shape their attitudes at work and elsewhere. Even if they edited the book together and agreed on the general objectives, Friedmann and Naville nevertheless adopted and promoted quite different points of view. While Naville and his team were mostly interested in automation and its consequences, Friedmann and his collaborators concentrated on the analysis of the evolution of skills apprehended at the workshop level. Both prominent scholars deeply marked the speciality with their scientific and institutional activity, but Friedmann's perspective became dominant and is now often called the "classical" sociology of work. Even if it can easily be shown that other perspectives have always existed, until the end of the 1970s the core of research undertaken in this "classical" sociology of work has been the study of the so-called "work situation." Most of the data were collected during an usually short period of time through interviews or observations of the way work was organized and actually done at workshop level,

---

[1]This section is particularly schematic; for a much more detailed account of that period, see Rose (1979).
[2]For a detailed analysis of the *Traité*, see La Rosa (1979) and Rose (1987).

establishing a link between this context and the condition of the working class.

The priority given to this topic can be explained by different factors (Rose, 1979; Tripier, 1994): the theoretical and philosophical–political tradition in which sociology of work takes place; the characteristics of the social demand and, in particular, available funds; and the dominant social groups that at the time produced representations of work and society (blue-collar workers and unions, engineers and middle-range managers directly involved in industrial production).

Three main features can be identified in this classical tradition. First, work is conceived as some kind of "substance" that can be analyzed as such, and exists as an abstract reality that becomes social only when embodied in the activity of the individual worker. Second, the studies refer to a state that is related to Proudhon's "complete worker": some nostalgic representation of craft industry as a "lost paradise" to be regained (Rose, 1987). Friedmann (1978), for example, judged that technological developments imply more worker polyvalence, and saw this as a revalorization of work. Finally, from a more methodological point of view, if what happens in the firm (or in the workshop) can sometimes be explained by variables exerting an influence from the outside, the problems that arise at that level can or could be solved from the inside (by acting upon the motivation of workers, through participation, wages, changes in the organization of work, etc.). According to this line of thought, the relationship between work and technology was given central importance in the analysis of work and industrial society; the evolution of the organization of work is seen as also having implications on a "worker's consciousness" and movement, as in Alain Touraine's early work (1962; 1971).

The main differences between Friedmann's perspective and the tradition promoted by Naville can be apprehended by examining the way each, in a famous controversy at the end of the 1950s, answered the question: Is it the work or the worker that is skilled? Naville considered that it is the worker, not the work that is skilled, and chose as the main criterion the time spent in education to measure this skill. In opposition, Friedmann and Reynaud thought it more fruitful to say that work is skilled, and tried to define a multidimensional way to establish a classification of jobs. Naville questioned this position, mainly on the basis that, in modern industry, it had become impossible to define such a hierarchy in an objective way. For him, skill was not some kind of substance created by the technical characteristics of the job but instead expressed a relation between technical operations and a social judgment that referred to the differential value of the different kinds of work and led to a hierarchy of workers. This implies that skill is not the immediate product of individual abilities but, rather, expresses a relationship between different categories of workers.

These discussions remain relevant in sociology of work today, and, when it comes to the study of "work situations," the dominant tradition is still marked by Friedmann's ideas. Some authors have nevertheless supported Naville's point of view and his "relational" definition of skill and the centrality he gave to the analysis of the labor process and wage payment as a point of departure to design new perspectives (Alaluf, 1986; Rolle, 1988, 1996; Tripier, 1991). They have particularly stressed the interest of adopting a research strategy no longer centered on the workshop or on the firm. In this way, they contributed to the development of the sociology of employment described in this chapter.

New Themes

The Societal Effect. International comparisons became more common after the pioneering work conducted since 1972 in France and Germany (and later Japan) by the "Aix-en-Provence school." The authors of that study tried to overcome what they considered to be the shortcomings of traditional international comparative research in order to be able to "compare what is uncomparable" (Maurice, 1995; Maurice, Sellier, and Silvestre, 1986). This means that one has to avoid a "blind" comparison of components of a social system and try to understand the differences between the elements in the framework of the social relations that produce those differences, as well as the specific features of the system. To reach that objective, relying on both an institutional analysis and case studies in various industries, these researchers identified what they called a "societal effect," which is a "coherence" resulting from a specific national configuration of interdependent social relations in three related fields: in the organization itself, in the industrial relations sphere, and in the socialization process (education system). This implies tackling the opposition between "macro" and "micro", which is here superseded by taking into consideration the way the actors, and the "social spaces" in which they act, are defined (and sometimes changed) in their relations with society as a whole. Micro and macro are built by each other. The notion of "skill space" is a good example of this perspective. It was first used as an empirical notion to describe the way German workers acquired and develop their skill: The features of the educational system explained the existence of a continuity in the "skill space," from the skilled worker to the engineer, and this continuity, of course, had consequences in terms of the mobility processes. This notion of "space" appeared to appropriately conceptualize in a dialectical way the relations between actor and social structure, and was later used in different settings: organization, industrial relations, technological innovation.

Even if more traditional, culturalist inspired research persists in international comparisons, the Aix school has been very influential and is still widely discussed (Maurice and Sorge, 2000). One of the shortcomings that was stressed is that this framework led to such complexity that it rendered very difficult the combination of both transversal and longitudinal analysis: The dynamics and the genesis of the rules and institutions did not receive enough attention. Some studies, less ambitious than Maurice, Sellier and Silvestre's (1986) founding work, were nevertheless able to include a more developed time dimension in the analysis. In a comparison between France, Sweden, and the United Kingdom, Anne-Marie Daune-Richard (1998) used, for example, statistical data and documents to show usefulness of the notion of societal effect in understanding the way part-time work is defined in each country and, above all, stressed the different roles played by employment status in the life cycle of female workers in both the labor market and the framework of family policies.

Work and the Family.   To try to analyze the relationships between work and family is another interesting, new perspective that has its roots in research into women's work and employment, and also migrant workers. Work conducted since the end of 1960s has used various data and methods: surveys, case studies, interviews, and documents. Here, too, international comparisons were helpful in understanding the variety of links that could exist between the different spheres to which individuals belong. Defining "work" as a whole comprising both paid and unpaid family work, and the "family" as the place where "work" is regulated and, in particular, allocated to each member of the family unit, Marie-Agnès Barrère-Maurisson (2000) describes the process of the "family division of labor," which can be seen at work at different levels and in different places: in the family itself, of course, but also in the employment sphere. The individual manages the relationship between his or her family and working life. Members of the family share unpaid and paid work. A similar rule applies inside the firm, when it comes to the way categories of workers are allocated to jobs, or in the labor market, where a link is established between categories of jobs and categories of workers. Relying upon in-depth analysis of the army and agriculture, life histories of women, case studies of firms, and secondary analyses of large surveys, one can also discern a relationship between a dominant family type and categories of economic activity or even countries. The analysis of the family division of labor can be analyzed from both a historical point of view and an international comparative perspective. In both cases, the features and interactions of individual, organizational, and institutional actors reveal the way the process is regulated and the variety of roles played by public policies.

Labor   Markets,   Work,   and   Occupations: Interactionist Perspectives.   The sociological study of occupations and professionalization, as conceived in the 1950s by E. C. Hughes, has been very influential in redesigning the framework of the French-language sociology of work in the last 20 years. This framework was used to give time a more central place in the analysis (mainly through the use of the notions of "career" and "life history") and, as was true for Hughes, found that studies conducted on atypical occupations were useful to single out features of more often studied occupations that otherwise would have remained unnoticed. Studies conducted on craft workers (e.g., bakers, farmers) or transportation workers (truck or train drivers, sailors) have also presented another opportunity to draw attention to the close link between work and nonwork, and, more specifically, between work and the lifestyles. Case studies, interviews, and participant observation are the methods used in most of those studies.

Research into work in the transport sector (Tripier, 1986) has been particularly fruitful in bringing to light the fact that to understand individual and collective behavior of the workers, one has to consider not only their working conditions but also the socialization processes specific to the occupation and, in particular, the relationships between know how and experience. These studies also have contributed to show how "nonwork" activities contribute to the functioning of the work system itself. The role of the family has also been particularly stressed; for example, when it helps to overcome the barriers that may protect access to a specific labor market, or comes into play in the organization of mobility processes or transfer of entrepreunerial responsibilities. Studies of transport have also led to the conclusion that the occupations one encounters in the sector are less homogenous than commonly thought. There are significant differences inside an occupation, for example, between wage workers and nonwage workers, or between sedentary and traveling workers. Those differences and the boundaries between the categories are partly created by public policies and can sometimes generate tensions between the holders of the different kinds of status. Finally, these studies revealed the way the organization and the function of labor markets can change. They reiterate that at stake here is the control an occupation has on its labor market, whether in terms of demographic regulation and/or the definition of mandates and competition.

The growing interest in individualistic and interactionist perspectives can also be found in other spheres of the sociology of work. Inside the firm, Jean-Daniel Reynaud delineates the difference between two opposite strategies. The first is organized around workers' activity and has been called "autonomous regulation," in opposition to "control regulation" by management, which is organized around prescribed tasks. Work, as it appears in the firm, is an equilibrium between the two, which is called "joint regulation" (Reynaud, 1989). Sometimes, what is at stake in an industrial conflict, says Reynaud, is the system of rules itself, but usually, both rationalities' underlying regulations follow established "rules of the game." Putting a series of conflicts under scrutiny, for example, Reynaud and Adam used this framework to analyze industrial relations in different countries, showing that in some of them, negotiation of the rules was more frequent. Gilbert de Terssac (1992) used the "joint regulation" perspective to stress that informal organization of work plays a key role in the regulation of sophisticated technical processes he studied through observation and surveys conducted mainly in the chemical, glass, and cement industries. Catherine Paradeise (1988) also takes this interactionist point of view to deal with labor markets and, more particularly, "closed" labor markets (i.e., labor markets in which one can only enter at the bottom, and hiring and promotion are subordinated to impersonal rules). Paradeise shows that the genesis of such markets can be explained by a "super rule" articulating the interests of employees and employers.

The Firm.   During the second half of the 1980s, some sociologists of work considered that the firm had not received the attention it deserved and decided to develop what they called a sociology of the firm(s). The journal *Sociologie du Travail* devoted a special issue to the topic in 1986, and Denis Segrestin (1992) published a synthesis of research in the field. This wish to analyze the firm in all its aspects, in itself (and in its relation to society), and no more as the place where "other things" can be observed appeared in a period during which the image of the firm was widely changing in French society. Formerly considered the place where exploitation has its roots, the firm was considered to be the source of wealth of society and even a place where workers could gain citizenship while the firm also functioned in harmony with society and aimed at the general interest. The resurgence of this conception of the firm in a context of reengineering, high redundancies, growing temporary employment, and closings led some authors to question its managerial orientation. Others had some doubts about the fruitfulness of this perspective because the new personnel policies rendered the boundaries of the firm fuzzier than ever.

While its difference with the sociology of organizations remains unclear for many sociologists of work, the sociology of the firm aims at defining some concepts that could be used to think of the firm as simultaneously a unit elaborated around one project and an entity in which one encounters conflict of interests, cliques, and contrasted rationalities—to think of its autonomy as well as its links with its environment; to think of its economic role as well as its role as social institution. This implies that research has to take into consideration not only the way norms are defined and changed in the firm but also the relationships the firm entertain with other institutions of the social world, such as the family, education and training, and local networks. In that perspective, some sociologists of the firm have discussions with members of other disciplines, such as management scientists, economists, and lawyers.

Post- or neo-Taylorism? The idea formulated by Naville at the beginning of the 1960s—that process industries' organization of work would become more and more common—even if it rested at the time upon a lean empirical basis, was insightful: For many workers, direct contact with materials has become less frequent and work often means conduct and control of automated processes and management of information. These observations rely mainly on data gathered in big firms and lead some authors to consider that a radical change has occurred in the organization of work, and to claim "the end of Taylorism." According to them, management and anticipation of unpredictable events are the core of modern work and require new organizational choices. What becomes more and more important is the ability of workers to exchange information, and conformity to predefined rules and norms becomes less important. Creativity, responsibility, communication, and autonomy are the key words of this "new productive model" (Francfort et al., 1995; Veltz and Zarifian, 1993). From this point of view, only objectives are prescribed, not means.

Other authors are skeptical about these conclusions and plead for at least more caution, especially concerning the fact that one faces the "end of Taylorism." They consider that work has indeed changed but note that the gap between conception and execution remains, even in the case of conduct and control of automated processes; these tasks have also often become fragmented and routinized. Management does not seem ready to forget the basic principles of taylorist organization of work; however, it has begun to develop policies aimed at changing the identities of the workers in order to lead them to make theirs the values of the firm and to forget more traditional (craft or class) values (see, e.g., Linhart, 1991, who synthetized studies conducted in various industries).

Skills and Identity. Even if some studies that rely upon data gathered during the 1970s have already stressed important differences between the identities shown by workers employed at similar tasks, during recent years, this topic has been more deeply investigated and related to the changes in personnel management policies. Renaud Sainsaulieu (1988), for example, has used participant observation and interviews in medium-sized and large companies and public administrations to design a typology of the attitudes of actors toward work. He makes a distinction between four types: integration in a solidary group of peers, valorization of interpersonal relationships, negotiation of the position in the organization, and withdrawal from work (which is then considered in an instrumental manner). Particular attention has also been given to occupational socialization and its links with job positions (and job changes), unemployment, and vocational training. Nondirective interviewing of wage earners in six large firms involved in modernization processes, case studies of two nuclear plants, and interviews with young, poorly educated people have, for example, allowed Claude Dubar (1995) to build a typology combining the two main ways people describe their own biography (as a continuous or discontinuous process), and the two main ways the same persons evaluate whether the firms in which they are involved acknowledge (or do not acknowledge) their qualities. Dubar stresses the opposition between the identities in which aknowledgment of qualities does not exist and those in which the qualities of the worker are recognized, one way or another. The latter types are seen as manifestations of the importance in firms using flexibility and individual procedures to assess know-how and commitment, and as a threat against traditional collective bargaining procedures. The growing importance given to individual abilities and tacit skills in management policies has been researched and assessed in a critical manner: Behind this evolution, it appears that the relative value allocated to a task makes an ability or knowledge visible or invisible (Ropé and Tanguy, 1993; Stroobants, 1993).

Work, Education, and Training.   The relationships between education and work have also been carefuly studied since the 1970s when the *Centre d'Études et de Recherches sur les Qualifications* (Céreq) launched large surveys aimed at gathering data on the position of young degree holders in the labor market. It is probably in this field that the most sophisticated statistical techniques have been used, since large data sets were available. Generally speaking, the results show a link between levels of education or degrees and employment that is much looser than predicted by many economic or even sociological theories. This has led to a consideration of the relationship between education and employment as "undiscoverable" (Tanguy, 1986). Education certainly continues to provide protection against unemployment and guarantees better access to continuing education and career opportunities. But it has also been shown that the improvement of the educational level of the population parallels access to employment that is more and more difficult, especially when unemployment is high. Research has been conducted on how that kind of transition becomes more and more organized, especially for young people, involving the definition of new positions, institutions, and processes, which may vary from one country to another (Jobert, Marry, and Tanguy, 1995; Rose, 1998). Another part of the research into education and training deals with their links with work itself. Here, the results of studies relying mainly upon direct (and sometimes participant) observation in various industry and service sectors show that the use of knowledge cannot be separated from the circumstances in which it is put into action (i.e., from work). At the same time, work activity creates new knowledge. The relationship between these two aspects of the problem has led to a new brand of investigations into the learning process, professional knowledge, and the language at work, in a framework that rests upon ethnomethodology and aims to build links with the cognitive sciences (Borzeix and Conein, 1994; Boutet, 1995).

A Sociology of Employment. In the mid-1980s, some authors considered that a new direction had to be taken and that there was a need for sociological analysis of labor markets (Tripier, 1991). This new orientation, called "sociology of employment" (Maruani and Reynaud, 1993), was meant to deal sociologically with processes that, until then were mainly analyzed by labor economics. The goal is to study the social construction of labor markets and the social relations related to employment (and unemployment). For example, Margaret Maruani and Chantal Nicole-Drancourt (1989) tried to understand the development of part-time work using statistical data, documents, interviews, and case studies in retail trade and the rubber industry. They showed that part-time jobs are less skilled than full-time jobs and are concentrated in some sectors. And in those jobs, women have almost a monopoly. Moreover, they are designed as "women job positions": Social status is directly related to the status of the job. This example stresses the way social norms and representations may explain labor market segmentation. The social status of the job also sheds some light upon the hierarchy of the workers and the differentiation of working conditions in the firm. Part-time workers usually have less career opportunities and lower wages. The position of their job in occupational classifications is also worse, even when the contents of the work and the level of education are the same. This confirms that employment status contributes to the definition of skills level.

Activity rates, unemployment levels, "new" job positions, gender division of labor, hiring and redundancy policies, flexibility, occupational classifications, labor market stratification, and the effects of public measures designed to combat unemployment all have now been investigated in the framework of the sociology of employment, which has also strengthened its relationships with other disciplines (labor economics, law, history, etc.) and other sociologies (of education, of the family, and so on) (Maruani, 1998). When compared to the point of view traditionally used by sociology of work, this developing perspective may be characterized by three main features (Maruani and Reynaud, 1993). It is a sociology of the active population more than a sociology of workers. It studies the labor market more than the firm. And the evolution of forms of (un)employment is given a more central role than "work situations" or the contents of the job. In their study of a newspaper company, for example Maruani and Nicole-Drancourt (1989) stressed the importance of the institutional dimensions of labor markets by showing that the same tasks were allocated to women and men but with different wages and places in the hierarchy.

THE INSTITUTIONAL CONTEXT

In France, the development of the sociology of work parallels the implementation of sociology in the academic world after World War II. The public administration *Centre National de la Recherche Scientifique* (CNRS) played a major role in these developments by funding specialized research teams. Even if there are agencies similar to the French CNRS in Belgium and Switzerland, they never provided important support for research in the sociology of work. The most important part of the available funds come from the ministeries and are often more dedicated to policy-oriented studies than to basic research. In all these countries, even if the variety of national or local funding agencies has now become larger than 20 years ago, money from international organizations such as the European Union (EU) itself but also EU satellite organizations as the European Institute for the Improvement of Working Conditions, or the *Centre Européen pour le Développement de la Formation Professionnelle* (CEDEFOP) is becoming more and more important. In Belgium and in France, national authorities now frequently try to build their research agendas in accordance with the most important European programs.

Since Friedmann's famous postwar seminar gathering together civil servants, managers, trade unionists, and researchers, many sociologists of work have maintained relationships with persons and organizations interested in the outcomes of scientific research and the way they might be used in their practical activities and the definition of their policies. Even if during the recent years some of these links have become weaker, there are new initiatives in the field, such as *Recherches, Société, and Syndicalisme* (RESSY) in France, that bring together social scientists from various disciplines and trade unionists from different organizations to think over the future of work and trade unionism (Kergoat et al., 1998).

The journal *Sociologie du Travail* was established in 1959. Other specialized journals have appeared more recently, the most important of which are published by public administrations: *Formation–emploi* (published by the *Centre d'Études et de Recherches sur les Qualifications* [Céreq]) and *Travail et Emploi* (published by the French Ministry of Labour). General sociological journals (as the *Revue Française de Sociologie, Sociétés Contemporaines, Actes de la Recherche en sciences Sociales, L'année Sociologique*) also publish articles in the field and, from time to time, special issues on work, employment, and related problems. *Travail, Genre et Sociétés* is a more recently created interdisciplinary journal devoted primarily to gender issues.

Some meetings have played, and still play, an important role in recent developments of the French-language sociology of work in Europe. The two *Colloques de Dourdan* (Colloque de Dourdan, 1978; Dourdan, 1982) have been milestones in the discussions on the renewal of the speciality. Since 1986, the *Journées de Sociologie du Travail* have been, and are, opportunities for the specialists of the field to share ideas and assess current research. These study days are organized around one topic and welcome recent results and contributions from young researchers. The five first editions of these *Journées* took place in France. Belgium and Italy hosted recent meetings.

CONCLUSION

The main feature of European French-language sociology of work has always been its will to develop theory on a strong empirical basis and to reach an understanding of modern society based upon the hypothesis that work plays an important role in shaping society. Since its beginnings as a speciality, research has been conducted in a huge variety of settings, even if the work situation of the male blue-collar worker has for a long time remained the core of the discipline.

Among the developments in recent years, two seem of particular importance. First is the renewed interest in the firm, and second is the shift from work to employment. Researchers into both fields consider their point of view as able to overcome the limits and shortcomings of the classical sociology of work. In both orientations, there is also a will to develop a cooperation with other disciplines or subdisciplines, such as management science, labor economics, labor law, sociology of education, and sociology of the family.

As in other countries, the future of work has received much attention in French-language European sociology of work; most aspects of these discussions are no different than what one encounters in other countries. Reich's *Future of Work* has been translated into French and discussed at length in relation to other publications originating in various disciplines, one of the most original being Robert Castel's (1995) sociohistorical account of the growth and the evolution of the wage work system in France. In the same vein, other thinkers have also discussed recent transformations of labor, social protection and labor markets, in order to try to define the alternatives to marginalization and social exclusion (see, e.g., Friot, 1998; Rolle, 1996).

Even if a little more memory or curiosity would sometimes have led some authors to be more careful when pursuing novelty or change, French-speaking sociologists of work have very much cared about progress in their speciality. They wonder regularly if the changes they describe are real transformations or the products of different points of view. Owing to somes studies that strike the balance and list what is still left on the agenda (see, e.g., Erbès-Seguin, 1988; Rolle, 1988), after some years, during which the multiplication of perspectives, as well as the questions about the "end of the centrality of work," generated a feeling of crisis in the discipline, most researchers today consider that there is a future for *sociologie du travail*.

REFERENCES

Alaluf, Mateo. 1986. *Le temps du labeur: Formation, emploi et qualification en sociologie du travail*. Brussels: Editions de l'université de Bruxelles.

Barrère-Maurisson, Marie-Agnès. [1992] 2000. *The Family Division of Labour: Lives Lived in Duality*. Amsterdam: SISWO.

Borzeix, Anni, and Bernard Conein, Eds. 1994. Travail et cognition. *Sociologie du Travail*, 4(Special Issue).

Boutet, Josiane, Ed. 1995. *Paroles au travail*. Paris: L'Harmattan.

Castel, Robert. 1995. *Les métamorphoses de la question sociale*. Paris: Fayard.

Colloque de Dourdan. 1978. *La division du travail*. Paris: Galilée.

Daune-Richard, Anne-Marie. 1998. "How Soes the Societal Effect Shape the Use of Part-Time Work in France, the UK and Sweden?" Pp. 219–231 in *Part-Time Prospects*, edited by Jacqueline O'Reilly and Colette Fagan. London: Routledge.

Dourdan. 1982. *L'emploi: Enjeux économiques et sociaux*. Paris: François Maspéro.

Dubar, Claude. [1991] 1995. *La socialisation: Construction des identités sociales et professionnelles*. Paris: Armand Colin.

Erbès-Seguin, Sabine. 1988. *Bilan de la sociologie du travail: Tome 2. Le travail dans la société*. Grenoble: Presses Universitaires de Grenoble.

Francfort, Isabelle, Florence Osty, Renaud Sainsaulieu, and Marc Uhalde. 1995. *Les mondes sociaux de l'entreprise*. Paris: Desclée de Brouwer.

Friedmann, Georges. [1946] 1955. *Industrial Society: The Emergence of the Human Problems of Automation*. Glencoe, IL: Free Press.

Friedmann, Georges. [1956] 1978. *The Anatomy of Work: Labor, Leisure, and the Implications of Automation*. Westport, CT: Greenwood Press.

Friedmann, Georges, and Pierre Naville. 1961–1962. *Traité de sociologie du travail*, 2 vols. Paris: Armand Colin.

Friot, Bernard. 1998. *Puissances du salariat*. Paris: La Dispute.

Jobert, Annette, Catherine Marry, and Lucie Tanguy. 1995. *Education et travail en Grande-Bretagne, Allemagne et Italie*. Paris: Armand Colin.

Kergoat, Jacques, Josiane Boutet, Henri Jacot, and Danièle Linhart, Eds. 1998. *Le monde du travail*. Paris: La Découverte.

Lafargue, Paul. [1883] 1907. *The Right to Be Lazy, and Other Studies*. Chicago: Charles H. Kerr.

La Rosa, Michele. 1979. *La sociologia del lavoro in Italia e in Francia*. Milan: Franco Angeli.

Linhart, Danièle. 1991. *Le torticolis de l'autruche: L'éternelle modernisation des entreprises françaises*. Paris: Le Seuil.

Maruani, Margaret, Ed. 1998. *Les nouvelles frontières de l'inégalité: Hommes et femmes sur le marché du travail*. Paris: La Découverte and Syros.

Maruani, Margaret, and Chantal Nicole-Drancourt. 1989. *Au labeur des dames: Métiers masculins, emplois féminins*. Paris: Syros.

Maruani, Margaret, and Emmanuèle Reynaud. 1993. *Sociologie de l'emploi*. Paris: La Découverte.

Maurice, Marc, François Sellier. and Jean-Jacques Silvestre. [1982] 1986. *The Social Foundations of Industrial Power: A comparison of France and Germany*. Cambridge, MA: MIT Press.

Maurice, Marc. 1995. "Convergence and/or Societal Effect for the Europe of the Future?" Pp. 28–40 in *Work and Employment in Europe: A New Convergence?*, edited by Paul Jones and Bryn Jones. London: Routledge.

Maurice, Marc, and Arndt Sorge, Eds. 2000. *Embedding Organizations: Societal Analysis of Actor, Organizations and Socio-economic Context*. Advances in Organization Studies 4. Amsterdam: John Benjamins and New York: De Gruyter.

Paradeise, Catherine. 1988. "Acteurs et institutions: La dynamique des marchés du travail." *Sociologie du travail* 1:79–105

Proudhon, Pierre-Joseph. 1969. *Selected Writings of Pierre-Joseph Proudhon*. London: Macmillan.

Reynaud, Jean-Daniel. 1989. *Les règles du jeu: L'action collective et la régulation sociale*. Paris: Armand Colin.

Rolle, Pierre. 1988. *Bilan de la sociologie du travail: Tome 1. Travail et salariat*. Grenoble: Presses Universitaires de Grenoble.

Rolle, Pierre. 1996. *Où va le salariat?* Lausanne: Page Deux.

Ropé, Françoise, and Lucie Tanguy. 1993. *Savoirs et compétences: De l'usage social de ces notions dans l'école et l'entreprise*. Paris: L'Harmattan.

Rose, José. 1998. *Les jeunes face à l'emploi*. Paris: Desclée de Brouwer.

Rose, Michael. 1979. *Servants of Post-Industrial Power? Sociologie du Travail in Modern France*. London: Macmillan.

Rose, Michael, Ed. [1985] 1987. *Industrial Sociology: Work in the French Tradition*. London: Sage.

Sainsaulieu, Renaud. [1977] 1988. *L'identité au travail*, 3rd ed. Paris: Presses de la Fondation Nationale des Sciences Politiques.

Segrestin, Denis. 1992. *Sociologie de l'entreprise*. Paris: Armand Colin.

Stroobants, Marcelle. 1993. *Savoir-faire et compétences au travail: Une sociologie de la fabrication des aptitudes*. Brussels: Editions de l'Université de Bruxelles.

Tanguy, Lucie, Ed. 1986. *L'introuvable relation formation-emploi: Un état des recherches en France*. Paris: La Documentation Française.

Terssac, Gilbert de. 1992. *Autonomie dans le travail*. Paris: Presses Universitaires de France.

Touraine, Alain. 1962. "A Historical Theory of the Evolution of Industrial Skills." Pp. 425–437 in *Modern Technology and Civilization*, edited by C. R. Walker. New York: McGraw-Hill.

Touraine, Alain. [1969] 1971. *The Post-Industrial Society*. New York: Random House.

Tripier, Pierre, Ed. 1986. *Travailler dans le transport: Recherches économiques, historiques, sociologiques*. Paris: L'Harmattan.

Tripier, Pierre. 1991. *Du travail à l'emploi: Paradigmes, idéologies et interactions*. Brussels: Editions de l'Université de Bruxelles.

Tripier, Pierre. 1994. "La sociologie du travail à travers ses paradigmes." Pp. 29–67 in
    Traité de sociologie du travail, eidted by Michel De Coster and François Pichault.
    Brussels: De Boeck.

Veltz, Pierre, and Philippe Zarifian. 1993. "Vers de nouveaux modèles d'organisation."
    Sociologie du Travail 1:3–25.

APPENDIX: CONTACTS

Research Institutes in French-Language Sociology of Work in Europe.

Centre d'Études et de Recherches sur les Qualifications (Céreq)
10, Place de la Joliette BP 176
13474 Marseille cedex 02
France
Phone: + 33 4 91 13 28 28
Fax: + 33 4 91 13 28 80
E-mail: webmaster@cereq.fr

Centre Lillois d'Études et de Recherches Sociologiques et Économiques (CLERSE)
Université Lille I
Faculté des sciences économiques et sociales
bat. SH2
59655 Villeneuve d'Ascq cedex
France
Phone: + 33 3 20 43 66 40
Fax: + 33 3 20 33 71 87
E-mail: bruno.duriez@univ-lille1.fr

Centre Pierre Naville
Université d'Évry Val d'Essonne
Bd. des Coquibus 4
91 000 Évry cedex
France
Phone: + 33 1 69 47 70 96
Fax: + 33 1 69 47 70 08
E-mail: cpn@socio.univ-evry.fr

Centre de Recherche en Gestion (CRG)
Rue Descartes 1
75005 Paris
France
Phone: + 33 1 46 34 34 27
Fax: + 33 1 46 34 34 44
E-mail: crg@poly.polytechnique.fr

Centre de Recherche: Innovation Sociotechnique et Organisations Industrielles (CRISTO)
Université Grenoble 2
Domaine Universitaire
B.P. 47
1041 Rue des résidences
38040 Grenoble cedex 9
France
Phone: + 33 4 76 82 55 35
Fax: + 33 4 76 82 58 43
E-mail: cristo@upmf-grenoble.fr

Centre de Sociologie du Travail, de l'Emploi et de la Formation (TEF)
Institut de sociologie - Institut du travail
Université Libre de Bruxelles
Av. F.D. Roosevelt 50 - CP 124
1050 Bruxelles
Belgium
Phone: + 32 2 650 91 14
Fax: + 32 2 650 91 18
E-mail: asiot@ulb.ac.be

Groupe d'Étude sur la Division Sociale et Sexuelle du Travail (GEDISST)
CNRS-IRESCO
59 Rue Pouchet
75849 Paris cedex 17
France
Phone: + 33 1 40 25 12 06
Fax: + 33 1 40 25 12 03
E-mail: coutras@iresco.fr

Groupe Lyonnais de Sociologie Industrielle (GLYSI)
Maison Rhône-Alpes des Sciences de l'Homme
14 Av Berthelot
69363 Lyon cedex 07
France
Phone: + 33 4 72 72 64 00
Fax: + 33 4 72 80 00 08
E-mail: glysi@mrash.fr

Groupe de Recherche sur l'Éducation et l'Emploi (GREE)
Université Nancy 2
23, Boulevard Albert 1er
BP 3397

54015 Nancy cedex
France
Phone: + 33 3 83 96 70 80
Fax: + 33 3 83 96 70 79
E-mail: Francois.Legendre@clsh.univ-nancy2.fr

Institut des Sciences du Travail
Université Catholique de Lauvain
Place des Doyens, 1
1348 Louvain-la-Neuve
Belgium
Phone: + 32 10 47 39 11
Fax: + 3210 47.39.14
E-mail: info@trav.ucl.ac.be

Institut de Sociologie des Communications de Masse
Université de Lausanne
BFSH2
1015 Lausanne
Switzerland
Phone: + 41 21 692 32 10
Fax: + 41 21 692 32 15
E-mail: Mireille.Bovey@iscm.unil.ch

Laboratoire d'Économie et de Sociologie du Travail (LEST)
35 Av Jules Ferry
13626 Aix en Provence
France
Phone: + 33 4 42 37 85 00
Fax: + 33 4 42 26 79 37
E-mail: lest@univ-aix.fr

Laboratoire d'Études sur les Nouvelles Technologies de l'Information, la Communi-
    cation et les Industries Culturelles (LENTIC)
Université de Liège
Boulevard du Rectorat, 19, Bât. B51
4000 Liège 1
Belgium
Phone: + 32 4 366.30.70
Fax: + 32 4 366.29.47
E-mail: lentic@ulg.ac.be

Laboratoire Georges Friedmann
Conservatoire National des Arts et Métiers
Institut des Sciences Sociales du Travail

16 Boulevard Carnot
92340 Bourg la Reine
France
Phone: + 33 1 46 65 70 80
Fax: + 33 1 46 65 70 81

Laboratoire Techniques, Territoires et Sociétés (LATTS)
Ecole nationale des ponts et chaussées
Cité Descartes
6/8 Av Blaise Pascal
77455 Marne la Vallée cedex 2
France
Phone: + 33 1 64 15 30 00
Fax: + 33 1 64 15 38 47
E-mail: veltz@latts.enpc.fr

Marché du Travail et Genre (MAGE)
IRESCO - CNRS
59-61 Rue Pouchet
75017 Paris
France
Phone: + 33 1 40 25 10 37
Fax: + 33 1 40 25 11 70
E-mail: mage @iresco.fr

Modélisations Appliquées aux Trajectoires Institutionnelles et aux Stratégies Socio-
       Économiques (MATISSE)
Université de Paris I - CNRS
Boulevard de l'Hôpital 106-112
75647 Paris cedex 13
France
Phone: + 33 1 55 43 41 82
Fax: + 33 1 55 43 41 83
E-mail: metiscom@asterix.univ-paris1.fr

Professions, Institutions, Temporalités (PRINTEMPS)
Université Versailles Saint-Quentin
47 Bvd Vauban
78047 Guyancourt cedex
France
Phone: + 33 1 39 25 56 50
Fax: + 33 1 39 25 56 55
E-mail: Danielle.Bonnot@printemps.uvsq.fr

Travail et Mobilités (TEM)
Université Paris 10
bat. G - bureau 505
200 Av de la République
92001 Nanterre cedex
France
Phone: + 33 1 40 97 71 33
Fax: + 33 1 40 97 71 35
E-mail: linhart@u-paris10.fr

Unité de Recherche Migrations et Sociétés (URMIS)
Université Paris 7
Casier 7027
Tour Centrale - 6 etg - P 608
2 Place Jussieu
75251 Paris cedex 05
France
Phone: + 33 1 44 27 56 66
Fax: + 33 1 44 27 78 87
E-mail: urmis@paris7.jussieu.fr

11

Germany

Walther Müller-Jentsch

INTRODUCTION

Studies on work and industry have a long tradition in Germany. A country in which the industrial revolution started somewhat later (about 1835) than in England and France, Germany remained highly dependent on foreign technology into the 1870s. But it was the first industrial revolution in which the introduction of the railroads shaped the pattern of early national industrialization. The huge demand for coal and iron stimulated heavy industry to rapid growth and development. In addition, an active state promoted the industrialization process, including state backing for investment banks. These and other conditions provided a favorable climate for the development of large firms and business corporations. "By the 1870s gigantic firms like Krupp dominated much of German metallurgy and mining, with branches extending from the mines through smelting and refining of metal to the production of armaments and ships" (Stearns, 1993:47). The relatively late start of German industrialization was followed by rapid speed that gathered momentum especially during the second industrial revolution toward the end of the 19th

Walther Müller-Jentsch · Professor of Sociology, Ruhr University of Bochum, 044780 Bochum, Germany.

Worlds of Work: Building an International Sociology of Work, edited by Daniel B. Cornfield and Randy Hodson. Kluwer Academic/Plenum Publishers, New York, 2002.

century. By the 1910s, Germany had obviously succeeded in overtaking the first industrial nation, Britain (Kindleberger, 1975).

Studies about work and industry in Germany go back to the founding fathers of industrial sociology: Karl Marx (1818–1883) and Max Weber (1864–1920). Of course, the work of Marx primarily reflected experiences in English industry, whereas Weber stimulated the first systematic research in German industry. Although much less known than the two authors mentioned, Goetz Briefs (1889–1974) must be added to the list of early German analysts who laid the foundations of studying work and industry from a sociological point of view. Briefs elaborated a new social science called *Betriebssoziologie* ("sociology of establishment" or "plant sociology"), which became a major approach of research during the 1920s and 1930s, institutionally backed by his foundation of the Institut für Betriebssoziologie und Soziale Betriebslehre at the technical university of Berlin in 1928.

Two distinctive features of the study of work in Germany have to be kept in mind.

1. From its very beginning, German industrial sociology should be regarded within a historical frame of reference. Its dominant themes were often shaped by the prevailing conditions of industry and society, especially by the respective roles of organized labor. Whereas Marx explicitly addressed his theory to a working class still in the making, most of his successors undertook their research at least with the awareness of the presence of a strong labor movement, ideologically influenced by Marxism and determined to achieve fundamental societal change or, later, radical social reforms. However explicitly or implicitly, this movement exerted great influence on the research agenda of the sociology of work not only during the Kaiserreich (1871–1918) but also during the interwar years (Weimar period) and even during the first decades after World War II. At the turn of the century, industrial unrest, large-scale strikes, and the pressure for radical political change motivated the ruling elite to initiate social research and to implement social reforms as counterinsurgent remedies. Later, during the interwar and postwar periods, social and political reforms (and also applied research linked to them) were undertaken with the collaboration of the labor movement, especially the trade unions, which in fact formulated their own research programs and established their own research institutes.

2. German industrial sociology includes a much broader field of study and research than in the Anglo–American countries (e.g., industrial relations, labor economics, and labor law). In the past, industrial sociology was closely connected with general sociology and social philosophy, for industrialization was regarded as a driving force of social change and therefore a pillar of sociological theories of society. Thus, Marx and Weber understood themselves to

be general sociologists with strong interests in industrial and organizational sociology. The latter specialization demanded its prize. Of the industrial sociologists on a "part-time basis"—Schelsky, Dahrendorf, Offe, and Beck—only Dahrendorf left his traces in this discipline .

HISTORY

The Early Period

The founders of the sociology of work and industry (Marx, Weber, Briefs) determined not only the early research themes but also the research agenda of their successors. Marx's concern with the dual character of the capitalist labor process, with cooperation and division of labor as well as technology and alienation, and, ultimately, his analysis of the dynamics of class relations in the production process (e.g., described in Chapters 5 and 11–13 of his principal work, *The Capital*, Vol. I) laid the foundations for the analytical framework of German industrial sociology for many decades. The posthumous publication of the so-called economic–philosophical manuscripts (1932/1953), with their Hegel-inspired deep insights into alienated labor, had considerable impact on the social philosophy of work. The very notion of alienated labor became a diagnostic tool for sociological inquiry.

In a way, Max Weber was the bourgeois counterpart of Karl Marx. His research on work started with studies on the social conditions of agrarian laborers in East Germany (Ostelbien) at the close of the century and continued with investigations into the life and conditions of industrial workers. He became a driving force and methodologist of the first empirical research on industrial work in large German firms under the patronage of the Verein für Socialpolitik (founded in 1872 by academics of the German "historical school" with the intention to establish social fairness between capital and labor). During the period 1873-1892 the Verein für Socialpolitik had arranged social inquiries (*Sozialenqueten*) on a broad range of questions such as factory rules, apprenticeship, housing, domestic industry, outwork, and agricultural laborers. These early inquiries were still in the tradition of the English surveys and inquiries of the 1830s and 1840s. Similar to their English model, their aim was to initiate social policy enactment by special analysis of a particular question on a broad material base (reports and interviews of experts, statistical material).

A new, major inquiry of the Verein für Socialpolitik was launched by Max and Alfred Weber, Karl Bücher, and Heinrich Herkner in the first decade of the 20th century: "inquiries into the selection and adjustment of workers in different branches of large industry" (*Untersuchungen über Auslese und Anpassung (Berufswahl und Berufsschicksal) der Arbeiter in den verschiedenen*

Zweigen der Großindustrie). This research project was the beginning of systematic industrial research in Germany. The principal question leading the inquiry was the following: What kind of men are shaped by the modern industry and which job prospects (and indirectly, which life chances) does big industry offer them? One of the new features of the inquiry was the interest in the effects of factory work on the worker's psychology. Knowledge of the subjective perspective of workers was scarce at that time compared to the objective conditions of factory work.

Max Weber wrote a lengthy methodological introduction to that research project, which served as instructions for the collaborators of the inquiry. He elaborated a number of questions, among them the social and geographical origin of the workers; the principles of their selection; the physical and psychological conditions of the work processes, job performance; preconditions and prospects of carrier; social structure of the workforce; the ways and degrees of workers' adjustment to factory life; but also questions related to the family situation and leisure time of the workers. These and other research questions had to be answered by operationalized interview questions. However, this was only one of the methodological instruments. The collaborators were also requested to interview employers and management, to observe production technology, and to gather statistics on working time, distribution of breaks, and wage systems.

The inquiry resulted in more than a dozen single studies, published in four volumes, between 1910 and in 1915. But the results were rather scanty. Only a tiny proportion of the 12,000 questionnaires were returned. The main reason for the poor performance of the workers' survey was the widespread mistrust among workers of bourgeois academics and their institutions. Another paper of Weber also belongs to this context: "about the psycho-physics of industrial work" (*Zur Psychophysik der industriellen Arbeit*, 1908/1909), which contained not only a detailed and critical review of the literature on the physiology and psychology of work, but also his own research into the fluctuating performance of weavers working in his uncle's mill. One of his main concern was the productivity of the individual worker. Thus he discussed many factors affecting worker's performance (among them wage level, humidity, noise, alcohol, sexual activity, regional origin, denomination, and the trade union membership).

With his seminal article on "industrial sociology" ("Betriebssoziologie") Goetz Briefs (1931) laid the theoretical foundations for analyses of the internal relations in business organizations and especially of the role of labor in the hierarchically organized production process. With no less intensity than the writings of Marx, he emphasized the phenomenon of alienation with its numerous facets :

> The notion of heteronomy (*Fremdbestimmtheit*) most clearly circumscribes the position of the worker in enterprise and establishment. Heteronomous is the workplace, the mode to work and further the intensity and special method of work, working hours, working instruments, the purpose of work and the work organization; heteronomous is also the output of the labor process and its market selling. (Briefs, 1927:1111; my translation)

If there was a common paradigm of these early sociologists of work, it was the understanding that industrial production is the hub of modern capitalism, being organized in privately owned firms by vertical and horizontal division of labor and according to the principles of rationality and profitability. Since the core of production was dependent wage labor, working under the authority of private entrepreneurs, more or less emphasis was also given to the questions of exploitation and alienation of labor in a class-divided society. This certainly was the understanding of Marx and Briefs (both were much closer in their analyses than their respective political beliefs would have let be suspected[1]). In contrast, alienation and exploitation were not Max Weber's themes. Despite being a class-conscious bourgeois, he nevertheless recognized that the capitalist employment relationship was a relation of dominance (*Herrschaftsverhältnis*), in which, however, the entrepreneur's authority was a legitimate one because of the workers willingness to enter into the employment relationship. Furthermore, the administrative process (bureaucracy) attracted him more than the labor process—the core of Marx's theory.

The Interwar Period

Although having been an authoritarian state, the Prussian Kaiserreich was nevertheless endowed with a farseeing ("Weberian") bureaucracy that, facing a growing and radical labor movement, showed great concern in solving the "social question." Bismarck's social insurance scheme was one of the obvious outcomes. Even docile trade unions had a place in their blueprint. This floor had been paved by Lujo Brentano (1844–1931), an early liberal economist and antipode of Marx and Engels, who argued that trade unions play a constitutive role in market economies since they empower employees to behave like sellers of commodities; to his mind, only the union enabled wage laborers to adjust their supply according to the market conditions (Brentano, 1909). But at that time trade unions had been recognized only in some handicraft industries; the authoritarian entrepreneurs of heavy and big industry accepted trade unions and collective bargaining not before the revolution of 1918/19.

---

[1]Briefs, a social minded liberal academic, was influenced by Christian social policy. In 1934, he emigrated to the USA.

During the first days of the "November revolution" influential representatives of both sides of industry signed an agreement (*Stinnes–Legien–
Abkommen*, 1918) on the recognition of trade unions, collective agreements,
and workplace representation. As a consequence of this agreement, the revolutionary councils movement was canalized into works councils (Works Councils Act, 1920). But the established institutional arrangements of works councils and free collective bargaining did not bear fruit because of political turmoil,
economic pressures, and antagonistic orientations of the actors in question.
During the postrevolutionary years issues of work organization, productive
rationalization, and labor productivity superimposed the search for consen-
sual industrial relations.

The research on the works councils during the Weimar period is scant.
Only Kurt Brigl-Matthiaß's thorough analysis ([1926] 1978) gives us valuable
information about their role in working life. According to his conclusions, the
legislator as well as the unions and the employers wanted to subordinate them
to the (less radical) unions and to limit their responsibility for the supervision
and the implementation of the collective agreements. Their common goal was
the "unionization of the works councils" notwithstanding their legal status as
workplace institutions representing the whole workforce. The majority of the
employers who did not like the new institution anyway tried either to para-
lyze or to assimilate it.

There existing much more research literature on the social and human
dimensions of industrial work, the shop floor organization, and plant hierarchy.

In 1931 Adolph Geck, who worked as research associate with Goetz Briefs
at the Berlin Institut für Betriebssoziologie und soziale Betriebsführung, published his work, *Social Labor Relations in the Course of Time* (*Die sozialen Arbeitsverhältnisse im Wandel der Zeit*). The book contained a historical account of the
development of work and of labor relations from the eve of the industrial revolution to the modern factory system. Subject matters were industrial hierarchy
and bureaucracy, the different styles of entrepreneurial authority, various forms
of personnel policy and labor relations, the role of the state for the employment
relationship, and the company-based social policy (*betriebliche Sozialpolitik*).

Walter Jost, another research associate of Briefs, published *The Social Life
of the Industrial Firm* (*Das Sozialleben des industriellen Betriebs*) in 1932. He was
the first to analyze the process of factory cooperation in detail. According to
him, cooperation is the skeleton of the social life of work organization. The
smallest unity of cooperation is the work group: Its members work physically
together and interlock their mutual behavior to achieve a concrete collective
product. A modern factory is differentiated in two ways: by the "primary differentiation" between leading and executing job tasks, and by further functional specialization of the latter ("secondary differentiation"). The industrial
firm consists of a system of work groups; several work groups form a shop or

a department, which is a work group of secondary order, by further successive combinations, we end at the company as the whole. Several authors, especially Popitz et al. (see the section on the postwar period), took up this productive approach for their own analyses of work organization.

The analytical perspective of the books by Geck and Jost was in common with that of Briefs. It was based on the strictly sociological understanding of *Betrieb* (a word that can be interpreted as establishment, plant, work organization, shop floor) as a social organization *sui generis,* with different groups of people working together under the (legitimized) authority of management. The social dimensions in which the authors were interested, and which determined their analyses, were, apart from the division of labor, the concern with cooperation and industrial conflict as well as class relations in industry. Besides the implications for industrial sociology, the authors' works were inspired by ideas of social reforms of work and labor relations.

Their social and human concern was shared by those authors whose major theme was "group fabrication" instead of Taylorist forms of division of labor. The works of Willy Hellpach and Richard Lang, *Gruppenfabrikation* (1922), and Eugen Rosenstock-Huessy, *Werkstattaussiedlung* (1922), regarded *soziale Betriebsführung* (socially minded management) and group fabrication as remedies for anomie in industry produced by extreme forms of division of labor.

Ergonomics and rationalization became major fields of scientific research and industrial implementation during the Weimar republic. A replica of the American "efficiency craze" (Haber, 1964) spread over the country, even taking grip of the trade unions. In 1921, the German Productivity Center (*Rationalisierungs-Kuratorium der Deutschen Wirtschaft,* RKW) was founded by industry, trade unions, and academic institutions, with the intention to increase productivity and efficiency especially in small- and medium-sized companies. A special institution for time and motion studies, the Imperial Committee for Time Studies (*Reichsausschuß für Arbeitszeitermittlung,* REFA) was founded by employers and industrial engineers in 1924.

Among the books on Fordism and industrial rationalization published in the Weimar republic, those of von Gottl-Ottlilienfeld (1926; 1929) have to be mentioned first. His research on rationalization, technology, and work organization culminated in the condemnation of Taylorism ("a tragedy of the skilled worker" [1926:8]) on the one hand and in the praise of Fordism on the other. To him, Henry Ford was the "Grand Master of technological reason" (1926:4) because of the following four principles: (1) the concentration on a key product; (2) the combined measures of reducing prices and raising wages at the same time; (3) the reinvestment of all profits; and (4) the unlimited and continuous rationalization of the production process (1926:63). He also praised Ford's paternalistic idea of the company being a community of leader and followers, which he appreciated as a kind of "white socialism" or *Führersozialismus.*

The latter idea became a cornerstone of the *Betriebsgemeinschaft* during the Nazi regime. According to the 1934 Act regulating the national labor (*Gesetz zur Ordnung der nationalen Arbeit*), the employer became the leader (*Führer*) and the employees the followers (*Gefolgschaft*). Trade unions and employers' associations were dissolved; instead the German Labor Front (*Deutsche Arbeitsfront*) became the compulsory organization of both sides of industry. But it did not completely work as an instrument of Hitler's totalitarian regime. Reacting to the workers' complaints and morale, it also functioned as a quasi trade union, and in this role, paradoxically, it fulfilled much better its task of integrating the working class. In contrast to the Communist and Socialist activists the bulk of the workers were not at all opponents of the *Führer*. New jobs, better pay, and social policy made the working class docile, especially during the early years of the Third Reich.

Although many sociologists (two-thirds of university professors) emigrated for racist and/or political reasons, sociology survived as a distinct "German" sociology, being no longer a sociology of groups, classes, and industrialism but a holistic science of the "community of the people" (*Volkgemeinschaft*), in which a mythic image of the peasant maintained a special place. This bastardized German sociology was mainly the work of the Leipzig sociologist, Hans Freyer, whose thoughts had already exposed great affinity to the fascist ideology before 1933. But, in general, theoretical discussion soon gave way to practical social research. Sociology became an applied science and, moreover, an explicit weapon in the defense of the system by observing the internal and external enemies, and by developing methods of maintaining social order (Rammstedt, 1986).

After World War II

The breaking-up and reorganization of the highly centralized coal and steel industry by the British Allied Forces immediately after the war had great impact on the German industrial relations system, for the measures were accompanied by the establishment of strong institutions of codetermination. In 1951, the trade unions put pressure on the German Parliament to ratify the facts by passing a law for steel and coal companies with more than 1,000 employees. Its regulations provided for full-parity representation of capital and labor at the supervisory board, and for the appointment of a labor director to be nominated by the workers' representatives.[2] The legal reestablishment of

---

[2]There exist three different forms of representation at the board level in Germany: (1) equal representation in the coal and steel industry (*Montanmitbestimmung*) under legislation from 1951; (2) one-third representation in companies with 500 to 2,000 employees under the Works Constitution Act of 1952; and (3) subparity representation in companies with more than 2,000 employees under the Codetermination Act of 1976. For the unions, *Montanmitbestimmung* was

works councils followed only a year later. Formally, the dual-channel system of industrywide collective bargaining by unions and shop-floor representation by works councils had already been existed during the Weimar period. But only after World War II did it become a success story—mainly due to the codetermination system in the steel and coal industry. Just this very industry, with its ill fame of authoritarian management and fierce resistance to trade unionism and collectivism, became a postwar laboratory of management-labor cooperation and—in combination with the "social market economy"—the nucleus of "social partnership" in German industry. As a genuine German creation, social market economy has a double goal: economic freedom on the one hand, and social balance and fairness on the other. Initially, the unions opposed market economy; but they gradually came to terms with it. Today, they find themselves in the role of defending it against market radicalism á la Hayek.

After the end of the Nazi Reich, sociology was gradually (re)established as an academic discipline at many universities in West Germany.[3] No less than 69 chairs of sociology were established during the period of 1947–1970 (Kern, 1982:220). But it took a long time to create a solid base for empirical social research. By the mid-1950s, only few research institutions had been established at the universities of Frankfurt (Max Horkheimer and Theodor W. Adorno), Cologne (René König), and Münster (Helmut Schelsky). At that time, official financial support was rare, and research projects were mostly undertaken by freelance researchers.

The first institute to become active in research on work and industry during the early postwar period was the Sozialforschungsstelle (Center for Social Research) in Dortmund, founded in 1946. Situated in the Ruhr area,[4] it primarily developed research projects in heavy industry. Two imaginative research projects were realized by the group working at this institution—Heinrich Popitz, Hans Paul Bahrdt, Ernst August Jüres, and Hanno Kesting. One was on the interplay between technology and industrial work (*Technik und Industriearbeit*, 1957); the other was on the worker's image of society (*Das Gesellschaftsbild des Arbeiters*, 1957). *Sociological Research in Steel Industry* was the common subtitle of both books. In the first book, the authors asked how technology changes the character of work on the basis of observations and

---

the most important model with the strongest codetermination rights. They were dissatisfied with the codetermination rights of the 1976 Act because they remained below full parity even though 50% of the supervisory board members were workforce representatives; but the chair, who was appointed by the shareholders, has a casting vote, and at least one employee representative had to be elected from among the executives ("leitende Angestellte").

[3]In East Germany sociology was kept subordinated under the Marxist "science of society."

[4]Because of the economic importance of the coal and steel industry, the Ruhr area, with its highly concentrated heavy industry, has played in major role in German economic and political history from the Kaiserreich to the post-war period.

interviews. The focus of their analyses was cooperation on the shop floor; they distinguished between two forms of cooperation: (1) the loosely structured team which leaves the individual workers room for mutual help; and (2) the technologically structured work group, in which technology determines pace and performance of the converging action. In general, the latter is complementary to advanced production technology. The second book, based on oral interviews, describes in great detail the steel workers' perception of work, technology, white-collar work, and their images of class structure and society. The authors came to the conclusion that the majority of workers still had a class awareness of society as a dichotomy of "them" and "us." Both books are regarded as exemplary works giving evidence for the blossom of industrial sociology in the early postwar period.

Two other research groups also investigated the conditions of work and workers' attitudes and expectations, especially toward codetermination in the heavy industry. The first group (Pirker, Braun, Lutz) came from the research institute of the German Confederation of Trade Unions (DGB), the second group (von Friedeburg, Teschner, Weltz) was affiliated with the Frankfurt Institute of Social Research (see Pirker et al., 1952; Institut für Sozialforschung 1955). At that time, the research field was clearly dominated by the coal and steel industry in the Ruhr area, and by the questions of codetermination and managerial authority. This is also true for Otto Neuloh's research on the development of the German works constitution (1956) and on the "new managerial style" (1960).

As early as 1956, Ralf Dahrendorf published the first textbook on industrial sociology (*Industrie- und Betriebssoziologie*, [1956] 1962), and only 3 years later, the first postwar systematic account of the social structure of the establishment (*Sozialstruktur des Betriebs*, 1959). Nevertheless, it was impossible to consolidate this early blossoming of industrial sociology. One of the reasons was that the precarious situation the research institutes maintained; since they could not offer career opportunities, excellent researchers moved away to the universities (for details, see Kern 1982:137f.).

Some foresighted studies, however, heralded new important themes at the turn of the decade. The publications to be mentioned included Hans Paul Bahrdt's book on "industrial bureaucracy" (*Industriebürokratie*, 1958) and Theo Pirker's investigation into the mechanization and automation of office work (*Büro und Maschine*, 1962). The most advanced piece was Friedrich Pollock's early study on the economic and social effects of automation ([1956] 1964). The author analyzed the real development and the academic discussion of this topic in the United States and in selected European countries (including the Soviet Union). Pirker and Pollock were mainly concerned about the risks of ongoing automation (technological unemployment and downgrading of occupational qualifications) but stressed also its opportunities. Both authors, too, expected a coming polarization of occupations as a consequence of automation. At the same time, the automation debate became a major focus of two international conferences (1963 and 1965) of the biggest German trade union, the IG Metall. There, union activists, politicians and academics aired their views on the fears and hopes for work, jobs, and standards of living.

The Expansionist Period

During the late 1960s, industrial sociology made a great leap forward and expanded rapidly during the 1970s. This was caused by three major events: (1) by the renaissance of Marxist thinking in sociological research, especially in industrial sociology under the impact of the radical students' movement; (2) by an effective institutional promotion of empirical research on work and industry; and (3) by the ambitious research program, Humanization of Working Life, launched by the SPD-led government in the early 1970s.

1. The main institutes involved in the neo-Marxist discussion were, first of all, the famous Institut für Sozialforschung in Frankfurt (at that time led by Gerhard Brandt and Ludwig von Friedeburg) and the two newly founded research institutes—Sociological Research Institute (SOFI) in Göttingen (since 1968), with Horst Kern and Michael Schuman as leading figures and at that time still, young researchers, and the Institute for Social Research in Munich (since 1965) under Burkart Lutz and Norbert Altmann.

At that time, the research programs of the three institutes were focused on studies about workers' organizations, actions, and consciousness on the one hand and on studies about production technology, work organization and managerial strategies on the other. A common theoretical concern, on the societal level was the problem of the integration of the working class and its organizations into the neocapitalist, affluent society. Thus, the role of trade unions, works councils, strikes, and workers' consciousness determined their research agenda. On the company level, particular emphasis was given to the production process and the organization of work. Many research projects were led by the question of the effects of technological and organizational structures on work and workers, accompanied by an extensive theoretical debate on the "economy of time," as well as on upgrading and downgrading of the skilled worker, in general: on the future of the German *Facharbeiter*.

The publication and early German translation of Harry Braverman's book, *Labor and Monopoly Capital* (1974) was a forceful amplifier of this theoretical discussion, which oscillated between the "production theorem" (a variant of technological determinism) and the "capital subsumption theory" (which understood production technology as a weapon of capitalist management against the workforce). Generally, the paradigm in industrial sociology shifted from the understanding of production technology as an independent variable ("force of production") to a dependent variable ("capitalistic managerial strategy").

2. The second factor responsible for the boom of industrial sociology during the 1970s was the financial support of two institutions that sponsored many large-scale research projects. The first was the semistate organization, Rationalisierungskuratorium der Deutschen Wirtschaft (RKW) (German Productivity Center), which triggered a series of research projects on the economic, industrial, and social aspects of technological change, among them the key project in industrial sociology of that decade (Kern and Schumann, 1970). The other institution was the Deutsche Forschungsgemeinschaft (DFG) (German Research Community), which established a special research program on industrial, workplace, and organizational sociology (Industrie-, Betriebs- und Organisationssoziologie) for a period of 10 years, and launched a *Sonderforschungsbereich* (special research field) called "Theoretical Principles of Labor Market and Occupational Research." Both had ample research funds for more than 50 research projects.

3. A further push came from the reform era of the social–liberal government, which intended to substantiate its policy by social sciences. The Federal ministries and their newly established research departments made available huge financial sources for industrial research and experiments in new forms of work. Firms, academics, and associations received a lot of money from them. Most important was the government's research program, Humanization of Working Life, which promoted basic as well as applied research. This program was strongly advocated by the trade unions and their confederation. Ministries with large research funds (Department of Employment, Department of Research and Technology) were led by former trade unionist. The unions also organized conferences at which politicians, workers' representatives, and academics exchanged their views on the improvement of working conditions and the increase of productivity. Furthermore, in 1971, the Federal government appointed the Kommission für wirtschaftlichen und sozialen Wandel (Committee for Economic and Social Change), with representatives of both sides of industry and academics. The Committee's task was to inquire into the consequences of the technical, economic, and social change, and to indicate what kinds of measures should be taken to shape the future development of society. One of its main instruments was to commission research projects.

Characteristic of that period was a general awareness and public debate on the need to modernize economy and society, and create a favorable climate for social reforms and the demand for democratization of all societal subsystems (industry, universities, schools, and even military forces). During that decade, industrial sociology in West Germany expanded rapidly. Compared to the 1960s, the financial resources increased seven fold during the 1970s

(Kern, 1982:242). The research staff at the institutes and universities increased considerably. The major projects of that period were conducted at the three research institutes mentioned earlier.

At the SOFI in Göttingen, Kern and Schumann investigated industrial work and workers' consciousness (*Industriearbeit und Arbeiterbewußtsein*, 1970). Obviously, their project's approach was similar to that of the early projects conducted by Popitz et al. (1957a, 1957b), but this time, not limited to the steel industry. The published research report contained precis and systematic observations of workplaces, and a detailed typology of industrial work. The two central results were the following: (1) As a consequence of rising mechanization and automation, job requirements and workers' qualifications are polarized between a smaller proportion of workers being upgraded and larger one being downgraded (polarization thesis); (2) the consciousness of the workers expresses a growing differentiation in accordance with the increasing divergence of work situations and work experiences. Contrary to Popitz et al., the authors gathered only data on attitudes toward work and technological change, not on the workers' images of society. That was made up by a later research project at the university of Erlangen (Kudera et al., 1979). Other research projects of the SOFI included investigations into automated industries (Mickler et al., 1977) and shipyards (Schumann et al., 1982). The Institute for Social Research in Munich started its research on work, and industry from two main strands. One was the interplay between technology, work and managerial authority (Altmann and Bechtle, 1971); the other was the relations between the educational and the employment system (Lutz, 1976), resulting in studies on labor market segmentation (Sengenberger, 1978). The institute conducted many research projects of great variety, mainly by means of industrial case studies (*Betriebsfallstudien*). Among them were studies on managerial strategy, personnel policy and planning; the *Facharbeiter* question, especially on initial and further occupational training; on modernization of public administration; and labor markets and new forms of work organization.

The Frankfurt Institute of Social Research, traditionally not particularly interested in industrial sociology, also became a center of major research on work and industry. Ludwig von Friedeburg initiated a large-scale research project on the politics and organization of the trade unions and the attitudes of union officers (Bergmann et al., [1974] 1977; Bergmann and Müller-Jentsch, 1977). Two connected studies investigated workplace bargaining (Teschner, 1977) and the historical development of wage-bargaining (Schmiede and Schudlich, 1976). Gerhard Brandt, the other director, promoted an early research project on computerization of work in the steel industry and banking (Brandt et al., 1978).

Besides the three institutes mentioned, other, newly founded or reactivated institutes gained from the boom in industrial sociology. The reactivated

Sozialforschungsstelle in Dortmund acquired new relevance with studies about trade unions, codetermination, and strikes. Among the newly established research institutes was the Institute for Research on Social Opportunities in Cologne and the Wissenschaftszentrum in Berlin. Two other research institutes were established by public authorities: the Institute for Employment Research (Institut für Arbeitsmarkt- und Berufsforschung, IAB) and the Federal Institute for Occupational Research (Bundesinstitut für Berufsforschung) in Berlin. At the universities, too, initatives were taken to engage in the booming research on work and industry.

New Themes: The 1980s and 1990s

Since the end of the 1970s some of the old research themes have gradually withered away and been replaced by new ones. Sociology of work and industry expanded further and dispersed into new fields.

Work in the Service Sector.   Compared with other Western countries, Germany still has a large manufacturing sector. Nevertheless, with the growth of the third sector, and of white-collar employment in general, the share of salaried employees in the working population has exceeded the share of the blue-collar workers since the late 1970s. Although some authors had dealt with the "new serving class" already in the Weimar Republic after Word War II, the white-collar workers were not rediscovered until the late 1970s—with the exception of Bahrdt's book on "industrial bureaucracy" (1958).

Besides the engineers ("technical intelligence") work in the banking and insurance industry and also in retail trade, became a major focus of empirical research. Initially, the widespread assumption was that white-collar work was undergoing profound rationalization and Taylorization. At the same time, it was recognized that white-collar workers, although bound to undergo similar processes of degradation as blue-collar workers, had a different class awareness than their blue-collar counterparts; this was simply explained by the "false consciousness" of salaried employees. The deterioration of the labor market and the introduction of computer-based office technology, which had led to dismissals of large numbers of salaried employees were understood by some industrial sociologist as an industrialization of office work and the coming proletarization of white-collar workers (see, e.g., Kadritzke, 1982).

Empirical research of the 1980s concealed a quite different panorama of the effects of rationalization on administrative work. Baethge and Oberbeck used the rich information of their case studies in 17 "technologically advanced enterprises" (1984:54) to draw a differentiated picture of the characteristic features of white-collar employment in industry, banking and insurance, retail trade, and local government. Far from finding a uniform development, they noticed ample scope for different paths of rationalization open to micropolitical processes of the actors involved. Similarly, Littek and Heisig (1986:1995), in case studies on technical and administrative white-collar work, disapproved of the unilateral downgrading hypothesis and instead established a skills-oriented modernization thesis.

Small- and Medium-Sized Businesses. The internal structures and processes of small- and medium-sized firms were not considered to be a serious theme for mainstream industrial sociology until the 1980s. Companies of this size were generally regarded as a kind of underdeveloped organization, with unsophisticated technology and deficient or no collective representation. Small firms were simply identified with sweatshops. The publication of Piore and Sabel's book, *The Second Industrial Divide* (1984), with the German translation published only 1 year later, and the debate on the job creation by small business firms in the United States, changed the evaluation to the reverse. Now the innovative potential for nonbureaucratic, flexible production and for job creation became a major focus of the new research in small business.

Surprisingly, the discussion of the necessity to decentralize large companies suddenly exposed some economic advantages of the smaller ones. And even the deficient interest representation seemed to gain a compensation by what Hilbert and Sperling (1990) dubbed "shadow participation" (i.e., the informal voice and involvement of workers). The most important result of the new research about small companies (Hilbert and Sperling, 1990; Kotthoff and Reindl, 1990; Mendius et al., 1987) was that no universal type could be found, but a spectrum reaching from high-tech, innovative firms (e.g., software and machine–tool companies) to sweatshops. Most recent research focuses on small businesses in the service industry.

Labor Market Segmentation/Erosion of Normalarbeitsverhältnis. Due to the long tradition of the dual system of training for skilled workers, occupation and qualification are significant dimensions of German industrial sociology. The skilled worker (*Facharbeiter*) is regarded as the backbone of the trade unions and one of the assets of Germany's economic power. Most debates on rationalization are explicitly or implicitly centered around the future of the *Facharbeiter*, which will also be affected by the erosion of regular employment.

The *Normalarbeitsverhältnis* indicates the regular employment relationship, that is, full-time employment of skilled (also semiskilled) male employees on a permanent job with full coverage of social security. The majority of male employment enjoyed this form of regular employment relationship for more than three decades during the postwar period before it has gradually become eroded by the increase of part-time and temporary employment, marginal work, and other atypical forms of employment. The increasing participation of women in the labor market has also contributed to the further segmentation of labor markets.

Werner Sengenberger, from the Institute for Social Research in Munich, modified and adjusted the dual labor market model of Doeringer and Piore (1971) to the German situation by distinguishing between three ideal types of labor markets: (1) a market for laborers with low-level general skills and high mobility; (2) an occupational market for workers with certified vocational qualifications and interfirm mobility; and (3) a firm-internal market for workers with firm-specific skills and low interfirm and high intrafirm mobility (Sengenberger, 1978, 1992). The latter two types are labor markets that allocate skilled workers. The internal markets are typical for large companies interested in a stable core labor force and a flexible internal allocation of labor, whereas the occupational market is dominant in the small craft business sector (*Handwerk*). In reality, "many labor markets exhibit elements both from occupational and firm-internal allocational structures" (Sengenberger, 1992:249). The segmentation of labor markets was mainly discussed as an aspect of flexibilization of labor. With deregulation, a new aspect became relevant: the disintegration of the constituent elements of the regular employment relationship and the growth of atypical forms of employment (Mückenberger, 1985), especially among women. Labor market segmentation became a main focus of gender studies on unequal opportunities (e.g., Beck-Gernsheim, 1976) and of the debate on the special "female work ability" (*Arbeitsvermögen*) (Beck-Gernsheim and Ostner, 1977).

New Technology and the Structuring of Workplaces. The microelectronic revolution provided the technological basis for a far-reaching implementation of information technology in the workplace in many industries. This development stimulated a profound debate on the effects of the new technology on work contents, qualification, skills, work organization, and worker control. The relevance of technology for industrial relations systems, since Dunlop (1958) a recognized fact, was also rediscovered (Sorge and Streeck, 1988). In the context of the neo-Marxist debate (discussed earlier), some sociologists defended an "apocalyptic version of the subsumption theory" (Brandt, 1990:263) arguing that the new technology would completely subjugate the worker by degrading him to an appendage of machinery (Benz-Overhage et al., 1982). David Noble's (1979) American case study on the introduction of automatically controlled machinery seemed to support this assertion. But others supported the perception of the new technology as an elastic potential, open to different solutions (Altmann et al., 1992:pts. II and III; Berger, 1991). And a third group understood the implementation of technology as a result of micropolitical bargaining processes (Müller-Jentsch et al., 1997; Ortmann et al., 1990).

Comparative research projects (Düll and Lutz, 1989; Heidenreich, 1995; Müller-Jentsch et al., 1997; Sorge et al., 1982) supported the thesis that information technology leaves room for different solutions. Some gender studies explored the interplay of gender, technology and work in offices, and computer-based industries (Becker-Schmidt, 1994; Gottschall, 1990).

Restructuring of Labor Process, Work Organization, and Companies (New Production Concepts vs. Systemic Rationalization). With the publication of "The End of the Division of Labor?" by Kern and Schumann (1984), the restructuring of work has become a major topic of sociological research and debate since the mid-1980s. The analytical focus of the book was the production process in three manufacturing industries (automobile, machine tools, chemicals). What both authors had called the "new production concepts" indicated a radical change in the traditional mode of industrial rationalization, in other words, a recognition by management that sophisticated production technology demanded somethings other than simply standardized (Taylorist and Fordist) concepts of the technical division of labor. Although Kern and Schumann emphasized the trend toward a reintegration of the skilled worker into the immediate production process, they delineated an uneven development, with winners and losers of the rationalization measures. A new category of multiskilled worker—the so-called "system regulator"—was among the winners. But a quantitatively oriented follow-up study (Schumann et al., 1994; English summary, 1995) showed that this new kind of production worker was still far away from being or becoming the dominant type (except in chemical industry, roughly half of the workers of the production line could be ascribed to it; in the automotive industry, less than 10% [1994:644]). Another finding of the follow-up research of Schumann and his colleagues was the spread of new production teams, which aroused expectations of a coming innovative personnel management (Schumann, 1993).

Altmann and his colleagues from the Munich Institute (Altmann et al., 1986, 1992) also noticed a paradigmatic change of rationalization, but, looking beyond the immediate production process, they called it 'systemic rationalization' as a new pattern of technology-centered rationalization embracing all departments of the whole company and their relevant networks with supplying and distributing firms. These alternative interpretations about the trajectory of rationalization turned out to be only a prelude to the debate about lean production, business reengineering, total quality management, and learning organizations that followed the publication of *The Machine That Changed the World* (Womack, Jones, and Roos, 1990).

Schumann himself has claimed that both interpretations were not contradictory but rather complementary perspectives of the ongoing rationalization process. Some of the following research projects started with a much broader understanding of rationalization. The whole business organization and its networks of supplier and delivery firms, too, became subject matter of empirical research on rationalization and innovation. Thus processes of decentralization in companies (Faust et al., 1994; Hirsch-Kreinsen, 1995) as well as complete restructuring of businesses (Pries, 1998; Sauer and Döhl, 1997) and of building strategic networks between companies (Sydow, 1992; Sydow and Windeler, 1994) were empirically investigated. The flourishing research in the reorganization of companies included comparative studies (Deiß and Döhl, 1992; Jürgens, Malsch, and Dohse, 1993; Sorge and Warner, 1986). Especially Japan and the United States became the favorite reference cases. In general, new reflections on the subject matter have conveyed new insights into the facets, myths, and dimensions of rationalization (Bechtle, 1994; Deutschmann, 1997; Minssen, 1992).

Since occupation has been regarded as a basis of personal self-confidence, the experience of work and the process of occupational socialization have played major roles in the research of workers' biographies (Brose, 1983). As a consequence of the profound reorganization and flexibilization of work and production, the boundaries of occupation are fading and the occupational identity is being eroded (Baethge and Baethge-Kinsky, 1998). In the advanced sectors, a new type of an individualized "worker–manager" (*Arbeitskraftunternehmer*) has been identified (Voß and Pongratz, 1998). Similar to Sennet's flexible character (1998), he or she becomes responsible for structuring and organizing his or her entire everyday lifestyle under the priority of employment opportunities.

Sociology of Management/New Public Management. As long as the neo-Marxist debate dominated German industrial sociology, there was no special interest in sociological research on management, because the so-called *Ableitungs-Marxismus* (deductive Marxism) was fully satisfied with the textbook tenets that capitalist management is only in existence for intensification of labor exploitation and maximization of profits. Early empirical studies on the "German entrepreneur" by Hartmann (1968) and the social reality of the "managers of capitalism" by Pross and Boetticher (1971) sank into oblivion. It was the Anglo–American labor process debate and a late rediscovery of Child's (1971) concept of "strategic choice" that generated new interest in management. Ganter and Schienstock's collective volume on the "sociology of management" (1993) included a broad spectrum of chapters that gave empirical evidence about the world of management. Furthermore, the American concepts of human resource management were well received by German authors (Fischer and Weitbrecht, 1995; Staehle, 1989). In 1991, Wolfgang Staehle founded a special yearbook on *Managementforschung* (management research), which offers academics of different disciplines (business administration, sociology, politics, law) a forum for their research findings. It has to be added that the modernization of the public sector is also on the research agenda, since "new public management" has recently become a topic of sociological research (special issue of *Managementforschung*: 1998).

Industrial and Labor Relations. Codetermination, trade unions, and workplace representation have been enduring themes, but a systematic approach to research on industrial relations systems was unknown until the late 1970s. During the 1950s and 1960s, there was ample research on codetermination (for an overview, see Funder, 1995), and during the 1970s, a series of major research projects focused on trade unions (Bergmann, 1979; Bergmann et al., [1974] 1977; Brandt et al., 1982; Streeck, 1981) and on large strikes and lockouts. The Anglo–American industrial relations approach became a discussion theme at the 1979 Convention of the German Society of Sociology in Berlin.

During the 1980s, the first textbooks with systematic accounts of the German industrial relations system were published (Keller, [1991] 1997; Müller-Jentsch, 1986), after Friedrich Fürstenberg (1975), the former president of the International Industrial Relations Association, and Hansjörg Weitbrecht (1969), had prepared the ground with their publications. Industrial relations has become a newly established, interdisciplinary field of research and university teaching (shared by industrial sociology, political science, labor law, business studies), with standard textbooks, an interdisciplinary quarterly (*Industrielle Beziehungen*), and a book series (*Schriftenreihe Industrielle Beziehungen*, edited by W. Müller-Jentsch). The point of departure for most research studies is now the "dual system" approach (see, e.g., Bergmann and Müller-Jentsch [1975] 1983; Jacobi et al., [1992] 1998; Thelen, 1991)—developed by researchers at the Frankfurt Institute. The dual system of interest representation consist of two arenas: (1) *free collective bargaining* by unions and employers' associations and (2) *codetermination by works councils* (codetermination at the supervisory board now fulfills rather a supplementary function for the works councils). Both arenas are functionally separated according to interests, actors and modes of enforcement (for further details, see Jacobi et al., [1992] 1998:190f.)

With the decentralization of companies and the diffusion of worker participation during the 1990s, works councils and teamworking became major research themes. With regard to the research on works councils, Kotthoff (1981; 1994), Osterloh (1993), and Bosch (1997) have submitted authoritative studies giving evidence of the proliferation of the councilors' functions and tasks. The first workplace surveys (Müller-Jentsch and Seitz, 1998; WSI-Projektgruppe, 1998) confirm these findings. The research on workers' participation (teamwork, quality circles) has also flourished parallel to their real growth (Binckelmann et al. 1993; Greifenstein et al., 1993; Minssen, 1999; Sperling, 1994; 1997).

Transformation of East Germany.   A huge research program on transformation of the economic and political structures of East Germany was initiated and organized by the Committee for the Investigation into the Social and
Political Change in the New Bundeslander (Kommission für die Erforschung
des sozialen und politischen Wandels in den neuen Bundesländern, KSPW).
More than 200 research projects have been commissioned. The empirical findings have been summarized in six reports on different research fields: (1)
work, labor market, and companies (Lutz et al., 1996); (2) inequality and social policy; (3) political system; (4) individual development, education, and
occupational careers; (5) cities and regions; and (6) transformation of legal
regulation of work and social policy. Dozens of separate volumes have been
published as contributions to the reports, for example, on industrial relations
(Bergmann and Schmidt, 1996), on management (Pohlmann and Schmidt,
1996), and on works councils (Förster and Röbenack, 1996).

The empirical findings expose a relatively successful transfer of the western political, legal, and socioeconomic institutions to the eastern part of Germany. Many reports on work structures, management, labor relations, and
labor markets show that the east is gradually keeping up with the west, although the rate of unemployment is still considerably higher (especially among
women) and the average incomes are lower. Following the pattern of Japanese
transplants, Opel and Volkswagen have set up Greenfield sites with advanced
technology and a labor force strictly selected by criteria of age and efficiency
(Mickler et al. 1996). In spite of these modern transplants ("cathedrals in the
desert"), East Germany will remain a dependent economy for the foreseeable
future.

Crisis of the "German Model."   The most recent debate is on the crisis
of the "German model" of production and labor regulation. The former means
the integration of skilled workers in the production process, and the latter,
the dual system of collective interest representation. Under the impact of globalization and Europeanization, some academics argue, the two dual systems
(occupational training and that interest representation) have turned out to be
barriers against flexibility and innovations. To their minds the "German vir-
tues" have become obsolete in a globalized economy (Jürgens and Naschold,
1994; Kern and Sabel, 1994; Streeck, 1998).

Other authors refer to the potentials of adjustability of both systems and
look forward to the emerging transnational level of work regulation. They
expect that the European works councils and the very beginnings of the social
dialog between the social partners in the European Union indicate a suprana-
tional industrial relations system in the making (Dörre, 1999; Lecher and Rüb,
1999).

INSTITUTIONAL CONTEXT

The framework constituting the institutional context in which sociology of work and industry has its place in Germany is determined by the corporatist tradition that goes back to the period of paternalistic social reforms under Bismarck. At that time, corporatism was an arrangement primarily between the authoritarian government and big industry, which excluded organized labor. In contrast, the corporatism of the early years of the Weimar period was strongly labor-oriented. New forms of corporatist governance emerged in the coal and steel industry of the Ruhr area during the postwar period. The strong provisions of codetermination changed the traditionally adversarial climate between capital and labor and strengthened the dual system of interest representation far beyond the coal and steel industry. Furthermore, the concept and practice of social market economy, which was ultimately accepted by the labor movement, and the dual system of training, became essential pillars of postwar corporatism. The richness of institutions regulating labor on macro- and microlevels is a historical heritage quite different from that in the United States and the United Kingdom. The governing of work in society and industry relies on a deep-rooted societal consensus. It cannot be ignored without major social conflicts.

Research on work could always count on strong support by public authorities, universities, and other institutions. Since 1909, the year when the German Sociological Association (Deutsche Gesellschaft für Soziologie) was founded with the active support of Max Weber, professional research on work has been conducted by a variety of public and academic research institutes which have already been mentioned.

The main sponsors of this research have been the Deutsche Forschungsgemeinschaft (DFG; German Research Community), the Volkswagen Foundation, and some private foundations. The DFG, especially, has financed large research programs on industrial and organizational sociology, the labor market, structural change of industrial relations, the restructuring of work under the impact of globalization, and so on. The Federal Department of Labor and the German Productivity Center (RKW), as well the government committees on economic and social change, have sponsored many research projects.

After World War II the major projects in research on work and industry were initiated by the Sozialforschungsstelle in Dortmund and by the Frankfurt Institute of Social Research. During the 1960s and 1970s, the Sociological Research Institute (Soziologisches Forschungsinstitut, SOFI) in Göttingen, and the Institute for Social Research (Institut für Sozialwissenschaftliche Forschung) in Munich, also became important research centers. The Sozialforschungsstelle has given up its leading position to the three other institutes since the late 1960s; during the 1980s, the Frankfurt Institute of Social Research also lost ground. Besides the Sozialforschungsstelle, which is a foundation of the state of Nordrhine–Westfalia, the other three institutes are private, although linked to universities and partly subsidizes by public funds.

Other institutes engaged in research on work are the Science Center Berlin (Wissenschaftszentrum, WZB), the Institute for Employment Research (IAB) in Nuremberg, the Max-Planck Institut für Gesellschaftsforschung (MPIfG) in Cologne, the Institute of Labor and Technology (IAT) in Gelsenkirchen (all four publicly financed); the Institute for Social Research and Social Economy in Saarbrücken, and the Institut for Work, Technology and Culture in Tübingen (both privately financed), and the research institute WSI of the DGB in Düsseldorf. Professional industrial research has also been conducted at many universities and university institutes in East and West Germany (see Appendix).

REFERENCES

Altmann, Norbert, and Günter Bechtle. 1971. *Betriebliche Herrschaftsstruktur und industrielle Gesellschaft*. München: Hanser.

Altmann, Norbert, Manfred Deiß, Volker Döhl, and Dieter Sauer. 1986. "Ein 'Neuer Rationalisierungstyp'—neue Anforderungen an die Industriesoziologie." *Soziale Welt* 37:191–206

Altmann, Norbert, Christoph Köhler, and Pamela Meil, eds. 1992. *Technology and Work in German Industry*. London: Routledge

Baethge, Martin, and Volker Baethge-Kinsky. 1998. "Jenseits von Beruf und Beruflichkeit?" *Mitteilungen aus der Arbeitsmarkt- und Berufsforschung* 31:461–472

Baethge, Martin, and Herbert Oberbeck. 1984. *Zukunft der Angestellten: Neue Technologien und berufliche Perpektiven in Büro und Verwaltung*. Frankfurt/New York: Campus

Bahrdt, Hans Paul. 1958. *Industriebürokratie: Versuch einer Soziologie des industrialisierten Bürobetriebes und seiner Angestellten*. Stuttgart: Enke.

Bechtle, Günter. 1994. "Systemische Rationalisierung als neues Paradigma industriesoziologischer Forschung?" Pp. 45–64 in *Umbrüche gesellschaftlicher Arbeit. Soziale Welt, Sonderband 9*, edited by Niels Beckenbach and Weiner van Treeck. Göttingen: Schwartz.

Beckenbach, Niels, and Werner van Treeck, eds. 1994. *Umbrüche gesellschaftlicher Arbeit. Soziale Welt, Sonderband 9*. Göttingen: Schwartz.

Becker-Schmidt, Regina. 1994. "Geschlechterverhältnis, Technologieentwicklung und androzentristische Ideologieproduktion." Pp. 527–538 in *Umbrüche gesellschaftlicher Arbeit. Soziale Welt, Sonderband 9*, edited by Niels Beckenbach and Weiner van Treeck. Göttingen: Schwartz.

Beck-Gernsheim, Elisabeth. 1976. *Der geschlechtsspezifische Arbeitsmarkt.* Frankfurt/ New York: Campus.

Beck-Gernsheim, Elisabeth, and Ilona Ostner. 1977. "Der Gegensatz von Beruf und Hausarbeit als Konstitutionsbedingung weiblichen Arbeitsvermögens." Pp. 25– 53 in *Die soziale Konstitution der Berufe,* Vol. 2, edited by Ulrich Beck and Michael Brater.

Benz-Overhage, Karin, Eva Brumlop, Thomas von Freyberg, and, Zissis Papadimitriou. 1982. *Neue Technologien und alternative Arbeitsgestaltung: Auswirkungen des Computereinsatzes in der industriellen Produktion.* Frankfurt/New York: Campus.

Berger, Peter. 1991. *Gestaltete Technik: Die Genese der Informationstechnik als Basis einer politischen Gestaltungsstrategie.* Frankfurt/New York: Campus.

Bergmann, Joachim, ed. 1979. *Soziologie der Gewerkschaften.* Frankfurt: Suhrkamp.

Bergmann, Joachim, Otto Jacobi, and Walther Müller-Jentsch. [1974] 1977. *Gewerkschaften in der Bundesrepublik: Vol. 1. Gewerkschaftliche Lohnpolitik zwischen Mitgliederinteressen und ökonomischen Systemzwängen,* 2nd ed. Frankfurt: Aspekte.

Bergmann, Joachim, and Walther Müller-Jentsch 1975/1983. "The Federal Republic of Germany: Cooperative Unionism and Dual Bargaining System Challenged." Pp. 229–277 in *Worker Militancy and Its Consequences,* 2nd ed., edited by Solomon Barkin. New York: Praeger.

Bergmann, Joachim, and Walther Müller-Jentsch. 1977. *Gewerkschaften in der Bundesrepublik: Vol. 2. Lohnpolitik im Bewußtsein der Funktionäre.* Frankfurt: Aspekte.

Bergmann, Joachim, and Rudi Schmidt, eds. 1996. *Industrielle Beziehungen: Institutionalisierung und Praxis unter Krisenbedingungen.* Opladen: Leske and Budrich.

Binckelmann, Peter, Hans-Joachim Braczyk, and Rüdiger Seltz. 1993. *Entwicklung der Gruppenarbeit in Deutschland.* Frankfurt/New York: Campus.

Bosch, Aida. 1997. *Vom Interessenkonflikt zur Kultur der Rationalität: Neue Verhandlungsbeziehungen zwischen Management und Betriebsrat.* München/Mering: Hampp.

Brandt, Gerhard. 1990. *Arbeit, Technik und gesellschaftliche Entwicklung: Aufsätze 1971– 1987.* Frankfurt: Suhrkamp.

Brandt, Gerhard, Otto Jacobi, and Walther Müller-Jentsch. 1982. *Anpassung an die Krise: Gewerkschaften in den siebziger Jahren.* Frankfurt/New York: Campus.

Brandt, Gerhard, Bernard Kündig, Zissis Papadimitriou, and Jutta Thomae. 1978. *Computer und Arbeitsprozeß.* Frankfurt/New York: Campus.

Braverman, Harry. 1974. *Labor and Monopoly Capital.* New York: Monthly Review Press.

Brentano, Lujo. 1909. "Gewerkvereine." Pp. 1106–1119 in *Handwörterbuch der Staatswissenschaften,* Vol. 4, 3rd ed., edited by J. Conrad, L. Elster, W. Lexis, and E. Loering. Jena: Verlag von Gustav Fischer.

Briefs, Goetz. 1927. "Gewerkschaftswesen und Gewerkschaftspolitik." Pp. 1108–1150 in *Handwörterbuch der Staatswissenschaften,* Vol. 4, 4th ed., edited by L Elster, Al WEver, and Wieser. Jena: Verlag von Gustav Fischer.

Briefs, Goetz. 1931. Betriebssoziologie. Pp. 31–52 in *Handwörterbuch der Soziologie,* edited by Alfred Vierkandt. Stuttgart: Enke.

Brigl-Matthiaß, Kurt. [1926] 1978. *Das Betriebsräteproblem.* Berlin: Olle & Wolter.

Brose, Hanns-Georg. 1983. *Die Erfahrung der Arbeit: Zum berufsbiographischen Erwerb von Handlungsmustern bei Industriearbeitern.* Opladen: Westdeutscher Verlag.

Child, John. 1971. "Organizational Structure, Environment and Performance: The Role of Strategic Choice." *Sociology* 6:1–22.

Dahrendorf, Ralf. 1959. *Sozialstruktur des Betriebes.* Wiebaden: Gabler.

Dahrendorf, Ralf. [1956] 1962. *Industrie- und Betriebssoziologie,* 2nd ed. Berlin: de Gruyter.

Deiß, Manfred, and Volker Döhl, eds. 1992. *Vernetzte Produktion: Automobilzulieferer zwischen Kontrolle und Autonomie.* Frankfurt/New York: Campus.

Deutschmann, Christoph. 1997. "Die Mythenspirale: Eine wissenssoziologische Interpretation industrieller Rationalisierung." *Soziale Welt* 47:55–70

Doeringer, Peter B., and Michael J. Piore. 1971. *Internal Labor Markets and Manpower Analysis.* Lexington, MA: Heath

Dörre, Klaus. 1999. "Industrielle Beziehungen im Spannungsfeld von Globalisierung und europäischer Mehrebenen-Regulation." Pp. 297–324 in *Konfliktpartnerschaft. Akteure und Institutionen der industriellen Beziehungen,* 3rd ed., edited by Walther Müller-Jentsch. München/Mering: Hampp.

Düll, Klaus, and Burkart Lutz, ed. 1989. *Technikentwicklung und Arbeitsteilung im internationalen Vergleich.* Frankfurt: Campus.

Dunlop, John T. 1958. *Industrial Relations Systems.* New York: Holt.

Faust, Michael, Peter Jauch, Karin Brünnecke, and Christoph Deutschmann. 1994. *Dezentralisierung von Unternehmen.* München/Mering: Hampp.

Ferner, Anthony, and Richard Hyman, eds. [1992] 1998. *Changing Industrial Relations in Europe,* 2nd ed. Oxford, UK: Blackwell.

Fischer, Stephan, and Hansjörg Weitbrecht. 1995. "Individualism and Collectivism: Two Dimensions of Human Resource Management and Industrial Relations." *Industrielle Beziehungen* 2:367–394.

Förster, Heike, Röbenack, and Silke. 1996. *Wandel betrieblicher Interessenvertretungen in Ostdeutschland.* KSPW Berlin: Graue Reihe.

Funder, Maria. 1995. *Stand und Perspektiven der Mitbestimmung.* Düsseldorf: Hans–Böckler–Stiftung (Manuskripte 187).

Fürstenberg, Friedrich. 1975. *Industrielle Arbeitsbeziehungen.* Wien: Manzsche Verlag.

Ganter, Hans-Dieter, and Gerd Schienstock, eds.1993. *Management aus soziologischer Sicht.* Wiesbaden: Gabler.

Geck, L. H. Adolph. 1931. *Die sozialen Arbeitsverhältnisse im Wandel der Zeit: Eine geschichtliche Einführung in die Betriebsoziologie.* Berlin: Springer.

Gottschall, Karin. 1990. *Frauenarbeit und Bürorationalisierung.* Frankfurt/New York: Campus.

Greifenstein, Ralf, Peter Jansen, and Leo Kißler. 1993. *Gemanagte Partizipation: Qualitätszirkel in der deutschen und der französischen Automobilindustrie.* München/Mering: Hampp.

Haber, Samuel. 1964. *Efficiency and Uplift. Scientific Management in the Progressive Era 1890–1920.* Chicago: The University of Chicago Press

Hartmann, Heinz. 1968. *Der deutsche Unternehmer.* Frankfurt: Europäische Verlagsanstalt.

Heidenreich, Martin. 1995. *Informatisierung und Kultur. Eine vergleichende Analyse der Einführung und Nutzung von Informationssystemen in italienischen, französischen und westdeutschen Unternehmen.* Opladen: Westdeutscher Verlag

Hellpach, Willy, and Richard Lang. 1922. *Gruppenfabrikation.* Berlin: Springer.

Hilbert, Josef, and Hans Joachim Sperling. 1990. *Die kleine Fabrik.* München/Mering: Hampp.

Hirsch-Kreinsen, Hartmut. 1995. "Dezentralisierung: Unternehmen zwischen Stabilität und Desintegration." *Zeitschrift für Soziologie* 24:422–435

Hirsch-Kreinsen, Hartmut, and Harald Wolf, eds. 1998. *Arbeit, Gesellschaft, Kritik: Orientierungen wider den Zeitgeist.* Berlin: Sigma.

Institut für Sozialforschung. 1955. *Betriebsklima.* Frankfurt: Europäische Verlangsanstalt.

Jacobi, Otto, Berndt Keller, and Walther Müller-Jentsch. [1992] 1998. "Germany: Facing New Challenges." Pp. 190–238 in *Changing Industrial Relations in Europe,* 2nd ed., edited by Anthony Feiner and Richard Hyman. Oxford, UK: Blackwell.

Jost, Walter. 1932. *Das Sozialleben des industriellen Betriebes.* Berlin: Springer.

Jürgens, Ulrich, Thomas Malsch, and Knut Dohse. 1993. *Breaking from Taylorism: Changing Forms of Work in the Automobil Industry.* Cambridge, UK: Cambridge University Press.

Jürgens, Ulrich, and Frieder Naschold. 1994. "Arbeits- und industriepolitische Entwicklungsengpässe der deutschen Industrie in den 90er Jahren." Pp. 239–270 in *Institutionenvergleich und Institutionendynamik,* edited by Wolfgang Zapf and Meinolf Dierkes. Berlin: Sigma.

Kadritzke, Ulf. 1982. "Angestellte als Lohnarbeiter: Kritischer Nachruf auf die deutsche Kragenlinie." Pp. 219–249 in *Materialien zur Industriesoziologie: Kölner Zeitschrift für Soziologie und Sozialpsychologie, Sonderheft 24,* edited by G. Schmidt, H.-J. Braczyk, and J. Knesebeck. Opladen: Westdeutscher Verlag.

Keller, Berndt. [1991] 1997. *Einführung in die Arbeitspolitik,* 5th ed. München/Wien: Oldenbourg.

Kern, Horst. 1982. *Empirische Sozialforschung: Ursprünge, Ansätze, Entwicklungslinien.* München: Beck.

Kern Horst, and Charles F. Sabel. 1994. "Verblaßte Tugenden: Zur Krise des deutschen Produktionsmodells." Pp. 605–624 in *Umbrüche gesellschaftlicher Arbeit. Soziale Welt, Sonderband 9,* edited by Niels Beckenbach and Weiner van Treeck. Göttingen: Schwartz.

Kern, Horst, and Michael Schumann. 1970. *Industriearbeit und Arbeiterbewußtsein.* Frankfurt: Europäische Verlagsanstalt.

Kern, Horst, and Michael Schumann. 1984. *Das Ende der Arbeitsteilung? Rationalisierung in der industriellen Produktion.* München: Beck.

Kindleberger, Charles P. 1975. Germany's Overtaking of England, 1806–1914. *Weltwirtschaftliches Archiv* 111:253–281, 477–504.

Kotthoff, Hermann. 1981. *Betriebsräte und betriebliche Herrschaft: Eine Typologie von Partizipationsmustern im Industriebetrieb.* Frankfurt/New York: Campus

Kotthoff, Hermann. 1994. *Betriebsräte und Bürgerstatus: Wandel und Kontinuität betrieblicher Mitbestimmung.* München/Mering: Hampp.

Kotthoff, Hermann, and Josef Reindl. 1990. *Die soziale Welt kleiner Betriebe.* Göttingen: Schwartz.

Kudera, Werner, Werner Mangold, Konrad Ruff, Rudi Schmidt, and Theodor Wentzke.

1979. *Gesellschaftliches und politisches Bewußtsein von Arbeitern.* Frankfurt: Europäische Verlagsanstalt.

Lecher, Wolfgang, and Stefan Rüb. 1999. "The Constitution of European Works Councils: From Information Forum to Social Actor?" *European Journal of Industrial Relations* 5:7–25

Littek, Wolfgang, and Tony Charles, eds. 1995. *The New Division of Labour: Emerging Forms of Work Organisation in International Perspective.* Berlin/NewYork: de Gruyter.

Littek, Wolfgang, and Ulrich Heisig. 1986. Rationalisierung von Arbeit als Aushandlungsprozeß: Beteiligung bei Rationalisierungsverläufen im Angestelltenbereich. *Soziale Welt* 37:237–262.

Littek, Wolfgang, and Ulrich Heisig. 1995. "Taylorism Never Got Hold of Skilled White-Collar Work in Germany." Pp. 373–395 in *The New Division of Labour: Emerging Forms of Work Organisation in International Perspective,* edited by W. Littek and T. Charles. Berlin/NewYork: de Gruyter.

Littek, Wolfgang, Werner Rammert, and Günther Wachtler, eds. 1982: *Einführung in die Arbeits-und Industriesoziologie,* 2nd ed. Frankfurt/New York: Campus.

Lutz, Burkart. 1976. "Bildunggssystem und Beschäftigungsstruktur in Deutschland und Frankreich." Pp. 83–115 in *Betrieb–Arbeitsmarkt–Qualifikation,* edited by Institut für Sozialwissenschaftliche Forschung. Frankfurt/New York: Campus.

Lutz, Burkart. 1992. "Education and Job Hierarchies: Contrasting Evidence from France and Germany." Pp. 257–273 in *Technology and Work in German Industry,* edited by N. Altmann, C. Köhler, and P. Meil. London: Routledge.

Lutz, Burkart, Hildegard M. Nickel, Rudi Schmidt, and Arndt Sorge. 1996. *Arbeit, Arbeitsmarkt und Betriebe.* Opladen: Leske und Budrich.

Managementforschung. 1991ff. Yearbook, vols. 1–11. Berlin: de Gruyter.

Marx, Karl. [1867] 1962. *Das Kapital: Kritik der politischen Ökonomie.* Erster Band. Marx–Engels-Werke, Vol. 23. Berlin: Dietz..

Marx, Karl. 1953. *Die Frühschriften.* Stuttgart: Kröner.

Mendius, Hans Gerhard, Werner Sengenberger, and Stefan Weimer. 1987. *Arbeitskräfteprobleme und Humanisierungspotentiale in Kleinbetrieben.* Frankfurt/New York: Campus.

Mickler, Otfried, Eckhard Dittrich, Uwe Neumann, Wilma Mohr, and Ulf Kadritzke. 1977. *Produktion und Qualifikation,* 2 vols. Göttingen: Forschungsbericht.

Mickler, Otfried, Norbert Engelhard, Ralph Lungwitz, and Bettina Walker. 1996. *Nach der Trabi-Ära: Arbeiten in schlanken Fabriken. Modernisierung der ostdeutschen Autoindustrie.* Berlin: Sigma.

Minssen, Heiner. 1992. *Die Rationalität der Rationalisierung. Betrieblicher Wandel und Industriesoziologie.* Stuttgart: Enke.

Minssen, Heiner. 1999. Direkte Partizipation contra Mitbestimmung? Herausforderung durch diskursive Koordinierung. Pp. 129–156 in *Konfliktpartnerschaft. Akteure und Institutionen der industriellen Beziehungen,* 3rd ed., edited by Walther Müller-Jentsch. München/Mering: Hampp.

Mückenberger, Ulrich. 1985. "Die Krise des Normalarbeitsverhältnisses: Hat das Arbeitsrecht noch Zukunft?" *Zeitschrift für Sozialreform* 31:415–434; 457–475.

Müller-Jentsch, Walther. [1986] 1997. *Soziologie der Industriellen Beziehungen: Eine Einführung,* 2nd ed. Frankfurt/New York: Campus.

Müller-Jentsch, Walther, ed. [1993] 1999. *Konfliktpartnerschaft: Akteure und Institutionen der industriellen Beziehungen*, 3rd ed. München/Mering: Hampp.
Müller-Jentsch, Walther, and Beate Seitz. 1998. "Betriebsräte gewinnen Konturen: Ergebnisse einer Betriebsräte-Befragung im Maschinenbau." *Industrielle Beziehungen* 5:361–387.
Müller-Jentsch, Walther, Hans Joachim Sperling, and Irmgard Weyrather. 1997. *Neue Technologie in der Verhandlungsarena: Schweden, Großbritannien und Deutschland im Vergleich.* München/Mering: Hampp.
Neuloh, Otto. 1956. *Die deutsche Betriebsverfassung und ihre Sozialformen bis zur Mitbestimmung.* Tübingen: Mohr.
Neuloh, Otto. 1960. *Der neue Betriebsstil.* Tübingen: Mohr.
Noble, David F. 1979. "Social Choice in Machine Design: The Case of Automatically Controlled Machine Tools." Pp. 18–50 in *Case Studies in the Labor Process*, edited by Andrew S. Zimbalist. New York: Monthly Review Press.
Osterloh, Margit. 1993. *Interpretative Organisations- und Mitbestimmungsforschung.* Stuttgart: Schäffer-Poeschel.
Ortmann, Günther, Arnold Windeler, Albrecht Becker, and Hans-Joachim Schulz. 1990. *Computer und Macht in Organisationen: Mikropolitische Analysen.* Opladen: Westdeutscher Verlag.
Piore, Michael J., and Charles F. Sabel. 1984. *The Second Industrial Divide.* New York: Basic Books.
Pirker, Theo. 1962. *Büro und Maschine.* Tübingen: Mohr.
Pirker, Theo, Siegfried Braun, Burkart Lutz, and Fro Hammelrath. 1952. *Arbeiter, Management, Mitbestimmung.* Stuttgart/Düsseldorf: Ring.
Pohlmann, Markus, and Rudi Schmidt, eds. 1996. *Management in der ostdeutschen Industrie.* Opladen: Leske & Budrich.
Pollock, Friedrch. [1956] 1964. *Automation: Materialien zur Beurteilung der ökonomischen und sozialen Folgen.* Frankfurt/Main: Europäische Verlagsanstalt.
Popitz, Heinrich, Hans Paul Bahrdt, Ernst August Jüres, and Hanno Kesting. 1957a. *Technik und Industriearbeit.* Tübingen: Mohr.
Popitz, Heinrich, Hans Paul Bahrdt, Ernst August Jüres, and Hanno Kesting. 1957b. *Das Gesellschaftsbild des Arbeiters.* Tübingen: Mohr.
Prics, Ludger. [1991] 1998. *Betrieblicher Wandel in der Risikogesellschaft.* München/Mering: Hampp.
Pross, Helge, and Karl W. Boetticher. 1971. *Manager des Kapitalismus: Untersuchung über leitende Angestellte in Großunternehmen.* Frankfurt: Suhrkamp.
Rammstedt, Otthein. 1986. *Deutsche Soziologie 1933–1945.* Frankfurt/Main: Suhrkamp.
Rosenstock-Huessy, Eugen. 1922. *Werkstattaussiedlung: Untersuchungen über den Lebensraum des Industriearbeiters.* Berlin: Springer.
Sauer, Dieter, Manfred Deiß, Volker Döhl, Daniel Bieber, and Norbert Altmann. 1992. "Systemic Rationalization and Inter-Company Division of Labour." Pp. 46–59 in *Technology and Work in German Industry*, edited by N. Altmann, C. Köhler, and P. Meil. London: Routledge.
Sauer, Dieter, and Volker Döhl. 1997. "Die Auflösung des Unternehmens?– Entwicklungstendenzen der Unternehmensreorganisation in den 90er Jahren." Pp. 19–76 in *Jahrbuch sozialwissenschaftliche Technikberichterstattung.* Berlin: Sigma.

Schmiede, Rudi, and Edwin Schudlich. 1976. *Die Entwicklung der Leistungsentlohnung in Deutschland.* Frankfurt/New York: Campus.

Schmidt, Gert, Hans-Joachim Braczyk, and Jost von dem Knesebeck, eds. 1982. *Materialien zur Industriesoziologie: Kölner Zeitschrift für Soziologie und Sozialpsychologie, Sonderheft 24.* Opladen: Westdeutscher Verlag.

Schumann, Michael. 1993. "Gruppenarbeit und neue Produktionskonzepte." Pp. 186–203 in *Entwicklung den Gruppenarbeit in Deutschland,* edited by P. Birkelman, H.-J. Bracqyk, and R. Seltz. Frankfurt and New York: Campus.

Schumann, Michael, Volker Baethge-Kinsky, Martin Kuhlmann, Constanze Kurz, and Uwe Neumann. 1994. *Trendreport Rationalisierung: Automobilindustrie, Werkzeugmaschinenbau, Chemische Industrie.* Berlin: Sigma.

Schumann, Michael, Volker Baethge-Kinsky, Martin Kuhlmann, Constanze Kurz, and Uwe Neumann. 1995. "New Production Concepts and the Restructuring of Work." Pp. 95–135 in *The New Division of Labour: Emerging Forms of Work Organisation in International Perspective,* edited by W. Littek and T. Charles. Berlin/NewYork: de Gruyter.

Schumann, Michael, Edgar Einemann, Christa Siebel-Rebell, and Klaus Peter Wittemann. 1982. *Rationalisierung, Krise, Arbeiter: Eine empirische Untersuchung aus der Werft.* Frankfurt/New York: Campus.

Sengenberger, Werner, ed. 1978. *Der gespaltene Arbeitsmarkt: Probleme der Arbeitsmarktsegmentation.* Frankfurt/New York: Campus.

Sengenberger, Werner. 1992. "Vocational Training, Job Structures and the Labour Market – An International Perspective." Pp. 245–256 in *Technology and Work in German Industry,* edited by N. Altmann, C. Köhler, and P. Meil. London: Routledge.

Sennet, Richard. 1998. *The Corrosion of Character.* New York: Norton.

Sorge, Arndt, Gert Hartmann, Malcolm Warner, and Ian Nicholas. 1982. *Mikroelektronik und Arbeit in der Industrie: Erfahrungen beim Einsatz von CNC-Werkzeugmaschinen in Großbritannien und der Bundesrepublik Deutschland.* Frankfurt: Campus

Sorge, Arndt, and Wolfgang Streeck. 1988. "Industrial Relations and Technical Change: Perspective." Pp. 19–47 in *New Technology and Industrial Relations,* edited by Richard Hyman and Wolfgang Streeck. Oxford, UK: Blackwell.

Sorge, Arndt, and Malcom Warner. 1986. *Comparative Factory Organisation: An Anglo-German Comparison of Management and Manpower in Manufacturing.* Aldershot: Gower.

Sperling, Hans Joachim. 1994. *Innovative Arbeitsorganisation und intelligentes Partizipationsmanagement: Trend-Report Partizipation und Organisation.* Marburg: Schüren.

Sperling, Hans Joachim. 1997. *Restrukturierung von Unternehmens- und Arbeitsorganisation—eine Zwischenbilanz. Trend-Report Partizipation und Organisation II.* Marburg: Schüren.

Staehle, Wolfgang. 1989. "Human Resource Management und Unternehmensstrategie." *Mitteilungen aus der Arbeitsmarkt- und Berufsforschung* 22:388–396.

Stearns, Peter N. 1993. *The Industrial Revolution in World History.* Boulder, CO: Westview Press.

Streeck, Wolfgang. 1981. *Gewerkschaftliche Organisationsprobleme in der sozialstaatlichen*

Demokratie. Königstein: Athenäum.

Streeck, Wolfgang.1998. "Industrielle Beziehungen in einer internationalisierten Wirtschaft." Pp. 169–202 in *Politik der Globalisierung,* edited by Ulrich Beck. Frankfurt: Suhrkamp.

Sydow, Jörg. 1992. *Strategische Netzwerke: Evolution und Organisation.* Wiesbaden: Gabler.

Sydow, Jörg, and Arnold Windeler, eds. 1994. *Management interorganisationaler Beziehungen: Vertrauen, Kontrolle und Informationstechnik.* Opladen: Westdeutscher Verlag.

Teschner, Eckart. 1977. *Lohnpolitik im Betrieb.* Frankfurt/New York: Campus.

Thelen, Kathleen A. 1991. *Union of Parts. Labor Politics in Postwar Germany.* Ithaca, NY: Cornell University Press.

von Friedeburg, Ludwig. 1963. *Soziologie des Betriebsklimas.* Frankfurt: Europäische Verlagsanstalt.

von Gottl-Ottlilienfeld, Friedrich. 1926. *Fordismus: Über Industrie und technische Vernunft,* 3rd ed. Jena: Fischer

von Gottl-Ottlilienfeld, Friedrich. 1929. *Vom Sinn der Rationalisierung.* Jena: Fischer

Voß, G. Günther, and Hans J. Pongratz. 1998. "Der Arbeitskraftunternehmer: Eine neue Grundform der 'Ware Arbeitskraft'?" *Kölner Zeitschrift für Soziologie und Sozialpsychologie* 50:131–158.

Weber, Max. 1908–1909/1995. *Zur Psychophysik der industriellen Arbeit. Schriften und Reden 1908–1912: Gesamtausgabe,* Vol. 11. Tübingen: Mohr.

Weitbrecht, Hansjörg. 1969. *Effektivität und Legitimität der Tarifautonomie.* Berlin: Duncker & Humblot.

WSI-Projektgruppe. 1998. Ausgewählte Ergebnisse der WSI-Befragung von Betriebs- und Personalräten 1997/98. *WSI-Mitteilungen* 51:653–667.

Womack, James P., Daniel T. Jones, and Daniel Roos. 1990. *The Machine that Changed the World.* New York: Rawson.

APPENDIX: CONTACTS

Major Research Centers Concerned with the Study of Work in Germany

Center for Social Research Dortmund (SFS)
(Sozialforschungsstelle Dortmund)
http://www.sfs-dortmund.de/
Director: Gerd Peter
E-mail: sfs@sfs-dortmund.de

Fraunhofer Institute for Industrial Engineering
(Fraunhofer Institut Arbeitswirtschaft und Organisation)
http://www.iao.fhg.de/activities-en.html
Director: Hans-Jörg Bullinger
E-mail: Hans-Joerg.Bullinger@iao.fhg.de
Phone: (0711) 9702000

Institute for Economic and Social Research in the Hans-Böckler-Foundation (WSI)
(Wirtschafts- und Sozialwissenschaftliches Institut in der Hans-Böckler-Stiftung)
http://www.wsi.de
Director: Heide Pfarr
Managment: Harmut Seifert
Bertha-von-Suttner-Platz 1
D-40227 Düsseldorf
Phone: (0211) 77780
Fax: (0211) 7778225
E-mail: Hartmut-Seifert@boekler.de

Institute for Employment Research (IAB)
(Institut für Arbeitsmarkt und Berufsforschung der Bundesanstalt für Arbeit)
http://www.iab.de
Director: Gerhard Kleinhenz
Regensburger Str. 104
D-90327 Nürnberg
Phone: (0911) 179-3023
Fax: (0911) 179-3258
E-mail: iab.ba@t-online.de

Institute for Social Research (ISF Munich)
(Institut für sozialwissenschaftliche Forschung e.V.)
Jakob-Klar-Straße 9
-80796 München
Phone: (089) 272921-0
Fax: (089) 272921-60
E-mail: isf@lrz.uni-muenchen.de

Institute for Social Research and Social Economy (ISO)
(Institut für Sozialforschung und Sozialwirtschaft e.V.)
Director: Hermann Kotthoff
Trillerweg 68; D-66117 Saarbrücken
Phone: (0681) 954240
Fax: (0681) 9542427
E-mail: iso-institut@hit.handshake.de

Institute for Work and Technology (IAT)
(Institut Arbeit und Technik)
Director: F. Lehner
Munscheidstr. 14; D-45886 Gelsenkirchen
Phone: (0209) 1707-113
Fax: (0209) 1707-110
E-mail: lehner@iatge.de

Max-Planck-Institute for the Study of Societies
(Max-Planck-Institut für Gesellschaftsforschung)
Directors:. Fritz W. Scharpf and Wolfgang Streeck
Lothringer Strasse 78; D-50677 Köln
Phone: (0221) 33605-25
Fax.: (0221) 33605-55
E-mail (Contact Raymund Werle): werle@mpi-fg-koeln.mpg.de

Research Institute for Work, Technology and Culture e.V. (FATK)
(Forschungsinstitut für Arbeit, Technik und Kultur e.V.)
Management: Reinhard Bahnmüller
Haußerstr. 43; D-72076 Tübingen
Phone: (07071) 2974214
Fax: (07071) 27467
E-mail: reinhard.bahnmueller@uni-tuebingen.de

Science Center Berlin for Social Research (WZB)
(Wissenschaftszentrum Berlin für Sozialforschung)
http://www.wz-berlin.de
President: Jürgen Kocka
Reichpietschufer 50
D-10785 Berlin
Phone: (030) 25491-0
Fax: (030) 25491-684
E-mail: wzb@wz-berlin.de

Sociological Research Institute (SOFI)
(Soziologisches Forschungsinstitut e.V.)
Presidents: Horst Kern and Michael Schumann
Directors: Martin Baethge and Volker Wittke
Friedländer Weg 31
D-37085 Göttingen
Phone: (0551) 522050
Fax: (0551) 5220588
E-mail: dgsf@gwdg.de

University of Bochum: Chair of Codetermination and Organisation
(Ruhr-Universität Bochum: Lehrstuhl Mitbestimmung und Organisation)
http://homepage.ruhr-uni-bochum.de/W.Mueller-Jentsch/
Chair: Walther Müller-Jentsch
Fakultät für Sozialwissenschaft
D-44780 Bochum
Phone: (0234) 7005429
Fax: (0234) 7094446
E-mail: w.mueller-jentsch@ruhr-uni-bochum.de

University of Dortmund: Chair of Technology and Society
(Universität Dortmund: Lehrstuhl Technik und Gesellschaft)
Chair: Hartmut Hirsch-Kreinsen
Phone: (0231) 7553718
Fax: (0231) 7553280
E-mail: H.Hirsch-Kreinsen@wiso-uni-dortmund.de

University of Erlangen-Nuremberg: Institute of Sociology
(Universität Erlangen-Nürnberg: Institut für Soziologie)
Chair: Gert Schmidt
Kochstr. 4
D-91054 Erlangen
Phone: (09131) 852 3378
Fax: (09131) 852 3372
E-mail: gschmidt@phil.uni-erlangen.de

University of Jena: Institute for Sociology of Work, Industry and Economy
(Universität Jena: Institut für Arbeits-, Industrie- und Wirtschaftssoziologie)
Chair: Rudi Schmidt
Otto-Schott-Str. 41
D-07740 Jena
Phone: (03641) 945510
Fax: (03641) 9455512
E-mail: Schmidt@soziologie.uni-jena.de

University of Trier: Institute of Labor Law and Industrial Relations
    in the European Community
(Institut für Arbeitsrechts und Arbeitsbeziehungen in der EG)
http://www.iaaeg.uni-trier.de/
Directors: Rolf Birk
Email: birk@iaaeg.uni-trier.de
Dr. Dieter Sadowski
E-mail: sado@iaaeg.uni-trier.de
Schloßstr. 140; D-54293 Trier
Phone: (0651) 9666-129
Fax: (0651) 9666200

12

Great Britain

Paul Edwards and Carol Wolkowitz

INTRODUCTION

The sociology of employment in Great Britain differs from its Continental and North American counterparts in several respects. We have the advantage of being able to draw upon a range of perspectives, including not only the empirical traditions of British sociology but also developments in English-language sociology more generally and, increasingly, research linked to networks established across the European Union. Perhaps partly for these reasons, British sociology of employment has tended not to produce overarching schemes of the kinds associated with the concepts of de-skilling, flexible specialization, *régulation,* or alternatives to lean production. Its main contribution has been to pursue empirical research, often based on case studies, that tests out and frequently challenges such schemes. In doing so, it has been aided by relatively fluid lines between it and students of subjects such as industrial relations. Many sociologists (one of the present authors included) practice their trade in business schools and publish in industrial relations, organization studies, or human resource management journals. This fluidity has cer-

Paul Edwards • Industrial Relations Research Unit, University of Warwick, Coventry CV4 7AL England. Carol Wolkowitz • Department of Sociology, University of Warwick, Coventry CV4 7AL England.

Worlds of Work: Building an International Sociology of Work, edited by Daniel B. Cornfield and Randy Hodson. Kluwer Academic/Plenum Publishers, New York, 2002.

tainly strengthened these fields. A good illustration is Hyman's (1982) celebrated critique of the work of American industrial relations scholar Thomas Kochan for neglecting sociological and historical analyses of the nature of the employment contract and the social organization of conflict and consent. Sociological perspectives have enriched other disciplines, which have in turn fed back into debates in sociology. Other sociologists work within university departments of sociology or interdisciplinary centers; many of them combine a specialist interest in work and employment with research in other substantive areas, such as gender, race relations, or migration. Some researchers have a long tradition of providing further education for trade unionists. Hence, debates on work and employment with a broadly sociological tone are wide spread in the United Kingdom (see further the section on Instititional Context).

In reviewing these debates, we have deliberately taken a selective approach, focusing on paid employment rather than work in all its forms, though one strand of research has analyzed linkages between employment and domestic life, and its contribution will be noted. We also avoid repeating lines of debate already covered in the United States. We identify some key themes and try to draw out the contribution of leading studies (with a bias toward citing materials such as books and other reports that may not be readily found through bibliographical searches). Fuller surveys can be found in the work of Richard Brown (1992, 1997a, 1997b).

KEY THEMES

In the case of Great Britain, many enduring themes can be identified, for example how workers respond to technical change, and concepts developed in the context of industrial administration or industrial psychology (e.g., Baldamus, 1961; Wootton, 1962) are still deployed. But researchers in the sociology of employment would not usually be very concerned to locate their work in relation to such long-standing traditions. Rather, the overwhelming impression is one of change, which has been of three kinds. First, the economic and social context has altered particularly dramatically, with deindustrialization and economic restructuring being sharper than in many countries and heightened by the political revolutions of the Conservative governments of 1979–1997. Second, new substantive research issues have arisen. Third, new analytical perspectives associated with feminism and postmodernism have been introduced, and the connections between sociology and other disciplines have been constructively explored. We thus characterize briefly the perspectives of the 1960s before explaining how these have evolved.

Up to the 1970s, the main "dependent variable" was workers' attitude to work, with two lines of explanation being found in the technical organization of work (as represented by the work of Joan Woodward, and later the Aston School) and "orientations to work" which were forged outside the workplace (notably, the Luton studies, led by Goldthorpe and Lockwood). (For discussion and bibliographic detail, the reader is referred to Brown, 1992). The main arguments of the Luton studies are that workers formed a prototypical new working class shaped by narrow instrumental orientations, and that they were often separated from traditional community sources of solidarity and cohesion. Several conclusions stand out in retrospect. First, many of these researchers were interested in attitudes (perceptions of management, views of the class structure) and not behavior (what workers actually did to control their work effort). Second, in a restudy of Luton, Devine (1992) found that Luton workers were much less individualized than had been claimed and that, in comparing Luton with an idealized picture of working-class communities of the past, the original researchers exaggerated the extent of change in working-class lifestyles. More generally, a large body of research showed orientations to be variable, multifaceted, and shifting. Third, "workers" were mainly male manual employees in factories.

Dissatisfaction with the first two issues emerged in what might be called homegrown studies, most famously Beynon's *Working for Ford* (1973). Though concerned with male auto plant workers, the study departed from the earlier tradition in terms of method (informal observation, lengthy discussions with shop stewards as opposed to structured questionnaires) and focus (workers' day-to-day struggles with managers over discipline and workloads). Such studies were homegrown in that they responded to shop floor militancy and used a broadly Marxist approach derived from long-established European traditions. They were further encouraged by American work on de-skilling and models of labor control. The dominant tendency, however, soon became the critique of such models, and a series of studies claiming to "test" a de-skilling model were undertaken. Armstrong's (1988) conclusions on this endeavor remain pertinent. Many "tests" had an impoverished view of skill (technical knowledge, not control of the work process) and used such short time frames that it was not surprising that they could find little de-skilling.

The third problem, the male-centered model of work, began to come under critical attack beginning in the mid-1970s, initially through a series of ethnographic studies of women workers (often, though, still those employed in semi-skilled factory jobs) that showed how gender divisions are both created and reinforced in the workplace (see discussion in Pollert, 1996; Thompson, 1989). Ethnographies such as these were complemented by the demonstration of systematic differences between men and women in a variety of work situations. These differences were conceptualized through the distinction between vertical and horizontal occupational segregation (i.e., segregation into the lower range of occupations and within specific sectors in the labor market). They were contextualized through sociologically informed economists' assessments of employers' labor market practices, including discrimination and gender pay inequality (Rubery, 1994). Such assessments drew on familiar ideas of segmented labor markets but developed them by stressing the role of trade unions and other actors in enforcing particular lines of division. Sociologists were particularly important in exposing the connections between men's and women's differential occupational opportunities, rather than assuming that men and women were on different trajectories from the outset. For instance, Crompton and Jones's (1984) study of white-collar jobs showed how men's occupational advancement from the clerical ranks often rested on the continued concentration of women in lower-grade jobs. It was also shown that, rather than being an objective category of jobs, the concept of skills was "saturated with sex," used to downgrade women's skills and defend male preserves from the incursion of women (Cockburn, 1991). Partly because of its success in pinpointing gender as a source of power (as against or in the context of capitalist social relations), the concept of patriarchy was a common reference point (Walby, 1990), although its early promise has been eroded, partly because it has provided less purchase on changes in patterns of employment, or on the intersection of gender with class, racial, and ethnic divisions. Pollert (1996) has addressed this point, also arguing that the early ethnographies had a greater theoretical content, particularly regarding the negotiation of gender identities, than has commonly been recognized.

During the 1980s, perhaps the major research was the Social Change and Economic Life Initiative (SCELI) conducted in 1986 (though publications continued to appear up to 8 years later) and based on six local labor markets. A core survey of over 6,000 employees was complemented by specific-issue studies in each labor market. The finding on skills (as measured by such factors as qualifications, training periods, and self-perceptions) was that overall skills levels had risen, but that some relatively small groups, particularly the already low-skilled, were most likely to lose skills, so that there was a clear but limited process of skills polarization (Gallie, 1994; other SCELI volumes include Rubery and Wilkinson, 1994). Such work provided other important results, notably on gender and social class differences in qualifications. But the SCELI results, like others, indicated that skills changes often went along with new demands on workers to work harder; though rejecting a crude work-intensification thesis, the authors acknowledged that work reorganization may have brought costs as well as benefits. Other researchers put more weight on these costs, with increasing working hours and stress becoming common themes of the 1990s.

This last point drove much research in the 1990s. It is increasingly argued that traditional patterns of work are fragmenting, with the growth of temporary and part-time jobs, variable patterns of work in place of the standard 40-hour week, the growth of unemployment, and a division between "work-rich" and "work-poor" households. Research has also continued to go beyond traditional locales to study employees in the service sector, managers, homeworkers, and the small-firm sector. Much research focuses on the question of which (if any) of these developments increased workers' autonomy in the workplace or independence in the labor market. Surveys following the SCELI have presented relatively optimistic views of the pattern of skill (especially Gallie et al., 1998), whereas case studies have tended to stress work intensification and employer control, which is explained in terms of employer assertiveness, the policies of the Conservative Government (1979–1997), and the weakening of trade unions.

The outcome of this widening of interest has naturally been the difficulty of reaching clear-cut, overall conclusions. The difficulty has been heightened by the widespread preference for case studies, which have been conducted in different sites using different methods, with evident problems of generalization. Some writers see such problems as inherent in the case method. However, such a view is too extreme. In some subfields, one can discern the development of a research program that offers generalization of two kinds (see Edwards, 1992). First, there is better understanding of the nature of the phenomenon under study. Second, the conditions leading to certain outcomes are being specified. The literature on small firms illustrates these two points (Scase, 1995). Up to around 1990, debate was dominated by two models: "small is beautiful" and "autocracy and management control." Researchers increasingly found that many small firms fitted neither model, with there instead being a negotiation of order in which principles of conflict and cooperation were intertwined. Thus, the phenomenon of worker behavior was better specified. As for conditions leading to certain outcomes, several distinct types of relationship in small firms, such as fraternalism and negotiated paternalism, were developed and applied to firms with different ownership structures and industrial locations. Though a full-scale framework does not exist (and, arguably, could not exist), general understanding has developed.

Similar results appear in another growth area, the study of "Japanization" and the effects of new work practices such as teamwork and total quality management (TQM). There was never much more than a sceptical reception among researchers to ideas of flexible specialization. The predominant initial tendency was to stress work intensification and tighter managerial control. The tendency may reflect something of the British intellectual tradition, with its empiricism and doubts about Grand Theory (especially that from overseas). But, more importantly, it represented an important aspect of the British political economy. Successive Conservative governments were determined to deregulate labor markets, and their early economic policies produced in the early 1980s one of the sharpest recessions on record. Job losses and retrenchment, rather than up-skilling, were the result in large parts of the economy.

In the context of factory employment, there were two broad interpretations of work reorganization during the 1980s and 1990s, focused on developments such as multiskilling, which were not always properly distinguished. The first was that these were successful means by which managers attacked workers' job controls and intensified their labor. The second, drawing on widespread evidence that multiskilling was in fact little practiced, argued that there were contradictions and uncertainties at the heart of many change programs and that results were at best patchy. In relation to particular firms, notably, Japanese transplants, and to wider initiatives such as TQM, writers began to argue that Japanization and TQM both had contradictory elements (e.g., between the alleged empowerment of workers and the need to tighter performance measurement in the case of TQM) and also that there were contradictions between innovation and other aspects of management practice (notably, that Japanese management systems ran up against the limitations of British management and the peculiarities of the British labor market, while TQM threatened existing hierarchies and was thus likely to be opposed by managers). As more developed contributions on Japanization (Elger and Smith, 1998) and TQM (Wilkinson, Godfrey, and Marchington, 1997) have shown, there is a reorganization of work that embraces elements of intensification and empowerment, workers continue to be able to shape some aspects of their work, and rather than there being one outcome, there is a spread of results reflecting the nature of the product market, the job security available to workers, and workers' own expectations.

Some of this work was connected with studies of trade unions. Not surprisingly, a great deal of work focused on the conditions for and consequences of trade union decline. Yet one strand of work argued that the widespread trend toward the decentralization of industrial relations gave unions opportunities as well as challenges. Fairbrother (1996) in particular argued that this trend in the public sector meant that issues formerly resolved in remote national-level institutions were now returned to the local level; appraising and grading, for example, were matters in which local trade unionists could actively engage. Other writers detected "rigor mortis" rather than "renewal" (see Colling and Ferner, 1995). It may be that these different outcomes reflect different conditions, such as the determination of managements to press through change, and the resilience and organization of unions at the local level, though the relevant causal mechanisms remain to be identified. Other research on unions in the private sector commonly detected either exclusion from managerial debates on restructuring or, at best, marginalization. Some writers began to advocate what was increasingly termed *social partnership*, a concept derived from European terminology and meaning, in the UK, the search for cooperation with management in the implementation of new forms of work organization. Some scholars, notably, John Kelly (1996), continued to insist on the value of retaining a distance from management and pursuing traditional class-struggle objectives. Other trade union themes emerged in comparative work, as discussed later.

A new strand of research looked at the ideological aspects of the control of workers, in addition to the economic and political resources stressed earlier. Drawing in particular on interest in Michel Foucault (and running against the usual hostility to foreign philosophies), writers argued that power was embedded in the day-to-day practices and the very fabric of society. As Warhurst and Thompson (1998:7) remark sardonically, "British universities . . . are producing generations of graduate students who can spot a panopticon, a disciplinary practice or a power/knowledge discourse at fifty paces." An initiative such as TQM might at one level be welcomed by workers, but it was nonetheless drawing them into a managerial way of thinking and establishing an ideological terrain from which there was little escape.

The response to Foucault often was either fevered excitement or hostility. One benefit of this interest was the reminder that power often lies in the interstices of organizational practice (see McKinlay and Starkey, 1997). We say "reminder" because any sensible reading of a large body of workplace studies (of which Armstrong, Goodman, and Hyman, 1981, is particularly pertinent, not least because it is unduly neglected) would be well aware of the point. Among the key problems with the interest in Foucault was a focus on the micropolitics of meaning, sometimes juxtaposed with sweeping references to the "disciplinary society." Orthodox accounts of cause and effect, and of the different ways in which workers behave lost out to accounts of surveillance that shifted alarmingly from the general to the particular. (The irony of the parallel with the Luton studies, which had also shifted from a single locale to arguments about prototypicality, is striking.)

Other sociologists have picked up on poststructuralist currents in other ways. For instance, students of women's employment had long been aware that power in the workplace is not necessarily a zero-sum game, but this perspective is increasingly evident, for example, in studies of sexuality in the workplace. While the earlier focus on sexual harassment has not been rejected (Brant and Too, 1994), it has been supplemented by arguments about women's involvement in the deployment of workplace sexuality and the construction of the workplace as a site of pleasure (Gherardi, 1995; McDowell, 1997).

This research coincides with several other changes in research on gender and employment, in which the earlier focus on workplace gender structures has been amplified by an even more explicit interest in gendered identities and gender symbolism. This three-sided definition of gender, taken by Cynthia

Cockburn (1993) from the writing of the American feminist philosopher Sandra Harding, has been particularly useful in highlighting the cultural processes through which apparently gender-neutral technical processes are constructed through the social relations of gender and appropriated for masculinity (see also Wajcman, 1991). With the expanding influence of the poststructuralist emphasis on meaning and culture, the concept of identity has been brought still further to the fore in some of the recent studies of gender and management (discussed later).

Another aspect of research in the 1990s is the rejection of analyses of either women or men as homogeneous categories. For instance, Walby's (1997) work identifies a degree of convergence in the opportunities for younger women and men, along with growing polarization between women of different generations. She argues that while some younger, better educated women are now using the "qualifications lever" (Crompton and Sanderson, 1990) to establish careers in management and the professions, women whose work trajectories are limited by domestic obligations remain locked into segregated, often part-time employment. The political implications of different explanations of disparities among women are one reason for the acrimonious debate over essays by Catherine Hakim, who has argued that lingering gender inequalities in employment reflect mainly the low commitment to work of some women rather than evidence of continuing discrimination or constraint (Ginn et al., 1996; Hakim, 1996). Inequalities among women are also central to the literature on race and ethnicity in employment, which provides, for both men and women, evidence of differences in opportunities within, as well as between, ethnically and racially defined categories, as well as the centrality of ethnic businesses and other workplaces to work experience (Brah and Shaw, 1992; Westwood and Bhachu, 1988).

Fracturing analytical categories is also seen in studies of male employment. Once the presumption of men as the universal category was overtly challenged, it was recognized that some of the earlier workplace studies—such as Benyon's *Working for Ford* (1973), mentioned earlier—could be reread for insight into the ways in which masculine bonding is used as a resource to achieve social closure against women, or to sustain solidarity against management (Morgan, 1992). However, recent research, which stresses the production of a plurality of hierarchically ordered work-based masculinities (Collinson and Hearn, 1996), is problematic for those who remain convinced that most men benefit at least indirectly from the privileging of male culture.

Finally, research on gender in employment continues to give attention to the family–work interface (e.g., Brannen, Moss, Poland, and Mesaros, 1994). Here women's continuing, time-consuming physical and emotional responsibility for children and other dependents is well-documented, as is men's relative freedom in this respect. However, the earlier British contribution to debates about women's unpaid labor in the home (recently updated by Gardiner, 1997) has been partly supplanted by research on caring that highlights the work of paid carergivers outside as well as within the home (Gregson and Lowe, 1994), surveys of various forms of men's and women's home-located paid employment (Phizacklea and Wolkowitz, 1995), and studies of occupations that seem to depend on the exploitation of women's and men's conjugal ties (Adkins, 1995). All of these reject treating home and work as dichotomous categories or entirely separate domains.

The development of research into new areas in tandem with the development of new themes is especially well illustrated by the study of managers. There were scattered studies from as early as the 1930s, but managers had not become a central focus. The SCELI studies, for example, contained no projects dedicated to managers. But by 1990, managerial labor had become more interesting in light of the downsizing and delayering that were common on both sides of the Atlantic. (To the extent that these processes were particularly marked in Anglo–Saxon countries, the study of managers is more likely to be advanced here than in other countries.) Studies began to explore the effects of these changes on managers' views of not only their jobs but also their perceptions of society as a whole. Some were interview-based (e.g., Scase and Goffee, 1989), while others deployed ethnographic methods to explore the day-to-day realities of work (notably, Watson, 1994). Key conclusions were that managers shared many of the uncertainties experienced by other workers. They naturally felt discontented about reduced job security but often accepted the need to work long hours. They felt distanced from top management and expressed scepticism about new changes in management techniques but still saw themselves as managers and separate from the workers they controlled.

Interest in gender issues also found expression in studies of managers. Research in Great Britain, as elsewhere, draws attention to the "glass ceiling" and to the familiar dual burden. There has nonetheless been a notable advance of women in some managerial and (particularly) professional occupations. Yet barriers remain, particularly at the very top levels of management. Wajcman's (1998) study importantly compared men and women within the same middle- to senior-management grades and showed that there were no differences in commitment to work, and also that involvement in housework did not explain women's lack of progression. Instead, cultural assumptions within management were crucial to the existence of a glass ceiling. Other studies have shown that women managers in different sectors negotiate a different balance between family and career commitments, with women in credentialized professions, such as doctors, more likely to have children, to have more children, and to integrate family and work goals than, say, women in banking (Crompton and Harris, 1998; Halford, Savage, and Witz, 1997).

Interest in gender, subjectivity, and identity is also playing an important role in studies of male managerial and professional work cultures (Cockburn 1991; Collinson and Hearn, 1996; Roper, 1994).

Key themes have emerged from such work. First, gender is a resource, since male managers use "homosociability" to reinforce a sense of group identity. Second, the emphasis on emotion work and the insecurities of managers undermines images of the firm as rationally organized and strategically directed. Management is about the construction of meaning in an uncertain and fragile world.

Though many of these themes parallel work in North America, some theoretical work is distinctive. Goldthorpe (1995) has developed his model of classes to place increasing stress on the distinction between the service class, which embraces managers and professionals, and other occupations. For Goldthorpe, the distinctive features of the service class are a relatively long-term and diffuse relationship with the employer and the exercise of delegated authority or specialized knowledge and expertise. The importance of this view is that it provides a framework for understanding service class work, for, rather than take a category for granted, it focuses on underlying relationships of trust. The limitation is that it is not very clear who is being served: The relationship between the service class and the owners of capital is not discussed. Other work (notably, Armstrong, 1989) has explored the nature of the trust relationship and the contradictions that it can entail: Trusting a subordinate can reduce the capitalist's control, and performance monitoring and direct surveillance are likely to exist in an uneasy balance with trust. Relatedly, the service class concept is rather static and does not directly provide purchase on trends toward the restructuring of hierarchy and careers. It needs to be complemented with approaches stressing the contradictions and tensions of capitalism, and the creation and decay of particular occupational categories (Hanlon, 1998). The experience of British managers—their increasing vulnerability to downsizing and to pressures for increased work hours, combined with greater performance monitoring through appraisal and performance-related pay—sharply illustrates the shifting balance of trust and monitoring as economic and social conditions change.

As some researchers have shifted their focus from the factory to the expanding service sector, so others have redeployed British expertise in studying shop-floor relations in the development of comparative research programs. For instance, the research on workplace industrial relations in Russia undertaken by Simon Clarke and his Russian and British colleagues (e.g., Clarke 1995, 1996) is based largely on longitudinal case studies, which have introduced ethnographic methods to Russian industrial relations research, but, as in much sociology of employment within Britain, set within an analysis of wider class relations. But the growing number of comparative studies covering employment in Western Europe has been fostered mainly by the post-Maastricht completion of the single European market in 1992 (e.g., Cockburn and Fürst-Dilic, 1994; Hyman and Ferner, 1994; Rubery and Fagan 1995; Rubery et al., 1998). A developing research method has been to conduct case studies within a given sector or occupation in different countries, for example, O'Reilly's work on part-timers in Britain and France (1992), and the four-nation study of doctors and bank workers by Crompton and Harris (1998). Such work has allowed distinctive features of a national social system to be addressed. Hantrais and Mangen (1996) have provided an overview of the key issues in the methodology of cross-national research, including problems of differing national perspectives and even definitions of terms.

More recently, debates on globalization have shaped research. The work inthe 1980s on Japanization was extended, with attention to lean production and the role of multinational companies (MNCs). It was commonly remarked that Great Britain is a distinctively open economy, as reflected in inward investment and the extent to which British-based MNCs have operations across the globe. Research began to explore the relationship between global forces and national systems of regulation, including the effects of European integration on MNCs' operations (Ferner, 1997). Research also addressed the extent to which distinctively British systems of trade union organization, based on the workplace, and lacking legal or other institutional support, obstructed effective intervention in new forms of work organization and thus contrasted with the position of the rest of Europe (Ortiz, 1998).

Finally we can mention research that, while recognizably dealing with issues of work and livelihood, is not always accepted as existing within the sociology of employment. While the emotional labor involved in the management of the service encounter is usually recognized as part of the labor process in service sector employment, other types of work remain at the fringes of sociology of employment as this is usually understood, for instance, studies of care work (Lee-Treweek, 1997), child labor (Lavalette, 1994), and sex work and prostitution (O'Connell Davidson, 1995). There are also many studies of the work experience of particular categories, such as lone mothers or older people (Duncan and Edwards, 1997), that have a different agenda than most workplace-based research.

It will be clear from the previous discussion that a range of methods has been deployed. One notable trend has been the growth of quantitative studies, some using newly generated data sets (e.g., SCELI and its successor, the Employment in Britain Survey; see Gallie et al., 1998), and some relying on existing data sets (e.g., the National Child Development Study, which is a longitudinal study of all children born in a single week in 1958, who have been tracked throughout their lives). Particular note should be taken of the Samples of Anonymized Records from the 1991 census; these samples provide very large numbers that can be used, as Hakim (1995) shows, to address a range of issues on employment and labor market experience. There are also links with the well-known debates on class analysis, in which the links between class position and employment status have been a central issue and in which quantitative analysis has played a key role (see Rose and O'Reilly, 1997).

Case study and ethnographic work has also progressed. There has been a particular concern to understand people's subjective experience of work and to relate this to managerial policies and to the economic and social context. The contrast with the rather flat sociologies of occupations of the 1960s and 1970s is striking. As several of these studies demonstrate, there has also been an effort to move into international comparative work, either on the basis of case study comparisons of workplaces or through the use of case study and survey techniques to examine specific occupations or forms of labor.

INSTITUTIONAL CONTEXT

The main funder of sociological research is the publicly funded Economic and Social Research Council (ESRC), which covers research projects and postgraduate student awards at masters' and doctoral levels in all the social sciences. About two-thirds of the ESRC's £65 million budget is spent on research. Research projects are organized in three ways: in long-term research centers; within initiatives on specific themes; and under the "response mode" wherein researchers propose their own topics of inquiry. Research centers covering employment include the Centre for Economic Performance at the London School of Economics (primarily with an economics focus) and the multidisciplinary Center for Skills, Knowledge and Organizational Performance, at Oxford and Warwick universities. A major initiative in the employment field is the Future of Work Program, which has a budget of £4 million over a 5-year period. In July 1998, the first 19 projects were funded under the program, with most of the social science disciplines being represented. The ESRC website (www.esrc.ac.uk) contains both valuable details on current programs and useful links to government departments and other funders of social science.

Research is also funded by government departments and by charities. Much government-sponsored research was initially under the wing of the Department of Employment and published in its research series; the two successor departments, Education and Employment, and Trade and Industry, now have their own research series. As for charities, some of the work on Japanization discussed earlier was funded by the Leverhulme Trust, which functions similarly to the ESRC response mode and initiatives. The Nuffield Foundation and the Joseph Rowntree Trust also fund some work in this area.

Researchers have increasingly sought funds under a wide variety of projects sponsored either by the European Union (EU) or its specialist agencies. In 1999, the EU's Fifth Framework Program was launched, with a dedicated social science budget of about £100 million over 4 years. Several ESRC programs, such as the East–West Initiative, also have international issues at their core. The ability to build networks with colleagues in Europe is an increasingly important attribute.

Great Britain is well-served with organizations operating between pure academic research and the business world. The leading example, the Institute of Employment Studies (IES), located at Sussex University, conducts regular studies of the labor market and of particular occupations around themes such as career development, and recruitment and selection. The IES is funded largely through subscriptions and its own research income. Other bodies include the Policy Studies Institute, still celebrated for its innovative studies of race discrimination in the 1960s, the Institute for Public Policy Research; and the Employment Policy Institute. Other public bodies, such as the Equal Opportunities Commission, have relatively small research budgets and fund research and organize seminars.

The late 1980s and 1990s saw an upsurge in new journals publishing work on the sociology of employment. The main new journals with dates of first publication include: *Gender, Work and Organisations* (1994), *Human Resource Management Journal* (1991), *International Journal of Human Resource Management* (1990), *Organization* (1994), and *Work, Employment and Society* (1987). As their titles imply, two of these journals focus on human resource management (HRM), though each publishes a fair number of articles with a sociological perspective. The other three journals adopt a broadly sociological view, though *Organization* has a particular concern with organization theory and thus goes outside the field of work and employment. All these journals have a catholic approach to methods, though the two HRM journals avoid heavily quantitative papers, while *Organization* tends to favor theoretical and case study work. A study of the mainstream U.K. sociology journals finds that *Work, Employment and Society* has the greatest proportion of quantitative articles (Bechhofer, 1996), but it is probably the case that most U.K. sociology journals are less quantitative than their U.S. counterparts, and there is a very strong expectation that articles be comprehensible to readers without quantitative expertise and address issues of genuine sociological import.

A major forum for debate has been the annual International Conference on the Organization and Control of the Labour Process, which began at Manchester University in 1983, and alternated between that university and Aston University in Birmingham, before embracing some other locations. Numerous edited books based on the conferences have appeared, of which some of the more notable are based on *Making Quality Critical* (Wilkinson and

Willmott, 1995), new work organization and trade unions (Ackers, Smith, and Smith, 1996) and new forms of workplace organization (Thompson and Warhurst, 1998). Other forums include the annual conference of the British Sociological Association, which nearly always includes a stream on work and employment, conferences sponsored by journals, including *Work, Employment and Society* (every 3 years) and *Gender, Work and Organization*, and those organized by various university business schools from time to time.

A potentially important source is the series of Workplace Industrial Relations Surveys, which began in 1980 and provides a representative sample of around 2,000 British workplaces. These surveys have been used mainly by economists and industrial relations scholars to assess issues such as the union–nonunion pay gap. But the 1998 surveys (now called "employee" rather than "industrial" relations) included surveys of employees, as well as the managers and employee representatives of earlier surveys (Cully et al., 1998; see the website, www.dti.gov.uk/er/emar, for more details). Sociologists might well use these surveys to assess the effects of change on employees.

CONCLUSIONS

British studies of work continue to provide a vigorous and informative analysis of workplace transformation. They are particularly strong on detailed case study inquiry, which embraces a welcome revival of ethnographic methods. They are also helped by the input from industrial relations and (some small parts of) economics, leading to an effective portrait of workplace change and its consequences. They can also draw upon the insights into continuities and changes in the occupational structure highlighted by those who focus on class relations. Finally, and more controversially, researchers are responding to recent challenges to the centrality of work as a sociological category in a number of ways—by ignoring them, by continuing to argue for the centrality of work to personal identity, or by incorporating some of the new interests in, for instance, consumption or embodiment, into their own work.

If there is one theme running through this research, it is that of complexity and variation. Assessments of the changing pattern of employment now routinely place themselves between the extremes of optimism and pessimism. Some analyses are beginning to explore the conditions producing specific outcomes, including the circumstances of particular companies, and the wider social and political context of Great Britain. On the first of these, it is argued that many companies lack the resources and managerial commitment for "empowerment" to be the outcome for any substantial numbers of employees. On the second, the British context of short-term, market-driven capitalism is widely seen as further undermining long-term up-skilling.

The key challenge is to explain the diverse trends that are taking place. The Foucauldian tradition tended to identify one path toward increased surveillance and one mechanism (managerial control of knowledge). Yet there has been a growing diversity of experience (Gallie et al., 1998). At one extreme are workers in relatively sophisticated firms, who have accepted new management techniques. It is wrong to suppose that these techniques simply entail costs for workers. A growing view of these firms suggests that workers may well welcome changes that increase both job security and immediate involvement in work, even at the cost of closer monitoring and the need to work harder (Rosenthal, Hill, and Peccei, 1997). At the other extreme are persons with no jobs at all (the growth of the totally workless household was a significant feature of the 1980s and 1990s), those with a succession of insecure employment, and homeworkers. For such groups, work is managed through traditional managerial disciplines. Yet even these groups are not homogeneous, for people working at or from home include well-paid professionals as well as low-paid sweated labor. Analysis of these groups has certainly explained a great deal. For example, there are good explanations of changing patterns of security and insecurity in the labor market and of why the labor process continues to reflect discipline and control as much as "empowerment." Yet the complexity and diversity of experience has militiated against explanations in terms of simple models or patterns. The challenge is to develop theoretical accounts that respect diversity and yet offer analytical purchase and generalizable conclusions.

REFERENCES

Ackers, Peter, Chris Smith, and Paul Smith, eds. 1996. *The New Workplace and Trade Unionism*. London: Routledge.

Adkins, Lisa.1995. *Gendered Work*. Buckingham: Open University Press.

Armstrong, Peter. 1988. "Labour and Monopoly Capital" in *New Technology and Industrial Relations*, edited by Richard Hyman and Wolfgang Streeck. Oxford: Blackwell.

Armstrong, Peter. 1989. "Management, Labour Process and Agency." *Work, Employment and Society* 3:307–322.

Armstrong, Peter, J. F. B. Goodman, and J. D. Hyman, 1981. *Ideology and Shopfloor Industrial Relations*. London: Croom Helm.

Baldamus, W. 1961. *Efficiency and Effort: An Analysis of Industrial Administration*. London: Tavistock.

Bechhofer, Frank. 1996. "Quantitative Research in British Sociology: Substantive Dogs and Methodological Tails Revisited." *Sociology* 30:583–592.

Beynon, Huw. 1973. *Working for Ford*. Hammondsworth: Penguin.

Brah, Avatar, and Sabia Shah, S. 1994. *Working Choices: South Asian Young Muslim Women and the Labour Market*. London: Department of Employment.

Brannen, Julia, P. Moss, G. Poland, and G. Mesaros. 1994. *Employment and Family Life: A Review of Research in the UK, 1980–1994*. Research Series No. 41. London: Department of Employment.

Brant, C., and Y. Too, eds. 1994. *Rethinking Sexual Harassment*. London: Pluto.

Brown, Richard K. 1992. *Understanding Industrial Organisations*. London: Routledge.

Brown, Richard K. 1997a. "Work, Employment and Society: Los diez primeros años." *Sociologia del Trabajo* 31:57–84.

Brown, Richard K., ed. 1997b. *The Changing Shape of Work*. Basingstoke: Macmillan.

Clarke, Simon, ed. 1995. *Management and Industry in Russia.*. Aldershot: Edward Elgar.

Clarke, Simon, ed. 1996. *The Russian Enterprise in Transition*. Aldershot: Edward Elgar.

Cockburn, Cynthia.1991. *In the Way of Women*. Basingstoke: Macmillan.

Cockburn, Cynthia.1993. *Brothers*. London: Pluto.

Cockburn, Cynthia, and Ruth Fürst-Dilic, eds. 1994. *Bringing Technology Home: Gender and Technology in a Changing Europe*. Buckingham: Open University Press.

Colling, Trevor, and Anthony Ferner. 1995. "Privatization and Marketization." In *Industrial Relations* edited by Paul Edwards. Oxford: Blackwell.

Collinson, David, and Jeff Hearn, eds. 1996. *Men as Managers, Managers as Men*. London: Sage.

Crompton, Rosemary, and Fiona Harris.1998. "Gender Relations and Employment: The Impact of Occupation." *Work, Employment and Society* 12:297–315.

Crompton, Rosemary, and Gareth Jones.1984. *White-Collar Proletariat*. London: Macmillan.

Crompton, Rosemary, and Kay Sanderson. 1990. *Gendered Jobs and Social Change*. London: Unwin Hyman.

Cully, Mark, Andrew O'Reilly, Neil Millward, John Forth, Stephen Woodland, Gill Dix, and Alex Bryson. 1998. *The 1998 Workplace Employee Relations Survey: First Findings*. London: Department of Trade and Industry.

Devine, Fiona.1992. *Affluent Workers Revisited*. Edinburgh: Edinburgh University Press.

Duncan, Simon, and Rosalind Edwards, eds. 1997. *Single Mothers in an International Context*. London: UCL Press.

Edwards, P. K. 1992. "La recherche comparative: L'apport de la tradition ethnographique." *Relations industrielles* 47:411–438.

Elger, Tony, and Chris Smith. 1998. "Exit, Voice and 'Mandate'." *British Journal of Industrial Relations* 36:185–208.

Fairbrother, Peter. 1996. "Workplace Trade Unionism in the State Sector." In *The Workplace and Trade Unionism*, edited by P. Ackers, C. Smith, and P. Smith. London: Routledge.

Ferner, Anthony. 1997. "Country of Origin Effects and HRM in Multinational Companies." *Human Resource Management Journal* 7:19–37.

Gallie, Duncan. 1994. "Patterns of Skill Change." In *Skill and Occupational Change*, edited by Roger Penn, Michael Rose, and Jill Ruberg. Oxford, UK: Oxford University Press.

Gallie, Duncan, Michael White, Yuen Cheng, and Mark Tomlinson. 1998. *Restructuring the Employment Relationship*. Oxford, UK: Clarendon.

Gardiner, Jean. 1997. *Gender, Care and Economics*. Basingstoke: Macmillan.

Gherardi, Silvia. 1995. *Gender, Symbolism and Organizational Cultures*. London: Sage.

Ginn, Jay, et al. 1996. "Feminist Fallacies: A Reply to Hakim on Women's Employment." *British Journal of Sociology* 47:167–174.

Goldthorpe, John H. 1995. "The Service Class Revisited." In *Social Change and the Middle Classes,* edited by Tim Butler and Mike Savage. London: UCL Press.

Gregson, Nicki, and Michelle Lowe. 1994. *Servicing the Middle Class.* London: Routledge.

Hakim, Catherine. 1995. "1991 Census SARs." *Work, Employment and Society* 9:569–582.

Hakim, Catherine. 1996. *Key Issues in Women's Work.* London: Athlone.

Halford, Susan, Mike Savage, and Anne Witz. 1997. *Gender, Careers and Organisations.* Basingstoke: Macmillan.

Hanlon, Gerard. 1998. "Professionalism as Enterprise." *Sociology* 32:43–64.

Hantrais, Linda, and Steen Mangen, eds. 1996. *Cross-National Research Methods In The Social Sciences.* London: Pinter.

Hyman, Richard. 1982. Contribution to Symposium. *Industrial Relations* 21:73–122.

Hyman, Richard and Anthony Ferner, eds. 1994. *New Frontiers in European Industrial Relations.* Oxford: Blackwell.

Kelly, John. 1996. "Union Militancy and Social Partnership." In *The Workplace and Trade Unionism,* edited by P. Ackers, C. Smith, and P. Smith. London: Routledge.

Lavalette, Michael. 1994. *Child Labour in the Capitalist Market.* Aldershot: Avebury.

Lee-Treweek, Geraldine. 1997. "Women, Resistance and Care: An Ethnographic Study Of Nursing Work." *Work, Employment and Society* 11:47–64.

McDowell, Linda. 1997. *Capital Culture.* Oxford, UK: Blackwell.

McKinlay, Alan and Ken Starkey. 1997. *Foucault, Management and Organisation.* London: Sage.

Morgan, David. 1992. *Discovering Men.* London: Routledge.

O'Connell Davidson, Julia. 1995. "The Anatomy of Free Choice Prostitution." *Gender, Work and Organization* 2:1–10.

O'Reilly, Jacqueline. 1992. "Where Do You Draw the Line? Functional Flexibility, Training and Skill in Britain and France." *Work, Employment and Society* 6:369-96.

Ortiz, Luis. 1998. "Union Response to Teamwork: The Case of Opel Spain." *Industrial Relations Journal* 29:42–57.

Phizacklea, Annie, and Carol Wolkowitz. 1995. *Homeworking Women: Gender, Class and Racism at Work.* London: Sage.

Pollert, Anna. 1996. "Gender and Class Revisited." *Sociology* 30:639–659.

Roper, Michael. 1994. *Masculinity and the British Organization Man since 1945.* Oxford: Oxford University Press.

Rose, David, and Karen O'Reilly. 1997. *Constructing Classes.* Swindon: ESRC/ONS.

Rosenthal, Patrice, Stephen Hill, and Riccardo Peccei. 1997. "Checking Out Service: Evaluating Excellence, HRM and TQM in Retailing." *Work, Employment and Society* 11:481–503.

Rubery, Jill. 1994. "Internal and External Labour Markets." In *Employer Strategy and the Labour Market,* edited by J. Rubery and F. Wilkinson. Oxford, UK: Oxford University Press.

Rubery, Jill and Collette Fagan. 1995. "Gender Segregation in Societal Context." *Work, Employment and Society* 9:213–240.

Rubery, Jill, Mark Smith, Colette Fagan, and Damian Grimshaw. 1998. *Women and European Employment*. London: Routledge.

Rubery, Jill, and Frank Wilkinson, eds. 1994. *Employer Strategy and the Labour Market.* Oxford, UK: Oxford University Press.

Scase, Richard. 1995. "Employment Relations in Small Firms" in *Industrial Relations in Britain,* edited by Paul Edwards. Oxford, UK: Blackwell.

Scase, Richard and Robert Goffee. 1989. *Reluctant Managers.* London: Unwin Hyman.

Thompson, Paul.1989. *The Nature of Work,* 2nd ed. Basingstoke: Macmillan.

Thompson, Paul, and Chris Warhurst, eds. 1998. *Workplaces of the Future.* Basingstoke, UK: Macmillan.

Wajcman, Judy. 1991. *Feminism Confronts Technology.* Cambridge, UK: Polity.

Wajcman, Judy. 1998. *Managing Like a Man.* Cambridge, UK: Polity.

Walby, Sylvia. 1990. *Theorizing Patriarchy.* Oxford, UK: Blackwell.

Walby, Sylvia.1997. *Gender Transformations.* London: Routledge.

Warhurst, Chris, and Paul Thompson. 1998. "Hands, Hearts and Minds." In *Workplaces of the Future,* edited by P. Thompson and C. Warhurst. Basingstoke, UK: Macmillan.

Watson, Tony. 1994. *In Search of Management.* London: Routledge.

Westwood, Sallie, and Parminder Bhachu, eds. 1988. *Enterprising Women.* London: Routledge.

Wilkinson, Adrian, and Hugh Willmott, eds. 1995. *Making Quality Critical.* London: Routledge.

Wilkinson, Adrian, Graham Godfrey, and Mick Marchington. 1997. "Bouquets, Brickbats and Blinkers: Total Quality Management and Employee Involvement in Practice." *Organization Studies* 18:799–820.

Wootton, Barbara.1962. *The Social Foundations of Wage Policy,* 2nd ed. London: Unwin University Books.

APPENDIX: CONTACTS

Research Centers in Work and Employment

Aston University, Business School
Aston Triangle
Birmingham B4 7ET
Contacts: Fred Steward and Michael West

Bath University, School of Social Sciences
Claverton Down
Bath BA2 7AY
Contacts: Peter Cressey and Michael Rose

*Contact in a related department, which is named if known)
Note. Most of these institutions have websites that can be accessed via www.[name].ac.uk, where [name] is the name of the university, e.g. www.Warwick.ac.uk.

Bristol University, Department of Sociology
12 Woodland Road
Bristol BS8 1UQ
Contact: Harriet Bradley

Cambridge University
Sociological Research Group,
Free School Lane,
Cambridge CB2 3RQ
Contacts: Bob Blackburn and Christel Lane

Cardiff University
School of SocialSciences
50 Park Place
Cardiff CF10 3AT
& 21 Senghennydd Road
Cardiff CF24 4AG
Contacts: Huw Beynon, Rick Delbridge * (Business School), Peter Fairbrother, Ralph
    Fevre, Tony Lane *(Seafarers International Research Centre), Theo Nichols *

City University, Department of Sociology
Northampton Square
London EC1V 0HB
Contacts: Cynthia Cockburn, Rosemary Crompton, Angela Coyle, Carolyn Vogler

Edinburgh University, Deptment of Sociology,
18 Buccleuch Place
Edinburgh EH8 9LN
Contacts: John MacInnes and Janette Webb

Essex University, Department of Sociology
Wivenhoe Park
Colchester CO4 3 SQ
Contacts: Miriam Glucksmann, Lydia Morris, and David Rose

Institute of Education
Thomas Coram Research Unit
27/28 Woburn Square
London WC1H 0AA
Contacts: Julia Brannen and Peter Moss

Leicester University
Centre for Labour Market Studies
7-9 Salisbury Road
Leicester LE1 7QR
Contact: Alan Felstead

Leeds University
ESRC Future of Work Programme
11-15 Blenheim Terrace
Leeds LS2 9JT
Contact: Peter Nolan

London School of Economics, Department of Sociology
Houghton Street
London WC2A 2AE
Contacts: Catherine Hakim, Stephen Hill, Richard Hyman, John Kelly * (Industrial
    Relations), and Patrick McGovern

Manchester School of Management
UMIST
P.O. Box 88
Manchester M60 1 QD
Contacts: John Hassard, Mick Marchington, Jill Rubery, and Hugh Willmott

Manchester University, Department of Sociology
Manchester M13 9PL
Contacts: Angela Dale * (Centre for Census and Survey Research), Fiona Devine,
    Colette Fagan, Jamie Peck *(Geography), and Karel Williams * (Accounting)

Skills, Knowledge and Organizational Performance Centre
Institute of Economics and Statistics
St. Cross Building
Manor Road
Oxford OX1 3UL
Contacts: Ken Mayhew (Oxford), Ewart Keep (SKOPE, WBS, Warwick University,
    Coventry CV4 7AL)

Strathclyde University, Department of Human Resource Management
Graham Hills Building
50 Richmond Street
Glasgow G1 1XT
Contacts: Paul Thompson and Anne Witz

Nuffield College
Oxford OX1 1NF
Contact: Duncan Gallie

Swansea University, Department of Sociology and Anthropology
Singleton Park
Swansea, West Glam SA2 8PP
Contact: Nicky Charles

Warwick University
(a) Centre for Comparative Labour Studies, Department of Sociology
(b) Industrial Relations Research Unit
Coventry CV4 7AL
Contacts: (a) Simon Clarke, (b) David Collinson, (b) Paul Edwards, (a)Tony Elger,
    (a)Annie Phizacklea, and (a) Carol Wolkowitz

University of West of England
Faculty of Economics and Social Science
Coldharbour Lane,
West of England
Frenchay, Bristol BS16 1QU
Contacts: Andy Danford, Kate Purcell, and Paul Stewart

13

Hungary

György Lengyel and László Neumann

INTRODUCTION

In our study, we have set a double goal. On the one hand, we wish to present the findings of sociological research on work by both Hungarian scholars and some foreigners conducting research in Hungary; on the other hand, we wish to refer to the economic and social conditions upon which these works reflect.

First, we outline the tradition of work sociology and fact-finding, descriptive sociography, which responded first of all to the state and stratification of the peasantry, and to the differentiation of peasant roles.

Next, we embark on the main institutional and structural conditions of the state socialist transformation, and on the changing role of sociology under these changed circumstances. We touch on collectivization, the second economy, and the segmentation of the labor market and the informal wage bargain. We present case-study investigations whose major aim was to find out how enterprises actually function in reality.

György Lengyel • Department of Sociology, Budapest University of Economic Sciences and Public Administration, 1093 Budapest, Hungary.   **László Neumann** • Research Fellow, National Labor and Research Centre, Budapest, Hungary.

Worlds of Work: Building an International Sociology of Work, edited by Daniel B. Cornfield and Randy Hodson. Kluwer Academic/Plenum Publishers, New York, 2002.

Analyzing the work-related sociological aspects of the major social transformation of the 1990s, we survey the impacts of the spread of private property, the dominance of the service sector and unemployment. Reference is made to the emergence of the entrepreneurial class, the dualization of the labor market, fears about unemployment, and the decline of internal labor markets.

Information concerning the workshops of work-related sociology is presented in the Appendix.

EARLY INDUSTRIALIZATION, FORERUNNERS' WORK

The prehistory of research into work in Hungary belongs to social criticism and sociography. On the whole, it has one general feature: It is primarily problem-oriented, not paradigm-oriented. On the one hand, its conceptual frames are less subtly elaborated, but on the other, it has a deep insight into reality and is responsive to social problems. Accordingly, the studies written around the turn of the 20th century have two features in common: a drive to improve society and a descriptive character. Outstanding among the early works are Manó Somogyi's studies (1900), Lajos Leopold's critical work ([1917] 1988), and the account of the lord lieutenant of Csongrád county, Andor Vadnay, about the "laborer question" in the Great Plain (1900). Good overviews of such exploratory efforts on this subject can be found in "the first Hungarian workshop of sociology" and "Hungarian sociographies of workers" (Litván, 1974; Litván and Szücs, 1973).

These studies at the turn of the 20th century, which mainly aroused leftist and liberal thinkers, found their continuation in sociographic writings about the peasantry in the 1920s and 1930s. Public discourse was much influenced by the social polemics of these "populist" writers and sociographers.

The political climate of the conservative right-wing regime after the loss of World War I, the unsuccessful bourgeois democratic and socialist revolutions of 1918–1919, and the ensuing immense loss of territory and population was not in favor of such worker-related themes. Although the Socialist Democratic Party was a legal parliamentary party, and the manufacturing trade unions were not banned, their influence was marginal in the entire period. While industry's contribution to the national income was gradually increasing and that of agriculture dropped from two-thirds in 1900 to one-fourth in 1941, the rate of the population employed in agriculture remained above 50%. Thus, the peasantry remained a massive social formation implying grave problems. One of the major topics of the public discourse was the living conditions of various layers of the rural society. The poorest stratum of the peasantry was envisioned as an underclass with the heaviest social burdens.

Typical figures among the "populist" writers and sociographers in the interwar period were first-generation intellectuals who came from peasant families. Hence, their natural milieu, self-interpretation, and problem-orientation were all focused around various groups of the peasantry. The work of highest literary merit in this group is Gyula Illyés's *People of the Puszta*, an accurate and at times highly upsetting account of the living conditions, inner relations, and motives of manorial laborers living in the venue of his childhood, a large estate ([1936] 1979).

At the other end of the spectrum is Ferenc Erdei's several works including *Drifting Sand* (1937) and *Hungarian Peasant Society* (1942). Erdei's sociographies are characterized by scientific precision and the sensitive analysis of a sharp-eyed observer. He describes various forms of landless rural society, from servants to day-wagers and agricultural laborers, to skilled workers in agriculture. What differentiated them from the landed peasant was not only the lack of land ownership but also a significant feature of their way of living and attitude: they were employees whereas the farmers were "their own masters," who had to make decisions concerning their economic activity and control the work of others. The ambivalence of the situation of an agricultural laborer, Erdei claims, derived from the fact that his employer, the landed peasant, expected him to behave in accordance with the peasant work ethic (i.e., all-round subordination to work) but at the same time, the agricultural laborer felt exonerated from the obligations of care traditionally devolved upon him.

In *The Situation in Tard* (1937), a description of a village in Northern Hungary, Zoltán Szabó grasped the tension fed by the feeling: "It's not worth being a peasant; you have no chance of rising." In his next writing, *Spiffy Misery* (1938), he also provided insight into transitory situations, the lives of North Hungarian miners and metalworkers, which constituted two separate groups of the labor force that had been transferred to colonies, workers hostels or barracks, and who commuted from nearby villages for temporary and permanent work. The latter lived from the work of the mine, but not as miners. Knowledge of local prestige relations and hierarchies, enabled Szabó to realize with acumen that the large enterprise brought capitalism to this region and adjusted to feudalism there.

The autobiography of the *avant-garde* artist and writer Lajos Kassák evoked a working-class milieu is a worthy parallel to Gyula Illyés's work about the poor peasantry (Kassák, [1928] 1983).

A pioneering work, Gyula Rézler's (1938) wrote an account of the Hungarian manufacturing workers who evolved as a class at the end of the 19th and early 20th centuries. Although he stressed aspects of political history, he devoted a separate chapter to the relationship between the working class and other social groups. Relying on reports by industrial inspectors at the end of the 19th century, he tried to outline an empirically well-founded picture of the social position of the emerging working class. This aspect was elaborated in more detail in another volume edited and lengthily prefaced by Rézler (1942) whose chapters, one by one, are devoted to the workers in various branches of industry. Though by different authors, the chapters have a unified structure and discuss the production and employment conditions of each branch, the situation of the trade unions, the development of working time and wages, and at the end, the welfare situation. Under this heading, some chapters touch on questions of family income, diet, and housing.

SOCIOLOGY OF WORK DURING STATE SOCIALISM

Collectivization, Restructuring the Workforce, and Reforms

The war economy, the loss of World War I, the German, then Soviet, occupation of the country, the nationalization of the industrial enterprises at the end of the 1940s and the emergence of the monolithic one-party regime, followed by the collectivization of agriculture, provided new institutional frames for the period of reconstruction (Jánossy, [1966] 1971). Its main effects with relevance to our theme, in the early phase of planned economy, are the prevalence of employee status without property, obligatory work, and a shortage of labor (Kornai, 1992), together with a substantial drop in agricultural employment to below one-fifth in 1970 (Andorka, 1982). About half the considerably boosted industrial labor lived in villages, and many laborers commuted between their work and home (Vági, 1982).

The other impact of the political turn was the blocking of sociological fact-finding research. Research, however, that highlighted work returned relatively soon, around the mid-1960s. At this time, the importance of sociological research lay in ushering the public discourse toward reality, without touching on the basic ideological tenets, including the question of "the power of the working class." In their book, András Hegedűs and Mária Márkus, for example, devoted a separate chapter to the labor turnover and concluded, on the basis of empirical investigations, that there might be structural and justifiable personal reasons for mobility, with only few of the reasons being "socially unacceptable" (1966:236). This realistic tone also implied a criticism of direct state control over the labor market. The authors argued in a similar vein in support of the second economy, stating that professional ambitions impossible to realize at the full-time main job, could be acted upon within it. Social historical research from these years described the working class of the interwar period in statistical terms (Laczkó, 1968). All this effort to transform the ideology and the public discourse was connected to the economic political debates preparing the reform of 1968.

The economic reform aimed at indirect enterprise control, intensive development and enterprise efficiency entailed two structural corollaries affecting the labor market. One was the appearance of industrial- and construction-oriented subsidiary units in agricultural cooperatives, which, owing to their flexibility, were lucrative. By some calculation, they produced more than half the added value of cooperatives and could offer more favorable wages to skilled workers (Rupp, 1983).

The other development was also partly related to cooperatives: to the exploitation of the household plots of the coop employees (Juhász, 1982). These agricultural households, which originally producing for their own subsistence, began increasingly to produce for the market from the 1970s onward and became a leading component of the second economy. Specialists estimated the working hours spent in the second economy at about one-fourth that spent in the first, with second economy income amounting to a one-fifth of the gross domestic product (GDP) (Gábor and Galasi, 1981).

The findings of research into the segmentation of the labor market were presented in *The Structure and Working of the Labor Market in Hungary* (Galasi, 1982) and a selection of writings in English (Galasi and Sziráczki, 1985). Researchers have exposed the peculiarities derived from the dysfunctional features of a "labor market without a capital market" (Fazekas and Köllő, 1990, Gábor and Kovári, 1990). The state wanted to achieve desirable labor allocation with a market-imitative tool, the influence of wages, which meant that it restricted wages to be paid by state enterprises.

Since there was full employment, the labor demand of enterprises were inflexible, with the lack of sensitivity to expenditure on wages. The wrangling about wages and performance derived from labor shortage resulted simultaneously in the pressure of wage inflation and waves of correction via state intervention.

How Did Enterprises Really Work?

The empirical organization studies launched parallel with and closely connected to the economic reform drives of the 1960s wished to explore the dysfunction of the typical economic organization of the age, the state-owned enterprise. The most influential researcher of Hungarian work sociology, István Kemény, probably extended this basically economic research. Reviving the tradition of pre–World War I worker sociographies, he described the inner stratification of the industrial labor force, the most populous class of Hungarian society by 1970.

Kemény's best-known work is the *Assembly-Line in the Motorbike Factory* ([1968] 1978). The control of technology over man planned by the "Scientific Management" was absolutely not typical of the Hungarian variant of the assembly line. Lacking the conditions of the ideal Taylorist–Fordist organization, the worker was able to mold technology for his own benefit in order to assert his own interests. A degree of workers' autonomy derived from the "disorganization" of the economy of shortage, which led to wage and effort bargaining.

His study revealed what family household income strategies the intrafactory behavior types fitted, and what role the second economy played, as well as the roads of mobility along which the actors arrived at their current status. A highly elaborate analysis of the social status of preceding generations afforded him the background against which to describe both the traditional working layers of artisan-origin and the various agrarian groups that left agriculture for industry (Kemény, [1972]: 1979). With his colleagues, Kemény also conducted a survey in which one of the largest Hungarian firms at that time was involved in investigating the inner stratification of the working (Kemény and Kozák, 1971a, b).

His method, the case studies of enterprises, became the basic instrument of research in the next decades, particularly through the endeavors of reform economists. On the border of economics and sociology, an empirical school— for want of a better term—emerged and became an important constituent of reform economics. The research themes of the "economic mechanism" no longer focused only on the dysfunctions of an enterprise's inner working but also emphasized the investigation of the environment of the firm, with special regard to the bargaining mechanisms between the party–state center and the firm (Laki, 1979; Laky, 1979; Tardos, 1978). The meticulous analytic elaboration of a number of partial phenomena of the economic system of state socialism (e.g., shortage, rush periods of production, development decisions and bargaining for investment funds) paved the way for the systematic description of the socialist economic system in the 1980s (Kornai, 1980, 1992).

The other research launched in the late 1960s is associated with two young sociologists, Lajos Héthy and Csaba Makó. They relied on the technique of sociometry in their investigation of informal organizations. First they examined the behavior of the sheetmetal workers in a railway coach factory, and second, the electricians of a construction company. At both places, the informal organization enabled workers to fend off, with concerted effort (performance maneuvering), the so-called norm–settlement, an action by the enterprise management that threatened their customary advantages (Héthy-Makó, [1972] 1989).

In the early 1970s, the book that made the greatest stir abroad was the sociography of a young writer: *A Worker in a Worker's State"* (Haraszti, [1979] 1989). The book, written by a participating observer, described the piecework system prevalent in Hungary. (The original title of the book was *Piece-Wages*.) It presented the everyday practices of a factory in which the allocation of work and income deviated from the formal directives, including the tendentious distribution of "good jobs" and "bad jobs," the privileged role of head foremen, and the specific form of workers' reaction: "looting," which meant the flouting of all technology, quality, and safety requirements in their pursuit of performance percentage rewarded by the wages system. The author, continuing the tradition of fact-finding journalism, introduced the organization, the social gap between workers and leaders, from the vantage point of the lowermost position in the hierarchy. The manuscript was confiscated by police and Haraszti was brought to court. Haraszti's critical approach confronted the ideology of the system with reality. The unpublished works of Kemény, Haraszti, and others were circulated in Hungary as *samizdat* literature.

In the 1970s, the practitioners of labor economics revived the research into worker behavior. They approached the topic from the angle of rational employee behavior: Workers wish to realize the largest gain with the smallest effort, or, to put it in another way, to maximize the relative net advantage. Although the worker is restricted in his decisions about length of time spent in work, acceptable wages, and work intensity by various other conditions, they argued that neither the macroeconomic polity nor an enterprise's wage and labor policy could ignore such rational employee behavior (Gábor and Galasi, 1981). The first attempt to analyze the value system of workers also started in the 1970s (Hankiss, 1978).

István Márkus continued the sociographic tradition. Still a pupil of Ferenc Erdei, he began the investigation of a market town in the Great Plain, Nagykrös, then repeated the field work in the seventies. He applied the term *after-peasantry* to the local conditions and provided meticulous descriptions about variants of the workers' newly adopted ways of living (Márkus, 1979). From the tradition of sociographic fiction, we emphasize the work of Zsolt Csalog, whose method rested on a collection of original interviews. Apart from his representations of Gypsies and peasants, his portraiture of four workers is redolent with firsthand experience (Csalog, 1981). The writing of Sándor Tar, about young Hungarian guest laborers in East Germany, made a stir with its explosive, critical tone (Tar, 1977). In the 1970s, his work won the sociographic competition of a periodical but could not be published because of its delicate contents. It was circulated in a *samizdat* publication entitled *Profile*. Tar has devoted several volumes of short stories to themes of workers.

In the 1980s, the impact of work organization and technology on interest protection was examined. The core–periphery dichotomy was introduced to describe various bargaining positions of the workers in the organization (Makó, 1985). Another investigation showed that changing the products, work organization, or external factors transformed the informal organization of the workers; that is, their positions were very vulnerable (Simonyi, 1978).

A set of case studies conducted in different fields in the 1970s and 1980s aimed precisely at showing the differences in the position of workers and exposing the factors that explained the differences in bargaining power. János Köllő's study about female workers in a cotton mill revealed value preferences that relegated behavior to maximize the net advantage to second place and prevented collective action (Köllő, 1981). In one of our largest vehicle factories, Károly Fazekas (1982) investigated attempts to solve the shortage of labor (performance press, incorporation of "rural" units, etc.), examining their effects upon the internal labor market and workers' behavior.

The two most momentous discoveries in Hungarian economic sociology of the 1970s were the phenomenon of informal wage bargaining in the factory and the doubling of the labor market. In addition to the labor shortage in the first economy, extraenterprise income sources became stabilized. By the mid-1980s, the labor–economics approach realized that various employee strategies also offered the enterprise a variety of choices. The different handling of workers with different training, motivation, and social background led to the enterprise's adaptability and the rational economy of labor costs (Galasi, 1982; Kertesi-Sziráczki, [1983] 1988).

This approach was strongly inspired by the theory of internal labor markets; however, the specificity lay in the preponderance of informal regulation and the resultant instability. True, the Hungarian elite worker also had some job control and advantages derived from seniority, but these were not supported by either trade union bargains or written enterprise rules. The differences between the two economic systems and work organizations were explored in depth by comparative studies triggered by Michael Burawoy's and David Stark's writings in the second half of the 1980s.

Burawoy and János Lukács compared prevalent opinions ("mythologies") chiefly detrimental to socialist enterprises with reality, and with the findings of Burawoy's investigations of similar fields in America. A major insight of their research is that the environment of the capitalist enterprise causes the insecurity of employment, while the rules of the internal labor market create wage security. The opposite applies to the socialist organization: Employment is guaranteed but wages are insecure. In his similar, mirroring opposition, Stark presented differences in the internal labor markets of the capitalist and socialist enterprises through the operation of the Work Partnerships within the Enterprise (WPEs). (The WPEs were the mass outcome of transformation in economic organizations over the 1980s: A select group of privileged workers could become sub-contractors to their full-time employer and work overtime.) While the insecurities of a capitalist enterprise originate in the market, those of a socialist enterprise are bureaucratic in origin. Consequently, the compensating mechanism is bureaucratic in the former and adjusted to the market in the latter. The aim in both cases is the retention of "valuable" employees, but while the capitalist enterprise achieves it by guaranteed wages and fixed rules of promotion, in a socialist enterprise, flexible work organization, based on informal operation and the institutions of selective wage bargaining, provides for the enterprise's adaptability (Stark, 1986).

Finally, an outcome of research in the 1980s was a new wave of studies into labor history. Tamás Gyekiczki exposed the nature of repression by analyzing the sabotage trials against workers in the 1950s: The early state socialist regime penalized not only former prominent socialist democratic activists but also victimized hosts of the most helpless in the labor segmentation (Gyekiczki, 1986). László Varga analyzed the position of the skilled workers' elite and especially the foremen of the period (Varga, 1984). In this wave of labor history Gábor Gyáni investigated archive materials concerning housing and living conditions of workers in the late 19th and early 20th century (Gyáni, 1992).

SOCIOLOGY OF WORK AND THE SOCIAL TRANSFORMATION

Major Trends Shaping the Labor Process

The central factors influencing the labor process in the current period of social transformation include the spread of private property and private enterprises, the appearance of unemployment, and the predominance of the services sector.

By the mid-1990s, nearly two-thirds of the labor force was employed by privately owned firms. The predominance of the private sector also applies to industry, since, by the latter half of the 1990s, privatization of this sector was practically completed.

Statistics registered nearly one million enterprises in 1997, 70% of which were actually active. It is also noteworthy that 75% of the enterprises comprised the self-employed, roughly 33% of the entrepreneurs were only part-time, and a mere 3% of enterprise had an employed staff of over 10 people. Thus, the spectacular achievements during the emergence of the private sector had only a restricted labor-absorbing effect up to the mid-1990s.

In the early 1990s, the unemployment rate was 10–13%. Local unemployment rates in heavy industry districts and in agrarian areas, where cooperatives ceased to exist and tiny cut up family plots did not offer mass employment, surpassed the national average two or three times (Laky, 1997b). About half of the unemployed remained out of work over time, not finding employment after the dole ran out. This group constituted the core of the marginalized masses (Csoba, 1994). The Roma (Gypsy) population is massively overrepresented in this group (Ábrahám and Kertesi, [1998] 2001). The unemployment rate was suppressed below 10% by the second half of the 1990s and the reemployment chances of the lastingly unemployed also improved somewhat (Lázár and Székely, 1996). The unemployment rate of men has been higher than that of women, because the structure of female employment by branches is different from the men's, and also, women became inactive at a higher rate, while far fewer of them applied for the dole (Nagy, 1994; Tardos, 1994). A corollary phenomenon is that in the 1990s, the rate of the inactive population surpassed the rate of the economically active in the adult population. The rate of those afraid of losing their jobs (thus, subjectively defined as potentially unemployed) was one-sixth at the end of the 1980s, and one-fourth in the late 1990s.

While 40% of earners in the 1980s worked in the tertiary sector, this rate was 60% in the mid-1990s. Thus, the services sector became predominant, employing more than industry and agriculture together. The rate of the latter plummeted more sharply, from 18% in 1990, to a mere 8% in 1996, while industrial employment dropped only slightly, remaining around 33%. The tertiary sector is however itself very complex, with financial institutions of large staffs on the one end of the scale and self-employed in services and retailers on the other. This polarization throws the dualization processes felt in the whole of economy into deeper relief in the tertiary sector (Gábor, 1997). While in the late phase of planned economy the duality of the first and second economies meant dual economic roles on a mass scale, in the phase of transitional economy, dualization took place between the segments of large and small firms. In the second half of the 1990s, more than one-half of the employees of small firms, and one-third of the employees of large enterprises, earned below the average income. The position of the latter was more favorable in terms of both income and job security, and hence chances of promotion. What small entrepreneurs felt to be their advantage over large-company employees was a somewhat greater decision-making competence and control over the work process.

As regards the action potential of labor representation in the second half of the 1990s, only about 50% of the active population was willing to take part in permitted demonstrations or labor strikes, with the rate growing slightly from the beginning of the decade, but the number of real actions was insignificant. The rate of those willing to emigrate or try to find a job abroad was very low, at 2–4%, with great temporal stability.

Enterprise Restructuring during Transformation from State Socialism

From 1989 on, a profound institutional transformation of the economy was triggered, together with a grave economic recession, which started in the early 1980s and lasted until the mid-1990s. Former full employment ceased to exist during this critical period and several "atypical" work relations appeared. With privatization coming to a head, and with the influx of foreign capital, the ratio of various sectors of ownership changed substantially. Within the private sector, which rose to predominance, firms owned by foreigners produced 43% of the added value of the enterprises and employed 25% of the labor force.

As one outcome of the economic change, the differences between workers further increased, in terms of both the chances of getting a job and income differences within a staff. This is revealed by the secondary analysis of official figures of the jobless and the employed carried out by Kertesi, Köllő, Fazekas and Nagy. Their statistical analysis included wage differences between enterprises, occupations, and regions; correlations between wages and unemployment; and characteristic features of employment at foreign-owned firms (Kertesi and Köllő, 1995; Köllő-Fazekas, 1998, 1997). In addition to the tangible spread of macrostatistical methods, micromethods used earlier proved well suited to the exploration of new phenomena within the economic transformation. Thus, the radical changes in the economic and organizational environment of the labor process came into focus with studies of the decentralization and privatization of the typical, large, state-owned enterprises and cooperatives of state socialism, followed by the appearance of multinational enterprises.

The range of empirical microeconomic research tried to keep track of the adaptability and transformation of firms with several case studies. Among studies into economic adaptation, the typology of Mihály Laki deserves mention, together with case studies of the history of the restructuring or privatization of certain enterprises (Laki, 1993). Within the trend we would call the "mechanism research," Éva Voszka deserves special mention. Through case studies and analyses, she followed the entire process of privatization, various techniques of privatization, and the emergence of the state-run agencies of privatization (Voszka, 1997). Investigations highlighting the insiders-turned-owners or conflicts that arose from such conversions were closer to the work process. An article by Gabriella Fogarassy and Zoltán Szántó (1996) tackled the questions of managers acquiring property. They tried to explore the sociological nature of the conflict among the actors through the application of the theory of triads (Fogarassy and Szántó, 1996). Dorottya Boda relied heavily in her analyses on former organizational researchers, which enabled her to pinpoint the selective nature of becoming owners and even surviving the segmentation of the internal labor market within enterprises transferred from state to employee ownership. In Hungary, however, employee ownership is initiated by the firm managers, and the predominance of managers both in ownership and control delimits the possibilities of the democratization of the work organization from the very beginning in most enterprises (Boda, 1996; Neumann, 1997).

The dismantling of the state sector affected the labor force of former large enterprises directly and on a mass scale: Nearly one million "typical" jobs were abolished. A case study exposed the inner conflicts of an early firm liquidation and revealed the selective treatment of laid-off workers and the complete lack of safeguarding the interests of the weakest workers (Bódis, 1994). Other researchers followed the process, in the course of which former employees of a disintegrated large electronic company tried to organize into small enterprises on a mass scale to keep alive the market of a rural town. Not only the unfolding or dying away of the earlier entrepreneurial gains deserve attention, but also the powerful differentiation that took place in the very first or second business years, both between and inside the enterprises (Leveleki, 1994).

As can be deduced from the previous discussion, the main area of informal bargaining between management and employees was the transformation of the enterprise setup: Various units becoming independent, acquisition of property by employees and managers in the course of privatization, and mass cutbacks in personnel all provided a chance to use the skills acquired in former bargaining. At the same time, sweeping organizational changes and the radical transformation of the environment, as many authors have noted, threatened a great part of the elite workers with the loss of their vulnerable positions.

To what extent does the change of ownership affect the positions developed in the previously informal wage–effort bargains and the former attitudes of the workers? That was the main question targeted in research led by the late László Csontos (1994), who tried to reformulate in the idiom of up-to-date sociological theories the experiences of previous decades. Will rent seeking by workers or worker groups monopolizing certain posts in the process survive? In the end, Lajos Bódis's almost anthropologically meticulous researches in a large clothing factory answered in the affirmative. There is still strong differentiation in the distribution of wages not justified by differences in performance, and this can only be leveled out in the long run. The informal organization tagged by the author as "insurance-like" recompensed the young worker for their inputs only decades later (Bódis, 1997). In a machine manufacturing firm of long standing, another member of the research team found that although the just-arrived foreign management tried to deprive the workers with specific knowledge of their privileges, the disastrous consequences made them recant (Janky, 1996).

The case is different when there is an owner with more ambitious changes in personnel policy, technology and organization; when the domestic traditions are confronted with Western practices, or, as will be touched on later, when multinationals carry out "Greenfield" investment or introduce standard technologies (Swaan, 1994). Reports about these might suggest that the former tools of individual interest protection, the wage and effort bargaining, have limited possibilities. The emergence of oversupply in the labor market and the abolition of wage regulation brought about a substantial change in the evaluation of formerly "dual status" employees. High degrees of absenteeism are no longer tolerated during agricultural peaks. "Presence bonus" as an incentive is incorporated in the wage system; those with high absenteeism are given the sack. This change in managerial attitude is not restricted to foreign-owned firms, and the Hungarian employers also try to utilize the, for them, favorable transformation of the labor market. It is an indication of the rudimentary character of manpower policies that case studies in a sample of 14 firms did not find significant differences between state-owned and privatized enterprises, and to different kinds of owners (Whitley et al., 1997). The authors conclude that the private owners' control over the newly acquired enterprise has limited influence upon the employment and work management practices of the firms—for a variety of reasons.

A relatively new area of research without antecedents is the description and analysis of the industrial relations of the emerging market economy. Since, in state socialism, independent trade unions and employers' organization only existed informally, no effective reconciliation of interests could exist. Neither did a strong unionist movement evolve during the period of transition. Neither the legacy of the state socialist system nor the changed labor market situation of the small-scale units of employment gaining ascendancy during the economic changes facilitated such an evolution. About one-fifth of employees noted membership in some trade union, the corresponding rate being below one-twentieth among the jobless. This is one reason why strikes are very rare in the country, and the majority of trade unions are considerably cooperative. Since the systemic change, the efforts of the government, employers, and trade unions all concentrated on building and developing of national and sectoral interest reconciliation. The majority of research on this topic addresses these institutions and the participants of these negotiations, the national employers' organizations and trade unions (Héthy, 1994; Ladó and Tóth, 1996).

Though there is far less coverage of company-level industrial relations and trade union action within enterprises, it can be concluded that there is strong polarization among the employers. A smaller segment of employers consolidated collective bargaining. They regularly signed collective agreements regulating wages, work hours, terms, and conditions of employment. The institutional way of collective interest representation can, however, only be trodden by a minority of employees, mainly those working in large enterprises or the state sector. In small- and medium-scale enterprises, and certain multinational companies, there is no trade union or collective agreement at all. In the study of the industrial relations of an enterprise, the approach from the angle of labor law is predominant, with relatively few empirical studies being conducted at the firm level. Possibly the reason is that such researches have no precedents in Hungary. The only possible exception is the works council introduced by the Labor Code of 1992, whose implementation stirred much attention (Tóth, 1997).

Precisely 60 years after the publication of his first book, Gyula Rézler held his inaugural lecture as the external member of the Hungarian Academy of Sciences, with the title "The Sociology of Arbitrage," elaborating his experiences gained as participatory observer over the decades in America.

Research was also launched into exploring the changing roles, internal organization and actions of trade unions (Makó, 1998). The work organization of multinational automobile manufacturing firms are in the focus of attention both in Hungary and abroad, since they provide almost laboratory circumstances of how the worldwide applied technologies and work management ideas (just-in-time production, teamwork, etc.) can be put into practice amid the cultural and production traditions of a particular country. In his study comparing the assembly lines of Suzuki and GM Opel, however, Tóth also discovered substantial differences in the practices of the two plants. The two firms employ worker layers of diverse social backgrounds, pursue different work management practices, and, as a result, implement the work organizational principles of their industry differently (Tóth, 1999).

With the breakup of large enterprises, the role of small- and medium-scale firms has been promoted in employment. Yet little is known about their labor relations. The "labor policy" of small firms is rarely touched on by research into small entrepreneurship, since small firms are often practically self-employing; that is, their extra labor power is that of the family. Should they hire non-family-members, the selection criteria are stronger. The result is higher levels of training and more personal and caring boss–staff relations. In return, the employee is expected to produce higher work intensity and loyalty (Kuczi, 1994; Laki, 1998). However, there is a segment of small- and medium-sized enterprises that is said by labor inspectorate reports, supported by trade union complaints, to elicit different opinions. These are believed to exploit frequently the helplessness of the employees when it comes to remedying the violation of their rights or interests.

Relying on the empirical traditions of research into the former second economy, it has become a significant trend to study the activity forms and markets of the informal economy. The empirical investigation of the "grey economy" is in part connected to the examination of migration and commuting even beyond the frontier. The latter has become an important research topic recently, with the protracted economic crisis of the East European countries and the hope that Hungary will join the European Union (Gagyi and Oláh, 1998; Hárs, 1995; Sík, [1982] 1998).

Empirical research into "atypical" employment practices has just started. Case studies explore the traditions and variety of seasonal work, and also uncover the typical situations of employers and employees that facilitate this type of legal or semilegal employment (Simonyi, 1997). Writings based on secondary analysis touching "atypical" work relations (part-time job, putting out, casual work, etc.) deal with the description of the legal environment, statistical registration, educational background, or presentation of the possibilities provided by the government employment policy (Laky, 1997; Tímár, 1996).

Finally, it is also to be noted that an important achievement of the 1990s was the Social Scientific Elaboration of 1956. The spontaneous contribution of the organizations and workers' participation was specifically emphatic here. One of the early analyses is by a foreigner, Bill Lomax (1976), who devoted great attention to the history of workers' councils. In the vein of the sociographic tradition, the Hungarian researchers have published interviews and analyses about the leaders of onetime workers' councils (Kozák, Molnár, and Kőrösi, 1993; Valluch, 1996). A separate volume is devoted to the history of the armed groups of a Budapest district, with some portraits of the participants added (Eörsi, 1997). A sociological investigation concerned with the events in 1956 (Tyekvicska, 1996) and the spread of information and structuration of events, stressed the role of railwaymen, commuters, and family networks in the life of a village.

CONCLUSION

The prehistory of Hungarian research into work and workers can be retraced to the turn of the 20th century. The features shared by the early researchers are their problem-oriented and critical social attitudes. The greatest achievement of Hungarian sociology of work is tied to the examination of informal bargaining between economic actors and the second economy, formulated more or less consciously in opposition to the official ideology propagating a society free from conflicts of interests. This approach continued in the early 20th-century sociological tradition characterized by a sensitivity to social problems in its choice of topics and a critical call for change, while its method was chiefly that of sociographic fiction. At the same time, the economics of work also largely influenced the sociology of work; thus, the two became closely intertwined.

The drive to change the political and economic systems coming into prominence at the end of the 1980s considerably changed the role, themes, and methods of sociology of work studies. The economic foundation for this change was undoubtedly the abolition of full employment and the relegation of labor done in the classical Taylorist work organization in factories and cooperatives. The political–ideological background was provided by the waning importance of the "question of the working class," given high priority by both the official position and its opponents. During the emergence of the institutions and actors of a market economy and the restructuring of the economy, the conditions of labor, the situation of the employees, and the collective interest representation of employees are not important public issues. As a result, a shift in the choice of research subjects can be detected in the 1990s: away from social problems and the focus on labor organization, and toward sensitive problems affecting macroeconomic performance and policymaking (e.g., employment, unemployment, small firms, and corporatism). As for the chosen method, the sociographic case-study approaches are giving way to mathematical–statistical and survey methods.

REFERENCES

Ábrahá, Árpód, and Gábor Kertesi [1998] 2001. Regional Unemplyment Rate Differentials in Hungary, 1990–1995: The Changing Role of Race and Human Capital. In *The Samll Transformation Society, Economy and Politics in Hungary and the New European Architecture.* Edited by G. Lengyel and Z. Rostováliyi. Budapest: Akadémiai,

Andorka, Rudolf. 1982. *A társadalmi mobilitás változásai Magyarországon.* [*Changes of Social Mobility in Hungary*]. Budapest: Gondolat.

Boda, Dorottya. 1996. Tulajdonnal megerősített munkavállalói pozíciók [Employee Positions Reinforced by Ownership]. *Külgazdaság* 4:62–75.

Bódis, Lajos. 1994. A létszámleépítés körüli alkuk jellemzői egy hazai középvállalatnál [Typical Features of Bargaining about Staff Cutbacks at the Hungarian Medium-Scale Enterprise]. In *A jövo munkahelyeiért. Munkatudományi tanulmányok* [*For the Jobs of the Future: Labour Studies*] (pp. 175–187), edited by G. Kovári. Struktúra, Budapest: Munkaügyi Kiadó.

Bódis, Lajos. 1997. Privatizáció, munkaszervezet és bérelosztási mechanizmusok egy nagyüzemi varrodában, Vols. I-II. [Privatization, Work Organization and Wage Distributing Mechanisms in the Large Sewing Enterprise] *Közgazdasági Szemle,* 8:689–717; 9:799–818.

Burawoy, Michael, and Lukács, János. 1992. *The Radiant Past.* Chicago: University of Chicago Press.

Csalog, Zsolt. 1981. *A tengert akartam látni: Négy munkásportré* [I wanted to see the sea. Portraits of four workers]. Budapest: Szépirodalmi.

Csoba, Judit. 1994. "Job-hunters and the Work-Shy: Permanent Unemployment and the Willingness to Take Up Work." *Szociológiai Szemle* 2:115–136.

Csontos, László. 1994. "Szempontok a privatizáció és a hierarchikus gazdasági szervezetek belső szerkezetének változásai közti összefüggések tanulmányozásához" [Viewpoints to Study Correlations between Privatization and the Changes of the Internal Structure of Hierarchical Economic Organizations]. *Szociológiai Szemle* 4:83–96.

Eörsi, László. 1997. *Ferencváros 1956: A kerület fegyveres csoportjai* [*Ferencváros, 1956: The Armed Groups of the District*], Budapest: Intézet.

Erdei, Ferenc. 1937. *Futóhomok* [*Drifting Sand*]. Budapest: Atheneum.

Erdei, Ferenc. 1942. *A magyar paraszttársadalom* [Hungarian Peasant Society]. Budapest: Franklin.

Fazekas, Károly. 1982. Bérteljesítményalku a belső munkaerőpiacon [Wage and Effort Bargaining in the Internal Labour Market]. In *Munkaerőpiac szerkezete és működése Magyarországon,* edited by P. Galasi. Budapest: Közgazdasági és Jogi.

Fazekas, Károly, and János Köllő. 1990. *Munkaerőpiac tőkepiac nélkül* [Labour Market Without Capital! Market]. Budapest: Közgazdasági és Jogi.

Fogarassy, Gabriella, and Zoltán Szántó. 1996. "Privatizáció és a neveto harmadik" [Privatization and the Tertius Gardens]. *Szociológiai Szemle* 2:71–80.

Gábor, R. István. 1997. Belso versus foglalkozási munkaeropiac—a posztszocialista átalakulás elhanyagolt dimenziója [Internal versus Occupational Labour Markets— A Neglected Dimension of Post-Socialist Transformation]. *Közgazdasági Szemle* 6.

Gábor, R. István, and Galasi Péter. 1981. *A "második gazdaság": tények és hipotézisek* [The "Second Economy": Facts and Hypotheses]. Budapest: Közgazdasági és Jogi.

Gábor R., and György István-Kovári. 1990. *Beválthatók-e a bérreform ígéretei?* [Can the Promises of the Wages Reform be Realized?]. Budapest: Közgazdasági és Jogi.

Gayi, József, and Sándor Oláh. 1998. "Vendégmunkások utazási formái Maros megyébol Magyarországra" [Guest/Workers' Travels from Maros County to Hungary]. In *Idegenek magyarországon* [Aliens in Hungary], edited by Sik Endre. Budapest: MTA PTI Nemzetközi Migrációs Kutatócsoport.

Galasi, Péter, ed. 1982. *Munkaerőpiac szerkezete és működése Magyarországon.* [The Structure and Operation of the Labor Market in Hungary]. Budapest: Közgazdasági és Jogi.

Galasi, Péter, and György Sziráczki eds. 1985. *Labour Market and Second Economy in Hungary* Frankfurt New York: Campus Verlag.

Gyáni, Gábor. 1992. *Bérkaszárnya és nyomortelep* [Tenement House and Slum]. Budapest: Magvető.

Gyekiczky, Tamàs. 1986. *A munkafegyelem joyi szabályozásàuuk tàrsadalmi hàttere az 1952-es èv Magyarországàu* [Social backgroud of the legal regulation of work discipline in Hungary in 1952.] Budapest: MM.

Hankiss, Elemér. 1978. *Értékszociológiai kísérlet (Az ipari dolgozók néhány rétegének értékrendjérol)* [An Experiment in Value Sociology (on the Value System of Some Layers of Industrial Workers)]. Budapest: Népművelési Propaganda Iroda.

Haraszti, Miklós. [1979] 1989. *Darabbér: Egy munkás a munkásállamban* [Piece-Wage: A Worker in a Worker's State]. Budapest: Téka.

Hárs, Ágnes. 1995. "The Alien Population and Its Presence in the Workforce." *Europa Forum* [Special Issue]:84–97.

Hegedűs, András, and Mária Márkus. 1966. *Ember, munka, közösség* [Man, Work, Community]. Budapest: Közgazdasági és Jogi.

Héthy, Lajos. 1994. "Tripartism in Eastern Europe." In *New Frontiers in European Industrial Relations,* edited by R. Hymanand and A. Ferner. Oxford, UK: Blackwell.

Héthy, Lajos, and Csaba Makó. [1972] 1989. *Patterns of Workers' Behavior and the Business Enterprise.* Budapest: HAS, HSOWL.

Illyés, Gyula. [1936] 1979. *People of the puszta.* Budapest: Corvina.

Janky, Béla. 1996. Övé a gyár—magadnak épített! [His Is the Factory—You're Building It for Yourself!]. *Szociológiai Szemle* 3–4:223–248.

Jánossy, Ferenc. [1996] 1971. *The End of the Economic Miracle. Appearance and Reality in Economic Development.* White Plains, NY: Books on Demand.

Juhász, Pál. 1982. "Agrárpiac, kisüzem, nagyüzem" [Agrarian Market, Small Enterprise, Large Enterprise] *Medvetánc* 1: 117–139.

Kassák, Lajos. [1928] 1983. *Egy ember élete* [*The Life of a Man*]. Budapest: Magveto.

Kemény, István, and Gyula Kozák. 1971a. Csepel Vas és Fémművek munkásai. [Workers of the Csepel Iron and Metal Works]. Budapest: Társadalomtudományi Intézet

Kemény, István, and Gyula Kozák. 1971b. *Pest megye munkásai* [*Workers of Pest county*]. Budapest: Társadalomtudományi Intézet.

Kemény, István. [1968] 1990. *Velük nevelkedett a gép. Magyar munkások a hetvenes évek elején* [*The Machine Grew Up with Them: Hungarian Workers in the Early '70s*]. Budapest: Művelődéskutató Intézet.

Kemény, István. [1968] 1978. "La chaîne dans une usine hongroise." *Actes de la Reserche en Sciences Sociales* 24 (November).

Kemény, István. 1985. *Ouvriers hongrois.* Paris: L'Harmattan.

Kertesi, Gábor, and György Sziráczki. [1983] 1988. "Workers Behaviour on the Labour Market. In *On Work*, edited by R. E. Pahl. London: Basil Blackwell.

Köllő, János. 1981. "Taktikázás és alkudozás az ipari üzemben: Kétségek és próbálkozások egy szövöde leírása közben" [Maneuvering and Bargaining in an Industrial Factory. Doubts and Attempts While Describing a Spinning Mill]. *Közgazdasági Szemle* 7–8.

Köllo, János. 1998. "Regionális bérkülönbségek, 1989–95."[Regional Wage Differences, 1989–95] In *A munkaeropiac az átmenet idoszakában* [*The Labour Market in the Period of Transition*], edited by K. Fazekas. Budapest: MTA Közgazdaságtudományi Intézet.

Köllo, János, and Gyula Nagy. 1995. Bérek munkanélküliség előtt és után. [Wages before and after Unemployment]. *Közgazdasági Szemle* 4:325–357.

Kornai, János. 1980. *Economics of Shortage.* Amsterdam: North-Holland.

Kornai, János. 1992. *The Socialist System. The Political Economy of Communism.* Oxford, UK: Clarendon Press.

Kozák, Gyula, Adrien Molnár, and Korösi Zsuzsa, eds. 1993. "Szuronyok hegyén nem lehet dolgozni" [You Can't Work at the Point of Bayonets]. Budapest: Századvég.

Kuczi, Tibor. 1994. "Which 'Ready/Made' Relations Contribute to the Intra-Enterprise Relations?" *Szociológiai Szemle* 2:87–94.

Laczkó, Miklós. 1968. *A magyar munkásosztály fejlodésének fo vonásai a tokés korszakban* [*Major Characteristics of the Development of Working Class in the Capitalist Period*]. Budapest.

Ladó, Mária, and Ferenc Tóth. 1996. *Helyzetkép az érdekegyeztetésről* (1990–1994): A tényfeltáró bizottság zárójelentése [The Reconciliation of the Interests in Hungary 1990–1994. An Overview of the Current Situation]. ÉT titkárság - PHARE Társadalmi Párbeszéd Projekt.

Laki, Mihály. 1979. *Év végi hajrá az iparban* [*End-of-the-Year Rushwork in Industry*]. Budapest: Magvető.

Laki, Mihály. 1998. *Kisvállalkozások a szocializmus után* [*Small Enterprises after Socialism*]. Budapest: Közgazdasági Szemle Alapítvány.

Laki, Mihály. 1992. "A vállalati magatartás változása és a gazdasági válság." [Changes in Enterprise Behaviour and the Economic Recession]. *Közgazdasági Szemle* 6:565–578.

Laki, Mihály. 1993. "Vállalati viselkedés elhúzódó gazdasági visszaesés idején". [Enterprise Behaviour at the Time or Protracted Recession]. *Külgazdaság* 11:23–34.

Laky, Teréz. 1979. *A recentralizáció rejtett mechanizmusai [The Hidden Mechanisms of Recentralization]*. Budapest: KJK.

Laky, Teréz, ed. 1997a. "Atipikus foglalkoztatási formák." [Atypical Forms of Employment]. *Európai tükör* No. 25, Integrációs Stratégiai Munkacsoport.

Laky, Teréz. 1997b. *Munkaerőpiaci helyzetjelentés [Situation Report about the Labour Market]* Budapest: Munkaügyi Kutatóintézet.

Lázár, György, and Judit Székely. 1996. *Részletes jelentés a munkanélküli ellátásra való jogosultságukat 1995.évben kimeritettek követéses vizsgálatának eredményeirol. [Report of the Findings of a Follow-Up Investigation of Those Who Exhausted the Unempoloyment Entittlement Benefit in 1995]*. Budapest: OMK

Leopold, Lajos. [1917] 1988. "Szinlelt kapitalizmus" [Simulated Capitalism]. *Medvetánc* 2–3:321–355

Leveleki, Magdolna. 1994. Les Fleurs du Mal: "As Videoton Was Falling to Pieces More and More of Them Came to Us. . . . " *Szociológiai Szemle* 2:137–148.

Litván, György, ed. 1974. *Magyar munkásszociográfiák, 1888–1945* [Hungarian Sociographies of Workers]. Budapest: Kossuth.

Litván, György, and László Szucs, eds. 1973. *A szociológia első magyar műhelye. A Huszadik Század köre* [The First Hungarian Workshop of Sociology: The Circle of Huszadik Század]. Budapest: Gondolat.

Lomax, Bill. 1976. *Hungary 1956.* London: Allison and Busby.

Makó, Csaba. 1985. *A társadalmi viszonyok erotere: A munkafolyamat [Labor Process as the Hub of Social Relations]*. Budapest: KJK.

Makó, Csaba. 1998. Conclusion: Some Impacts for Trade Unions. In *Workers, Firms and Unions: Industrial Relations in Transition,* edited by Roderick Martin, Akihiro Ishikawa, Csaba Makó, and Francesco Consoli. Bern, Frankfurt, New York: Peter Lang.

Márkus, István. 1979. *Nagykőrös.* Budapest: Szépirodalmi.

Medgyesi Márton, and Péter Róbert. 1998. *A munka-attitűdök időbeli változása 1989–1997 között [Changes of Work-Attitudes between 1989–1997]* Budapest: Tárki.

Nagy, Beáta. 1994. "Women in Management." *Szociológiai Szemle* 2:95–114.

Neumann, László. 1997. "Circumventing Trade Unions in Hungary: Old and New Channels of Wage Bargaining." *European Journal of Industrial Relations* 3(2):181–200.

Rézler, Gyula. 1938. *A magyar nagyipari munkásság kialakulása, 1867–1914 [Emergence of the Hungarian Manufacturing Workers, 1867–1914]*. Budapest: Rekord.

Rézler, Gyula. 1942. *Magyar gyáripari munkásság: Szociális helyzetkép [Hungarian Factory Workers: Social Situation]*. Budapest: M. Közgazdasági Társaság.

Rupp, Kálmán. 1983. *Entrepreneurs in Red: Structural and Organizational Innovation in the Centrally Planned Economy.* Albany: State University of New York.

Sík, Endre. [1982] 1988. "A munkacsere a mai magyar gazdaságban." In [Exchange of Work in Today's Hungarian Economy]. *Gazdaságpolitika, gazdasági szervezet [Economic policy, economic organization]*, edited by Iván Major. Budapest: MTA

Közgazdaságtudományi Intézet.

Sík, Endre, and Judit Tóth. 1998. From Improvisation toward Awareness. *Yearbook of the Group of International Migration.* Budapest: Institute of Political Sciences of the Hungarian Academy of Sciences.

Simonyi, Ágnes. 1978. "Központból a perifériába" [From Core to Periphery]. *Valóság* 1:89–98.

Simonyi, Ágnes. 1997. "Szezonális foglalkoztatás" [Seasonal employment]. In *Atipikus műhelytanulmànyok* [Atypical Forms of Employment], edited by Laky Teréz *Európai tükör.* No. 25. Budapest: Integrációs Stratégiai Munkacsoport.

Somogyi, Manó. 1900. *Szociálpolitikai tanulmányok* [Studies in Welfare Policy]. Budapest: Hirlap.

Stark, David. 1986. Rethinking Internal Labor Markets: New Insights from a Comparative Perspective. *American Sociological Review* 51:492–504.

Swaan, Wim. 1994. "Tudás, tranzakciós költségek és a transzformációs válság." [Knowledge, Transaction Costs and the Crisis of Transformation]. *Közgazdasági Szemle* 10:845–858.

Szabó, Zoltán. 1937. *A tardi helyzet* [*The Situation in Tard*]. Budapest: Cserépfalvi.

Szabó, Zoltán. 1938. *Cifra Nyomorúság: A Cserhát, Mátra, Bükk, földje és népe* [*Spiffy Misery: The Land and People of the Cserhát, Mátra, Bükk*]. Cserépfalvi.

Szelényi, Iván. 1988. *Socialist Entrepreneurs.* Madison: University of Wisconsin Press.

Tar, Sándor. 1977. "Tájékoztató" [Information]. In *Profil: Válogatás 34 szerzo nyilvánosságra szánt, de meg nem jelent írásaiból.* [*Profile: Selection of 34 Authors' Unpublished Manuscripts*]. Összeállította: Kenedi János.

Tardos, Katalin. 1994. "Marginal Groups in the Labour Market: Those Refused Unemployment Benefits." *Szociológiai Szemle* 2:149–159.

Tardos, Márton, ed. 1978. *Vállalati magatartás—vállalati környezet* [Enterprise Behavior—Enterprise Environment]. Budapest: Vözgazdasàgi es Fogi.

Tímár, János. 1996. Munkaerő kereslet és -kinálat, 1995–2010 [Demand and Supply of Workforce, 1995–2010]. In *Munkaero kereslet és -kinálat, 1995–2010* [Demand and Supply of Workforce, 1995–2010], edited by János Gállos. Budapest: Ministry of Labour–The World Bank; Human Resource Development Program.

Tóth, András. 1997. The Invention of Works Councils in Hungary. *European Journal of Industrial Relations,* 3(2):329–356.

Tóth, András. 1999. "Building Unions of Autotransplants in Hungary." In *Globalization of Work,* edited by Jeremy Weddington. London: Mansell.

Tyekvicska, Árpád. 1996. "Local Revolution." *Hungarian Sociological Review* [Special Issue], pp. 104–128.

Vadnay, Andor. 1900. *A Tiszamellékről. Tanulmány az alföldi munkáskérdésrol* [About the Tisza region: Study on the Issue of Workers in the Great Plain. Budapest: Rákosi.

Vági, Gábor. 1982. *Versengés a fejlesztési forrásokért* [Rivalry for the Sources of Development] Budapest: Közgazdasági és Jogi.

Valluch, Tibor. 1996. *Ötvenhatosok* [*Fifty-Sixers*]. Debrecen: Cívis

Varga, László. 1984. *Pató Pálok vagy sztahanovisták?* Budapest: Magvető.

Voszka, Éva. 1997. *A dinoszauruszok esélyei: Nagyvállalati szerkezetváltás és privatizáció*

[*Chances of Dinosaurs: Restructuring and Privatization of Large Enterprises*]. Budapest: Pénzügykutató.

Whitley, Richard, et al. 1996. "Enterprise Change and the Management of Labour in a Transforming Society: The Case of Hungary." In *State, Market and Organizational Form,* edited by Ayse Bugra and Behlül Üsdiken. Berlin/ New York: Walter de Gruyter.

Zsille, Zoltán. 1988. *A létező kecske* [*The Existing Goat*]. Wien: Kosmos.

APPENDIX: INSTITUTIONAL CONTEXT OF RESEARCH

The International Labour Organization of the United Nations supports targeted researches and reports. Basic research is financed by the Hungarian National Science Foundation and the Research Support Scheme of the Soros Foundation.

Major Workshops of Relevant Research

Department of Human Resources, Budapest University of Economic Sciences (BUES)
Department Head: Gyula Nagy

Department of Social Policy, Janus Pannonius University of Sciences, Pécs
Department Head: Endre Nagy

Department of Sociology and Social Policy, BUES
Department Head: György Lengyel,

Department of Sociology, József Attila Pannonius University of Sciences, Szeged,
Department Head: Gábor Feleky

Department of Sociology, Kossuth Lajos University of Sciences, Debrecen
Department Head: Csaba Béres

Department of Sociology, Miskolc University of Sciences
Department Head: Béla Kolozsi

Institute of Economics, Hungarian Academy of Sciences
Institute Head: Jeno Koltay

Institute of Sociology and Social Policy, Eötvös Loránd University of Sciences (ELTE)
Institute Head: Tomas Rudas

Institute of Sociology, Hungarian Academy of Sciences
Institute Head: Pál Tamás

National Labor Center
Center Head: Judit Székely

National Labor Center, Research Unit (formerly Labor Research Institute)
Center Head: Máaria Ladó

Committees

Committee of Labor Studies of the Hungarian Academy of Sciences (Honorary President: János Tímár; President: György Kővári; Secretary: Ildikó Ékes)

Committee of Sociology of Hungarian Academy of Sciences (President: Péter Somlai; Secretary: Péter Róbert)

Committee of Economic Sociology of the Hungarian Sociological Association (President: Teréz Laky; secretary: Ágnes Crakó)

Hungarian Industrial Relations Association (President: Mária Ladó; Secretary: Erziébet Berki)

Subcommittee of Labour Issues of the Task Force for European Integration (of the Prime Minister) (President: Teréz Laky)

14

Portugal

Ilona Kovács and António Brandão Moniz

The first 10 years of democracy in Portugal (1974–1984) produced an interesting bibliography in the fields of social stratification, labor conflict, and social history. However, since the mid-1980s, significant changes have occurred and are manifested not only in the theoretical diversity but also the preoccupation with the development of more professional teaching of the discipline. At the same time, there was a growing preference for practical intervention and an increase in the amount of research projects and publications. At this time, the first students to graduate in sociology appeared on the labor market, working in municipalities, industrial firms, public health institutions, schools, and research and development (R&D) units. The Portuguese Association for the Sociology of Industry, Organization and Work (APSIOT) was established in 1984. This association has organized many scientific meetings; debates with unionists, managers, and politicians; and has published its scholarly journal, *Organizações e Trabalho* (*Organization and Work*), since 1989.

New research practices have emerged in collaboration with different social actors (entrepreneurs, trade unionists, government entities, local councils, etc.) in the hope that research results will influence the decisions of these

Ilona Kovács • Department of Social Sciences, Faculty for Economics and Management, Technical University of Lisbon, 1200 Lisbon, Portugal. **António Brandão Moniz** • Industrial Psychology Section, Faculty of Sciences and Technology, New University of Lisbon, P-2825-114 Caparica, Portugal.

Worlds of Work: Building an International Sociology of Work, edited by Daniel B. Cornfield and Randy Hodson. Kluwer Academic/Plenum Publishers, New York, 2002.

social actors. We can speak of the emergence and diffusion of a professional culture of sociologists that associates science and occupation not only with scientific quality but also with technical competence and social responsibility.

Some present challenges to sociology of work in Portugal concern the training of sociologists and other specialists who enter into the work sphere. Other challenges point to the evolution of the international division of labor in the context of globalization and the analysis of the activity of transnational firms in Portugal. Even the critical analysis of the ideology and practices of competitiveness has produced increased interest.

But this field of sociology is also increasingly in competition with other related specialties. These are applying remedies of social techniques proposed by the "management gurus." At the same time, we can attest to the participation of sociologists in the social and organizational molding of new technologies in order to promote alternative production systems to computerized Taylorism. It is not compulsory, but the specialists in sociology of work agree that the participation in the revitalization of the economy and of social life is made possible by promoting new work organizational experiences, and not just by prescribing organizational models dominant in the modern industrialized systems.

BRIEF CHARACTERIZATION OF THE EVOLUTION OF THE SOCIOLOGY OF WORK IN PORTUGAL

The Initial Phase of the Sociology of Work (1974–1986)

Portugal, as a member of the European Union, finds itself in this last decade in a specific and complex situation in which modernization implies postindustrial problems, without, however, having yet resolved problems connected to industrialization. And this variety of problems emerges in a context of increasing competition at the European and world levels.

In 1974, a military uprising ended the Salazar dictatorship, in power since 1936. The context in 1974 was characterized first by increasing criticism from businessmen against the incapacity of the Portuguese economy to face the "modern times" that issued from the integration in the European Free Trade Association (EFTA) framework, and the need to increase integration in the European market. The second characteristic is manifested by the insoluble colonial war in Africa, where the midrange militaries were more and more upset and visualizing an impossible military and political end to the warfare. A third characteristic of this mid-1970s period was the growing activity of progressive labor movements. There were ups and downs during the 1960s, but beginning in the 1970s, strikes, labor conflicts, demonstrations, and police and paramilitary aggressive actions were a constant of daily life in both urban and rural areas.

Last, student activism increased, as was evident in the major 1969 national strike, influenced by the American antiwar movements and by the French movement in May 1968. But it was also influenced by the major probability that students had to enter the military forces and become involved in the colonial war. These movements were influential not only among university students but also among students in secondary schools.

Until 1974, the authoritarian regime found suspicious the few sociological activities held in Portugal and there were no university courses in sociology. These years (1960s and mid-1970s) were characterized by workforce emigration to France, as well as academic emigration. Not until the mid-1970s was the teaching of sociology institutionalized and research began to take place (cf. Almeida, 1990).

After the *coup d'état*, the political instability led to a shift in the social conflict process: Military officers (some conservative) headed the new provisional governments with some political left-wing leaders. The workers, with new political and civil conditions, could develop openly their demands (better salaries, rights expression, union organization inside the factories). The increase in conflictual situations (strikes; firms closing down; industrialists that, afraid, ran away to other countries with their assets) lasted until the end of 1975. From 1975 to 1980, the political situation was determined by the development of a social democracy supported by deficient economic structures. During this period, some sociological studies focused on labor conflicts and union movements (Cristóvam, 1982; Santos, Lima, and Ferreira, 1978).

The manufacturing industry, which normally used the raw materials from the colonies, had to restructure completely since 1973 inside a world framework of economic crisis. Many CEO's and property owners, with alliances in the former regime, tried to escape to Brazil, Spain, or other conservative regimes after 1974. In order to maintain national firms, the early government (with pressure from left-wing parties) started a process of nationalization that affected major companies in the steel industry, banking and insurance, cement and chemicals, and transportation and communications.

This process brought new industrial leadership to the "front." This leadership was composed of either military officers that developed administrative careers (or were second-rank seniors), or new political bureaucrats. This industrial leadership negotiated with the International Monetary Fund (IMF) (under the government of Mário Soares) the conditions to support economic restructuring (privatization, end of the agrarian reform, lowering of wage levels, high inflation). Agricultural employment rapidly declined (from around 1.3 million in 1974, to 0.9 million in 1986) and employment increased in the service sector (from 3.7 to 4.1 million), while, in industry, employment remained stable (around 34%).

An International Labor Organization (ILO) document on Portugal indicated that "the Revolution entailed a general increase of income in all socio-economic groups, more especially the wage and salary earners, and includes even the higher income groups." But, as stated in the document, "If the equilibrium in the balance of payments has to be established simultaneously with an employment increase of 8 per cent, average consumption per worker will have to decrease by 13 per cent" (Maton, 1979:109–110). In the late 1970s, living conditions had declined. The unemployment rate doubled between 1975 (4.4%) and 1983 (8.5%). The worsening situation was clearly related to female unemployment. For example, in 1974, the proportion of young unemployed females (ages 15–19 years) was 5.7%; this rate rose to 33.2% in 1978. Even in 1984, this rate was 25.5%. Unemployment was also high among male workers (3.2% in 1974, 16.3% in 1978, and 15.6% in 1984).

Nevertheless, at the end of this period, political expectations of the unions and workers' organizations were frustrated, living conditions worsened, and the economical restructuring, under IMF coordination and European Economic Community (EEC) distant supervision, was in a development stage. Some important foreign investments in automotive, electronics, and chemical industries took place and there was a shift on the export orientation: The European market was decisive for the Portuguese economy, when the EFTA model was no longer suitable.

Within this context the sociology of work emerged in Portugal. Its initial phase was similar in a way to the other areas of sociology: predominantly theoretical orientation linked to the strong influence of French sociology (most Portuguese specialists on labor sciences studied in France). But this orientation was related also to a prevailing mentality of the political and business sectors that only acknowledged the academic value of sociological research and ignored its practical usefulness.

The main research themes were linked to topics on Taylorism and worker consciousness, labor conflicts, cultural identities, changes in social relations in the workplace, and unionism (Cristóvam, 1984; Kovács, 1986; Lima et al., 1982; Patriarca, 1982). These themes reflect the radical changes in Portugal after 1974, namely, the institutional transformations, the institutionalization of industrial relations, and the spread of unionization in companies. Studies about labor conflict showed the effects of economic crisis on unemployment and the precariousness in the labor market, and on labor relations. After 1974, cooperatives and self-managed companies had strong political and social relevance (many achieved this strong legal change after employers gave up their responsibilities, or after strong conflicts that resulted in occupations that followed the need of production management continuity). The self-managing structures and participation thematic were also important research issues in sociology of work during this period (Baptista, Kovacs, and Antunes, 1985).

Many of these studies were descriptive, using qualitative methods of analysis, and applied to manufacturing industries. Surveys were much more difficult due the lack of available funds.

The lacking or relatively reduced financial support in Portugal for sociological research is due, above all, to the fact of attributing only an academic value to this scientific field. An underlying mechanistic and formalist–juridical perspective of the social systems ignored the role played by the social sciences in laying out a scientific basis as to the decisions and their practical usefulness in problem solving (Lima and Rodrigues, 1985).

This situation favored and continues to favor, an academic orientation above all, concerned more with the theoretical and methodological aspects of research and less with its application and a view to practical intervention to resolve social problems. Consequently, its promotion is limited to academic channels and to highly specialized journals.

Professional Identities and Scientific Developments in the Consolidation Phase

This second period may be characterized by a stronger development of the internationalization process in the Portuguese economy. At the end of the 1980s, the public debate emphasized one basic theme: the integration of the European market through the adhesion to EEC in 1986. Relationships with Spain increased significantly, with stronger economic exchanges and investments. The "agrarian issue" signified the end of the agrarian reform with the decrease of employment and investment in this sector. At the same time, public investment on infrastructures changed also the employment structure: Construction activities employed in this period around 8.5% of total civil employment (e.g., 7.3% in 1976), and the financing activities employed 6.4% in 1992.

There is a clear increase of employment in the service sectors (mainly, retail trade and tourism, and proximity services),[1] and a strong decrease in the primary sector (agriculture, fisheries, etc.).[2] However, in recent years, this primary sector increased its employment volume due to the fact many unemployed from industry "returned" to agriculture activity or became new "peasants" (mainly in the dairy sector, cattle producers, forestry, or even bioagriculture employers). Manufacturing industry maintained its importance (1.4 million workers in 1987 and 1997) and was the object of a new investment policy that would lead to a rapid process of modernization and technological development. The unemployment process decreased (5.7% in 1988, 4.1% in

---

[1]With 1.8 million workers in 1987 (43%), and one decade later (1997), 2.5 million (55%).
[2]From 0.9 million workers (22%) in 1987, to 0.6 (13.6) in 1997, according to the Organization for Economic Cooperation and Development (OECD).

1992, and in 6.7% in 1997), stabilizing at round the 6%, with a more equitable distribution among genders.

Yet, in this context, a traditional technocratic mentality was still dominant among policymakers and entrepreneurs that, on one hand, ignored social, organizational, and human factors of the economic efficiency and, on another hand, did not bother with the articulation of social and economical dimension of society. At the same time in the Portuguese industrial structure, there prevails the traditional organizational model, with authoritarian hierarchical relations, formalism, and a low degree of motivation and involvement of the workers. There persisted (and persists!) a technocentric perspective of the innovation, mystifying new technologies, and ignoring their social and organizational implications. A visible tendency toward the increased unemployment and the precariousness of jobs, affected particularly the young,[3] women and the poorly qualified people.[4] At the same time, traditional forms of labor relations, with limited negotiated content (mainly wages and career issues) continued.

To analyze these problems and to search for solutions, sociology of work, together with other specialized sociologies (e.g., sociology of organizations, sociology of employment, industrial sociology, or even women's studies and the sociology of social stratification), played an active role in terms of both teaching and research. However, the social sciences, and particularly sociology, in Portugal, faced greater difficulties than similar disciplines in other countries of the European Union. This difficulty concerns a relatively recent scientific area.

Yet, especially in the mid-1980s, significant changes arose, manifest in the influence of diversity of theoretical tendencies (beyond those of French sociology), reflecting a preoccupation with the development of more professional training, and also a growing wish for the practical intervention of sociologists of work. Kovács highlighted at that time the importance

> of empirical sociological studies, as well as inter-disciplinary studies, in order to influence social actors, showing the complexity of social problems raised by the introduction of new technologies. It is important also to contribute for an adaptation of technological development to social, economical and cultural conditions of the country, to prevent or minors negative consequences or even to contribute to the elaboration of vocational training policies in the field of re-qualification and education." (Kovács, 1986:513)

---

[3]In Portugal in 1996, the probability of young people from 16 to 29 years old would find a job was 50.3% (53.7% for men, and 46.5% for women). In the United States the same probability was 74.6% (Organization for Economic Cooperation and Development, 1998).

[4]For young male, one year after finishing the school, 54.5% will have a temporary job, and 9.2% in part-time. For females, this rates increase to 62.1% (temporary job) and 17.6% (part-time). In US these data are agregated, and are 21.3% for male, and 35.3% for female. All figures are related to 1996 (Organization for Economic Cooperation and Development, 1998).

These were some of the central issues and controversial themes on the role of scientific research sociologists in changing processes.

The part taken by APSIOT (member of International Sociological Association category "C" since 1985) in this debate was very relevant. One of the aims of this association was to promote communication and cooperation, not only among sociologists of the areas concerned, but also between sociologists and other specialists linked to the world of work, as well as between sociologists and diverse social actors.

Debates were organized on priority themes, such as industrial democracy, economic restructuring and the transformation of labor relations, new technologies and work organizations, social criteria for firm performance evaluation, and so on. The participants in these debates were sociologists, as well as representatives of both trade unions and management associations, and private and public companies. These meetings helped to remove some of the main obstacles in these specialized fields of sociology, such as the isolation of individual researchers. Obstacles were revealed by a lack of available field work (case studies, surveys), enclosure in the academic world by the exclusivity of teaching tasks, or institutional research oriented to historical aspects. Finally, these meetings revealed also the lack of dialogue between different actors and researchers (and between the social actors themselves or researchers from different institutions and regions).

One indicator of the sociology of work consolidation (with other related fields, or sociology of industry, organizations and work) in Portugal is the regular publication of the journal *Organizações e Trabalho* by APSIOT, with 22 issues published between 1989 and 1999. Also, there were eight national meetings, two conferences on university curricula issues and, also, a growing volume of research and other publications (newsletters, conference proceedings).

Portuguese society is slowly beginning to seek the specific competence (analytical and technical) of sociologists. Despite this slowness, the demand for new types of sociological research activity is increasing. The area of sociological intervention is expanding in accordance with the acknowledgment that the sociocultural dimension has a crucial role to play in the performance and revitalization of the economy. Its contribution is increasingly being sought in the solution of work and organizational problems.

Thus, in this new phase, apart from university or academic individuals, other professional figures are appearing, such as office consultants concerned with studies/projects, and specialized companies, as well as technicians integrated into public and private enterprises and into state organisms. Researchers seek to collaborate with different social actors (entrepreneurs, trade unionists, governmental associations, local councils, and European Union entities), hoping that the research results will coincide with decisions of these social actors.

The second Sociology of Industry, Organisation and Work (SIOW) in June 1985, closed a first large cycle of development and consolidation in Portugal (cf. Kovács and Moniz, 1987). In this meeting, the question of the professional identity of SIOW was an issue for a debate. This debate on deontology and perspectives for professional intervention included colleagues from other fields of sociology, and was approved in 1992 (at the second Portuguese Congress of Sociology) as the Deontological Code, common to the Portuguese Sociological Association (APS) and APSIOT.

The connection to other research networks outside Portugal as a basic need of the scientific growth of sociology of work in Portugal was a major objective of APSIOT from the beginning of this period (1984–1994). Later on, this aim was accomplished through the active affiliation to ISA. The regular contact and exchanges with North American sociologists began in recent years. As Ferreira de Almeida pointed out:

> Sociology as it has developed in Portugal is actually receptive to different influences, in fact it actively seeks and selects them, whether they come from the rest of Europe, North America or from other sources and areas. Sociology has had time to get used to living with multiple references, with more or less bodies of theory, and to propose different instruments and fields of research. (Portuguese Sociological Association, 1994:495–496)

The major influences, beside Marxianism and functionalism, were the regulation theories, ethnomethodology, and actionalism, among others. But also, as Almeida mentions, "We have no option but to keep a constant eye on the multifarious sociological output outside our own four walls, and to gather there all that which it seems to us will enrich our own world. The small size of our community, together with its open attitude, have prevented the field of sociology in Portugal from splintering into small schools and factions" (Almeida, 1998:87).

There is a strong orientation toward interventions concerning the change of values, mentalities, and work organizations, according to participative management and to motivating and qualifying labor principles. It is in this sense that one can speak of the emergence and diffusion of a professional culture of the sociologists who associate science and occupation (Costa, 1990; Kovács and Moniz, 1987), concerning themselves not merely with scientific quality, but equally with technical capacity and social responsibility.

The most studied themes in Portugal in this period are among others, the new socioeconomic dynamics and the changes in the labor market. Other themes are the new skills and vocational training system, participation and industrial democracy, management and trade union strategies, organizational and technological changes in industry, or job design in flexible production systems (cf. Kovács, 1996). Major diversity could be found not only in theoretical and methodological terms but also in financial sources terms. A part of the studies is also integrated into the European projects coordinated in the scope of CEDEFOP, FAST/TSER, ESPRIT, FORCE/Leonardo, and so on.[5] These kind of studies occur mostly in research centers and academia.

Mainly, the Institute of Employment and Vocational Training (IEFP) funds research projects related to changes in the labor market, new skills, and vocational training systems. More recently, INOFOR (Institute for Training Innovation) is also supporting these kind of studies. Both institutes belong to the Ministry of Labor and Solidarity (MLS). Typically, studies on these new socioeconomic dynamics are of either the new vocational and occupational profiles, or the new configurations of labor markets and the social economy. Maria João Rodrigues (1991) developed a critical perspective of the economics of the labor market, proposing a new framework of an employment system based on the regulation theory. Analyses of the changes that occurred in Portugal after 1974 are the main element of the empirical ground for these studies. Kovács et al. (1994) compared skill requirements according to employers with the labor offer. The unadjustments of the labor market are increasingly important in the context of technological and organizational changes, which are analyzed in different sectors (manufacturing, banking, and retail trade). Rodrigues and Neves (1994) applied these issues to the regional framework.

The main studies referred to next were based on empirical data and published in specialized journals or books. Most of them used the case study method, but others applied their own surveys. Less numerous are the studies based on government census data (essentially from the Statistical Department of the Ministry of Labor).

The participation and industrial democracy field was undertaken by several research centers, and increasingly involves interdisciplinary teams (sociology, psychology, and engineering). Some of this research stressed mostly the attitudes towards work (Cabral et al, 1998; Kovács and Moreno, 1992; Martins, 1996; Silva, 1998) or the learning organizations, focusing, for example, on training and work contents (Moniz et al., 1998). This type of research analyzed the new forms of work organization as semiautonomous working groups, parallel structures, *kaizen* methods for involvement, or even other participatory forms (Cabeças, 1994; Casaca, 1998; Kovács, 1997, 1989; Teixeira, 1994; Urze, 1996, 1998). But this thematic was developed also by computer scientists who cooperated with sociologists in this topic of participation (Moniz and Oliveira, 1996; Soares and Mendonça, 1998) using concepts of CSCW

[5]CEDEFOP (European Center for the Development of Vocational Training); FAST (Forecast and Assessment in Science & Technology); TSER (Targeted Socio-Economic Research; ESPRIT (Strategic Program of Research on Information Technology); FORCE/Leonardo (Programs on Training Innovation . . .).

(computer system for cooperative work) environments, virtual organizations, hybridization or DSS (decision support systems). These studies demonstrate a low level of participation, information, and consultation in the modernization process, either through workers unions or committees. But forms of direct participation related to quality improvement and operational flexibility issues are emerging.

The thematic on management and trade union strategies in the context of economic restructuring is being researched with the support of the Ebert Foundation, or the Foundation for Science and Technology (PRAXIS Program). Different specialists are studying the management strategy development: not only sociologists but also management scientists (Sousa, 1989; Ussman, 1998).

Trade union organization, the unionization of labor force, and the industrial relations systems in Portugal constitute another research theme for many sociologists, stressing organizational problems (Cerdeira, 1997; Cerdeira and Padilha, 1988; Rosa, 1992; Stoleroff, 1990; Stoleroff and Naumann, 1993) or strategies toward employment (Kovács, 1989b; Lima et al., 1992; Lima, 1991) and bargaining policy (Cerdeira, 1988; Dornelas, 1996; Mozzicafreddo, 1994). Since late 1980s, Cerdeira has studied both labor strategies (1998, on the employer organizations; 1997, on unions).

Findings on this theme include the late institutionalization of the labor movement, the weak role of the autonomous negotiation between employers and unions, and excessive intervention of public administration to solve labor conflicts. There is a weak involvement of unions in small and medium-sized enterprises (SMEs), which at the same time are a strong force in the industrial fabric. These firms have little influence in the public policies. A strong division and competition among union movements (CGTP and UGT, independent unions) and a limited range of the bargained collective agreements are also significant findings. Finally, there clearly exists a defensive union strategy around classical demands (wages, working time) and an absence of labor agreement on technological changes, work organization, vocational training, and occupational profiles.

Organizational and technological changes in industry are central issues of the research in sociology of work in Portugal. Most publications (articles or books) show that these research findings have built up in several industrial sectors. Examples can be found in electronics and telecommunications (Assunção and Bilhim, 1998; TDC/FUNDETEC/Dinâmia 1997; Leitão and Moniz, 1996), the printing sector (Reto et al., 1996), the plastics industry (Moura, 1996), the automotive sector (Lima et al., 1996; Moniz, 1998; Neves, 1996; Oliveira, 1996; Stoleroff and Casaca, 1996), and the textile/garment sector (Marques, 1998). Other researches are oriented toward the development of an information society in Portugal (Moniz, 1998; Kovács, 1998) or the organizational framework of technological innovation (Bilhim, 1995). Some general conclusions on this topic may be drawn from a rapid diffusion of information technologies and an evident integration of the industrial strategies into more global economic spaces (Iberian, European, and international). Another finding is related to a diversity of forms of work organization using new technologies. There is a low diffusion of new forms of work organization: Only one-fifth of firms apply non-Tayloristic organizational forms (Kovács, Moniz, and Cerdeira, 1992b). These rapid changes created a strong process of requalification. The employment structure tends to change because of an increased average level of labor force schooling and by unemployment among older and less skilled workers (mainly in electronics and textile sectors). Most of this research was nationally representative field studies, with some studies based on analysis of workplaces changes.

New investments in the automotive and metal engineering sectors were due to globalization of businesses and increased insertion of Portuguese SMEs in the internationalization process (mainly with European networks or transnational enterprises). The research topic on people, organization, and competitiveness (Rodrigues, 1991) overlapped another related, emergent topic: human resources management. Some very interesting studies published on the banking sector (Coelho and Moura, 1998; Machado, 1996) and the textile sector (Marques, 1997) used sectorial surveys and structured interviews of key actors.

A more micro-level research can be found. And, more recently, the issue "job design in flexible production systems" has been revealed as an interesting theme for sociologists of work (Cabeças, 1996; Moniz, 1990; Moniz and Oliveira, 1996). The published work is normally based on case studies, or developed with prototypical structures based on workplaces and firm analysis, using an interdisciplinary approach. In this case, the research involves mostly computer scientists or industrial production engineers and sociologists.

This research reveals the main changing trends (some contradictory in terms of regions or sectors), identifies the firm's labor demand needs confronted with the existent offer in the labor market, and contrasts employer and employee representations of industrial changes. A relevant number of studies presented systematic recommendations for implementation (by firms, social partners, and public administration) or policies development.

Thus, the two main research lines with more practical influence are the issues on skills, training, and labor markets, and the issues on technology design, organizational development, and new production systems. Both are based on surveys and other empirical data collection. The growing importance of this theme is indicated by its inclusion on the agenda of the major

[6]For example, the organization of seminars in computer-aided design (CAD), computer-aided manufacturing (CAM), and computer-aided planning (CAP), organized by the national association of engineers (Ordem dos Engenheiros), and the last ones with international participation, always had themes on "anthropocentric approaches" or "human-oriented production systems."

engineering activities,[6] by the officials from industrial support public agencies, and by those responsible for training and employment policy.

At the same time, some documentation centers recent national meetings with available information in this speciality of sociology,[7] presented bibliographical exhibitions. Diffusion of information organized by the *Boletim SIOT* (more than 40 issues were published by the year 2000), edited by APSIOT, occurred during the 1990s.

In spite of these achievements, some difficulties persist. As stated by J. Madureira Pinto in a Congress of Sociology, "The last years have been particularly difficult for universities. These are institutions that polarize decisive competencies and energies in the national scientific panorama; at the same time, the amount of financing instutions to research projects in our field is decreasing to a level that is worrisome (Pinto, 1993). The impact of this situation has been analyzed, and gave rise to a slight change on the social science policy designed in the corridors of the Ministry of Science and Technology. Some research programs are increasing the financial support to sociological analysis, and the SIOW field is one of the most important in Portugal for sociology (in terms of project funding and scholarships).

The increased market demand for rapidly applicable studies has made visible the need for coping with a pragmatic, empiricist, and economist orientation that reproduces ideas of the management ideology.

Recent Trends

In 1994, during the sixth National Meeting (ENSIOT) there occurred an overall survey of 10 years of associative life. It stressed the fact that this "second cycle of the development of SIOW in Portugal represented a phase of maturing in this scientific field" (Moniz, 1994, p. 7). The third phase, started from this sixth meeting, would make real the remaining objectives designed in 1984, that is, the adoption of a pragmatic site of concerted and united action, as referred by José Baptista (the first President of APSIOT). In the "agenda" concerning the intervention of sociologists, some problems were pointed out, in order to contribute to the better understanding of the sociocultural system of the organizations, the strategies of the social actors, and social relations at work. Other activities are designed to make the organizations more efficient via human-centered technical and organizational innovations (decentralization and participation) or even to avoid or minimize negative social conse-

[7]APSIOT's Documentation Fund (Lisbon); Instituto de Desenvolvimento de Novas Tecnologias-Centro de Robótica Inteligente Library (Monte de Caparica); Documentation Center 25 April (Coimbra); Social Research Center of University of Azores (Ponta Delgada); CIES Library (Lisbon), Centro de Investigação em Sociologica Económica e das Organizações Library (Lisbon), and more recently, the FDSI-JB (José Baptista Industrial Sociology Documentation Fund) at FCT-UNL (Monte de Caparica).

quences, to reduce social costs (unemployment, disqualification, the increase of social inequality) of economic restructuring (cf. Kovács, 1996).

New, related themes for research can be designed as new models of production, changing labor relations, direct participation, teleworking and job design, atypical employment, virtual enterprise and networking.

One can in recent years find several sociological studies and labor–economy research findings that feed one another strongly. These studies are on the emergence of new neighborhood services and its impact on employment (Evaristo, 1999; Simões, 1999), employability trends (Imaginário, 1998; Kovács, 1999; Oliveira, 1998), new qualifications and skills needs (Kovács et al., 1994; Moniz and Kovács, 1997; Rodrigues and Nieves, 1994), and on the effects of industry restructuring on labor markets (Almeida, 1996; Gomes, 1998; Neves, 1996; Oliveira, 1998; Parente, 1998; Rebelo, 1999; Reis et al., 1996; Rita, 1997; Rodrigues and Neves, 1994). Also noteworthy are the studies on nonstandard forms of work, such as part-time jobs (Janeiro, 1998), teleworking (Fiolhais, 1998), and independent jobs (Freire and Delgado, 1996). One conclusion is that increased attention is given to new aspects of employment, and not just to evaluation of impacts on unemployment levels or jobs de-skilling. The regional, juridical or economic approaches are strongly considered in sociology of work research.

On labor relations' issues, the more recent findings show that the major collective agreements become unadjusted to the changed conditions at the firm level due to technological or organizational changes as well as the prevalence of sector bargaining (there are no national or interprofessional agreements on the one hand, and no firm-level agreements on the other). There remains a strong employer protagonism in the modernization processes, when weakened bargaining power of the unions is evident and when the participation structures (workers' committees, safety councils) are weak. This situation can lead to a strong marginalization of the unions in this modernization process and a weakened social control mechanism.

In recent years, sociologists have developed the study of new models of production (Kovács, 1998; Kovács and Castillo, 1998), based on several case studies in different sectors. The study analyzes the most used or sound concepts of production management (e.g., total quality management, Just-in-Time Concepts, lean production, outsourcing, downsizing, anthropocentric systems, reflexive production, etc.), and their implementations in Portugal. The major finding supports the idea that new management and organization principles tend to be applied in firms worried about quality and innovation. Regularities are difficult to find except on the relation participatory structures/increment of productivity, or centralized organizations/disfunctionalities. However, it seems that there is no "one best model" in terms of production management strategy.

Some of "white papers" of the EEC also push the debate in these fields and introduce new references into this debate. Most significant were themes of "information society," "new partnerships for organizational changes," the "learning society and the long-life learning," "social policy and quality of living conditions," and "innovation and competitiveness."

In spite of the development of sociology of work, there are not enough postgraduate professionals in this field in Portugal. Efforts are being made to promote Ph.D.-level and other postgraduate courses, and the trend allows us to perceive a strong increase in the number and quality of experts in SIOW. Another contribution to this development is the fact that, through the fourth Framework Program on Science and Technology of the European Union (1994–1998), particularly its specific social science program, TSER (targeted socioeconomic research), many research teams were involved in international partnerships.

This pushes those teams in the direction of comparative methodologies, acquaintance with research techniques developed by other mature teams, and a better knowledge of their own research materials when facing information from abroad. Such a trend of research organization is restabilized with the new fifth Framework Program (1998–2002).

Whereas it was once usual to think of anything coming from another country as good (!), an attitude quite common among sociologists during the "first phase," this attitude is declining in popularity. There is increased attention toward results and problematic issues developed and presented within Portuguese research projects. Authors, recognized scholars, and researchers are more involved in public debate or, in some cases, in government tasks or other political activities. One can assist the increase in public importance of the specificity of sociological analysis of or research findings.

PRESENT CHALLENGES IN THE PORTUGUESE SOCIOLOGY OF WORK

The Training of Sociologists and Other Interventions in the Work Area

One of the main challenges, as mentioned earlier, is the training of sociologists in the sense of facilitating their integration into the labor market, and not just the academic sphere. Beyond training sociologists to achieve adequate competence, is the very important training of professionals whose activity is central to the shaping of the work sphere, such as economists, managers, and engineers, among others. In spite of the fact that, today, the social and psychological parameters are increasingly included in the training programs of these "interventionists" in the working world, a strong "technical" orientation continues to predominate.

Particularly important is the inclusion of the labor and organization sciences in the vocational training of those who conceive and/or adopt new technical solutions (information systems specialists, systems analysts, engineers, and technicians). These experts, in proceeding toward processes of computerization and automatization, do not limit themselves to altering the technical system but also interfere in the social system. Therefore, it is fundamental that, they either have training that enables them to intervene in the social dimension, or that they otherwise communicate and cooperate with other specialists who have the necessary knowledge relating to the social and organizational dimensions.

It is worth mentioning that the National Association of Engineers (Ordem dos Engenheiros) recommends sociology as a complementary training course for its own course work. This also represents a challenge to sociologists when they have to answer this kind of solicitation, and when a new path to cooperation is under way.

Dispute with Other Specialists

Increasingly applied sociological researchers competes with other specialists (economists, managers or "wide-scoped" consultants) in disputes over the same field of intervention (human resources management, organizational behavior). These specialists do not have a large and deep knowledge of sociology and are only familiar with the best-selling literature. The superficial assimilation of certain notions and discourses about human behavior by these specialists results in a simplified reductionism and mechanical application of promising techniques for change, elaborated by the amply promoted and publicized "gurus" of downsizing, reengineering, or benchmarking. An alternative approach and action when confronted with the remedies of social techniques, disembodied from a system of coherent knowledge (produced by sociology of work and other social sciences) constitutes one of the challenges to sociologists of labor.

Sociologists demonstrate that it is not possible to apply "techniques" of motivation, participation, or innovation successfully without understanding the attitudes, motivations, rationality forms, collective behavior (interactions, influences, communication), organizational structure, or the variable mechanisms of structures and mentalities changes.

Organizational change is not a question of the application of social techniques, which would please many managers and consultants alike. It is a question of comprehending the function of the sociocultural system and its different, and even contradictory, rationalities. The space of intervention of the sociologists is precisely that: It contributes to the comprehension and analysis of the sociocultural system, creating conditions for reflection on the problems, and on the choice between alternative solutions.

We can observe a trend of dilution of disciplinary boundaries. However, this process is ambiguous. In some cases it can promote cooperation among scientific fields, the creation of interdisciplinary teams, but in other cases it creates fractal situations when economists or management scientists develop research projects in the field of sociology or research of a sociological nature, without real interdisciplinary teams or cooperation with sociologists.

Participation of Sociologists in the Social and Organizational Molding of the New Technologies

The growing diffusion of the information technologies into several fields of activity, with its quantitative and qualitative implications at work, constitutes a challenge for sociologists: Do the new technologies create or destroy, qualify or disqualify employment, centralize or decentralize information and decisions? In relation to these questions are confrontations between optimistic and pessimistic conceptions. Some seek to prove that the new technologies lead to disqualification and to unemployment; others, on the contrary, announce the increase of employment in quantity and in quality.

In reality, there is not a single tendency; rather, both tendencies are verifiable in accordance with a series of organizational and sociopolitical variables, such as strategy of industrial development, labor market structure, cost of production factors, manpower policy, education and training systems, forms of work organization, management methods, and organizational culture, among others. There is not one, single, unique tendency, but there are many possible futures. One of the possible futures refers to computerized Taylorism, in which computerization systematically and permanently control men and machines, and in which one opts for centralist and determinist hardware and software structures associated with a neo-Taylorist work organization. In the face of this, it is very important to develop alternative, productive systems in which potentialities of computerized technology complement each other, with specifically human capacities associating themselves with new forms of work organization.

These alternative systems are directed toward the valorization of human abilities and skills in the context of participative and flexible organizations. This orientation implies the shaping of technology to improve competencies and decision-making capacity of people, allowing, at the same time, increased economic performance. Sociologists, in the context of the diffusion of new technologies, cannot only participate in the conception of alternative systems and pilot experiments in an interdisciplinary perspective, but can also evaluate advanced technological systems already functioning, using human–social criteria, and analyze and search out solutions for problems linked to the negative effects of the new technologies (cf. Kovács and Moniz, 1990a).

This kind of intervention needs the collaboration between work sociologists and psychologists, and entrepreneurs, managers, engineers, operators, and trade unionists, and requires a capacity for communication, learning, and work in multi- or interdisciplinary teams.

The fact that human and social aspects tend to be undervalued is due not only to the subsistence of a traditional mentality marked profoundly by Taylorism, but also the attitudes of the social scientists themselves. According to Chris Clegg and Martin Corbett (1987), social scientists themselves have contributed substantially to their own scanty influence. They have failed to persuade others as to the legitimacy and significance of the human aspects of the advanced technology of production. These lapses on the part of the social scientists are connected to the objectives of the research, with their emphases and their style.

The research projects concerning CIM (computer-integrated manufacturing), which, in Europe, are developed mostly at an international level in the scope of the ESPRIT Program, constitute an opportunity for the contribution of the social sciences. Various research groups have demonstrated the possibility of this participation.[8] The same applies in Portugal, as shown by the research projects developed by sociology teams working with engineers at the UNINOVA-CRI Intelligent Robotics Center, and at INESC-Porto (Institute of Systems and Computers Engineering). Some of these are joint projects, or projects with international teams. Relevantly, unions are increasingly more interested in these types of research activities and are involved in these projects.

Improved Competitiveness and the Sociology of Work

Another challenge concerns the participation of sociologists in the revitalization of the economy, above all, in the improvement of the competitiveness of enterprises. Sociologists can intervene in innovation processes at the firm level, most notably in work organization, as well as in evaluation of the results based in social criteria. They can indicate the principal malfunctions of the existing work organization, its costs, and suggest changes. They can show how taking advantage of the potentials of the new technologies promotes adequate changes in the work organization and increases participation.

This activity implies a divergence of interests and points of view when the entrepreneurs expect, first of all, the improvement of the competitiveness of their enterprise, even with high social costs. In turn, sociologists wish to reconcile improved in competitiveness and quality of life at work, and in society in general.

The preoccupation of sociologists with the quality of life in general and,

---

[8]Among others are the Institute of Science and Technology at the University of Manchester (UMIST) and the group of Social and Applied Psychology at the University of Sheffield (SAPU) in Great Britain, the Institut Arbeit und Technik (Gelsenkirchen) in Germany, the group of Sociology and Human Resources at the Danish Technological Institute (Taastrup).

particularly at work, is so much more important than how much an atmosphere of competitiveness exists as an aim in itself. The production model that, at present, generates the greatest fascination in the race toward competitiveness is the "lean production model." Fundamentally, this model contains various risks. In this context, it is important that work sociologists, in a critical position (Castillo, 1994) with respect to the Taylorist–Fordist model, do not turn into ideologists of the lean production model (Kovács, 1994; Kovács and Castillo, 1998).

It is important that sociological research call attention both to the ambiguity of some institutionalized forms of direct participation and some of new forms of work organization utilized. Frequently, promotion, in the technical perspective of some forms of direct participation, does not, in fact, increase participation, since it leaves intact the principal factors of nonparticipation linked to the existing work organization. The promotion of polyvalence and group work can be carried out with the objective to reduce the number of employees, without improving qualifications, maintaining the hierarchical relations and the content prior to the job. But these same forms can be intermediate in a process of innovation oriented toward the global transformation of the enterprise.

In spite of the upsurge of a certain consensus concerning the necessity of promoting participation, manifest in the great promotion and multiplication of its forms, participation might not in fact increase. Paradoxically, the promotion of participation in accordance with subjacent objectives can result in a mere formal participation that leads to apathy and even to increased pressure on, and control of, individuals and groups, resulting in the loss of autonomy (Casaca, 1995).

With increasingly precarious jobs, unemployment, abandonment of the full employment policy and social well-being programs in the name of competitiveness, we find ourselves confronted with a paradoxical evolution. For some, the job and the firm turn into a place of citizenship, sociability, and the expression of subjectivity. For others, a significant sector of the population, destined for the problems of poverty and social security, the right to work is denied at a time when financial resources are being increasingly reduced.

It is necessary to widen the research object into nonwork activities (leisure time, domestic and education activities, etc.) in its articulation with working activities to identify new needs of workers for flexible working hours and for new forms of work. This analysis also requires new, interdisciplinary approaches into anthropology, ergonomy, psychology, geography, and other sociological specialization (family, gender, culture).

The study of the evolution of the international division of labor in the context of a globalization of the economy also constitutes a challenge to the sociology of work. The constant search for the most advantageous localities for selling and producing products and services on the part of the transnational companies tends to lead toward segmentation of the productive process and to a spatial division of labor. It is important to know the location of knowledge-intensive and routine tasks—either among or within firms, or among or within regions.

In this process, professional work linked to a high technology is inclined to be situated in restricted areas of the world that are equipped with material infrastructures and advanced information–communication facilities. Routine operations are inclined to be either relocated to regions in which there is a cheap labor force, or to be otherwise automated in factories situated within the proximity of the social headquarters of the transnational company.

In this context, the dilemma for the sociologists is either to promote their teaching and research activities in a more critical perspective, or to make themselves more instrumental in the service of competitiveness.

The first option implies the distance that separates discourse (post-Fordism, information or knowledge of society, etc.) and the dominant practices by way of the study of concrete situations. And at the same time, that option should alert to the serious social consequences of the race in the direction of competitiveness, creating a greater awareness in respect to other humanized alternatives. The second option means an identification with the ideology of competitiveness and an orientation toward "human engineering," in the way that C. Wright Mills characterized (and criticized) it.

CONCLUSION

We can speak about the challenge of choice, on the part of the sociologists, between alternative functions. They can be social technicians for solving administrative problems, researchers channeled in the direction of "pure" or academic science, or even agents of change, that is to say, researchers involved in social innovation actions. As agents of change, they can consider themselves as specialists with a vocation toward the elaboration of change projects, ready to be applied in companies, or as participants and coauthors in processes of innovation—in this latter case, a new model of scientific research that breaks with the positivist–empiricist model. Rather than making a declaration of neutrality, the model compromises itself with certain values, such as the humanization of labor, the improvement of the quality of life at work (and quality of living conditions), and the democratization of organizations. It has been, as an objective, the development of the social competence of the nonscientists. In other words, in a manner different from that of the 1960s and of the 1970s, it is possible to unite critical perspectives and research oriented toward practical usefulness.

However, this orientation implies a latent conflict between decision makers and sociologists, due to their divergent interests. This relationship can become particularly quarrelsome when the decision makers expect from the researchers immediate help with their problems and, in turn, the researchers concern themselves with the transformation of social practices in accordance with new values. Even when informed people listen to sociological discourse acknowledging the usefulness of sociological research, the divergence of interests and points of view remains. For enlightened decision makers, social innovation in the first place is a means of improving economic results. For the socially committed researcher, innovation is first a way of improving the quality of working life.

REFERENCES

Almeida, J. F. 1990. Opening speech in Associaçã Portugesa de Sociologia: *A Sociologia e a Sociedade Portuguesa na viragem do Século. Actas do 1 Congresso Português de Sociologia,* Associação Portuguesa de Sociologia/Fragmentos, Lisbon.

Almeida, A. J. 1996. Sistema regional de inovação, desenvolvimento industrial e políticas municipais, in APSIOT: *Novas Dinâmicas Socioeconomicas,* Lisbon: CML-APSIOT-CML.

APSIOT. 1996. *Novas dinâmicas socioeconómicas.* Lisbon: APSIOT-CML.

APSIOT. 1998. *Formação, Trabalho e Tecnologia.* Oeiras: Celta.

Associaçao Portuguesa de Sociolgia. 1992a. *Perfil dos sociólogos presentes no 2º Congresso Português de Sociologia.* Lisbon: Author.

Associação Portuguesa de Sociolgia. 1992b. *Código deontológico.* Lisbon: Author.

Assunção, F., and Bilhim, J. 1998. Organização, tecnologia e actores sociais. In *Formação, Trabalho e Tecnologia,* edited by APSIOT. Oeiras: Celta.

Baptista, J., Kovács, I., and Antunes, C. L. 1985. *Uma gestão alternativa.* Lisbon: Relógio d'Água.

Bilhim, J. 1995. *Gestão de ciência e tecnologia.* Lisbon, ISCSP.

Cabeças, José M. 1994. "Estruturas paralelas em sistemas de produção industrial." *Organizações e Trabalho,* 12. APSIOT.

Cabral, M. V. et al. 1998. *Atitudes sociais dos portugueses: Orientações perante o trabalho.* Lisboa: ICS.

Capucha, L. 1998. "Exclusão social e acesso ao emprego: Paralelas que podem convergir." *Sociedade e Trabalho,* No. 3. Lisbon: MTS.

Casaca, S. F. 1995. "A socialização dos indivíduos e a ideologia empresarial," *Organizações e Trabalho.* No. 14. Lisbon: APSIOT.

Casaca, S. F. 1998. "O envolvimento dos trabalhadores no melhoramento contínuo (kaizen)." *Organizações & Trabalho,* Vol. 20. Lisbon: APSIOT.

Cerdeira, M. C., and E. Padilha. 1990. *A sindicalização e alguns comportamentos sindicais.* Lisbon: MESS.

Throughout the references, APISOT = Associação Portuguesa de Profissionais em Sociologia Industrial das Organizações e do Trabalho (Portuguese Association for Sociology of Industry, Organization, and Work); IEFP = Instituto de Emprego e Formação Profissional (Institute of Employment and Professional Training).

Cerdeira, M. C., 1997. *A evolução da sindicalização portuguesa de 1974 a 1995.* Lisbon: MQE.

Cerdeira, M. C. 1989. "Estratégias sindicais na concertação social e participação sindical no política económica." *Economia e Sociedade, Rivista do Centro de Estudos Economia e Sociedade, Lisbon, n°* 1:105–116.

Cerdeira, M. C. 1998. *O movimento associativo patronal português de 1834 a 1994.* Lisbon: MTS.

Clegg, C., and M. Corbett. 1987. "Research and Development into 'Humanizing' Advanced Manufacturing Technology. In *The Iluman Side of Advanced Manufacturing Technology*, edited by Wall, Clegg, and Kemp. Chichester, UK: Wiley.

Coelho, T., and R. Moura. 1998. "As novas competências emergentes: Estudo de caso no sector bancário." In *Formação, Trabalho e Tecnologia*, edited by APSIOT. Oeiras: Celta.

da Costa, A. F. 1990. "Cultura Profissional dos Sociólogos." In *A sociologia e a sociedade Portuguesa na Viragem do Século*, Fragmentos, Vol. I. Lisbon: IEFP.

Cristóvam, L. 1982. *Os conflitos de trabalho em 1979—Breve abordagem sociológica.* Lisbon: Ministério do Trabalbo e Soledariadeade.

de Almeida, João Ferreira. 1998. "Sociology: Some current problems." In *Terra Nostra: Challenges, Controversies and Languages for Sociology and the Social Sciences in the 21st Century*, edited by A. N. Almeida. ISA.

Dornelas, A. 1996. "Interrogações sobre a concertação social." In *Novas Dinâmicas Socioeconomicas*, edited by APSIOT. Lisbon: APSIOT-CML.

European Foundation for the Improvement of Living and Working Conditions. 1987. *Participation in Technological Change.* Dublin:

Evaristo, T. 1999. "Empregos e formação no âmbito dos serviços de proximidade." *Sociedade e Trabalho*, No. 5, Lisbon: Ministério do Trabalbo e Soledariadeade.

Ferreira, J. M. C. et al. 1996. *Entre a Economia e a Sociologia.* Oeiras: Celta.

Fiolhais, R. 1998. *Sobre as implicações jurídico-laborais do teletrabalho subordinado em Portugal.* Lisboa: IEFP.

Freire, J. 1993. *Sociologia do Trabalho: Uma introdução*, Porto: Afrontamento.

Freire, J. 1998. "Empresas e organizações: mudanças e modernização. In *Portugal, que modernidade?*, edited by J. M. L. Viegas and A. F. de Costa. Lisbon: Celta.

Freire, J., and L. Delgado. 1996. Os trabalhadores independentes. In *Novas Dinâmicas Socioeconomicas*, edited by APSIOT. Lisbon: APSIOT.

Gomes, C. T. 1998. "Caracterização do desemprego de longa duração numa área crítica a sul do Tejo." *Organizações & Trabalho*, No. 18/19. Lisbon: APSIOT.

Graça, L. 1985. "Condições de trabalho e saúde ocupacional: uma abordagem psicosocial." *Revista Portuguesa de Saúde Pública* 3(2). Lisbon: ENSP.

Imaginário, Luis. 1998. "Problemas de inserção profissional dos adultos pouco escolarizados." *Sociedade e Trabalho.* No. 2. Lisbon: Ministério do Trabalbo e Soledariadeade.

Janeiro, M. J. 1998. *O trabalho a tempo parcial na regulamentação colectiva.* Lisboa: MTS.

Kovács, I., M. C. Conceição, M. Barrida, and A. B. Moriz.. 1994. *Qualificações e Mercado de Trabalho.* Lisbon: IEFP.

Kovács, I. 1986. " Sociologia Industrial, das Organizações e do Trabalho em Portugal: Situação e perspectivas nos anos 80. *Pensamiento Iberoamericano 9.*

Kovács, I. 1996. "The Sociology of Work in Portugal: Situation and Perspective." *Proceedings of the World Meeting of Labor Studies and Sociology of Work*, Mayaquez: University of Puerto Rico.

Kovács, I. 1997. "Mudanças técnico-organizacionais do trabalho e participação." *Cadernos Noroeste*, 10(1):69–84.

Kovács, I. 1998. Trabalho, qualificações e aprendizagem ao longo da vida: Ilusões e problemas da sociedade da informação. In *Formação, Trabalho e Tecnologia*, edited by APSIOT. Oeiras: Celta.

Kovács, I. 1999. "Qualificação, formação e empregabilidade." *Sociedade e Trabalho* 4: Lisbon: Ministério do Trabalbo e Soledariadeade.

Kovács, I., and J. J. Castillo. 1998. *Novos modelos de produção*. Oeiras: Celta.

Kovács, I., and A. B. Moniz. (eds.) 1987. *Problemas da Sociologia Industrial, das Organizações e do Trabalho em Portugal*. Lisbon: APSIOT.

Kovács, I., and A. B. Moniz. 1990A. *Prospects for Anthropocentric Productions Systems in Portugal*, Commission of the European Communities, APS Research Papers Series Vol. 16, December 1990 (FOP 260).

Kovács, I., and A. B. Moniz. 1990b. "Trabalho e Organização no Sistema de Produção Integrada por Computador", in: Associação Portuguesa de Sociologia, *A Sociologia e a Sociedade Portuguesa na viragem do Século. Actas do 1⁰ Congresso Português de Sociologica*, Vol. II., pp. 45–61. Lisbon: Associação Portuguesa de Sociologia/ Framentos.

Kovács, I., and A. B. Moniz. 1992. "La introducción de sistemas antropocentricos automatizados en Portugal." *Sociología del Trabajo* 16, Madrid.

Kovács, I., and C. Moreno. 1992. Tecnologias de informação e valores: Atitudes face ao trabalho. *Organizações e Trabalho* 7–8: APSIOT.

Kovács, I., A. B. Moniz, and M. C. Cerdeira. 1992. *Mudança tecnológica e organizacional do trabalho na indústria*. CGTP, DGI.

Leitão, M., and A. B. Moniz. 1996. "Novas qualificações no sector de telecomunicações." In *Novas Dinâmicas Socioeconomicas*, edited by APSIOT. Lisbon: APSIOT-CML.

Lima, M. P. 1991. "Relações de trabalho, estratégias sindicais e emprego." *Análise Social* 26(114):1299–1366.

Lima, M. P., and M. J. Rodriques. 1985. "As Ciências Sociais em Portugal." *Análise Social*.

Lima, M. P. et al. 1982. "Notas para uma história da organização do trabalho em Portugal (1900–1980)." *Análise Social* 18(72–73–74).

Lima, M. P. et al. 1996. "Organização da indústria automóvel na península de Setúbal." In *Novas Dinâmicas Socioeconomicas*, edited by APSIOT. Lisbon:

Lima, M. P. et al. 1992. *A acção sindical e o desenvolvimento*. Lisbon: Salamandra.

Lopes, A., and L. Reto. 1992. *Cooperativismo e sindicalismo*. Lisbon: Inscoop.

Lopes, E. et al. 1989. *Portugal: o desafio dos anos 90*. Lisbon: Presença.

Machado, Carolina. 1996. "Os recursos humanos na banca: o desafio da mudança." In *Novas Dinâmicas Socioeconomicas*, edited by APSIOT. Lisboa: APSIOT-CML.

Marques, A. P. 1997. "Espaço de qualificação profissional." *Cadernos Noroeste* 10(1):

Marques, A. P. 1998. "Percursos socioprofissionais no sector têxtil." In *Formação, Trabalho e Tecnologia*, edited by APSIOT. Oeiras: Celta.

Martins, A. 1996. "Da escolha de uma profissão às atitudes perante o trabalho." In

Novas Dinâmicas Socioeconomicas, edited by APSIOT. Lisbon: CML-APSIOT.

Mateus, A.1989. "1992 :A realização do mercado interno e os desafios da construção de um espaço social europeu." *Economia e Sociedade* 1. Lisbon: APSIOT-CML

Maton, J. 1979. "Income distribution and income policy." In *Employment and basic needs in Portugal*, edited by International Labor Organization. Geneva: International Labor Organization, 1979.

Moniz, A. B. 1989. "Modernização da indústria portuguesa: Análise de um inquérito sociológico." *Economia e Sociedade* 1. Lisbon: APSIOT-CML.

Moniz, A. B. 1996. Discurso de Abetura do VI Encontro Nacional. Pp 7–9 in Apsiot, Novas Dinâmicas Socioeconómicas—Que desafios para a Sociologia Industrial, das Organizações e do Trabalho? VI Encontro Nacional Proceedings. Lisbon: CML-APSIOT.

Moniz, A. B. 1998. "Políticas de emprego e sociedade da informação: para uma sociedade do conhecimento." *Sociedade e Trabalho*, 2.

Moniz, A. B. 1998. "Novos modelos de produção na indústria automóvel? Análise de uma fábrica de motores." In *Formação, Trabalho e Tecnologia*, edited by APSIOT. Oeiras: Celta.

Moniz, A. B. 1990. Aplicação de robots em Portugal, *Organizações e Trabalho* 3/4:59–73.

Moniz, A. B., and I. Kovács. 1997. *Evolução das Qualificação e das Estruturas de Formação em Portugal*. Lisbon: OEFP.

Moniz, A. B., and P. Oliveira. 1996. "Hipóteses para uma hibridação de um sistema flexível de produção." In *Novas Dinâmicas Socioeconomicas*, edited by APSIOT. Lisbon: APSIOT-CML.

Moniz, A. B. et al. 1998. "Sobre o conteúdo formativo do trabalho." In *Formação, Trabalho e Tecnologia*, edited by APSIOT. Oeiras: Celta.

Moura, R. 1996. "Flexibilidade organizacional em ambiente de automação." In *Novas Dinâmicas Socioeconomicas*, edited by APSIOT. Lisbon: APSIOT-CML.

Mozzicafreddo, J. 1994. "Concertação social e exclusão social." *Organizações e Trabalho* 12.

Never, A. O. 1996. "Avaliação *ex ante* do impacte de grandes projectos sobre o desenvolvimento local: Um contributo metodológico a propósito do projecto Ford/VW." *Sociologia* 22:

Olivera, L. 1998. *Inserção profissional: O caso da reestruturação dos lanifícios na Covilhã*. Lisbon: Cosmos.

Olivera, L. et al. 1995. *Estudo socioeconómico da Marinha Grande e área envolvente*. Lisbon: OEFP.

Parenta, C. 1998. "Formação, competitividade empresarial e trajectórias profissionais." In *Formação, Trabalho e Tecnologia*, edited by APSIOT. Oeiras: Celta.

Patriarca, F. 1982. "Taylor no Purgatório: O trabalho na metalomecânica pesada." *Análise Social*, 18(71):432–530.

Pinto, J. M. 1993. "Discurso do Presidente da Associação Portuguesa de Sociologia." In *Estruturas sociais e desenvolvimento*, Vol. 1, edited by APS. Lisboa: Fragmentos.

Pinto, G. A. 1998. *O trabalho das crianças*. Oeiras: Celta.

The Portuguese Sociological Association. 1994. "The Round Table: Sociology in Portugal." *International Sociology* 9(4):

Rebelo, G. 1999. *A (in)Adaptação no Trabalho*. Oeiras: Celta.

Reis, J. et al. 1996. *Potencialidades e factores de dinamização do concelhos de Águeda e Estarreja,* Lisbon: OEFP.

Reto, L. et al. 1996. *O sector das indústrias gráficas e transformação do papel.* Lisbon: IEFP.

Rita, J. Palma. 1997. *As organizações públicas estatais na qualificação das regiões.* Lisbon: OEFP.

Rodrigues, A. N. 1994. "Cultura Organizacional e mudança na Administração Pública." *Organizações e Trabalho* 11.

Rodrigues, M. Jo. 1991. *Competitividade e recursos humanos.* Lisbon: Dom Quixote.

Rodrigues, M. J., and A. O. Neves. 1994. *Políticas de Reestruturação.* Lisbon: OEFP.

Rosa, T. 1991. "As mulheres e o sindicalismo." *Organizações e Trabalho* 5/6.

Rosa, T. 1998. *Relações Sociais de Trabalho e Sindicalismo Operário em Setúbal.* Porto: Edição Afrontamento.

Rosa, T. 1996. "A qualificação no trabalho." *Organizações e Trabalho* 15.

Santos, M. L. L., M. P. Lima, and V. M. Ferreira. 1978. *Movimentos Sociais e Conflitos Laborais em Portugal.* Porto: Afrontamento.

Serra, H. 1998. "Tecnologias de informação, emprego e organização do trabalho." In *Formação, Trabalho e Tecnologia,* edited by APSIOT. Oeiras: Celta.

Silva, R. B. 1998. "Para uma análise da satisfação com o trabalho." *Sociologia-Problemas e Práticas* 26:

Simões, F. 1999. "Serviços de proximidade." *Sociedade e Trabalho* 5:

Soares, A. L., and J. M. Mendonça. 1998. "Processos de desenvolvimento técnico-organizacional." In *Formação, Trabalho e Tecnologia,* edited by APSIOT. Oeiras: Celta.

Sousa, F. H. 1989. "Para uma abordagem sistémica da classe empresarial portuguesa." *Economia e Sociedade* 1:67–104.

Stolerhoff, A. 1990. *O Padrão de Relações Industriais emergentes em Portugal.*" *Organizações e Trabalho,* 2:49–79.

Stolerhoff, A. 1996. "Sociologia e a gestão dos recursos humanos." *Organizações e Trabalho* 15:105–113.

Stolerhoff, A., and S. F. Casaca. 1998. "Intensidade de trabalho e satisfação na produção magra." In *Formação, Trabalho e Tecnologia,* edited by APSIOT. Oeiras: Celta.

Stoleroff, A., and R. Naumann. 1993. "A sindicalização em Portugal: a sua medida e a sua distribuição." *Sociologia-Problemas e Práticas* 14.

TDC/FUNDETEC/Dinâmia. 1997. *As tecnologias de informação e electrónica em Portugal: Desenvolvimento competitivo e recursos humanos.,* Lisbon: DGI.

Teixeira, C. 1994. "Participação dos trabalhadores: evolução dos quadros de referência." *Organizações e Trabalho* 12:

Teixeira, C. 1996. *Organização do Trabalho e Factor Humano.* Lisbon: OEFP.

Urze, P. 1996. "Equipas de trabalho: Novas exigências na gestão dos recursos humanos," *Organizações e Trabalho,* 15:43–65.

Urze, P. 1998. "Equipas de trabalho: Condições de sucesso/insucesso (estudo de caso na indústria têxtil." In *Formação, Trabalho e Tecnologia,* edited by APSIOT. Oeiras: Celta.

Ussman, A. M. 1998. "Influências culturais sobre a função empresarial no feminino." *Organizações & Trabalho* 20.

Variz, P. E. 1998. *Fundamentos económicos e sociológicos das IPSS.* Lisbon: Ed. Vulgata.

APPENDIX: INSTITUTIONAL BASES OF SOCIOLOGY
OF WORK RESEARCH IN PORTUGAL

Research Centers

SOCIUS (ISEG-UTL)
Research Center on Sociology of Enterprise and Organizations
Institute for Economics and Management (ISEG)
Technical University of Lisbon (UTL)
Rua Miguel Lupi, 20
P-12+9-078 Lisbon
Phone: 351 213951787
Fax: 351 213951783
E-mail: *socius@iseg.utl.pt*
Website: http://www.iseg.utl.pt/socius/index

CIES (ISCTE)
Research Center for Sociological Studies
Institute for Work and Enterprise Sciences (ISCTE)
Av. Forças Armadas
P-1600 Lisboa
Phone: 351 217935050
Fax: 351 217964710
Website: http://www.cies.iscte.pt/

CRI (UNINOVA)
Research Unit on Social Implications of Automation
Center for Intelligent Robotics at UNINOVA
FCT Campus
P-2825 Monte de Caparica
Phone: 351 212948527
Fax: 351 2129557786
Website: http://www.uninova.pt/CRI/GSIA/

Dinâmia (ISCTE)
Research Center on Sociology of Enterprise and Organizations
Institute for Work and Enterprise Sciences (ISCTE)
Av. Forças Armadas
P-1649-026 Lisboa
Phone: 351 217938638
Fax: 351 217940042
E-mail: dinamia@dinamia.iscte.pt
Website: http://www.dinamia.iscte.pt/

CES-UA (University of Azores)
Center of Social Studies
Apartado 1422

Rua Mãe de Deus
P-9500-539 Ponta Delgada Codex
Phone: 351 296653155 / 296653582
Fax: 351 296653582
Website: http://www.uac.pt/Historia/ces.html

CES-UC (University of Coimbra)
Center of Social Studies
Colégio de S. Jerónimo
Praça D. Dinis, Apartado 3087
P-3000 Coimbra
Phone: 351 239826459
Fax: 351 239829076
E-mail: ces@sonata.fe.uc.pt

IS-FLUP (University of Porto)
Institute of Sociology
Faculty of Humanities (FL)
University of Porto (UP)
Rua do Campo Alegre, 1055
P-4150-564 Porto
Phone: 351 226077100
Fax: 351 226091610

ICS (University of Lisbon)
Institute for Social Sciences
Av. Forças Armadas, Edifício ISCTE - 1º andar
P-1600 Lisbon
Phone: 351 217995000
Fax: 351 217964953
Website: http://www.ics.ul.pt

ICS-UM (University of Minho)
Institute of Social Sciences (ICS)
Campus de Gualtar
P-4710-057 Braga
Phone: 351 2139350800
Fax: 351 253676966
Website: http://www.ics.um.pt/

Grant Agencies

Foundation for Science and Technology (FCT)
Av. D. Carlos I, 126 - 2º
P-1200 Lisboa
Phone:+351 213979021

Fax: 351 213907481
Website: http://www.fct-mct.pt

Institute of Employment and Vocational Training (IEFP)
Av. José Malhoa
P-1600 Lisboa
Phone: 351 217227000
Fax: 351 217270433
Website: http://www.iefp.pt

Luso-American Foundation for Development (FLAD)
Rua do Sacramento à Lapa 21
P-1249-090 Lisbon
Phone: 351 213935800
Fax: 351 213963358
E-mail: faldport@flad.pt

Foundation Calouste Gulbenkian (FCG)
Av. de Berna
P-1000 Lisboa
Phone: 351 217935131
Fax: 51 217935139
Website: http://www.fcg.pt

Institute for Training Innovation (INOFOR)
Ministry of Labor and Solidarity (MTS)
Rua Soeiro Pereira Gomes, 7
P-1600 Lisboa
Phone: 351 217946200
Fax: 351 217946201
E-mail: inofor@mail.telepac.pt
Website: http://www.inofor.mts.pt

Observatory of Employment and Vocational Training (OEFP)
Av. Defensores de Chaves, 95
P-1000 Lisboa
Phone: 351 217933301
Fax: 351 217954010
Website: http://oefp.iefp.pt

Institute for the Development and Inspection of Working Conditions (IDICT)
Ministry of Labor and Solidarity (MTS)
Praça de Alvalade, 1
P-1700 Lisbon
Phone: 351 217978051
Fax: 351 217934047
Website: http://www.idict.mts.pt

Directorate General for Employment and Vocational Training (DGEFP)
Ministry of Labor and Solidarity (MTS)
Praça de Londres, 2
P-1049-056 Lisbon
Phone: 351 218429010
Fax: 351 218465272
E-mail: dgefp@mail.telepac.pt

Observatory of Employment and Vocational Training of the Autonomous Region
    of Azores (OEFP-RAA)
Rua Margarida de Chaves, 135
P-9500-088 Ponta Delgada
Phone: 35196 304470
Fax: 35196 304488
E-mail: sreas.gt@mail.telepac.pt
Website: http://www.oefp-raa.pt/

Specialized Journals

Organizações e Trabalho
Semestral journal of APSIOT (Portuguese Association for Sociology of Industry, Or-
    ganizations and Work)
Editor: Celta Editora
Director: António Brandão Moniz
Rua de Xabregas 20, 3°, sala 14
1900-440 Lisbon
Phone: 351 218687941
Website: http://www.apsiot.pt/apsiot_4.htm

Sociedade e Trabalho
Trimestral Journal of the Ministry of Labor and Solidarity
Editor: DEPP-MTS
Director: António Oliveira das Neves
Praça de Londres, 2 - 2°
P-1049-056 Lisboa
Phone: tel. 351 218441220
Fax: 351 218406171
E-mail: depp.cides@deppmts.gov.pt
Website: http://www.deppmts.gov.html

Associations

APSIOT
Portuguese Association for Sociology of Industry, Organizations and Work
Rua de Xabregas 20. 3°, sala 14
P-1900-440 Lisbon
Phone: 351 218687941
Website: http://www.apsiot.pt

15

Sweden

Casten von Otter

INTRODUCTION

The distinguishing features of the once-celebrated "Swedish model" were national bargaining, full employment, and "solidaristic" wage policy. In conceptualizing and framing the discourse of this welfare regime, sociology of work was probably more deeply involved than in most countries. The eventual breakdown of this model and the negotiated consensus between the employers and the unions also meant a less prominent position for social research in general and sociology of work in particular. Now, in the shift to a new millennium, as we witness a certain reincarnation of a national consensus, we might ask whether this will again imply an active role for the social sciences.

For more than 50 of the last 60 years, the Government has been led by the Social Democrats. While firmly entrenched in the market economic system, the government has been trying to achieve a high standard in working life. The trade union movement holds a uniquely strong influence in politics. This is, of course, based on a high membership rate, around 80% for professionals and workers, men and women, as well as a well established, historic partnership with the Social Democratic party. The birth of the welfare state—

Caston von Otter • National Institute for Working Life, 84 Solna, Sweden.

Worlds of Work: Building an International Sociology of Work, edited by Daniel B. Cornfield and Randy Hodson. Kluwer Academic/Plenum Publishers, New York, 2002.

in the period between the wars—drew inspiration from the research community. Virtually all Swedish sociologists shared commitment to the reform agenda, to an active labor market policy, to industrial democracy, to decreased wage differentials, and so on.

It would be a gross exaggeration to claim that sociology of work set the agenda for *The Folkhem* ("The People's Home", a favorite metaphor of the Social Democrats), but it certainly affected it and constantly exchanged information with the political level of society. The purpose of this chapter is to attempt to show how sociology interacted with policy formation and implementation over different phases:

- In providing concepts and theories for a reformist political approach to working life.
- In articulating perspectives and factual descriptions from the shop floor.
- In analyzing technical and organizational alternatives.
- In developing work policy as a new regimen for working life.

The welfare state regimen passed its peak some 10 or 15 years ago. The period covered in this chapter extends from the establishment of sociology as an academic discipline to its marginalization from the political sphere and possible revival in the new century. The close involvement with policy has been discussed internationally (e.g., Allardt, Lysgaard, and Sörensen, 1988).

The unique position of Swedish sociology of work during its heyday was related to the privileged position researchers often acquire in small countries. However, it also benefited from easy access to the work sites and the many broad, national field programs organized by the industrial partners. The interest taken by Swedish politicians and employers, by trade unions and other social movements, in experimental social (action) research is rarely matched in most countries. While empirically rather strong, few Swedish theoretical contributions to international sociology of work have been deeply original or of lasting significance.

The Establishment of Academic Sociology

In the establishment of academic sociology in Sweden, sociology of work had a significant role. Clearly, human relations theory had to it that sizzling ring of usefulness that stimulated the appetites of both the business community and the public sector. The few previous attempts at sociology had little lasting impact. Modern history of sociology in Sweden begins with the ideas of Mayo *et consortes*, which were picked up by industry at an early stage. In 1938, a national, "Keynesian compromise agreement" was first reached and which manifested the partnership between capital and a labor. Shortly afterwards, the employers founded several research institutions to support the formation of new relations at work. Sociologists were expected to be the engineers of productivity, competitiveness, and social harmony.

In 1947, sociology was first established as an independent academic discipline. The first generation of professors, in Uppsala, Stockholm, and Gothenburg, had conducted major studies of industrial relations. Their research mapped terrain that was rather unknown to the upper classes. The new paradigm of consensus needed disinterested representations of working life in language and theories acceptable to the elite.

The happy days lasted a few decades. In more recent years, as Swedish politics has "normalized," sociology has been marginalized. When the economy and the labor market became less sheltered from forces of the global marketplace, the space for idiosyncratic policies diminished. Ideologically, the government has fallen in line behind other countries of the European community (Sweden, Finland, and Austria were the latest to join the European Union, or EU). Monetarist remedies were prescribed for Sweden's economy to meet the deep financial crisis in the 1990s.

Sociology of Work Today

Today, sociology of work is in a highly transitional phase, reflecting deep changes in society. Globalization has placed market competitiveness at the top of the agenda, and individual aspirations, rather than collective strategies of change, are in focus. Unemployment is now only slightly better than the European average, while it used to be extremely low. Reengineering, outsourcing, and so on, are the order of the day. International consultants are doing well, while the demand for sociologists is low. The faltering interest is also seen in publications in the leading Swedish professional journal, where articles on working life were down by one-third in the 1980s from the average for the preceding two decades (Allardt et al., 1988).

With the new millennium, however, there are faint indications of a resurgent interest in sociology of work. The 1990s were a period of rapid and exceptionally fundamental shift in working life in Sweden. Not only was there the deep labor market recession, but there were also repercussions following the new full membership in the EU, as well as a repositioning of multinational corporations for the global economy, including several mergers, rapid development of the new economy, and so on. All these developments were associated with changes in labor market processes. As the economy improved, concern developed rapidly over new occupational health hazards, regional imbalances, and increasing polarization in the labor market—fields of knowledge that might again bring sociology in to the picture.

IMPORTANT THEMES

A handful of themes have inspired important discussions in the academic as well as the broader community. The first period is related to the founding of the welfare state.

Vanguard of the Welfare State

The main impact of the first generation of surveys of working life was to establish a conceptual structure, making sociological perspectives familiar (e.g., Dahlström, 1954; Segerstedt and Lundquist, 1956). In the second stage, descriptions gave way to a more analytical period. What were the mechanisms behind turnover, absenteeism, a disciplined work organization, and so on? How should the role of supervisors be defined, or systems of payment by results be designed? Eventually, questions were also asked about the resistance of workers. With such scientific management, why are workers not content? The outstanding Scandinavian work here is by a Norwegian, Sverre Lysgaard (1961), who laid out a Merton-inspired analysis of the workers collective. He demonstrated how the workers need to protect themselves in the face of the "inexorable and insatiable pressures" created by the productivity squeeze, and how workers apply collective pressure to control individual members of the group. Lysgaard excellently called attention to the two-sidedness of the workers' collective.

This led to social critique, with issues of social tensions and cohesion explicitly on the agenda. When asked to advise the corporation on how to "adapt" the workers, many sociologist felt they could not be in the service of only one of the parties, or take a "neutral" scientific position. The trade unions started commissioning studies based on their definition of social problems. The first example of academic research collaboration with a trade union was a study of "technological change and work adaptation." It established technology as a non-neutral area and inspired research for technical alternatives (Dahlström et al., 1966).

A seminal contribution that laid the ground for a whole new school of empirically well-founded studies of welfare distribution in the following decades, and up to this day, was the Level of Living Study, headed by Sten Johansson (1979). The defined social indicators had a strong employment and work-oriented perspective that influenced similar studies by international organizations, for example, the Organization for Economic Cooperation and Development (OECD) and the United Nations (UN). It was not clear from the outset that work and employment (for men and women), including issues related to work organization and job design, would be seen as core aspects of well-being.

Employment and job experiences were treated on a level with economic utility and seen as the main determinants of the well-being of the individual and his or her family. The analysis demonstrated significant flaws in the welfare system. Also, in studies used for international comparative purposes demonstrated that labor reformism mattered significantly in welfare outcomes (Erikson, Goldthorpe, and Portocarero, 1979). The study was repeated in 1981, using the same panel (Erikson and Åberg, 1987) and in 1991 (Fritzell and Lundberg, 1994), and will again be conducted in the years to come.

In 1968, with an outburst of frustration from the privileged young and segments of the working class, the situation was totally incomprehensible to the national leadership. Protests were directed against social injustice in general and against working life specifically. Sociologists were there already, with empirical facts and explanations for what was going on. Many sociologists took a position in favor of the workers, deconstructing the concept of economic growth, the rhetoric of solidarity, and the presumption that *the Folkhem* was here and now.

While little about this debate was uniquely Swedish, the open and constructive response of the government and the economic establishment (initially), was probably more so. The 1970s were a period of radical reforms in working life that empowered the workers, ultimately at the price of the general consensus between employers and workers.

A widely acclaimed study from this period was that conducted by Walter Korpi, who had been asked by the metalworker's trade union to look into the problem of wildcat strikes—by all international comparisons a miniscule problem in Sweden but an irritating blemish to the national leaders. Korpi's results—in brief, "If there is a strike, there is a reason"—caused some instantaneous turbulence. More important was the long-term impact of the empirical evidence brought forward, which was analyzed in Korpi's monograph, *The Working Class in Welfare Capitalism* (1978). Korpi (1983) is one of the rather few researchers who also made important theoretical contributions internationally (e.g., to the theory of power, industrial conflicts and political mobilization of the working class).

From the 1970s on, sociologists of work pursued two different courses. One—here labeled "the work reform movement"—held on to the microlevel in industrial relations, however, with a broader and more directly reform-oriented ambition, working in partnership with employers and unions. The other radically and impatiently pursued the project of economic democracy.

Few Swedish sociologists argued against reformism in favor of extended market liberalism or a nonetatist Weberian civil society. The exception was Hans L. Zetterberg, the sociologist from Uppsala, who spent most of his career in sociology in the United States at Columbia University, and later became a leading conservative ideologue in Sweden.[1] He belonged to the Columbia group with Lazarsfeld and other *émigrés*. Zetterberg's sophisticated lifestyle approach to social differentiation, as opposed to class theory, was supported with rich empirical evidence (Zetterberg, 1977).

The Democratic Class Struggle

Sweden has always been a work-oriented society ("Work is to Swedes what sex was to Freud," claimed some foreign observer). In the fields of work and employment, explanations and remedies were sought for all sorts of social problems. The first half of the 1970s was a period of preparation and experiments for the "reform of the century," when standards for a decent working life, job security, occupational health, and industrial democracy would be established.

Several government commissions were appointed to look into economic and industrial democracy ("the third step," according to Prime Minister Olof Palme, after, first, the universal suffrage and, second, the social welfare reforms). The resulting package included new laws regulating workplace codetermination, job security, work environment, and so on. The commissions were staffed by social scientists, including several sociologists.

This all gave substantial impetus to a reform of the industrial relations system and to a period, the 1970s, that can well be described as the heyday of Swedish sociology of work. Clearly sociologists knew something about conflicts in society and could contribute to policy reform.

The unions managed to place industrial and economic democracy at the top of the political agenda. Rudolf Meidner, one of the foremost trade union intellectuals of the post–World War II era in Europe, was called back to Landsor/organizations (LO) (Sweden's Trade Union Congress) from an academic position to study models of labor capital formation. The active labor market policy, which actively promoted structural rationalizations, was incomplete without some form of worker ownership (Meidner, 1978). As an institutional economist, Meidner was probably more at ease among sociologists than among most of his neoclassical colleagues.

In the 1950s, Rudolf Meidner, along with his colleague at LO, Gösta Rehn, had already made important theoretical contributions to the economic policy of the welfare state (see Meidner, cited in Lundberg et al., 1952; Rehn, 1985). Their model for wage solidarity and active labor market policy was based on the idea of centralized bargaining, of not "subsidizing bad jobs by low pay," and active policy measures to support labor mobility and flexibility. Meidner

[1]Zetterberg is perhaps most remembered by the discipline for being, along with Talcott Parsons, the main target of Dennis Wrong in his seminal essay, "The Oversocialized Concept of Man in Modern Sociology" (1961).

designed a model according to which surplus profits would be taxed away to national wage earner funds, which would be controlled by the trade unions. Within a few decades, major parts of Swedish industry would be "socialized."

The issue of ownership and civilization of capitalism became the cleavage point of domestic Swedish politics for over a decade. Wage earners' funds, more than anything else, cracked the old consensus model from 1938 and raised an enormous debate, mobilized employers into the streets, and so on. Most surprising, here, is perhaps that the heated reaction from the business sector came as such a surprise to supporters of the project. At any rate, nothing better illustrates the historicist mode of labor intellectuals in this period. History was evolution, and now was the time for the third step: It would perhaps be met with resistance, as had parliamentary democracy, child benefits, and retirement pensions, but after a short while, according to the logic of the argument, it would be accepted and endorsed by all. Several sociologists contributed to the debate (Abrahamsson and Broström, 1980; Clement and Mahon, 1994; Pontusson, 1992).

During these years, new labor legislation concerning all major aspects (most of which until then had been regulated in national agreements) was passed and implemented. In 1976, as part of the bill of codetermination, public funding for work research was radically increased and new research and development (R&D) institutions established. Research in the field (e.g., by sociologists) could not depend on economic support from the employers alone. The wage earners' fund proposal was given up in the early 1990s.

Work Reform Movement

The other major response to the political and intellectual ferment of the late 1960s, was skepticism about structural changes in society of the kind debated by proponents of a class-based democratic reform. They saw the third step as reforms from above, likely to change little in shop-floor relations unless sustained by motivated workers who actively took part in the reform process. Without the offer of real alternative arrangements, workers would not care much about codetermination rights, or about who owns the company.

The academic core of this research was connected to the established Scandinavian approach to job design, which drew on earlier international research. Kurt Lewin's field experiments in the 1940s and Fred Emery's and Einar Thorsrud's work in the 1950s and 1960s had taught that social theories need to confront testing and input from real field situations (T. Sandberg, 1982).

The originality of these projects was due to the unique potential for action research in Scandinavia (i.e., Sweden and Norway). As pointed out by Björn Gustavsen, there is no inherent peacefulness or collaborative orientation in Scandinavian working life. Constructive forces have, however, been able to come to grips with the conflicts through the development of industrial relations that could, stepwise, gain sufficient legitimacy and support to be efficient (Gustavsen, 1992).

The first field program took place in the 1960s in Norway, in a series of experiments with autonomous work groups (Emery and Thorsrud, 1976). Soon, a similar project developed in Sweden was even more directly was linked to the debate on industrial democracy. These projects raised issues about industrial democracy at an operational level. Was it to be board representation, works councils? Or was it a matter of respect and self-control of each worker on the job (i.e., everyday conditions on the shop floor)? While many of these propositions today are commonplace, they were quite controversial at the time. Few believed that supervisors and other middlemen could be replaced by self-management. Others asked: Are job enlargement and job rotation what workers really want? Is democracy really concerned with the trivia of daily activities? Is the matter not about more solemn and consequential issues and principles?

This was a period of broad, systematic experimentation, with representation for all major social partners. The experiments were held within a common sociotechnical framework. The workers and shop-floor managers built each specific field project on active participation in the creative process.

The programs were based on a firm belief in the disseminating force of a "model case." Viewed more closely, this diffusion of good examples did not occur as expected. More broadly, however, a research process was set off, based on participative and active research strategies that 30 years later still carry considerable momentum (Toulmin and Gustavsen, 1996).

After the first set of bipartisan programs in Norway, and later in Sweden, the Swedish Employers Federation (SAF), with a selected group of sociologists and other organization specialists, set out on their own to design "the plant of the future" (Agurén and Edgren, 1980). This time, they did not seek collaboration with the national trade unions or the research community in general.

The program initiated some important innovative thinking, including the now-famous Volvo assembly plants. While the first set of projects had been restricted by the fact that established organizations could not easily be changed, and that the physical and technical properties of the old plant severely restricted the options for new career patterns for the workers, and so on, the new set of projects included Greenfield projects (Berggren, 1987).

The sociological research community, which largely had been excluded from participation in the "plant of the future" project, not surprisingly, responded by heavily criticizing this pioneering work done with the good aim of breaking the regime of the assembly line (Fordism). To a degree, they caught the ear of national union militants, and this progressive project was not as strongly endorsed as it should have been.

This initial set of projects was significant to the next generation of action research programs shaped in the mid-1980s. They found that diffusion of good examples was a problematic issue. The idea that the experiments would function as points of departure for broader processes of change did not materialize, at least not in the course of the program. Neither problems nor solutions emerged from the experiments in an immediate and sharply featured form. Formulating them was the result of a long discussion and process of clarification. Initially, the problems surfaced in the form of experimental difficulties in which it was not clear whether faulty ideas or inefficient practices were the problem (Gustavsen, 1992).

The 5-year LOM (Leadership, Organization, co-Management) program, with some 50 companies and public institutions, began in 1984. The vehicle of change was communication and suggestions for how networks could develop in the workplace (Naschold et al., 1993).

Subsequently, an even broader program, the 1990–1995 Working Life Fund (WLF), state funded by U.S. $2.5 billion, was initiated by the social partners nationally. Sociology of work provided a conceptual structure, and researchers worked closely with the program management agency. During the 5-year run of the program, a creative and experimental phase set in, and several thousand projects resulted. It is perhaps too early to ascertain the lasting influence of this outburst of energy, but indications are that Swedish companies are rather advanced in the application of new managerial concepts and information technology (Ennals and Gustavsen, 1999).

Stress and Working Life

A theory of work-related stress (the "Karasek model") developed by the American sociologist Robert Karasek, with Swedish colleagues Bertil Gardell, Töres Theorell, and others, demonstrated a strong statistical correlation between work organization and self-control, and job stress and various health problems. These researchers showed how psychological demands of work, skills uses, and task controls could predict a broad range of health and behavioral consequences. The results explained why people in senior positions suffered fewer health problems in spite of a heavy workload, while those in lower positions, because of low self-control, ran a greater health risk (Karasek and Theorell, 1990). These results were important politically as well as academically. They demonstrated that a reasonable degree of self-control was not only a "philosophic good" but also a requirement for good health. Thus, worker participation could be phrased as not just an ideological issue.

The theory helped identify specific problematic groups in the labor market. In order to maintain competitiveness while improving work organization, technological alternatives had to be developed. Bertil Gardell and others went on to design ambitious action projects in manufacturing, health care, and so on. The Almex report (Gardell and Svensson, 1981) is an account of a self-management program in one factory, initiated by the trade union local. An innovative wage policy was used to encourage not only narrow productivity but also aspirations for learning, self-management, and so on.

In another report, which is even more a landmark, work organization in the hospital was analyzed using the Karasek model of work-related stress. The inefficiency of the modern "assembly line" acute care model was demonstrated and an alternative model offered. The strong tensions between a managerial perspective and "nursing care" were worked out in codetermination teams with the unions. These discussions affected for years to come the perspective of the health care professions, and their unions and became the basis of totally new bargaining strategies.

Organization of work and wage policies are interdependent, and the traditional platform, which sees organization as a management prerogative, while, only compensation for work is a legitimate bipartisan issue, is invalid. At this stage, the unions, rather than the employers (the county councils), stood for the more advanced thinking in terms of what is good for both patients and even cost-effective health care (Gardell et al., 1979).

Technological Alternatives

The Swedish trade union movement has a reputation for its positive attitude to change and new technology. There are anecdotes of how visiting Swedish trade unionists in the United States pointed out to plant managers how they should rationalize work even further.

Trade-union-focused industrial research has become a field in which Swedish sociology of work has had, and continues to have, an international impact (Ehn, 1988; Göranzon, 1991; Sandberg et al., 1992). The researchers are interested in independent, local union activity, in contrast to both detailed management and supervision, and formalized codetermination in committees. They have been looking for a system in which workers truly can contribute their experience and perspectives on the development of new technology. The local union needs assistance to formulate their own demands and set a standard for skills requirements, and so on. Good jobs cannot be created *ex post facto*, after the technology is in place, with all the stable parameters fixed. Job design is integrally linked to the whole production process—the products, technology of production, tasks, information, buildings, and so on. Control of these factors has been guarded by management as key aspects of managerial control. The question of access to information for the local union, which was regulated in the 1976 Codetermination Act, is thus a key aspect for workers and researchers alike.

All the three national automakers, Volvo, Saab, and Scania were designing new plants, trying to humanize assembly line production, in order to become more attractive on the labor market in the then prevailing full-employment situation. "Volvoism" fed into the international discourse on Fordism, Toyotism, and so on. They claimed that the Swedish experience demonstrated that alternatives to repetitive work structures were not only socially desirable and economically valid, but also resulted in qualitative improvements and greater flexibility. Unique teamwork of behavioral scientists, engineers, and so on, followed. Workers come in different forms, sizes, and sexes. Tools, work positions, and so on, need to be flexible in order to adapt to a variety of situations. Sociological evaluations demonstrated the value of mixed teams, with men and women, to improve the work culture. According to Berggren (1987), Sweden's contributions to the discussion of car manufacturing technology have been marked by a distinctive shop-floor focus. It is a matter of dispute whether this also, in the end, includes a sufficiently strong focus on productivity (Sandberg, 1995).

Welfare State Transformation

Today, demand for sociology of work in the private sector has decreased; managers prefer the straightforward, know-it-all answers of international consultants to the inconsistent advice of researchers. Instead, research in the public sector has become a very significant instrument in assessing demand for services, effectiveness, and so on. One field that has grown increasingly stronger is research into welfare services, which in Sweden are to a very large degree delivered and financed in the public sector.

When the United States and the United Kingdom were talking about dismantling "the nanny state" and "getting government off our backs," an attempt was made in Sweden to reform the welfare policy system without losing the basic qualities of solidarity. The objective was to improve services and work organization in the public sector (which at the time represented about 40% of the labor force) (von Otter, 1981).

Over several decades, Sweden was a leader in *inventing* government, with public programs for child care, education, elder care, and so on. After the economic recession, *reinventing* government came as an inspiration from abroad but proved to be an arena in which the contribution of sociology of work was especially useful. Sociologist helped reconcile the new market-like instruments, which were badly needed, with a protective shield of social values.

A broadly backed program tried to lead the way for reform that acknowledged problems of state paternalism, high costs, and rigidity—using institutional economics, organizational theory, and sociology of work to shape a new interactive, dynamic rationality for the public delivery system (Naschold and von Otter, 1996). In one project, the preconditions for a participatory, dynamic, and service-oriented organization of public health services were studied using an institutional economic framework. Concepts such as planned markets, public firms, and civil democracy were launched as ingredients in an alternative health sector reform (Saltman and von Otter, 1992).

Gender: Opening New Territory

In most of the respected sociology of work studies in the 1960s and 1970s, the perspective was totally on men. A very early (well, depends on how one sees it) and important book was *The Changing Roles of Men and Women* (Dahlström et al., 1967). It clearly raised questions about opportunities for women at work, and which political reforms were needed to square the equation of combining work and family. The report is another clear case of research impact on policy, actually setting the agenda for the decade. The leading name in gender sociology at this time was Rita Liljeström, who worked closely with Edmund Dahlström the leading work sociologist. The trade union federation (LO) funded their large project on working-class women (Dahlström & Liljestrsöm, 1982). Liljeström's contribution at that period in time, was a sensitive mapping of the field, raising some new questions about women rights and demonstrating the unreasonable social and cultural determinants of life careers. However, she also raised the whole reproductive theme in a way that bore out an important critique against both the welfare state and its unrecognized patriarchal bias, and the corporate elite that neglected family needs in the organization of working life.

A summary assessment of "sociology of women" in Sweden concluded that the clearly dominating theme is women's work (as wage laborers). Of published articles from the 1970s and 1980s, 25% dealt with work and employment, which was three or four times the work on other subjects. The focus was on segregation, wage differential, and the general subordination of women in working life (Acker et al., 1992). As the new public sector of the labor market developed, and women filled positions as child care attendants, nurses, and so on, attention turned to how these jobs were organized, valued, and paid.

In an attempt to establish the unique features of the caring professions, some very important conceptual and philosophical issues were revived. No doubt, this research agenda broadened the perspectives of sociology of work in a significant way. Sociology of work, as union policies and labor legislation, had been disproportionately concerned with industrial manufacturing and full-time, male, blue-collar work, totally disregarding the service professions and other careers. Gender sociology has deepened the academic discourse in new, exciting directions. Thus, the work of Wittgenstein, Polany, Habermas, and others introduced an exploration of the nature of human service work.

NEW DIRECTIONS

Today, many sociologists have moved away from political and social engineering, either to micro-oriented theoretical issues or technical specialties such as personnel management. Of the former, rational choice and institutional theory are potentially significant themes as a sociological rejoinder to mainstream economics.

Institutional and economic processes of significance for new jobs and unemployment are another new direction that is attracting attention. "Development coalition," a more recently focused concept, pertains to the ability of organizations to learn, innovate, and change. To form a coalition all participants must gain an understanding of others, pool insights, and strive for joint solutions. Multidimensionality can be seen as a core characteristic of the European approach to work organization. Constructive development demands active cooperation, and pooling of ideas and resources among all actors (Ennals and Gustavsen, 1999).

Particularly important in this context is the way in which work organization is *created*. Work organization, in this approach, is linked to a participatory development process that in turn is linked to some kind of broader supportive environment. Making new forms of work organization real is mainly a practical project, not one of implementing universal reason. Theory is helpful, but it has to be independently tested against specific, local experiences.

Features recently emphasized (e.g., dialogue), convey the open and indeterminate character of the development process and focus on the process of change as such. In addition, there is strong emphasis on deconstruction of existing patterns, introducing notions that can utilize open learning situations. Sociologists have moved from implementation models to innovation-supportive models linked to workers' expectations to participate and contribute to change. While workers in more liberal market societies are empowered through the marketplace, in the Nordic countries, empowerment is related to coalition building and organization.

There is, however, also a more individualistic direction in sociology of work, focused on motives and attitudes rather than structures and manifest social patterns. Theories of value change are one new important strand, in which individual and collective behavior are analyzed using value theory and "life stories" (Danermark and Kullberg, 1999; Holmer et al., 1999).

INSTITUTIONAL CONTEXT

Academic institutions are public and financed by the state, with only one major exception (the Stockholm Business School). Most universities and many regional colleges conduct courses in sociology of work. However, the greatest number of students has enrolled in programs of personnel administration or labor market policy administration. Ph.D. programs in sociology—which include sociology of work—are offered at all universities.

The Swedish Institute of Social Research, SOFI, grew from a small labor market policy institution headed by Rudolf Meidner, and was later chaired by leading personalities in sociology (e.g., Gösta Rehn, Walter Korpi, and Sten Johansson). Over the years, SOFI has attracted a great number of leading, international sociologists studying welfare distribution, working life, social mobility, and so on.

In another important institution, the Swedish Institute for Working Life (Arbetslivsinstitutet, or ALI), sociology emanates from the Center for Working Life (Arbetslivscentrum), established to support the new legal institutions of the labor law reform of 1976. Arbetslivscentrum was intended to even out the balance in research resources between capital and labor. Most of its leading academics were sociologists who worked with new technology, information technology, gender studies, public sector organizations, trade unions, and so on, many with a positive inclination for action-oriented research strategies. Arbetslivscentrum was merged with the National Institute of Occupational Health to become *Arbetslivsinstitutet*, with some 400 researchers, of whom approximately 15% have a background in social or behavioral sciences.

There are four university-based chairs in sociology of work (including two in labor market sociology). Academically, the main difference 10–15 years ago was that most of the professors of sociology did sociology of work; today, sociology of work is much less visible within the core discipline, and sociological researchers interested in work have found more supportive environments in multidisciplinary groups and departments.

Public funding for work research has been very generous since the mid-1970s, and it would be unfair, especially in an international perspective, to claim that this is no longer the case. However, it has been reduced, and the available funds are used for a broader set of research problems. Of the social sciences, only economics has fared really well. While, some years ago, the ratio of chairs in sociology and economics numbered 1:2, the ratio today is more like 1:6 or 1:7.

Today, there is little articulated demand for sociology of work, as such, in industry. What at one time was the exclusive realm of sociologists is now addressed in a multidisciplinary, and multiprofessional way: work design (by psychologists and engineers); organization theory (by students of management, and so on); labor market and employment issues (by economists); labor market institutions, bargaining, and trade unions (by political scientists). This marginalization of sociology is perhaps a good thing for the discipline, necessary to define new approaches to new issues in a new economy that is information- rather than technology-driven.

Journals and Data Sources

There is no academic journal devoted purely to the sociology of work. The English-speaking forum for Nordic sociology since 1957 is *Acta Sociologica*, which now and then has featured a special issue on sociology of work and regularly publishes such articles. In recent years, an orientation toward rational choice sociology again placed the journal in an important arena for discussions of market systems, including the labor market.

Sociologisk Forskning (in Swedish) covers more or less the same ground as *Acta Sociologica*, though it is perhaps less traditional and more sensitive to new debates. Special issues have covered, for example, action research, sociology of organization, pay and incentives, and gender.

In addition, there is a set of broader, interdisciplinary journals. The *Journal of Economic and Industrial Democracy* is one of the oldest (now in its 20th year) and most renowned, with a thematic focus on workers' rights and so on, and a broad international coverage. Until recently, it was edited by Rudolf Meidner.

In 1996, a fairly new member of this set, *Concepts and Transformation— International Journal of Action Research and Organizational Renewal*—published its first volume, focusing on new relationships between theory and practice. The journal's focus is on contextual shifts in world of work and the mutuality of research and development. From the same group, there is a series of books, *Dialogues on Work and Innovation* (published by John Benjamins Publishing Company, Amsterdam).

A fairly new journal, *Arbetsmarknad & Arbetsliv* (in Swedish, with summaries in English), is published jointly by the National Labor Market Board and the National Institute of Working Life. It prints original contributions, and reprints articles from other (international) journals, and has a useful current debate section.

The National Bureau of Statistics (*Statistics Sweden*) is an excellent source of data, much of it presented also in English. Sweden has a unique history (back to the 17th century) in collecting data about the population. Several national registers for work-related parameters provide unmatched opportunities for longitudinal surveys and so on, and are much used by international scholars.

The *Swedish Institute* is the foremost source of basic summaries about economic and social affairs in Sweden. It provides overview articles of important debates and proposals, as well as systems and policy descriptions. The

National Labor Market organizations and agencies also often print the material in English.

CONCLUSIONS

Over the years, many Nordic sociological review groups have been organized. Several have made observations about the typical Scandinavian differences. While sociology in all the countries has characteristically been concerned with social development in the respective countries, the Swedes have typically worked closer to the state than colleagues in Norway or Denmark. Erik Allardt, leading Finnish sociologists, suggests that typical features of Swedish sociology are explained by the same processes that underlie the uniquely dominant position of social democracy in Sweden, and exactly why in Sweden the Nordic Welfare State has reached its highest manifestation.

In contrast to continental Europe, the state or the government is not experienced as a repressor. It is rather the reverse situation: A strong government is seen as protection for the individual against powerful (global) market forces (Allardt et al., 1988; Wolfe, 1989). Remarkably few sociologist have opposed the prevailing welfare paradigm (disregarding those who attacked from the left). The important exception is Hans L. Zetterberg.

During the period of social democratic utopianism, sociology of work could claim a privileged position as a guide and critic *vis-à-vis* the political and economic systems. Today, the development of work life is guided less by national policy programs and more by the business community, inspired by international consultants offering solutions to challenges supposedly unambiguously defined by international competition.

A whole range of issues related to unions, policies of workers' control and worker's rights, and so on, has become more or less obsolete, and the labor movement feeds little new energy into the sociology of work agenda. However, after the recovery in the economic situation, in the early years of the new century, there are indications that problems associated with "the new economy" are again posing important questions to sociologists of work.

Many of these issues deal with work-related stress and increased dissatisfaction with the uneven balance between demands for working life flexibility as compared to demands derived from family responsibilities. Equally important is the concern over increasing inequalities in income distribution and economic resources. While it is not obvious that sociology can come up with a fix for any of these predicaments, there is once again the kind of critical query from which interest in sociology spouts.

In this chapter, sociology of work in Sweden has been seen mainly from the perspective of an applied science and how the collaboration between the academic and the political spheres has changed over the years. Another story could have been told as well, focusing on strictly academic criteria (e.g., who appeared with what publications in the *American Journal of Sociology*, who introduced this or that international discourse). To me, it is clear that the contributions Swedish sociologists have made to the sociology of work, depend more on open access to field sites, the general cooperative mood, and their practical inventiveness than on theoretical creativity or empirical excellence.

REFERENCES

Abrahamsson, B., and A. Broström. 1980. *The Rights of Labor.* Beverly Hills, CA: Sage.

Acker, J., A. Bandi, U. Björnberg, and E. Dahlström 1992. *Kvinnors och mäns liv och arbete.* Stockholm: SNS.

Agurén, S., and J. Edgren. 1980. *New Factories: Job Design through Factory Planning in Sweden.* Stockholm: Swedish Employers' Confederation.

Allardt, E., S. Lysgaard, and A. Böttger Sörensen. 1988. *Sociologin i Sverige.* Uppsala: Swedish Science Press.

Berggren, C. 1987. *New Production Concepts in Final Assembly: The Swedish Experiences.* Stockholm: KTH.

Clement, W., and R. Mahon. 1994. *Swedish Social Democracy: A Model in Transition.* Toronto: Canadian Scholars Press.

Dahlström, E. 1954. *Management, Unions and Society: A Study of Salaried Employee Attitudes.* Stockholm: Studieförbundet Näringsliv och Samhälle.

Dahlström, E., B. Gardell, and B. Rundbland. 1966. *Teknisk förändring och arbetsanpassning: Ett sociologiskt bidrag till forsknings- och planeringsdebatten.* Stockholm: Prisma.

Dahlström, E., ed. 1967. *The Changing Roles of Men and Women.* London: Gerald Duckworth.

Dahlström, E., and L. Liljeström. 1982. *Working-Class Women and Human Reproduction.* Göteborg: Göteborg University, Sociology Deptartment.

Danermark, B., and C. Kullberg. 1999. *Samverkan: Välfärdsstatens nya arbetsform.* Lund: Studentlitteratur.

Ehn, P. 1988. *Work-Oriented Design of Computer Artifacts.* Stockholm: Arbetslivscentrum.

Emery, F., and E. Thorsrud. 1976. *Democracy at Work: The Report of the Norwegian Industrial Democracy Program.* Leiden: Nijhoff.

Ennals, R., and B. Gustavsen. 1999. *Work Organization and Europe as a Development Coalition.* Amsterdam: Benjamin.

Erikson, R., J. H. Goldthorpe, and L. Portocarero. 1979. "Intergenerational Class Mobility in Three Western European Societies." *British Journal of Sociology* 30(4):415–441.

Erikson, R., and R. Åberg, eds. 1987. *Welfare in Transition: A Survey of Living Conditions in Sweden 1968–1981.* Oxford, UK: Clarendon.

Fritzell, J., and O. Lundberg, eds. 1994. *Vardagens villkor.* Stockholm: Brombergs.

Gardell, B., and R. Å. Gustavsson. 1979. *Sjukvård på löpande band: Rapport från ett forskningsprojekt om sjukhusets vård och arbetsorganisation.* Stockholm: Prisma.

Gardell, B., and L. Svensson. 1981. *Medbestämmande och självstyre: En lokal facklig strategi för demokratisering av arbetsplatsen.* Stockholm: Prisma.

Göranzon, B. 1991. *The Practical Intellect: Computers and Skills.* London: Springer.

Gustavsen, B. 1992. *Dialogue and Development: Theory of Communication, Action Research and the Restructuring of Working Life.* Assen/Maastricht: Van Gorcum.

Holmer, J., Jan C. Karlsson, and B. Thomasson, eds. 1999. *Making Work Life Work: On Change, Competence and Participation.* Karlstad: Karlstad University Press.

Johansson, S. 1979. *Frame of Reference of the 1968 Survey of Levels of Living in Sweden.* Stockholm: Låginkomstutredningen.

Karasek, R., and T. Theorell. 1990. *Healthy Work, Stress, Productivity and the Reconstruction of Working Life.* New York: Basic Books.

Korpi, W. 1978. *The Working Class in Welfare Capitalism: Work, Unions and Politics in Sweden.* London: Routledge and Kegan Paul.

Korpi, W. 1983. *The Democratic Class Struggle.* London: Routledge and Kegan Paul.

Lundberg, E., R. Meidner, G., Rehn, and K. Wickman. 1952. *Wages Policy Under Full Employment.* London: W. Hodge.

Lysgaard, S. 1961. *Arbeiderkollektivet: En studie i de underordnedes sosiologi.* Oslo: Universitetsforl.

Meidner, R. 1978. *Employee Investment Funds: An Approach to Collective Capital Formation.* London: Allen and Unwin.

Naschold, F., R. E. Cole, B. Gustavson, and H. Van Beirum. 1993. *Constructing the New Industrial Society.* Assen: Van Gorcum.

Naschold, F., and C. von Otter. 1996. *Public Sector Transformation: Rethinking Markets and Hierarchies in Government.* Amsterdam: John Benjamins.

Otter von, C., ed. 1981. *Worker Participation in the Public Sector.* Uppsala: Almqvist and Wiksell International.

Pontusson, J. 1992. *The Limits of Social Democracy: Investment Politics in Sweden.* Ithaca, NY: Cornell University Press.

Rehn, G. 1985. Swedish Active Labor Market Policy: Retrospect and Prospect. *Industrial Relations* 1:62–89

Saltman, R. B., and C. von Otter. 1992. *Planned Markets and Public Competition.* Buckingham: Open University Press.

Sandberg, T. 1982. *Work Organization and Autonomous Groups.* Lund: Gleerups.

Sandberg, Å., ed. 1995. *Enriching Production: Perspectives on Volvo's Uddevalla Plant as an Alternative to Lean Production.* Aldershot: Avebury.

Sandberg, Å. et al. 1992. *Technological Change and Co-Determination in Sweden.* Philadelphia: Temple University Press.

Segerstedt, T. T., and A. Lundquist. 1956. *Man in Industrialized Society.* Stockholm: Studieförbundet Näringsliv och Samhälle.

Toulmin, S, and B. Gustavsen, eds. 1996. *Beyond Theory: Changing Organizations through Participation.* Amsterdam: John Benjamins

Wolfe, A. 1989. *Whose Keeper? Social Science and Moral Obligation.* Los Angeles: University of California Press.

Zetterberg, H. L. 1977. *Arbete, livsstil och motivation.* Stockholm: Swedish Employers' Confederation.

APPENDIX: CONTACTS

Major Research Centers and Organizations in Sweden

Center for Business and Policy Studies
Studiefrämjandet Näringsliv
och Samhälle (SNS)
Box 5629
S-114 86 Stockholm
E-mail: info@sns.se

Center for Work Research
(Centrum för Arbetsvetenskap)
Göteborgs Universitet
Box 700
S-405 30 Göteborg

Karlstad University
Center for Work Reseach (Centrum för Arbetsvetenskap)
Universitetsgatan 1
S-651 88 Karlstad
E-mail: kau@kau.se

Royal Institute of Technology
INDEK, Industriell ekonomi och Organisation
Valhallavägen 79
S-100 44 Stockholm
E-mail: info@admin.kth.se

Statistics Sweden (Statistiska Centralbyrån)
Box 24
300, S-10451 Stockholm
E-mail: scb@scb.se

Stockholm School of Economics
Institution for Management of Innovation and Technology (IMIT)
Box 65 01
S-113 83 Stockholm
E-mail: info@imit.se

Stockholm University
Department of Sociology
S-106 91 Stockholm
E-mail: sociologi@su.se

Swedish Institute for Social Research (SOFI)
Stockholm University
S-106 91
E-mail: sofi@ sofi.su.se

Swedish Institute for Working Life (Arbetslivsinsitutet)
S-112 79 Stockholm
E-mail: niwl@ niwl.se

Umeå University
Department of Sociology
Petrus Laestadius väg
S-910 87 Umeå
E-mail: umea.universitet@adm.umu.se

University of Halmstad
Centrum för Arbetslivsutveckling (CAU)
Box 823, S-301 18 Halmstad
E-mail: hhweb@inf.hh.se

Labor Market Partners

LO Swedish Trade Union Federation
Research Department
Barnhusgatan 18
S-105 53 Stockholm
Fax (46) 8 796 28 00
E-mail: LO@LO.se

TCO, The Swedish Central Organization of Salaried Employees
Linnégatan 14
S-114 94 Stockholm
Fax: (46) 8 663 75 20
E-mail: tco@tco.se

SAF, Confederation of Swedish Employers
Research department
S. Blasieholmshamnen
4A S-103 30 Stockholm
Fax: (46) 8 762 62 90
E-mail: saf@saf.se

V
Conclusion

16

The Sociology of Work Today
Looking Forward to the Future

Juan José Castillo

INTRODUCTION

This concluding chapter has been inspired by the chapters on the "state of the
art" of the sociology of work in the countries covered in this volume, as well as
a number of other, similar reviews published over the last 5 years in Europe
and Latin America. In it, I offer seven observations or reflections on the state
of the discipline, its social context, and the prospects for the future. I begin by
considering the different rhythms and levels of development of the sociology
of work and, closely related to these, the social, cultural, academic, and political contexts that shape research agendas and results. The evident trends toward convergence, often more academic than real, of research topics in the
different countries, then lead to a consideration of the continued importance
of national and international differences, and points of noncommunication
stemming from both disciplinary and linguistic divides. In this respect, I highlight what I see as some of the negative implications of the "Babelesque" character of an academic community that is fragmented by its various languages
of reference. The chapter ends with some thoughts on the distinct "national
paths" of presentation and argumentation that can be seen in the reports on

Juan José Castillo • Department of Sociology, Universidad Complutense de Madrid, Madrid
28223 Spain.

Worlds of Work: Building an International Sociology of Work, edited by Daniel B. Cornfield and
Randy Hodson. Kluwer Academic/Plenum Publishers, New York, 2002.

the different countries and their authors' discursive strategies. Finally, I conclude by pinpointing the trends identified in the different reports that constitute the surest signs of hope for the consolidation of a global academic community of sociologists of work.

The late 1990s saw the publication of a whole spate of articles on the "state of the art" and assessments of the strengths and weaknesses of the social sciences. More specifically, considerable attention was paid to the sociology of work, understood both in the broad sense of the term and in its narrower, academic definition.[1]

While the immediate roots of this already-long "reflexive wave" can be traced back, to mention just one particularly significant event, to the I Latin American Congress of the Sociology of Work, in Mexico City in 1993, there are certainly much earlier precedents. In this respect, mention should be made of two crucial texts for the development of the discipline, T. H. Marshall's *Sociology at the Crossroads and Other Essays,* first published in 1963, and Alvin Gouldner's 1970 classic, *The Coming Crisis of Western Sociology.*

This volume undoubtedly represents a major contribution to this ongoing task of reflection, to the evaluation and construction of the discipline and of a style of thinking. Since the 1993 congress in Mexico posed the question— "What future for the sociology of work?"—this line of thought and debate has been pursued in a whole series of meetings, conferences, congresses, and publications. Particular mention should be made here of the two "global" meetings chaired by Carlos Alá Santiago and the Research Committee 30, "Sociology of Work" in Puerto Rico, as well the crucial role that the International Sociological Association (ISA) "Sociology of Work" Committee has played in encouraging, supporting, and coordinating debate in this area. If any consensus has emerged from all this, it is on the need and potential for the sociology of work to broaden its outlook and research concerns.[2] In this sense, we now appear to be reaching the conclusion of a reflection that over the years has emerged as a common and crucial concern for the consolidation of the sociology of work today.

As will become apparent in the pages that follow, I am referring to a process of consolidation that is inherently precarious, contradictory, incom-

---

[1]See in particular, J. J. and S. Castillo (eds.), "Diez años de sociología del trabajo," special issue of *Sociología del Trabajo* 31, 1997; J. J. Castillo (ed.), "Which Way Forward for the Sociology of Work?", special issue of *Current Sociology* 47(2), 1999; and "Le ricerche in Sociologia del Lavoro in Italia e in Europa," special issue of *Sociologia del Lavoro* 76, 1999.

[2]Mention should be made here of J. J. Castillo (ed.), "La Sociología del Trabajo en América Latina," special issue of the *Revista de Economía y Sociología del Trabajo* 23–24, 1994, and Carlos A. Santiago, "Labor in the Americas," special issue of *Work and Occupations* 24(3), August 1997; the common origins of these reflections are considered in Dan Cornfield's "Editorial Introduction" to the second text.

plete. Not least because the protagonist of the process is an international scientific community that is very dispersed in every sense of the word. Dispersed, that is, not only in geographical terms but also due to the numerous fractures that constantly resurface within the discipline of sociology as a whole. Nonetheless, the current vitality and social presence of the sociology of work presages a promising future of debates, hopes, and necessary innovation.

The first and most obvious merit of *Worlds of Work* is, without any doubt, the fact that it combines evaluation and analysis of the state of the art, perspectives, and problems for the discipline. All this is accompanied by suggestions for further research and practical information on the main journals and institutions involved in studying the world of work in the countries covered in this book.

By now, readers will have formed their own global overview of the state of the discipline, presumably having begun with the chapter covering the country closest, in a scientific sense, to them (the book, of course, has been published precisely with this mind). In this way, readers will have sought an overview of the relevant country and the world of work in it, seen through the prism that the sociology of work provides into any society and its work. Other readers will have found information centers and identified possible partners for future international research projects.

Since there is little need to provide readers with a summary of what they have before them or have just read, in this short concluding chapter I merely try to highlight a handful of points, seven, or rather six observations plus a conclusion, suggested to me by a careful reading of the various national reviews published in this volume. At the same time, this text also returns to some of the points I raised in a recent review of the "state of the art in Spain,"[3] as well referring to the conclusions of various similar articles published over the course of the 1990s. In this way, I hope to contribute to the development of a reflexive sociology that analyzes itself as a necessary and simultaneous step to analyzing the society in which it is produced.

SIX OBSERVATIONS ON THE SOCIOLOGY OF WORK IN THE WORLD

First Observation

(Modern) times for the sociology of work are very different in different countries.

The dates, moments of inflection or rupture, and phases of progress or decline in the evolution of the sociology of work show the influence of na-

[3]See Castillo et al. (2000).

tional histories, political events, and the changing sway of different social actors and demands. So, for example, while there are few references to the origins or ruptures in the discipline in the chapter on the United Kingdom, it is quite apparent that the "Revolution of the Carnations" and the fall of the Salazar dictatorship, in 1974, marked a clear "before and after" in the case of Portugal. In fact, one could conclude from the chapter in this volume that sociology in Portugal was effectively reborn in 1974.

The social context in which scientific production takes place plays a similarly decisive role, despite the equally significant differences, in explaining the late consolidation of the sociology of work in Spain. Here, too, the discipline only really developed after 1975, when Franco's death marked the beginning of the end of the dictatorship. Moreover, consolidation, in the sense of reaching a critical mass, would only come after Spain joined what is now the European Union in 1986, with all that this meant for comparative research.

Other countries in which the evolution of the discipline has been marked by peculiar dates, dates that are deeply rooted in their respective national histories, include Korea. Here the workers' revolt of 1987 marks a key turning point and helps explain why, even now, sociology arouses only a little less suspicion than acts of subversion. In the words of the authors of the Korean report, "Sociology was regarded as a radical study field by the public in general and government policy makers in particular."[4] In Hungary, the key date is 1989, when the country began to reappear in the world of sociology, at the same time as the Berlin Wall disappeared.

In the case of the Latin American countries, and Brazil in particular, the upsurge of sociology and the development of specific interests and themes have also been shaped by the ebb and flow of politics. This is not just because some sociologists, to give just one example, saw research into the labor movement as a means of helping it survive or expand through periods of state terrorism. More importantly, this political chronology of the discipline also reflects the physical disappearance of sociologists, through emigration, persecution or elimination, whether in Brazil, Chile, Argentina, or any number of other countries, both in Latin America and the old continent.

Second Observation

These different rhythms of development highlight the way the sociology of work constitutes a mirror onto the social contexts in which it is produced.

As the Brazilian report observes, "Production in the sociology of work

---

[4]As noted in Chapter 8, it is still difficult to obtain authorization for the creation of departments in Korean universities. In fact, at the end of the 1900s, only 40 of the 100-odd universities in the country had a sociology department, while they all had economics departments.

largely reflects the orientations and vicissitudes of the process of industrial restructuring in Brazil." The same authors make a similar point in reference to the new unionism that developed at the end of the 1970s, which brought with it the need for the sociology of work to respond to new questions both within and outside Brazil. Even in terms of method and approach, change rarely comes about solely because of autonomous developments within the discipline, but rather as a result of encounters with the new demands of equally new actors. In this fact lies the importance attached to studying daily life in the workshop and factory and the preeminence of research carried out directly in the field, trends which also reflect the influence of what has come to be known as studies of the labor process.

Awareness of the difficulties involved in understanding the current state of the sociology of work, if one does not know the work to which this knowledge is actually applied, may explain why the Hungarian report presents a useful selection of data on the country (active population, unemployment rates, etc.). These data give the unfamiliar reader the minimum information required to compare the problems affecting work there with the research being carried out. It is quite patently impossible to grasp the full significance of the studies of work produced in South Africa, for example, if one does not even know how many people make up its active population.

The authors of the report on Australia are clearly well aware that the differences and similarities between countries have deep historical and institutional roots. Accordingly, they begin by setting the scene and emphasizing the importance that industrial or labor relations have had in shaping the state and structure of the discipline in Australia: so much so that industrial relations is identified as "the first and most significant thematic area," while the other two highlighted areas (inequality at work and the decentralization of work) are either very descriptive or have yet to establish themselves as distinct areas of research. As readers will recall, under the heading of industrial relations, the authors include studies of satisfaction with work, of the relation between technology and work—which can be negotiated, case studies and analyses of flexibility—which are also negotiable, and, hence, the preferred object of research from the institutional perspective.

Third Observation

In very different social contexts, there is a tendency toward nominal academic convergence.

I have already noted the way in which the evolution of the discipline has been shaped by its social context, exemplified by the cases of Portugal and Spain, where 1974 and 1975 marked the end of two seemingly never-ending dictatorships and paved the way for the rebirth of the social sciences. However, these domestic political events also coincided with the diffusion of Harry Braverman's influential work, *Labor and Monopoly Capitalism*, which revolutionized the social sciences of work, not just in the United States and the United Kingdom, but in Brazil and Mexico, and Spain and Portugal. Readers will have found numerous references to this seminal work in this volume. When discussing the new topics of research in the sociology of work, the chapter on Germany, for example, does not just mention the most influential texts by German authors but also refers to Braverman and others.

This helps explain why, in the case of Brazil, for example, we find that the 1980s were a period of excellence in research on the labor process. As we have argued here, this boom in research not only reflected the specific domestic social context but also coincided with a wave of research being carried out in the same period in Spain, Mexico, and the United Kingdom, to cite just three very different and distant cases.

Elsewhere, I have analyzed and criticized these tendencies toward concurrence or convergence in research topics as being the result of "imposition" by academic demand and research funding bodies from the major global centers of power.[5] In this sense, we learn from the relevant chapter in this volume that after 25 years of expansion, and in the midst of a phase of consolidation, so much of the sociology of work in Portugal is devoted to the research into the most advanced new technologies. In contrast, researchers appear to pay much less attention to other, more traditional, and evidently still socially unresolved, areas and problems, such as working conditions, employee involvement, or racial and gender discrimination at work.

At the same time, a reading of the various chapters in the *Worlds of Work* makes one begin to wonder whether a purely nominal comparison hides as much as it reveals. To give just one example, what does it really mean to say that research has been carried out and published on "productive chains," or what my research team, the Charles Babbage Seminar in the Social Sciences of Work, terms the reconstruction of complete labor processes? It is very difficult to compare the recent influence of this approach, which reconstructs the subcontracting networks and the spatial diffusion of the productive process in a bid to identify the collective worker who manufactures a given good or service in Mexico, with the body of research and studies carried out in Spain. Still less can this be compared with Italy, where this field of research (which first emerged in 1974) is so well developed that it forms part of the dominant paradigm of research.

This point is perhaps better illustrated by something that this reader, at least, found quite remarkable: The dominant themes and the new areas of research in the sociology of work in the United States coincide, point by point,

[5]See Castillo (1999b).

with those in Spain. This is all the more surprising given that these two scientific communities share neither the same academic tradition nor the same social demands. This issue that probably merits more detailed consideration and, in the case of the United States, breakdown in terms of different "scientific communities," possibly on a state-by-state basis: The sociology of work in Texas may not be the same at that produced in California.

Fourth Observation

The convergence of subjects and foci in countries that are very far apart cannot mask the persistent differences within individual countries and national scientific communities.

If we want the scientific community to continue down the promising international road depicted in this volume, divisions such as these oblige us to consider the real theoretical, or epistemological, limits of research practices that all too often are carried out in isolation from, and ignorance of, their counterparts, whether disciplinary cousins or fellow countrymen and women. The most striking example of this comes from Canada. The magnificent text by Giles and Bélanger paints a picture of two scientific communities completely divided by language, to the extent that this "state of the art" is in itself exceptional insofar as it treats the literature in both English and French as a whole, thereby constituting a major step forward in this essential pooling of knowledge.[6] As in many other countries, this divided discipline also pays the price of its estrangement from, and failure to take account of or refer to, research produced by social scientists in other disciplines. Finally, there is a further divide between those who a adopt an essentially inward-looking orientation, emphasizing the peculiarity of things Canadian, and those who try to show that what is taking place in the world of work in Canada or Quebec is the local manifestation of global changes that are taking place all over the world and, above all, in their southern neighbor, the United States. The Canadian case is merely an illustration of trends unfolding in other countries and scientific communities.

Fifth Observation

Is our scientific community a tower of Babel in which the multitude of languages hinders understanding?

---

[6]In an earlier text, "El paraíso perdido de la interdisciplinariedad: Volver a los clásicos" [Interdisciplinarity Paradise Lost: Coming Back to Classics], included in *A la búsqueda del trabajo perdido*, 1998, I mentioned an article by Chanlat in English and presenting Francophone studies of French Canada.

These national divergences are by no means an exclusively Canadian preserve, as I have just said. Rather, these divergences, fractures, and fragmentation in the social sciences of work highlight constant problems in the international academic community. These problems might be easier to face up to if we formed an ideal community for dialogue, whose members could express themselves in their own language and understand others talking in theirs. This might possibly be feasible if we are thinking in terms of a small cluster of languages, which, in the case of Europeans, would consist of four or five relatively closely related languages. This idea has long been the subject of debate within the ranks of the International Sociological Association (ISA), embraced and encouraged by Inmanuel Wallerstein during his presidency of the association. However, things become much more complicated if what we mean is access, without having to pass though the customs barrier of retranslation into English, for example, to the texts reproduced here, and published in Korean, Hungarian, Swedish, or to others that are sorely missed here in Japanese, Russian, Greek, and so on. In this case, obviously, much more serious problems are involved. We might be able to ask our colleagues, and ourselves, to make the effort to give serious attention to a scientific community that thinks and writes in Italian, Spanish, French, or German, and which meets, reads, and uses trade publications in these languages. Indeed, this in itself would constitute major progress and show a strong commitment to change. However, it does not seem reasonable, or justifiable, to expect a sociologist to develop a universal gift of languages.

To take the case of the United Kingdom as an example, the authors of Chapter 12 not only refer exclusively to their English roots but also only to work published in English. Rarely in these texts, or in those written in the United States or Australia, do we find references to authors writing in any other scientific community. And this, in turn, tends to imply ignoring the nature and achievements of other scientific communities.

Sixth (and Final) Observation

The presentation in society itself of each scientific community gives us an idea of its peculiarities, expectations, and future prospects.

Working from drafts in more or less advanced phases of production, I had the chance to read the splendid chapter on Brazil while still incomplete, in a state in which the two authors had yet to remove their messages to each other: "We should include such and such a point," "Give more references to that author," "Shall we include more of these critical texts?", and so on. Evidently, the authors of the chapter were thinking about how they wanted to present the sociology of work in Brazil, that is, about the image they wanted to give of it, without, of course, distorting reality. In this way, the spontaneity of these messages and notes raises the question of the structure of all the articles, including those in which the scaffolding is not so clearly visible.[7]

Take, for example, the Portuguese chapter, which illustrates the (semi) eternal dilemma of having to choose between being political or scientific, or as Weber would put it, whether to be critical or a servant of the system, to line up with the "consultants" or the real sociologists. In this chapter, the authors appear to be describing their exciting aspirations for the future of the sociology of work in Portugal rather than the reality of the discipline as it now stands.

These different "styles of presentation" are also apparent in the approaches taken by the authors, which, of course, lead to very different texts. So, for example, in his excellent chapter on Sweden, Casten von Otten makes it clear that he is not interested in telling the academic story of who introduced such and such a concept, or who was the first person to criticize Braverman and how. Rather, he had very different intentions, namely, to show how sociology has affected policy development and implementation by offering conceptual resources, providing descriptions and analyses of real work situations, and putting forward alternative proposals, all of which have helped shape and influence labor policy. In this way, he is also able to show how the rise and fall of the sociology of work has accompanied the rise of welfare policies in the past, and their dismemberment in the present.

These discursive strategies recall the Spanish philosopher Ortega y Gasset, whose books were always replete with prologues for his German or French readers; that is, it was as if texts should be written with a specific audience in mind. In the case of this volume, which initially at least, is only to be published in English, it appears that more than one author has written with an essentially English-speaking public in mind. I am not, of course, suggesting that this in itself is a defect, but merely trying to highlight some of its consequences. These are exemplified by the very informative chapter on France (and Belgium), which nonetheless does not manage to convey the very lively, and controversial, debates now going on in the discipline in France, or the wealth of research, analysis, and ideas currently coming out of the country.[8]

When reading the different chapters in this volume, the reader might find it interesting to consider the authors' objectives when writing their chapters, the ideas behind their presentation, and the points they have chosen to silence or magnify. By doing so, the reader will be in a better position to judge the extent to which the different chapters, and the book as a whole, contribute to the development of a new scientific community of sociologists of work.

[7]My knowledge of the works of the authors, some of them edited by myself, gives me a very sympathetic insight to this volume.
[8]See, for example, Boutet et al. (1999).

CONCLUSION

Turning now to the future, the expectations and prospects outlined by the authors of these chapters point us toward paths to take in the short term, and paths to build in the medium term. One obvious conclusion to be drawn from these chapters is that, given their distinct starting points and social contexts, individual countries and geographic regions can be expected to develop in different ways, even if all of them converge in the way desired by the editors.

First, for example, it is to be hoped that the various national or linguistic communities can learn from the different experiences and vicissitudes described in this volume. It is hardly necessary to stress that it is highly unlikely that merely by reading this book, politicians and policymakers responsible for labor, educational, or research policies will be convinced of the need to change their mentalities or strategies. However, this does not mean that we cannot speculate as to the direction the sociology of work in Portugal might take if, for example, the relevant decision makers opted for the path taken by the Federal Republic of Germany in the 1970s, and promoted programs devoted to the "humanization of working life." In fact, something of this kind does actually appear to have been happening over the last 5 or 10 years, as shown by Portugal's strong commitment to European policies for the modernization of labor relations, its involvement in the introduction of complex technological systems, participation in drafting of "green books" on the information society, the enthusiastic support of institutions such as the Instituto para a Inoraçao na Formaçao (INOFOR), the specialized institute for training, or the study and development of new qualifications, and so on.

In the same vein, it is interesting to see what is happening in Australia. While, on the one hand, the sociology of work, under that particular label, appears to be threatened by marginalization, on the other, the institutional context bodes well for the future development of the sociological approach to work, even if this is largely takes place under the label of "industrial relations."

In a number of other countries, such as South Africa, where it seems that everything remains to be done, and where social actors have an enormous thirst for knowledge and research, the discipline appears to have a bright future. In part, at least, this is precisely because it is starting out almost from scratch.

The chapter on Canada reveals the fundamental theoretical influence, in their respective linguistic spheres of influence, of the United States and the United Kingdom on the one hand, and France (or rather Paris) on the other. In this respect, Canadian sociologists might do well to start reading sociology of work published in Portugal, Brazil, Italy, Spain, Argentina, or Mexico. This might help to break down the existing divide between their own two fragmented communities, as well as to throw off the heavy burden of their obsession with the United States.

The various chapters in this volume, and the book as a whole, represent a major step forward in this direction. In this respect, I share the sentiments that Marshall expressed at the beginning of the reconstruction of the destroyed and demoralized Europe, then emerging from the World War II; that is, now, at the threshold of this new century, "I hope that, as sociology studies the map at the crossroads it will not choose a lonely road; the road sociology chooses should be one with busy traffic on it, and with company and conversation with others of a kindred spirit" (Marshall, 1963:24). Here, we are talking and debating in this volume about the sociology we have and the sociology we want. And this, of course, means that we are sharing our ideas about the world that we dream of building. This, at least, is my vision.

REFERENCES

Abramo, Laís. 1999. "Desafios Atuais da Sociologia do Trabahlo na América Latina: Algumas Hipótesis para a Discussâo." Paper presented to the International Seminar, "Los Retos Teóricos de los Estudios del Trabajo Hacia el Siglo xxi," Aguascalientes, Mexico, October.

Antunes, Ricardo. 1996. "Qual Crise da 'Sociedade do Trabalho'?" Paper presented to the 2nd Congreso Latinoamericano de Sociología del Trabajo, Aguas de Lindoia, São Paulo, Brasil, 1–5 December.

Aronowitz, Stanley, and Jonathan Cutler, eds. 1998. *Post-work: The Wages of Cibernation*. New York: Routledge.

Boisard, Pierre et al. 1997. *Le Travail, Quel Avenir?* París: Gallimard.

Borderias, Cristina. 1998. "Identidad Femenina y Recomposición del Trabajo." Pp. 47–65, in *El futuro del trabajo*, edited by A. Rodríguez et al. Bilbao: Bakea.

Boutet, Josiane et al. 1999. *Le Monde du Travail*. Paris: La Découverte.

Brown, Richard. 1992. *Understanding Industrial Organizations: Theoretical Perspectives in Industrial Sociology*. London and New York: Routledge.

Brown, Richard, ed. 1997. *The Changing Shape of Work*. Basingstoke: Macmillan.

Brown, Richard. 1998. "Succession or Cumulation? Some Comments on Changing Theoretical Approaches and Substantive Concerns in the Sociology of Work and Employment." Paper presented to the Congress organized by *Work, Employment and Society*, "The study of Work: Past and Future Trends," Cambridge, UK, 14–16 September.

Burris, Beverly H. 1998. "Computerization of the Workplace." *Annual Review of Sociology*, 24:141–157.

Castillo, Juan José. 1994a. *El Trabajo del Sociólogo*. Madrid: Editorial Complutense.

Castillo, Juan José, ed. 1994b "La Sociología del Trabajo en América Latina." Special issue of *Revista de Economía y Sociología del Trabajo* 23–24 (March–June):1–293.

Castillo, Juan José. 1996. *Sociología del Trabajo: Un Proyecto Docente.* Madrid: Centro de Investigaciones Sociológicas-Siglo XXI.

Castillo, Juan José. 1997. "Looking for the Meaning of Work." *Work and Occupations* 24(4):411–425.

Castillo, Juan José. 1998. *A la Búsqueda del Trabajo Perdido.* Madrid: Editorial Tecnos.

Castillo, Juan José, ed. 1999a. "Which Way Forward for the Sociology of Work?" Special issue of *Current Sociology* 47(2):

Castillo, Juan José. 1999b. "Sociology of Work at the Crossroads," in *Current Sociology* 47(2):

Castillo, Juan José, ed. 1999c. *El Futuro del Trabajo.* Madrid: Editorial Complutense.

Castillo, Juan José et al. 2000a. "La Sociología del Trabajo en España entre dos Siglos," *Sociología del Trabajo* 39:

Castillo, Juan José. 2000b. "Un Camino y cien Senderos. El Trabajo de Campo como Crisol de Disciplinas." Paper presented to the III Congreso Latinoamericano de Sociología del Trabajo, Buenos Aires, 17–20 May.

Castillo, Juan José (dir.). 2000c. "El Trabajo Invisible en España: Una Evaluación y Valoración del Trabajo Realmente Existente, de su Condición, Problemas y Esperanzas." Research Project 2000–2003, Madrid.

Castillo, Juan José, and Jesús Villena, eds. 1998. *Ergonomía: Conceptos y Métodos.* Madrid: Editorial Complutense.

Castillo, Juan José, and Santiago, eds. 1997. "Diez Años de Sociología del Trabajo." Special issue of *Sociología del Trabajo,* nueva época 31.

Castillo, Juan José, Arturo Lahera, Margarita Barañano, and Carlos Castillo. 2000. "La Sociologia del Lavoro in Spagna tra due Secoli." *Sociología del Lavoro* (Bolonia) 76:139–158.

Devine, Fiona. 1992. *Affluent Workers Revisited. Privatism and the Working Class.* Edinburgh: Edinburgh University Press.

Dudley, Kathryn Marie. 1994. *The End of the Line: Lost Jobs, New Lives in Postindustrial America,* Chicago, University of Chicago Press.

Durán, María-Angeles et al. 1998. "The Future of Work in Europe (Patterns of Gendered Time Distribution)." Summary of the report produced for the European Commission's Direction General V, Equality of Opportunities Unit, Madrid, May.

Faure-Guichard, Catherine. 1999. "L'Introuvable Centralité du Travail: Bilan Provisoire d'un Débat en Cours." *Le Temps Modernes* 54(603):141–162.

Garza, Enrique. 1999. "¿Fin del Trabajo o Trabajo sin fin?" Pp. 13–39 in *El trabajo del futuro,* edited by Juan José Castillo. Madrid: Editorial Complutense.

Goulder, Alvin. 1970. *The Coming Crisis of Western Sociology.* New York: Basic Books.

Green, Nancy L. 1997. *Ready-to-Wear and Ready-to-Work: A Century of Industry and Immigrants in Paris and New York.* Durham, NC: Duke University Press.

Grint, Keith, and Steve Woolgar. 1997. *The Machine at Work: Technology, Work and Organization.* Cambridge, UK: Polity Press.

Hodson, Randy, and Teresa A. Sullivan. 1995. *The Social Organization of Work.* Belmont, CA: Wadsworth.

"Labor in the Americas." 1997. Special issue of *Work and Occupations* 24(3).

Linhart, Danièle. 1997. "Travail: Défaire, Disent-ils: Note Critique." *Sociologie du Travail* 2:235–249.

Lupton, T. 1963. *On the Shop Floor. Two Studies of Workshop Organization and Output.* [Field Work, 1955–56]. Oxford, UK: Pergamon Press.

Marshall, T. H. 1963. *Sociology at the Crossroads and Other Essays.* London: Heinemann.

Moore, Henrietta L. 1995. "The future of work." *British Journal of Industrial Relations* 33(4):657–678.[Followed by replies by Ruth Milkman, pp. 679–683, and Ulrich Jürgens, pp. 685–687].

Panaia, Marta. comp. 1996. *Trabajo y Empleo. Un Abordaje Interdisciplinario.* Buenos Aires: Eudeba-PAITE.

Planell, Elsa, Juan José Castillo, and Carlos Alá Santiago, eds. 1998. *Estudios del tTabajo en El Caribe.* San Juan: Universidad de Puerto Rico, Proyecto Atlantea.

Pries, Ludger. 1995. La Reestructuración Productiva como Modernización Reflexiva: Análisis Empírico y Reflexiones Teóricas sobre "la Sociedad de Riesgo." Mexico: Universidad Autónoma Metropolitana-Iztapalapa.

Rabinbach, Anson. 1992. *The Human Motor: Energy, Fatigue, and the Origins of Modernity.* Berkeley and Los Angeles: University of California Press.

Revista Latinoamericana de Estudios del Trabajo, 5: 1997. "Trabalho e Sociedade: Desafios Teóricos." [Selected texts from the II Congreso Latinoamericano de Sociología del Trabajo, December 1996]

Rojas, Eduardo, and Ana Proietti. 1996. "La Sociología del Trabajo en América Latina: Una Crítica al Paradigma Politicista." Pp. 383–413 in *Trabajo y empleo: Un abordaje interdisciplinario,* compiled by M. Panaia. Buenos Aires: Eudeba-PAITE.

Santiago, Carlos Alá, ed. 1995–1996. "Primer Encuentro Latinoamericano de Estudios del Trabajo." Special issue of the *Revista de Administración Pública* (Universidad de Puerto Rico) 28.

Sociologia del Lavoro. 1999. "Le Ricerche in Sociologia del Lavoro in Italia e in Europa." Special issue of *Sociología del Lavoro* 76.

Supiot, Alain, ed. 1996. Reflexiones Cruzadas sobe el Trabajo y su Porvenir." *Revista Internacional del Trabajo* (OIT; special issue) 115(6).

Thomas, Robert J. 1994. *What Machines Can't Do: Politics and Technology in the Industrial Enterprise.* Berkeley: University of California Press.

Thompson, Paul, and Chris Warhurst, eds. 1998. *Workplaces of the Future.* London: Macmillan.

Warhurst, Chris, Paul Thompson. 1998. "Hands, Hearts and Minds: Changing Work and Workers at the End of the Century." Pp. 1–24 in *Workplaces of the Future,* edited by P. Thompson and C. Warhurst. Houndmills and London: Macmillan.

Wisner, Alain. 1997. *Anthropotechnologie: Vers un Monde Industriel Pluricentrique.* Toulouse: Octarès Éditions.

About the Contributors

Jacques Bélanger is Professor in the Département des relations industrielles, Université Laval, Québec. He is co-editor of *Workplace Industrial Relations and the Global Challenge* (1994) and *Being Local Worldwide: ABB and the Challenge of Global Management* (1999). From 1990 to 1996, he was Associate Editor of *Relations industrielles/Industrial Relations*.

Sharit K. Bhowmik is Professor of Sociology and Head of the Department of Sociology at the University of Mumbai (formerly Bombay). His research interests are in the sociology of work and sociology of organizations. He is the author of two books on plantation labor in India and a member of the editorial boards of *Sociological Bulletin* and *Indian Journal of Social Work*. He has published research papers on plantation labor, labor movement, worker cooperatives and labor in the urban informal sector in India.

Juan-José Castillo is Professor and Chair at the Departamento de Estructura Social, Universidad Complutense de Madrid, editor of *Sociología del Trabajo*, and past President of RC-30 of the International Sociological Association (1990–1998). A member of the International Steering Committee of GERPISA, International Network Program, his recent publications include *A la búsqueda del trabajo perdido* (1998), *El futuro del trabajo* (1999), and "Which way forward for the sociology of work?" *Current Sociology*, 47(2), 1999.

Daniel B. Cornfield is Professor of Sociology and Department Chair at Vanderbilt University and editor of *Work and Occupations*. A former Chair of the Section on Organizations, Occupations, and Work of the American Sociological Association, he is co-author with Bill Fletcher of "The U.S. Labor Movement: Toward a Sociology of Labor Revitalization," in Arne Kalleberg and Ivar

Berg (eds.), *Sourcebook on Labor Markets* (2001), and co-editor with Karen Campbell and Holly McCammon of *Working in Restructured Workplaces* (2001).

Enrique de la Garza Toledo is Professor of Sociology of Work, Director of the Ph D. Program on Social Studies at the Metropolitan University of Mexico, and Editor of *Trabajo*. He is the founding Editor of *Revista Latinoamericana de Estudios del Trabajo*, an official publication of the Asociación Latinoamericana de la Sociología del Trabajo. Among his recent publications are his edited volumes, *Tratado Latinoamericano de Sociologia del Trabajo* (2000) and *Los Retos Teóricos de los Estudios del Trabajo hacia el Siglo XXI* (1999).

Pierre Desmarez is Professor of Sociology and Director of the Centre de Sociologie du Travail de l'Emploi et de la Formation (TEF) at the Université de Bruxelles (Belgium). He is a member of the editorial board of *Sociologie du travail* (Paris). His research interests are the history of sociology, theory and methods in sociology of work, and the sociology of occupational systems. His publications include *La sociologie industrielle aux Etats-Unis* (1986).

Paul Edwards is Professor of Industrial Relations and Director of the Industrial Relations Research Unit, Warwick Business School, University of Warwick. He is a Fellow of the British Academy and edited *Work, Employment and Society* from 1996 to 1998. His research interests include workplace relations and the employment policies of multinational companies. He is co-editor of *The Global Economy: National States and the Regulation of Labour* (1999) and co-author of *Managers in the Making* (1997).

Anthony Giles is Professor in the Département des relations industrielles, Université Laval, Québec. He has published articles and book chapters on industrial relations theory, the history of industrial relations, globalization, comparative international relations, and the restructuring of work in multinational corporations. From 1995 to 1998, he was Associate Editor of *Relations industrielles/Industrial Relations*.

Nadya Araujo Guimarães is Doctor in Sociology, Professor at the University of São Paulo–Department of Sociology and CNPq Senior Researcher at Centro Brasileiro de Análise e Planejamento. A former co-editor of *Revista Latinoamericana de Estudios del Trabajo*, her recently published books include *Trabalho e Desigualdades Raciais: Negros e brancos no mercado de trabalho em Salvador* (1998); *A Ocupação na América Latina: Tempos mais duros* (1998); and *Competitividade e Desenvolvimento: Atores e instituições locais* (2001).

Sandra Harding, is Professor and Dean, Faculty of Business, at Queensland University of Technology, Brisbane, Australia. A sociologist, she has degrees from the Australian National University, University of Queensland, and North Carolina State University. Her interests include alternative forms of industrial organization and inequality at work. She is currently engaged in a large-scale national study, the Australian National Organisation Survey.

Randy Hodson, currently Professor of Sociology at Ohio State University, has a Ph.D. degree from the University of Wisconsin at Madison. His research interests include worker–management conflict, co-worker relations, and technological change. He is the author of *Dignity at Work* (2002), the co-author with Teresa A. Sullivan of *The Social Organization of Work*, 3rd ed. (2002), and the editor of the JAI Press annual series on *Research in the Sociology of Work*.

Arne L. Kalleberg is Kenan Professor of Sociology at the University of North Carolina at Chapel Hill. Co-editor of the Plenum book series Studies in Work and Industry, his current research focuses on U.S. organizations' use of non-standard work arrangements, cross-national differences in the work attitudes, work–life balance, high-performance work organizations, and changing employment relations in the United States and Norway. He is co-author, with Eileen Appelbaum, Thomas Bailey, and Peter Berg of *Manufacturing Advantage: Why High-Performance Work Systems Pay Off* (2000). His most recent book, edited with Ivar Berg, *is Sourcebook of Labor Markets* (2001).

Ilona Kovács is Professor of Sociology of Work at the Faculty of Economics and Management at the Technical University of Lisbon. A member of the editorial boards of *Organizações e Trabalho*, the official journal of the Portuguese Association of Professional Sociology of Industry, Organization, and Work, and *Sociología del Trabajo*, her recent publications include *Novos Modelos de Producao. Trabalho e Pessoas* (with Juan Jose Castillo) (1998), and *Pescas e Pescadores* (with Antonio B. Moniz and Manuel M. Godinho) (2000).

Kevin T. Leicht is Professor of Sociology and research scholar at the Obermann Center for Advanced Study at the University of Iowa. Editor of *Research in Social Stratification and Mobility* and *The Sociological Quarterly*, his research focuses on gender inequality among professionals and managers, career decision making, and organizational and political analyses of postindustrial society. He is finishing books on the social organization of professional work (with Mary Fennell) and on current issues in the study of labor markets (with Scott Eliason).

Marcia de Paula Leite is Doctor in Sociology, Professor at University of Campinas, Department of Social Sciences and Education. and Senior Researcher at Centro Brasileiro de Análise e Planejamento. A former co-editor of *Revista Latinoamericana de Estudios del Trabajo,* her recently published books include *Trabalho, Qualificação e Formação Profissional,* (1998), *O Trabalho em Movimento* (1997), and *O Futuro do Trabalho. Novas tecnologias e Subjetividade Operária* (1994).

György Lengyel is Professor and Chairman of the Department of Sociology at Budapest University. His recent research focuses on uncertainty, unemployment, and social action. He is the chairman of the editorial board of *Szociológiai Szemle* (*Review of Sociology*). His recent publications include *Elites after State Socialism,* edited with J. Higley (2000), and *Work in the European Context,* edited with R. Münch (1999).

António Brandão Moniz is Professor of Industrial Sociology at the New University of Lisbon and Editor of *Organizações e Trabalho,* the official journal of Associação Portuguesa de Profissionais em Sociologia Industrial, das Organizações e do Trabalho. Secretary of ISA Research Committee 30, he has served on the Mission for the Society of Information of the Portuguese Ministry of Labor and Solidarity and the Steering Committee for the European Social Survey of the European Science Foundation. His recent publications include *Inovação e Fomento do Emprego* (2000) and *Pescas e Pescadores,* with M. Godinho and I. Kovács (2000).

Walther Müller-Jentsch is Professor of Sociology at the Ruhr University of Bochum and holds degrees in sociology from the University of Frankfurt and in industrial relations from the London School of Economics. He is chairman of the German Industrial Relations Association. He is series editor of *Schriftenreihe Industrielle Beziehungen* and co-editor of the quarterly *Industrielle Beziehungen.* His recent books include: *Soziologie der Industriellen Beziehungen* (2nd ed., 1997) and *Konfliktpartnerschaft* (3rd ed., 1999).

László Neumann is a sociologist and research fellow at the National Labor Centre Research Unit. He has been an adviser to an independent union federation (LIGA), and gives lectures in industrial relations at the Institute of Sociology and Social Policy, Eötvös Lóránd University, Budapest. His current research interest include decentralized collective bargaining, foreign-owned companies, labor market impacts of Hungary's accession to the European Union, and teleworking.

Richard B Sappey, Ph.D., is Lecturer in Industrial Relations at Griffith University, Brisbane, Australia. An economist, he has degrees from Sydney, London, and Queensland universities. His research interests include the study of work intensification, emotional labor, the industrial relations of developing countries, the economic and social dimensions of labor markets, and the relationship between industrial relations and human resource management. He has recently published in *The International Journal of Employment Studies and Employee Relations*.

Song Ho Keun received his doctorate from Harvard University and is Associate Professor of Sociology at Seoul National University. He is currently Director of the Institute of Social Development and Policy Research, the publisher of the scholarly journal *Development and Society*. He is an author of many books in Korean in the fields of labor markets, labor movements, democratization, and welfare and social policy. He is presently researching the working poor and government poverty policy before and after the foreign debt crisis.

Doowon Suh is Assistant Professor in the Graduate School of International Studies of Korea University. Formerly a lecturer of sociology and a postdoctoral research fellow at the Center for Korean Studies, University of California at Berkeley, his research addresses white-collar unionism, the impact of new social movements on democratic consolidation, and labor transformations under neoliberalism. His recent publications include "Institutionalization of New Social Movements and Development of Democracy: Theories and Debates" (in Korean) and "Middle-Class Formation and Class Alliance" (forthcoming in *Social Science History*).

Casten von Otter holds a Ph.D. in sociology from University of Uppsala and is Professor at the National Institute for Working Life, Stockholm. He has been an advisor to the Swedish government on industrial relations and work policy and is former President of the Swedish Sociological Association. He is the editor of *Economic and Industrial Democracy*. His published work includes *Implementing Planned Markets in Health Care*, with R. B. Saltman, and *Public Sector Transformation: Rethinking Markets and Hierarchies in Government*, with F. Naschold.

Edward C. Webster is Professor of Sociology and Director of the Sociology of Work Unit at the University of the Witwatersrand, Johannesburg, South Africa. His current research interests include the evolving labor relations system in South Africa, labor market segmentation, and the impact of deep-level gold mining on the occupational culture of miners. He is a founding member of the *South African Labour Bulletin*. His most recent book, *Trade Unions and Democratization in South Africa*, was published by Macmillan in 1999.

Carol Wolkowitz is a lecturer in the Department of Sociology at the University of Warwick (in the United Kingdom). She is co-author of *A Glossary of Feminist Theory* (1997) and two books on homeworking and home-based work. She is currently writing a book on gender and embodiment in the labor process, as well as developing research based on Manhattan Project narratives. She was Reviews Editor of the journal *Work, Employment, and Society* from 1996 to 1998.

Index

PLENUM STUDIES IN WORK AND INDUSTRY
COMPLETE CHRONOLOGICAL LISTING

Series Editors:
Ivar Berg, *University of Pennsylvania, Philadelphia, Pennsylvania*
and Arne L. Kalleberg, *University of North Carolina, Chapel Hill, North Carolina*

PLENUM STUDIES IN WORK AND INDUSTRY
COMPLETE CHRONOLOGICAL LISTING